"Love to All, Scottie"

Graduation United States Naval Academy 1939

PLEBE TO WWII HERO

My Journey from Annapolis to Midway

CORRESPONDENCE FROM

Robert Scott Whitman Jr.

U.S.N.A. 1939 · LIEUTENANT (JG) U.S.N.

ANNOTATED BY

Robert Scott Whitman 2021

PARK PLACE PUBLICATIONS
Pacific Grove, California

Private letters from Robert Scott Whitman Jr.
Transcribed by Robert Scott Whitman Sr., father of Robert Scott Whitman Jr.
Annotated by Robert Scott Whitman, nephew of Robert Scott Whitman Jr.
Digital file by Gay Anne Himebaugh, Seaview Secretarial Solutions, Corona del Mar, CA
Interior design and layout by Patricia Hamilton, Park Place Publications, Pacific Grove, CA

PARK PLACE PUBLICATIONS
Pacific Grove, California

Published by
Park Place Publications
Pacific Grove, California
www.parkplacepublications.com

ISBN: 978-1-953120-38-0

Printed in U.S.A.

First U.S. Edition: 2021

DISCLAIMER

*This book contains personal, handwritten letters from Robert Scott Whitman Jr.
The stories, the experiences, and the words are the author's alone.
To preserve the author's memory, voice, and intent, no grammar nor any other
corrections have been made to the documents provided.*

*Scottie's father elected to replace selected names with initials, as was the
practice at that time to preserve anonymity of individuals.
Friend Ada is referred to at various times as "A". A..E.. and A..L..*

To Mother

ROBERT SCOTT WHITMAN
BINGHAMTON, NEW YORK

"Whit"   "Scottie"

HAILING from the apparently thriving climate of Binghamton, where men achieve bulk and vigor (and his drags are proud of it) he found the mechanical arts here less palatable than the liberal arts at college. By "jumping numbers" continuously since plebe year, he proved, however, that his mind was readily acclimated to the new curriculum. Either his impatience to put to sea or his early civilian independence netted him a month cruise not included in plebe training. Fortunately in later years he has been more judicious with nocturnal exploits over the mural obstructions. For two years he devoted his brawn to the gridiron, but an injury directed his attentions along literary lines. Equal versatility aboard and ashore will make him a grand shipmate.

Football 4, 3; Glee Club 4, 3, 2; Musical Club Show 3, 2; Assistant Director 2; Stunt Committee 2, 1; Chairman 1; Chairman Activities; Committee 1; Log Staff 4, 3, 2, 1; Feature Editor 1; Trident 2, 1; 1 Stripe.

Yearbook Entry:

Plebe Robert
Scott Whitman –
"Scottie," "Whit"

"Equal versity aboard
and ashore will
make him a grand
shipmate."

FOREWORD

The Battle of Midway is considered a major decisive Allied victory in World War II, as well as one of most significant battles in the entire history of naval warfare. The encounter in June of 1942 between the U.S. Pacific fleet and the Japanese navy dealt a stunning blow to the Japanese military just six months after the attack on Pearl Harbor.

The conflict resulted in 307 U.S. casualties. Among them was my uncle, Robert Scott Whitman, Jr.

My uncle was a war hero and a prolific letter-writer. From his days as a cadet at the Naval Academy at Annapolis to the time just before his death in the Battle of Midway, he sent a total of 268 letters to his father (my grandfather), Robert Scott Whitman. Over a span of seven years, he laboriously typed over 140,000 words on a manual typewriter—all they had in the way of "word processing" back in the late 1930s and early 1940s.

When his son lost his life in battle, my grandfather set about attempting to publish the letters as a book. I believe this must have been part of the grieving process. How heartbreaking it must have been for my grandfather and grandmother to lose their son—and my father to lose his older brother—a young man who was so loved and had such a promising future.

Eventually, I inherited the letters. I know at some point, my grandfather made good on his intention to turn the letters into a book, because they came to me wrapped in brown paper bearing a return address label from Simon and Schuster. I believe my grandfather mailed the letters to the big New York publisher hoping to have them released as a book, but for unknown reasons, Simon and Schuster turned down the project and returned the letters to my grandfather. Sadly, my grandfather died in 1944 and never had the chance to see his son's letters published as a book. He titled his book, "Love to all, Scottie" which you will see is how Scottie signed off on nearly all the letters he sent home. I changed the title to make it more descriptive of the content of the book.

The letters stayed in the family for decades until one day several years ago, a contractor was doing work at our home. My name is also Robert Scott Whitman. He asked me if I was any relation to the World War II Naval Aviator Robert Scott Whitman, Jr. It turned out this contractor was a history buff, with a special interest in the Battle of Midway. He recalled seeing a passage about my uncle in a book by Robert Cressman and Steve Ewing, *A Glorious Page in Our History: The Battle of Midway 4-6 June 1942.*

Intrigued, I obtained a copy of the book. On pages 73-74 I found two paragraphs describing my uncle's encounter with the enemy along with his picture. The caption reads, "Midshipman Robert Scott Whitman, circa 1939. Killed in action with floatplanes from *CHISTOSE* on 4 June when his PBY was shot down, he would be the only patrol plane commander to die in action in Midway."

Obviously, my uncle's legacy is known to others beyond the family. I began searching on the Internet and discovered multiple entries featuring my uncle's heroic service and sacrifice to his country. The "Find a Grave" website includes an entry about my uncle in its Memorial section. Several individuals made comments, including Jim Maddox, who wrote, "Scotty, I think about you frequently … every time I view the Quincy napkin ring you gave my family. Rest in peace and thank you for your service." I reached out to Jim Maddox and learned that his father, Bill Maddox, later commander of Destroyer Division 601, knew my uncle. In one of his letters, my uncle mentioned a visit to Bill and Betty Maddox in Key West, Florida.

In addition to my uncle's letters, I also inherited his Purple Heart (awarded posthumously), his engraved sword, and his naval certificates and diplomas.

I contacted the U.S. Naval Academy Museum in Annapolis to see if they would be interested in these artifacts, including the letters. They responded that yes, they would be interested.

Robert Scott Whitman Jr.'s Purple Heart, front and back, and engraved sword.

But then it occurred to me—instead of releasing the original hand-typed manuscript to the museum, why not publish them as a book, just like my grandfather wanted to do so many years ago? The book you now hold in your hands is the result of that decision.

My uncle—my namesake—went down with his plane in the line of duty nearly 80 years ago at the onset of the Battle of Midway, a major turning point in the War of the Pacific. He was considered a war hero and had a ship named after him, the *USS WHITMAN*. He is recognized in the U.S. Naval Academy Memorial Hall of Honor as one of 692 honorees killed in the line of duty in World War II and remembered for their service.

I hope you enjoy these insights into the day-to-day life of a naval cadet going through Annapolis prior to World War II, his journey to becoming a Naval Aviator, and the ultimate sacrifice he made for his country.

Robert Scott Whitman
2021

N. Nav. 199

United States of America.

Navy Department

By direction of the President of the United States you are hereby appointed a *Midshipman* in the United States Navy from the twenty-fourth day of August one thousand nine hundred and thirty-five

Given under my hand and seal of the Navy Department at the City of Washington, this 29th day of October one thousand nine hundred thirty-five

Claude A Swanson
Secretary of the Navy.

Midshipman

Robert Scott Whitman, Jr.
U. S. Navy.

Midshipman Appointment 1935.

CONTENTS

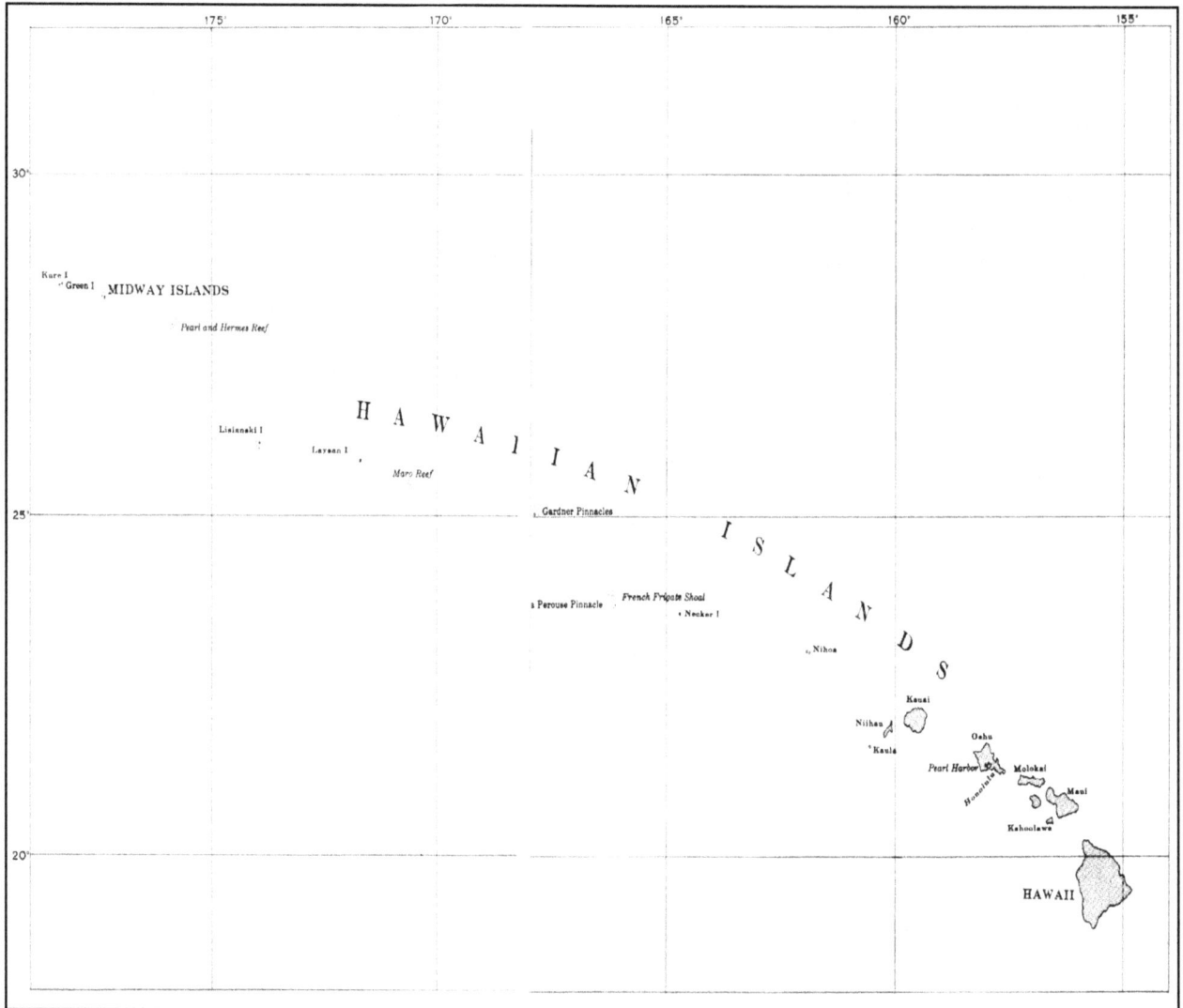

Map of Midway and the Hawaiian Islands.

ILLUSTRATIONS

Scottie - Graduation, Binghamton Central High School, 1933.

CORRESPONDENCE FROM

Robert Scott Whitman Jr.

U.S.N.A. 1939 · LIEUTENANT (JG) U.S.N.

Letters from "Scottie" to his family
Annapolis, 25 August 1935
to Honolulu, 21 May 1942

PLEBE YEAR
1935 - 1936

ROBERT SCOTT WHITMAN JR.

Annapolis, 25 August 1935

Dear Mother,

Well, I'm in and so up to my neck in work. I've been stenciling my name on equipment for almost two days and I'm not done yet.

I don't know when I start going to drills, probably Tuesday. Every Plebe on my deck has been helping me. They seem like a right good bunch.

I'm in a "harem," a room for three. One of the boys is from Kansas and the other from Massachusetts.

They give you everything and it is the best. Here are some of the things you wouldn't expect:

> pencils
> pen points and pen
> glue
> thumb tacks
> this stationary
> a knife
> all toilet articles
> slippers
> sneaks
> rubbers
> two pairs of Stetson shoes (high)
> shoe trees
> and ten billion other things.
> Oh, yes, and even stamps.

I had three shots in the arm yesterday, typhoid, small pox, and Shick test. No ill effects, thank goodness!

I think I'm going to like it very much.

I am sending my clothes home.

Please send me my own suitcase — no hurry, I won't get out for a long time.

There is another month before the "ac" [academic] year starts.

There is so much to tell and so little time.

Will write again soon.

> Love to all,
> Scottie.

Annapolis, 26 August 1935

Dear Family,

Both your swell letters came today. I'm pretty well settled and start work tomorrow.

I went out for football today and am dead tired right now. There are about three hundred boys out for the team and I have no idea how much of a chance I have of making the club. The rest of the boys have been out about a week already.

Before I forget it, there are several things I want:

1. my own suitcase immediately I have the keys
2. the keys to the Murrays' case
3. my watch repaired and fixed
4. my pipe
5. my typewriter if it can be mailed
        (if not I'll get it Christmas)
6. Magazines when you are through with them
7. There must be more than I will think of later.

There is so much to tell and yet so little. Everything is different. March to meals. March back. "Yes, sir". "No, sir". Turn square corners, and a million other rules.

We get to go to the Princeton, Penn., Notre Dame, and Army games away from home. The only one we miss is the Yale game.

There is "scuttle butt" around (rumor) that we go to the Olympics in Berlin next summer. We are going on a Northern European cruise anyway.

Please do me a favor and write Mrs. D..... a note and thank her for being so nice to me. You know it was Dr. D..... who introduced me to "Spike" Webb, who introduced me to "Rip" Miller.

A second classman by the name of Wengrovius from Binghamton looked me up today.

Well, I'm in the Navy. The Navy is getting into my blood. I imagine I'll growl a lot about it but deep down inside I think I am going to learn to love it just as much as every other man in the Academy does.

I hope I'll be able to justify all your hopes in me and make you all proud of me.

        Love to all,
        Scottie

PHOTOS FROM WHITMAN FAMILY ARCHIVES

Pop.

Pop and Scottie.

Pop.

Mother.

Scottie, Mother, and George.

Scottie with his younger brother George.

Annapolis, 27 August 1935

Dear George,

How're you doin', Old Boy? Still having lots of woman trouble, I'll bet. I do hope you had a swell time in Norwich. Mother says that it was a "snazzy" house at which you stayed.

I'm beginning to get settled down here. I have lots and lots to learn but sometime I'll know when to do what.

We march to all classes and drills. We march all the time, no matter whether alone or in battalion form.

You're interested in mechanical drawing. You should see my drawing outfit. It's worth about $40. Has everything in it that a draftsman could use, all cased in a leather box about 2 ft. by 1 ft. with a handle for carrying. That's just one thing. I have a million other things just as exciting and just as new to me.

They even give us a dictionary, Webster's Collegiate. Of course it all comes out of our pay. We don't get out of debt until about April next year and then we go back in again for uniforms.

It's a tough life but a good one.

They have some swell sea planes stationed here at the Academy. You would be interested to see them. There are about ten or twelve small planes and five large ones anchored in the Severn. The admiral (Sellers) has a special cabin job for his own personal use, just to taxi him around.

Well be a good boy.

     Love,
       Scottie

Annapolis, 28 August 1936

Dear Family,

Well, I'm getting more and more settled into the routine. I was last to enter but for about six. They are all here now. "ac" [academic] year starts the first of October. I have all my books. The Algebra is practically the same, the Trig. is the same [as at Dickinson College]. The English looks easy. Marine Engineering, Chemistry, and Seamanship are all new to me. I'm going to try to take German from Prof. Thomas [from Dickinson College]. He's here and I tried to call him. I'm going to try again as soon as I get a chance.

I went to rifle range today for the first time. It normally takes three days of rifle range before you can even see a gun. I took all the preliminary and qualified as a marksman all in one day.

To qualify you must get a score of 120 or better out of a possible 150, firing in prone, sitting, and prone rapid fire, all with regulation 30-30 Springfield rifles. They are small cannons. We fired at 200 yards. Great stuff! Telephone communications, movable targets and all.

I got on the water for the first time. The ranges are across the Severn and they took us over I motor launches.

There are more men in the Plebe class than there were in all of Dickinson College – 800 or more.

This sure is going to be a busy life. I know I'm going to like it.

There is not much more news now.

      Love to all,
       Scottie

Annapolis 1 September 1936

Dear Family,

Sunday again. I've been here just a week. Quarantined again until 1:30 today because of my second typhoid shot. We have to take three, one a week for three weeks.

Tomorrow we all go ashore. A.. E..... is coming down for the day and bringing a friend for whom I have secured a date.

We start on a new schedule today, less drill and more classes. We start Math. soon (solid mensuration, Geometry, I think).

It has been right cool today and yesterday.

I haven't been able to get out to one scrimmage yet. Quarantine or something has always held me in. I probably haven't a ghost of a chance of making the team. We have gymnasium four times a week.

I think I'll get out to the Wyoming (a battle wagon) which is anchored out in the bay today. It should be an interesting trip. In Seamanship the other day they took us all over one of the destroyers that are anchored here. It sure was interesting. Now I'd like to see one of the big boats and compare the two.

The one thing that impresses me about the Academy more than anything else (I don't know whether I have mentioned it before) is the completeness of the organization and equipment. We have our own fire trucks, fire boats, and equipment of all sorts for fighting fire. Every need of the Midshipman is taken care of and every bit of work except just that which leads to one goal, that of a commission, is done by either enlisted men or hired civilians.

Every Wednesday and Sunday we have formal room inspection. That means lockers, strong box, desk drawer must be open for inspection, and room must be in the same cleanly condition as for every day inspection.

There is a place for everything and it must be in its place ten hours out of every day.

All for now.

       Love to all
         Scottie

ROBERT SCOTT WHITMAN JR.

Annapolis, 4 September 1935

Dear Family,

I received all your letters yesterday and was sure glad to get them.

Things are becoming more natural for me around here now. I have had one set back though. As a football player I'm a complete washout. I don't know what is wrong with me. I guess I'm just not good enough; but I haven't even made the fourth team, which is the last team on the squad. I'm so ashamed of myself that it is not even funny. I want your advice. I can keep on playing on the "B" squad, but I have no desire to. I can't work up the old enthusiasm that I used to have. I've found that true from the first day out. I don't think I could stand playing on the scrubs and there isn't a chance of doing anything else. My only consolation is that I came out late, quite a bit later than the others, and that there are mostly ex college (big college and prep. school) stars on the Varsity Plebe squad.

I had the illusion that I was a fairly good ball player, but my illusion is a disillusion. I hope Dad won't be too disappointed in me. So much for the disappointment.

We have started Math. and are working on logs.

The Marine Engineering is fascinating, learning to use all sorts of drafting tools etc.

We'll be starting on Descriptive Geometry soon.

Our routine is about the same every day. Up at 6:15, chow, classes, recreation, study, chow, study, and bed at 10:00.

I've learned all the drill movements and have started on the manual of arms. We've been drilling as an awkward squad for some time. Next time we start drilling with our companies.

We received request cards for football tickets today. I can get any number of tickets for the Army game, or any other for that matter, at $4.40 a-piece. Please find out who of my friends would like them. I'll send in the request as quickly as possible. It must be in one month before the game and the sooner before that, the better the chance of seats. I can't guarantee how good seats will be, as we are allowed only two guaranteed side section seats at reduced price. The rest probably will be side, but not necessarily. Remember, I can get any number of them.

A.. L.. was down on Labor Day with a friend. We had a very

nice time. I got her friend a date with a boy from Texas. Her mother spoke of your "very, very nice note".

Uncle Charley Conrad, Kiss, Nance and young Chuck were here for Sunday. Gosh! It was nice to see them; and all Uncle Charley could say all the time he was here was, "Gosh! kid, I'm so glad!" It really is nice to have friends who appreciate one's good luck, isn't it? I took them over one of the destroyers and tried to show them the Academy, but I don't know much more about it than they do.

It's been raining all day and we've had to wear our cape rain coats and rain cap covers to class.

Wednesday P.M. and Saturday P.M. we have free, that is, practically free. All day Sunday is free, of course, except for meal formations and church.

All for now.

      Love to all,
       Scottie

Keep my civilian clothes. Give George what he wants, but keep my suits, coats etc. I'll need them on leave at Christmas and in September.

Scottie and Ada in front of
U.S.N.A. Mahan Hall.

Annapolis, 8 September 1935

Dear George,

Many happy returns of the day! I wish I could be home to help you celebrate the occasion.

Life is becoming very routine here now, very routine and very busy. We are studying Math. and will be every day from now on until two years and a half have passed.

Language starts next week. As you know, I'm taking German.

We're learning how to use slide rules in Math. You can do anything with the darn things, multiply, divide, logs or anything else.

There is really no news of interest. The Varsity football squad is back and practicing. Can't tell much how they are as yet. They've only been at it two days.

Just got through inspection and nothing was wrong. I'm keeping my fingers crossed. As yet I haven't been caught with anything out of place or dusty.

I do hope you all can sometime come down and see the Academy. It sure is an imposing place.

This is all for now. So long and best of luck.

     Love,
      Scottie

Annapolis, 9 September 1935

Dear Gram.,

Well, your grandson is now en embryo Naval Officer. After four long years of trying I finally made it and achieved the height of my dreams. I now have ahead of me four of the hardest years I expect to ever put in.

Mother writes that you sent me a new laundry bag for school. That was indeed very thoughtful of you and please realize that I appreciate it greatly.

Military or in this case naval discipline and training is new and at first a bit hard, but I know I am going to like it.

I start drilling tomorrow, and it is then that the hard work begins.

I have gone out for football and hope I can make the team.

I have no chance to get home until Christmas, and then none till September. That is all going to be very hard but I guess it is worth it.

I was issued every bit of equipment that I will need for my stay here. All my civilian clothes are sent home. I could have come in here with just the clothes on my back and in ten minutes would be just as well off as any millionaire's son.

I must close now but will write again soon.

       Love to all,
        Scottie

ROBERT SCOTT WHITMAN JR.

Annapolis, 10 September 1935

Hello Pop,

Congratulations. Many happy returns of the day and many of them! This is the first time I've not been home to help in the double celebration. Have a nice one anyway, won't you?

I'm getting so I can throw a rifle around in the manual of arms like nobody's business.

I made the training table of the Plebe squad after all, at least I think I made it. It hasn't started yet but will soon.

Your letters have been great and you can't possibly know how much I appreciate them.

The other night, the whole Plebe class went to see Annapolis Farewell, a new movie about the Naval Academy. It is fairly authentic, and a lot of the shots and scenes were taken here at the Academy. The lockers and rooms are accurate except in one or two very small details.

The uniforms are the actual stuff, and so are the drills.

You should all by all means see it if you want to see what sort of a place I live in. The plot and continuity is not so good, but it will give you all a fairly accurate picture of the Academy.

If you do see it notice the officer who swears in a bunch of Plebes. He is Commander Badger and the same man who swore me in.

If you would like to know just what sort of things we are studying I'm going to name the titles of my books as they are on my bookshelf. (From left to right)

1. Landing Force Manual (U. S. N.) 1927
2. Naval Customs, Traditions and Usage
3. Engineering Descriptive Geometry and Drawing
4. Webster's Collegiate Dictionary
5. Knight's Modern Seamanship
6. Manual of Athletic Requirements (U.S.N.A.)
7. Algebra, College Course
8. Smith's Introductory College Chemistry
9. Solid Mensuration
10. Makers of Naval Tradition
11. Writing Well

12. <u>Naval Terms</u>
13. <u>The Romantic Period of English Lit.</u>
14. <u>English Literature in Fact and Story</u>
15. <u>The Blue Jackets Manual</u> (1927)
16. <u>Small Arms Firing Regulations</u>
17. <u>The Boat Book of U.S. Navy</u>
18. <u>Plane and Spherical Trig.</u>
19. <u>Useful Tables</u>
20. <u>The Book of Navy Songs</u>

That is all I have at present, but we double the number before the year is over.

Some of the books on tradition etc. are grand and I shall bring the book home at Christmas time for you to see.

Well, Pop, you said I'd get in this place when we were standing there at the bus and I'm here sure enough. It's a grand school and I love it already. The Navy spirit has been instilled in us very deeply already. They say (and I'm sure it is true) that the whole Navy is built on loyalty, loyalty first to your Company, then to your Battalion, then to the Regiment and last, but not least, all for the Academy. That spirit, although dormant, is always a sleeping volcano that every now and then erupts and manifests itself.

I only hope that I can justify the confidence which my family has shown itself to at all times have in me.

Good luck and much love,
Scottie

Annapolis, 11 September 1936

Dear Mother,

Received your and Dad's letters. Thank you muchly and stuff.

I'm so glad you saw <u>Annapolis Farewell</u>. It should have given you a good idea about life at the Academy.

You have asked about the meals. They are excellent, plentiful and quite much better than one could possibly expect in a place so large. WE have turkey once a week and usually chicken once, ice cream at least three or four times a week, all the milk you can drink and then some, steak (tenderloin, if you please), roast beef, veal cutlets etc.

I am on the training table and so eat toast three times a day, beef or chicken broth once a day, steak more often than the rest, no coffee or tea, no dessert except when it's ice cream, two kinds of cereal instead of one for breakfast etc.

My roommates are Frederick Sturdevant from Wichitaw, Kansas and John Costello from Lawrence, Mass. They are both good eggs.

The only uniform we have is white works so far, the uniform you saw the Plebes drilling in. We wear leggings and caps to drill in, caps and white works to noon meal, and hats (with the blue band) to all other formations and to recitations.

Went to German for the first time today and it's going to be a pipe. Heard Dr. Thomas lecture on "Philology, the German Language, and Its Connection with English" for the second time.

Studying "Solid" in Math, not so hard, not so easy.

The most intriguing thing about Math. is the slide rules. You can do anything with the darn things, logs, square root, cube root, and inverse reciprocals etc.

      Love to all,
        Scottie

Annapolis, 17 September 1935

Dear Family,

Well, here's for another letter. There is no news in particular. Things are going along in regular routine.

I'm now on the second Plebe team. Was promoted once on Monday and again on Tuesday. How long it lasts I don't know. We play our first game this Saturday with the Varsity.

We will have finished Solid Geometry by the end of next week-then to Trig. I am taking beginning German from Thomas and to date it is a frightful bore.

You wanted to know where I room so here's a sketch of the side of Bancroft Hall in which I live now, showing my present home and my new one – we move up to the fourth deck when "ac" academic year starts.

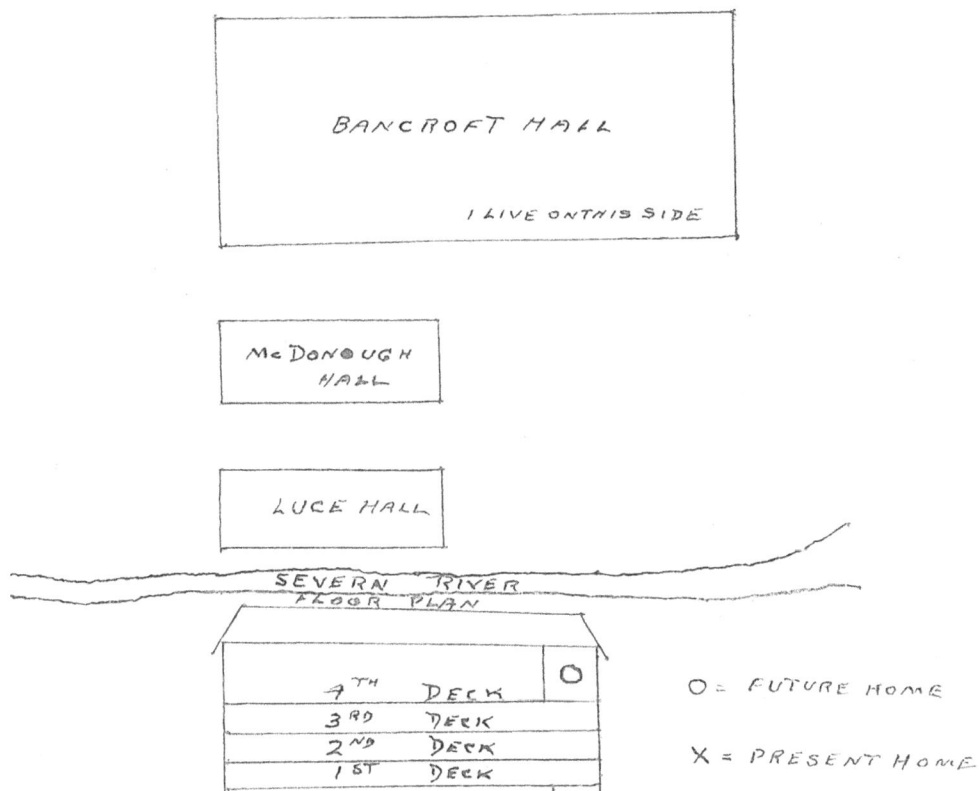

Bancroft Hall residence.

Both overlook Severn.

Quite an artist aren't I? I don't know whether you will be able to get anything from my rather crude attempt at art.

Just now we are waiting for noon formation which busts as 12:30- in just about ten minutes. At this meal it is necessary to wear a clean suit of whites and be immaculate in every where since it is at this formation that the personal inspection is made.

Oh, by the way, I wish you would send me my camera. I could get some good pictures if I only had it.

Time for lunch - finish later.

9:55

Taps busts in five minutes so I guess I'd better give up writing any more for a while.

> Love to all,
> Scottie

Scottie and the team.

PLEBE TO WWII HERO, MY JOURNEY FROM ANNAPOLIS TO MIDWAY

Annapolis, 20 September 1935

Dear Family,

There is really nothing to write about but I must use one of my new envelopes. They gave each of us on the football squad eight of them. [Special football covers, with football schedule, all in Navy Blue and Gold.]

We play our first game tomorrow (with the Varsity). It is a regularly scheduled game with outside officials and everything. I expect to see some action although I'm still on the second team, darn it.

Tomorrow we go into blue service (our regular blue uniforms). I have mine and it fits perfectly. I am going to try to get somebody to take my picture so I can send it to you.

I received Dad's letter with the applications. I can manage to get the required number, but for heaven's sake, tell him to lay off any more high pressure salesmanship.

We finished the Solid Mensuration book today and review for a week now until a week from Thursday. All our Math. here is strictly practical application - no proving of theorems etc. It makes it a lot more interesting.

Today I was on Watch. Technically, in Navy nomenclature, I was M.O.D. (Mate of the Deck). It was my duty to stand watch at intervals (being relieved by a second section at approved times) on the Terrace Deck of the First Battalion wing. (Bancroft Hall being divided into wings according to Battalions). I did not attend formation or drill and had as my duty the responsibility of delivering messages and orders to members of my Batt. both singly and as a unit, these orders coming from the Batt. office by voice tube. I had to make inspections after each formation had busted and make sure the deck was clear, that is, that every body who was supposed to be was at formation. It is a very tiresome job and I'm glad it is over. No more Watch until next year. The upper classes handle it while they are here.

I got my first delinquency report today, better known as "Pap". My bed was not properly turned back at reveille (mattress folded double, clothing and pillow on top). Of course the one time I forgot about it the D.O. (Duty Officer or Officer of Watch, a commissioned Lt. Comd.) had to inspect. It means three demerits. That is, of course, nothing to worry about. Plebes are allowed 300.

Yes, I see Charlie McCall once in a while. He is in another Batt. and consequently in another part of the building.

They certainly run their athletics in a big way down here. They have mokes (negroes) galore with special uniforms with the emblem N.A.A. on them (Navy Athletic Association) to do all the work. They take movies of every scrimmage to show us later and point out all our faults. The practice field (Varsity) is surrounded by a canvas wall with a Marine stationed at the entrance to keep all undesirable visitors out. It is really the biggest of big time and quite thrilling to a mere small college boy. The Plebe "A" squad has four coaches and the "B" squad two. Heaven knows how many the Varsity has. One thing gratifying-both the big shots for the Varsity, Miller and Hamilton, know me and call me "Whit".

I'm writing this during study hour 2000 to 2130 – 8:00 to 9:30 P.M. A plane just zoomed over the grounds and everybody's window went up and heads stuck out to see what it was. He has gone now. Probably an old grad. giving us the salute or saying "Hello" to somebody here in the yard.

Academic year begins a week from Monday. Then begins the time when Plebes rate everything unpleasant.

I'm going to beg my bathrobe on the Army – Navy game. We make the bets with the Kadets by mail and pay by mail. The Army bathrobes are real nice and I'd like one.

Well, I guess I go now.

Much love to all,

Scottie

Annapolis, 26 September 1935

Dear Family,

Well, I'm moved. My new room is 1439 and it is a honey. We have what is usually a First Class room. We are right in the corner facing the river view and up the river (two ways), a beautiful view and high up. I'm in a "B" room that is by myself. Two of us have these "B" rooms, each room being off the main room which the other two have. We have a shower and a large closet in our suite which makes it very nice. Of course we have four flights to climb but it is worth while.

The Varsity - Plebe game ended up with a score of 54 - 3 - guess in whose favor - I played about a half.

The whole D.....s family came to see me Sunday. They were on their way back from Delaware. It was their wedding anniversary and they had been on a long drive. I only saw them for about an hour but A.. is coming down again Sunday and I'm going to have dinner with her at Carvel Hall, the one nice hotel here.

I have bought a fountain pen on requisition, a new $7:50 Parker. It cost me $4:15. That is the kind of prices we get here.

The Plebes play their first game Sat. with Dean Academy from Mass. I probably won't see much of the game.

We haven't much to do today. No classes. Just rehearsal for our presentation to the Regiment tomorrow. Monday work begins in earnest.

A.. L.. has started at Goucher.

As you can see by the stamp on the back of the envelope, there is going to be a big time here on Oct. 10th. Our 90th anniversary, a sham battle, football game and about a million yards of "gold braid" around I guess.

This is all for now.

> Much love to all,
> Scottie

ROBERT SCOTT WHITMAN JR.

Annapolis, 3 October 1935

Dear Family,

I'm sorry to have let writing go longer than usual, but I have never been so busy in all my life.

We are down to a regular schedule – study, recite, study, recite, lunch, recite, drill, football, and bed.

Of course we Plebes are taking a beating and will from now till June week.

Today we had our final in Solid Mensuration. It was awfully tough and I have no idea how I came out. Next we take Trig. We are studying Descriptive Geometry in "Steam" (Marine Engineering), Unity Coherence and Emphasis in Bull, (English), Chemistry in "Juice" (Electrical Engineering), and <u>haben</u> and <u>sein</u> in "Dago" (German).

We have been practicing for the Sham Battle. It is going to be funny. It sure is too bad that only First Classmen rate playing dead. The lazy stiffs!

Of course we are wearing blue service all the time now. We, of course, wear separate starched collars and cuffs!!! and are the cuffs ever a bother! They hook on like a collar and are stiff as a board.

From what I hear we on the training table are very lucky. The rest of the Plebes lead a dismal life at meals. They are the target for a constant barrage of questions to which they must know the answers. All sorts of pranks. Of course we will get it at the end of the season. I hope by then they will have tamed down.

It is indeed a great life if you don't weaken – but I like it.

I'm sleepy – Goodnight.

Love,

Scottie

It would be real nice if sometime you could bake me some cookies or something. Anything to relieve the starved sweet tooth.

Annapolis, 6 October 1935

Dear Mother,

I believe today is the most dismal day I have encountered here as yet, dismal climatically I mean, not mentally. It is raining and has been doing so steadily all evening. It is one of those monotonous rains and should last quite a time.

The Plebes won again yesterday from Georgia Military College-37 - 2. I played about a quarter.

We saw almost a half of the Varsity game. It is such a change to be in a big school where spirit is so prevalent. You should hear the Regiment cheer. It has got Colgate beat a mile.

This is going to be just sort of a "rambly" letter so don't get discouraged if it lacks good old Unity Coherence and Emphasis.

As far as the spirit is concerned there are some interesting customs you might like to hear about.

Of course every Friday night is a big pep night. When we line up to go to chow, and the order is given for the companies to march off, each company, as it does squads right or left, to march off shouts in unison -

N - A - V - Y - F I G H T - F I G H T - F I G H T!

when we get into the mess hall, part of the 150 piece band is there, playing the "Navy Victory" Song. Of course everybody is singing and shouting. It took 15 minutes last Friday before they could get us quieted down long enough to seat us. The whole meal is in an uproar from beginning to end. Way at the end of the mess hall some table will give a cheer - then the next table and the next - up one side and down the other.

Every Saturday evening - if we win (I don't know what happens when we lose) we yell as we march off -

N - A - V - Y - F O U G H T L I K E H E L L!

some fun eh!

After dinner.

And it's cold too - I have been listening to the world series in my First Classman's room. Each Plebe has a First Classman to whom he reports before each meal formation. He sort of takes care of me. Never runs me, and is a sort of protector as is the case with every Plebe's First Classman. Mine is my Company Commander. Name is Riewe - Quite a good egg.

I met a Second Classman who knows Peg Harmes. He "spooned

on me". (Shook hands with me and therefore declares himself my friend and doesn't run me, and I am free to visit him at any time, listen to his radio, read his papers, and so forth.)

My instructor in Math. wrote both our Trig. book and Solid book. He is a whiz. I took the Solid exam on Thursday. I have no idea how I made out.

Every week the names of those Midshipmen who are "unsat" (unsatisfactory) in any subject are posted. So far I have stayed off the "tree," as it is called.

Tell Dad that I may have to disappoint some one of his friends about tickets – there is a great demand for them and I may have to cut down two on somebody. I'll know soon.

The "Naval Institute Proceedings", a monthly magazine put out by the Naval Institute, is devoted entirely to the Academy this month. It gives a fine picture of life here and I'm going to send a copy home.

We had our first lab in Chemistry the other day. I think I shall enjoy it very much.

The clippings you have sent have interested me greatly.

I would appreciate it very much if you would send me my English Rhetoric Book and my English Rhetoric Outlines – the course here is the same as the one at Dickinson and my book and outlines are much better than the one used here. I can crack a 4.0, I think, if I use a little time on it.

There is so much talk of "Bilging" [being dropped} out of this place that I really am scared. I'm going to work like the devil because my marks here effect directly my whole Naval Career.

This is all for now.

Much love to all,
Scottie

Annapolis, 9 October 1935

Dear Family,

I've just finished watching a dress rehearsal of the Sham Battle. We have a wonderful view of part of it from our windows, and, since the football squads are excused, I had about half of the squads both Plebe and Varsity, in my room watching the fun. The attack was made on the Parade Grounds from land, sea and air. Lots of noise and excitement.

The big day is tomorrow and I guess there will be really a lot of "Gold Braid" around.

I have finally got the pictures I had taken. They are horrible but you can see how I look in a uniform anyhow. I'm enclosing them with the negatives. They were taken after chapel on Sunday. Hence the white gloves.

It has been really cold here lately. We have not had to wear reefers, but we have been using two blankets at night.

I now have two blue uniforms, an overcoat, and a reefer. Full dress comes next.

I am sending a copy of the "Proceedings" under separate cover. It is quite the finest thing of its type I have ever seen. Please stop reading all sorts of things from my letters which are not there. I never liked any place as well as this and am getting along fine.

       Love to all,
        Scottie

ROBERT SCOTT WHITMAN JR.

Annapolis, 13 October 1935

Dear Family,

Well, two weeks of the academic year have passed. Seventy days to Christmas. Everyone here is looking forward to it already. This place is the greatest school in the world, but ten days out of it will be quite all right also.

The Plebes played Massanutten Military Academy yesterday and won 25 - 17. I think I'd put this year's Plebe team against any Prep School in the country and bet on them. I got to play a quarter and we scored once while I was in.

The Virginia game was as good a game as I have seen in a long time. Virginia led 7 - 6 at the end of the half; but once Navy got going there was no stopping them. It was a very, very exciting game from beginning to end and quite a suitable game to be played before the Alumni crowd that was here.

I didn't see much of the celebration Thursday as we Plebes had to play a game with the Varsity "B" squad in the morning. We won 14 - 0.

The next five weeks of football are going to be full of good games for the Navy. Yale, Notre Dame, Princeton, Penn., and Army, every one a strong team. There sure are going to be fireworks.

Next Saturday the Third and Fourth Batts go to New Haven. I don't go but we get to go to Princeton. Maybe I can collect my five bucks. [loaned to a Princeton friend]

From Notre Dame on we make every trip. Some fun!

I think George ought to think about coming here. He has quite a time yet and might be able to swing it. [George received an appointment later but failed the eye test.] It is possible that I may have some influence by that time. It is a thought anyway. He sure could get his fill of airplanes here.

A.. was to have come down today but she could not make it. I am hoping I can swing it to have her to the Army game. I think I possibly will be able to and it will go a long way toward repaying her and her family for their many, many kindnesses, besides being a more than pleasant relief from the more or less monastic existence one leads here. I still have nine dollars left from my last pay check and, if I can collect from Gross, I'll be able to do it.

"Toots" baked me a cake and sent it to me the other day and, surprise of surprises, it was darn good cake. She is going Tri Delt at Goucher and is quite happy there. I am very glad.

There has nothing of particular interest happened here. We went to Rifle Range on Friday and we Plebes worked the Butts for the Second Class, that is, we took care of the targets, ran them up and down, and signaled score and placement of hits. Whoever was on my target was lousy. He scored more "swaboes" (zeroes) than anything else.

I have sent the magazine. I hope you enjoy it.

  Much love to all,
   Scottie

Annapolis, 20 October 1935

Dear Family,

I fear you think I have fearfully neglected you during this last week. I have been getting busier and busier as each day passes and consequently have found less and less time to write. I'll try to catch up on the news now, however.

Last Friday we had our first monthly examination in "Bull". It was not especially hard and I am hoping I make a good mark in it. Tomorrow we take a monthly in "Steam" and Wednesday in "Skinny". The Steam is entirely Descriptive Geometry (orthographic projection). The Chemistry is quite interesting. Of course, as yet, we have not progressed very far in the course. They told us that the only object of the course was to teach us to test boiler waters and know about the manufacture of powder.

Yesterday the Plebes played "Kiski," rated usually as the best Prep School team in the country. We took them 27 - 0. I played some. Did rather well if I do say so. Busted up a couple of passes, recovered a fumble, and tackled men for losses a couple of times. I think I can be sure of making my numerals.

The custom here is to wear your Athletic Insignia on the back of your bathrobe.

A.. E........ was down today for the afternoon. I had special permission to "drag". The Plebe football players were allowed to "carry on" yesterday and today. Between "dragging" and "carrying on", I was a pretty "ratey" Plebe.

The Plebes don't have any games now for four weeks. Then we play Penn. State Frosh and Eramus High School of New York City.

Next week we go to Baltimore to the Notre Dame game. I hope we take those Irishers. They seem to play a pretty good brand of ball this year.

It was a darn shame that we had to lose at New Haven. We outplayed them most of the game. They pay of in points though - that's the hitch.

I am very sure that I'm going to have to cut down on Mr. Behan. Dad's friends can feel lucky they are getting any tickets at all. Each Midshipmen is to be limited to eight. I got some other boys to get some for me and it's lucky I did because now you can't find a soul who has any left on his applications. I know - I tried to get some for a cousin of Dr. D......

The score now is 40 days to Army, 61 to Christmas and 228 to graduation. You can see how they are looked forward to.

Outside the Gym there is a huge football schedule, and at the bottom the number of days to Army is posted every day.

We gave the team a big send off on Thursday evening – The whole Regiment turned out in front of Bancroft Hall and I never heard so much noise before in my life. This morning the whole Regiment was out at the No. 2 gate at 7:35 to welcome them back.

When the football season is all over I don't know what I'm going to do. My roommates all talk about the "beatings" they take at the tables. I just won't know the score when I leave the training table.

The whole D...... family will be at the Notre Dame game. I'll have about half an hour in the stadium after the game to see them.

I do hope the magazine interested you all.

By the way I was _not_ in the old time football game. The Plebe "B" squad took part in that. We had nothing to do with it.

Yesterday morning we stood a really tough room inspection. Luckily, although there was dirt, there was not enough to put us on the "Pap".

I have five demerits so far – three for not turning my bed back, and two for having a library book over due.

I see that Army took Harvard rather handily and how about that Penn. – Columbia touchdown spree? Looks like I'm going to see some good ball games this year. Some difference from last year's small time stuff!

I still think it would be a good idea if Mother would bake me some cookies or something when she can get a minute.

Every Saturday after our game a couple of other boys and I go into town and eat some slop – gooey sundaes etc.

Our room always buys 15¢ worth of magazines on Saturday. Collier, Saturday Post and Liberty. One of the boys MacGreggor subscribes to the Times so we get a good paper every day.

How is the High School team getting along? I see Dickinson won for a change yesterday. There is a Plebe in my Batt from Elmira. We are having a big argument as to the outcome of the Central – Elmira game.

I suppose it is quite cold in Binghamton now. The nights are very cool but the days are still very warm. We have not yet worn reefers or over-coats.

A.. L.. and I went in and took a look at J.P. Jones sarcophagus. They say the old boy had himself pickled in alcohol – that the coffin was filled with it.

Have you read the "Maudie" story about the Academy? It is quite good. How a <u>Ladies Home Journal</u> got into Bancroft Hall I have no idea, but somehow one got into our room and I read the story.

Well, Tattoo has busted and I have five minutes to get into bed.

Goodnight and love,
Scottie

Annapolis, 27 October 1935

Dear Family,

Well, yesterday we went to Baltimore and saw Navy take a beating. Notre Dame deserved to win, too. We were hopelessly outclassed. Notre Dame has a really fine team, as good as any I have seen.

We got up yesterday morning at 5:45, went to our classes at 7:00 instead of 8:00, and had lunch at 9:20. Immediately after that we left for Baltimore. Why we left so early I have no idea, because after we got there we stood in ranks for easily an hour and a half before we marched on to the field.

It gives a guy quite a thrill marching through the streets of Baltimore singing Navy songs and then marching onto the field behind a 100 piece band to the tune of "Anchors Aweigh" - 2000 of us. My company was the first to march into the stadium and of course everybody gave us a big ovation. We gave Notre Dame a cheer, then about faced and gave a Navy cheer, and then got to our seats.

At the half we put on the famous card stunts. I guess they were O.K. I had to take part - all Plebes do - and couldn't see them.

I saw A.. and her father and mother for about five minutes after the game.

Next week we go to Princeton. I was dead tired when I got back from Baltimore - what will it be after the Princeton trip?

The Navy - Notre Dame game was the largest I have seen. There were 63,000 people in the stadium.

I got a letter from Dot Sears today. She says that her father and mother and the three girls are going to Syracuse next week.

There is not much news around here. Four weeks of academic year have passed and I guess I'm doing all right so far. This place is a lot tougher on you in studies than any I have heard of, nevertheless.

It's only about 55 days to Christmas. If you are thinking anything about Christmas presents, think of nothing but money. Pass that on to the West. I want to spend the latter part of the vacation in Baltimore and I want to have enough money to have a good time. It's the only chance I'll have between the time I came in and June Week. Pass that word on to the West - it might do some good out there.

There is, as I say, no particular news so for the time being I'll close.

        Love to all,
          Scottie

Annapolis, 1 November 1935

Dear Mother,

If I don't run into the toughest luck! Two days before the Princeton game, and I have to come down with catarrhal fever and they shove me in to the hospital. Don't let that word hospital worry you. I am running only a little temperature and feel quite chipper. Around this place, if you aren't up to going to classes, there is no place for you but the hospital. Anywhere else I would be O.K. just staying in bed a couple of days. It is a Naval Academy regulation thought that you can't be sick and stay away from strict medical surveillance.

So here I am - I'll be out by Monday, in just enough time to miss the football trip.

Please don't worry - I'm not nearly as sick as I was this summer. I am getting a good rest, too.

I assure you it wasn't the cookies - they were the best of anything I've tasted in a long time, and they lasted just exactly fourteen minutes.

       Love to all,
        Scottie

Annapolis, 8 November 1935

Dear Family,

Well, I'm out and have been for two days. I feel fine again and ready to yell my lungs out at Philadelphia tomorrow. According to my definition with the help of A.. E........, catarrhal fever is acute "sinusitis" or a bad cold. Well, I had no bad cold. I had a little but not much. I had quite a fever and a headache. They fed me quinine – I guess it was quinine – and sprayed my nose and gave me cough syrup. Anyway, I feel fit as a fiddle again and got a good rest and re-read Work of Art and read The Inquisitor by Hugh Walpole.

My marks are all O. K. for the first month. As you know they mark on a basis of 4.0 as perfect. I got so far as I know the following:

> German 3.65
> English 3.34
> Chemistry 3.30
> Engineering 3.16
> Trig. 34.20 (approximate)

So you see although there is much room for improvement, I am getting along all right. I'd like to "star" (get the privilege to wear a star on the collar of my dress uniform), but I doubt if I make it. It requires a 3.4, and 3.4's are hard to get here – so much tougher than an "A" in college.

I do hope we can take Penn tomorrow. The team has a lot of potential power – much more than has been shown to date. Maybe they will click tomorrow.

We leave tomorrow morning at 8:30 – will get in Philly.....

I had to leave this in the middle to turn to and dust. The word was just passed to get cleaned up, there was going to be a "class A" inspection. Nothing has happened so far. I'm hoping nothing will.

I don't know whether there is any news of any interest. Last night we had movies. We have them every Thursday in Smoke Hall – a new reel, "Popeye", and a Grantland Rice sportlight. Then on Saturday we have a regular movie in Mahan Hall.

The Scientific American you sent me was greatly appreciated.

Today I received the certificate of my appointment, signed by the Secretary of the Navy. I don't know how to send it home but, if I can't find some way, I'll bring it with me Christmas.

The Army – Navy tickets should be coming along any day now. I still don't know how Mr. Behan is going to make out. I'm hoping he'll get all of them, but there is no way of telling.

I wonder how this place will seem after the excitement of the football season is over. Of course we are looking forward to the Army game already. Each day brings that big day closer. That is the day that we have all of four hours after the game to spend free from the Academy. Sounds funny, looking forward to getting away – you'd think we didn't like the place. That, of course, is as far from the truth as anything could possibly be. However, the infernal routine and discipline does get you down sometimes.

We had cutter drill today. We row out into the basin in cutters and then execute maneuvers by flag signals from one of the motor launches – just like the fleet, only it's harder on the backs and is conducive to blisters.

There is not much more to write now so

Aufwiedersehen, and much love,
Scottie

PLEBE TO WWII HERO, MY JOURNEY FROM ANNAPOLIS TO MIDWAY

Annapolis, 12 November 1935

Dear Family,

I received your two letters today and was indeed very glad to get them.

The game at Philly was quite as exciting as any game I have seen to date. I am till hoarse from yelling. On paper it does look as though Penn outplayed us, but it is not so much the case as it seems. True we got our first touchdown by help of a penalty, but we were kept from getting one by three straight fifteen-yard penalties. We carried the ball right back every time, only to be penalized. The fourth time we failed to make the necessary 25 yards in four downs. I believe though that we are going to have to do some mighty hard playing to beat Army.

Next week the second set of monthly exams come up. I hope I can get through them as well as I did the last time. I am constantly in a frightened condition about Academics – as is everyone else. There is so much talk of "bilging" (flunking out).

This Saturday the Plebes play the Penn State Frosh. This time we are going to play at eleven o'clock. That will give us a chance to see the Columbia game – which is very fine indeed.

As usual the subject of every bull session is either the Army game or Christmas leave. It is increasingly noticeable how everyone, including myself, live in the future here. The First Classmen live for graduation, and so on down the classes.

Every day we have during the last period in the afternoon what is called "P Work" or practical work. Usually three times a week it is either seamanship or executive. Executive may be infantry, rifle range, lecture, or, later in the year, dancing lessons. One day it is a long drill in "Steam" (Marine Engineering). The other day it is "Skinny" (Chemistry).

As you know, the day is divided into six periods, four in the morning with alternating study periods, and two in the afternoon.

So we are going to have both the Mayor and the ex-Mayor at the Army game. The tickets will be issued soon and will be sent immediately. They will all be sent to Dad. They were so mixed up on the applications that they could not be sent to the individuals.

No more now, Much love,

        Scottie

ROBERT SCOTT WHITMAN JR.

Annapolis, 17 November 1935

Dear Family,

Well, I guess Navy sort of walked over Columbia - walked all over them in fact. They really looked good yesterday. It was a horrid day to watch a football game though. A driving rain coming in from the bay and awfully cold. Consequently the crowd was not so good. The game was broadcast by W. M. C. A. I don't believe you could pick it up.

The monthly exams started Friday with English. Monday we have "Steam", Wednesday Chemistry, and Saturday the final in Trig. I hope I can hit them O. K.

There is nothing to write about that is the least bit interesting. It is still nasty out - raining and blowing.

A.. E........ and two friends are due to arrive in about half an hour. I just called Baltimore to see if they were coming and they are on the way. I got the two friends dates. All we can do is sit in the reception room.

I got one of the girls a date with a boy from Texas named Leroy Harris. She is going to Philadelphia with A.. L.. and Harris going to have a date with her. Today is a sort of get-acquainted party. I'm going to room with Leroy next year. He is an O. K. guy and much more my type than my present roommates. He has had two years at the U. of Texas.

I don't think there is any more news so I guess I'll quit writing.

Will write soon again.

> Love to all,
> Scottie.

Annapolis, 23 November 1935

Dear Mother,

Tomorrow I'm on watch and, being officially on tonight although not actually. I do not rate the movies, so I guess I'll write a letter.

The exams are all over now - thank goodness. This sure has been a hectic week. I guess I made out all right in all of them - I sure hope so anyway.

Today, we beat Erasmus Hall of Brooklyn 66 - 0. It was our last game. The second team started and made two touchdowns in about four minutes. That is all the time we played. The first team played about an equal time and the scrubs did the rest.

A week from tonight we will be in Philadelphia. It hardly seems possible. It has been so long that I have been looking forward to it.

You asked about Christmas leave. The leave starts at noon formation on Saturday, December 21. It ends at evening formation on January 1, 1936. That means we have just eleven days.

I don't' know anything about trains or bus schedules as yet. When I know them I can tell you better when to expect me.

It has been fearfully cold here for the last week. A cruel wind comes in from the ocean and makes it seem so very much colder than it really is. We have been wearing reefers to classes. Reefers are like mackinaws - half length coats. With these we wear gray gloves. With our overcoats (the finest thing we have and cost $89.00) we wear white gloves until we put on blue cap covers. Then we put on gray gloves. We put on blue cap covers after the Army game. It sure will be a drab place when that happens. The white caps look so much nicer. When I'm home I'm going to wear white cap covers. Do not be mistaken though - I'm not going to wear my uniform all over the place on leave. I want to wear my civilian clothes (if I have any) just as much as I can. One does get sick of the same uniform all the time.

I wonder if my clothes will fit me. I have lost about 15 pounds - I weight 205 now - of course they will fit me though.

I'm wondering how you will like me in my uniform. When I come home you will find me in the best condition I have ever been in.

Well, it's almost time to go to bed. As we are wont to say "another day another dollar".

      Love to all,
       Scottie

ROBERT SCOTT WHITMAN JR.

Annapolis, 30 November 1935

Dear Family,

Well, the tragic day is over. The less said about the game the better, except that in the second half, when it was too late, the boys snapped out of it and played circles around the Army.

Aside from the actual game, I had as good a time as ever I have had. We arrived in Philadelphia at about 11:15 and as soon as the other three battalions had arrived we marched to the field. At 12:15 sharp we marched on. The Regiment marched on first this year since we won last year. Of course there was the usual applause as we cheered Army, about faced, cheered the team, and then manned the stands. Since we entered first we got a chance to see the "Kaydets" march in. I must admit that they march infinitely better than we do. After all, that's all they'll do for the rest of their lives.

It was great fun to see the meeting of the goat and the mule and hear the razzings that were exchanged across the field. Finally I have seen all the color and glory of an Army – Navy game.

Right after the game, Harris and I went to A.. E.......'s and her friend's seats. We struggled through the crowd and went over to the hotel and got cleaned up and warm once more.

Then we went to the Hotel Pennsylvania and "dined and danced". It was awfully crowded, but we had a grand time. We were to leave at 9:15 and at 9:14 we got to the station. It was a close shave but no harm done.

All in all, it was a very successful day. We got back to the Academy at 1:30 A.M. A.. and her friend had a grand time as did Harris and I.

Now there are twenty more days to Christmas leave. Let's hope they go quickly.

Love to all,
Scottie

Annapolis, 6 December 1935

Dear Family,

Well, it's only two weeks away now, and it seems like two months. I don't know as yet how I'm coming home. I haven't had a chance to check up on train and bus schedules as yet. Tomorrow when I am out in town I'll stop in at the ticket office and get the dope. I do know that we get greatly reduced rates on the trains and probably the buses. I think it is round trip for fare and a dollar, but I am not sure.

A.. E........ wants me to spend a night with her before I come on home. If the schedules fit in that way I shall – otherwise I don't know. She is driving down on the 21st and is going to take me to Baltimore anyway. That will save me a lot of time getting out of here.

The training tables have, of course, broken up and I am sitting at one of the regular tables. The Plebes at the regular tables take pretty much of a beating, but it is really not so bad.

My marks for last month took a slump – undoubtedly due, partially at least, to my hospital time. However, I am satisfactory in everything and have nothing to worry about. Math. is my big trouble. Funny too – I thought it was going to be a snap at one time.

I have only about five minutes to make formation for a "Bull" class, so good-bye for the time being.

        Love to all,
         Scottie

Annapolis, 8 December 1935

Dear Family,

I've checked up on the train and bus schedules. There is only one possible bus I can take that will get me in at any reasonable hour. That is one that leaves Baltimore at 9:30 A.M. and arrives in Binghamton at 9:03 P.M. The tax is $10.90 round trip.

The time is really passing far more rapidly than I expected. We are so busy that there is hardly a free minute. Of course being busy makes the minutes fly.

Right now as usual I'm waiting for A.. L.. (as usual) I doubt very much if she comes down though. As happens every time when she comes, it is raining. It never fails.

Tonight at the table, two of us Plebes have to put on a skit for the entertainment of the upper classmen at our end of the table. It is entitled "Sherman's March to the Sea" – I have no idea what it will be as we have had no rehearsal.

The tables aren't so bad. Most of the "running" consists of their asking us questions about the Navy which, of course, is instructive and some of the things are really worth knowing.

I cannot think of anything else of interest.

      Love to all,
       Scottie

Annapolis, 18 December 1935

Dear Mother,

I'm sorry I haven't written sooner but we are in the midst of exams and I have been very busy. I received your letter with the fare month – I will arrive at 11:00 – whatever – it is, on Sunday evening via D. L. & W.

It sure is going to be grand to get home again. It seems so long since I got in here.

There is really no news of interest. Friday night we have our usual Christmas dinner. It is quite a festive occasions. Each man at the table chipped in 50¢ and we are going to have a little Christmas tree and everything.

I have to work now and take my last exam, Chemistry.

   Love to all,
    Scottie

Annapolis, 20 December 1935

Dear Mother,

    I'm packing. It doesn't seem possible that after all this time I actually am going to get away on leave.

    This is just a note to answer your question about Marsh and Mrs. Sheridan. If you are sure you can have them, all right – I think it would be awfully nice. Please do not do it if it will be any trouble.

    I'm as excited as a kid about getting home.

    Will be there as planned on Sunday evening.

    Love to all,

    Scottie
The only exam mark I know is English – 3.42.

Annapolis, 2 January 1936

Dear Family,

Back to work again. For the first few hours after I got back, I believe I never hated anything or any place as I did this. But, when I stopped to think how essentially worth while everything I do here is, how vital the whole thing is to the welfare of the rest of my days, I sort of stopped hating it.

There is, of course, no news of the Academy as yet – we have had one day of classes, Math., "Bull", and "Skinny".

The Severn is frozen over but melting fast in the rain that is falling. It is not cold. They had an awful lot of snow here and in Baltimore, but I think it will soon all disappear.

The laundry arrived this afternoon as did Dad's letter. He said he was enclosing a clipping and then evidently forgot to do so, at least, I found no trace of any.

The stay in Baltimore was a very pleasant one – as it always is. We went to several parties on New Years Eve, ending up at Trudi Evers. You remember my speaking of her – she went to Dickinson last year.

There is really nothing more to say. I so enjoyed being home. I don't think I realized how much I missed home until I came back.

I'll write again soon.

      Love to all,
        Scottie

Annapolis, 6 January 1936

Dear Mother,

Your letter came today. Have no fear I have snapped out of the fog - did so long ago. Everybody is blue after Christmas leave - at least I found a good many others in the same boat.

Have just finished writing an outline for a ten page English theme. I'm writing about a city in Tasmania, Hobart it is called. Used to be a center for sailing ships of all kinds. Sort of an interesting old place.

There is really no news of any value. The routine has settled down to normal and all is the same as before Christmas.

My watch has not varied a second since I arrived here. It's such a grand watch - I'm so proud of it. A lot of the boys have commented on it - voluntarily that is.

I got a letter off to Aunt Julie today.

Harris Rhode, another boy, and I had a fine game of bridge on Saturday afternoon. Skipped the basketball game. We went to the movie in the yard on Saturday evening. It was lousy.

I guess that is all for now.

Much love to all,
Scottie

Annapolis, 11 January 1936

Dear Family,

I have seen the movie in the yard, and so I'm staying home and taking things easy.

This afternoon I saw the Penn State – Navy basketball game – it was a corker. Navy, after trading the advantage with Penn State, finally came out ahead and won 36 – 30.

After the game I took care of Mr. Pinkerton's (First Class) drag while he played with the "B" squad. We went to the movies and had quite a nice time. I brought her back to him at 6:00.

I believe I wrote to you about my English theme. I'm quite proud of it. It's all finished and typed and ready to be handed in tomorrow. I found a fine map of Tasmania and copied it – decorating it with sailing ships and spouting whales etc. (all copied, of course). I really put quite a bit of work into it. I sure hope my "Prof" appreciates it. If I get it back, I shall send it home.

Yesterday I had the "guard" – acted as Assistant Mate of the Third Deck. The "Watch" is really quite a bore and I'm glad it's over for another twenty days.

You wrote about lighting. Early last week the new lamps were installed and are fine. The difference is quite noticeable. Your thoughts of a letter to the "Supe" are quite unnecessary therefore.

Term exams are coming up soon. They really are of no consequence to us Plebes however. We have only monthly exams in "Steam" and "Skinny" – no finals. These are the two bugaboos – and the exams this month will be just like those of others. We have a final in "Bull" and "Dago" and a subject exam in Algebra. I think I'm doing much better in Algebra than I did in the Solid or Trig. I have no way of actually finding out since Math. marks are posted only at the completion of the subject. I can, therefore, only hope I am right.

On February 8th, the Masqueraders put on their annual stage play. It is the first time that Plebes rate a week end drag – if I can find some money somewhere, I'm going to have A.. E........ come down for the week end. Naturally, all we Plebes are looking forward to it eagerly.

I have been smoking my Christmas pipe in preference to cigarettes, and it is already well broken in.

ROBERT SCOTT WHITMAN JR.

"Steam" has taken on a new angle now. We have commenced Elementary Drawing and the sketching of standard machine parts. It is our first contact with the actual engineering that we will come to know so intimately later in our years here. It is quite interesting but, as is all "Steam", at the same time difficult.

A funny thing happened today. You remember how Dot Sears stood me up that Sunday night while I was home? Today I received a box - quite a large one. It was filled with two kinds of fudge - very delicious and almost as good as Mother's. It was from Dot - with a very apologetic card. I'll bet her m other put it up to her. Oh, well, the chow was good. I think she wants to start a correspondence. I suppose I'll have to thank her for it.

Love to all,
Scottie

Plebe to WWII Hero, My Journey From Annapolis to Midway

Annapolis, 18 January 1936

Dear Family,

Another Saturday evening and time enough to write another letter. I've seen the show and doubt that, even had I not, I would go. There is so much comfort in just taking it easy and getting little things done that ought to be done. This evening I've stowed two clean batches of laundry and taken a long hot shower, and now feel down right at ease.

This afternoon Harris and I went for a long walk. Were both too broke to go to the movies, and now I'm glad we were, for we started out to see Annapolis. First we went down by the waterfront (the city's waterfront) and looked at the oyster boats, hundreds of them, all with the same dirty white paint, filthy decks cluttered with nets and empty oil barrels, stubby masts and dirty furled sails. They come in every week end with the week's catch and go out again early Monday morning.

From there we cruised around back into town and out again to the west. We hit West Annapolis finally and decided that we would try to find Dr. Thomas. After inquiring at several places we finally found out where he lived and, after walking ten minutes or so, we found his home. It is quite a nice place - out in the country, and it is beautifully furnished. Dr. Thomas was not in but his wife was and so our trip was not futile - I know her also. We had quite a chat. Tommy came in later.

I guess, all in all, we covered about twelve miles - and had a grand time.

All our drills in seamanship are inside drills now, and the things we do are quite interesting. Today, for instance, we had a lecture on putting boats over the side, and hoisting them aboard again. The "Chief" (boson's mate) had a little working model that showed us the complicated process quite simply. Then we had a talk about the "cradeling" of the boats, and other entirely disassociated things about the "battle wagons". There was a seven-foot, scale model of the New York (complete in every detail) to help him along. He pointed out the various things he told us about on it - such things as accommodation ladders, "jacob's ladders", davits, life lines, buoys etc.

Time before that, we had a lecture on the use of collision mats, mats made of canvas and coated with unraveled hemp - used to cover holes in the hulk below the water line in case of emergency. They do not keep the sea out, but break the force of the sea so it won't rush in and tear out bulkheads thereby flooding other compartments.

"Steam" is much more interesting now. I've told you we are "sketching and dimensioning" now. We are given models. From them we must make sketches and place upon them all dimensions accurately. Later on we are going to have to take these same sketches and make regular orthographic machine drawings from them.

We are reading poetry in "Bull" now, Burns and Wordsworth. My average for last week was either a 3.8 or a 3.7.

I just finished Main Street. I'd never read it, and decided I'd like to, so I did, grabbing a few pages now and then as I had time for it.

The first part of the German exam comes Tuesday. I think I told you that our only term exams at in "Bull" and "Dago". A regular subject exam in Math. and the rest monthly exams.

I believe I could get along with anybody now after living with these roommates of mine. The three are constantly bickering and quarreling. They are of three entirely different types, and naturally the temperaments clash. They cannot seem to overcome this obstacle. I keep out of it all, and get along with all of them. It does take a self control which I never knew I possessed – for I would love sometimes to bust in with both fists flying. As a rule, however, it bothers me not in the least. As long as they keep quiet during study hours – as they frequently don't – I'm satisfied.

Next year, Harris, Jenkins (a boy from Mo.), and Rhode (from Reading) and I are hoping to get together.

I'm about writ out for the time being.

       Love to all,
        Scottie

Annapolis, 25 January 1936

Dear Mother,

I went to the movie tonight, the first time for several weeks. It was "Here Come the Marines", an old picture, I understand, but it was very good.

This week we had two exams, "Dago" (first half), and Math. today. I got a 3.52 on the "Dago" and I approximate a 3.3 on the Math. Next Monday is "Steam", Thursday "Skinny", and Friday "Bull", and Tuesday the second half of the "Dago" exam. Then the first half of my Plebe year is over.

The time has really gone so fast. It doesn't seem that I've been here in the Academy five months, and yet it does seem so long since Christmas.

I think I'm a little home-sick tonight. Not as you may think for the good times and "gadding", but just for the opportunity to sit, to talk to you and Dad and Georgie, and be home.

I often think that maybe you all don't believe me to be aware of the wonderful opportunity I have now. I am, and I don't think it's quite fair that I should have all the luck. I seem to be the lucky one – and I shall make the most of it, so at least you can be proud of me.

I think so often of you and Dad struggling along in the same rut and never complaining and I'm glad you're my family.

This week we've been taking dancing lessons. It has all been quite amusing, especially the looks on the North Carolina wrestlers' faces as they came through "Smoke Hall", where we were taking our lessons and saw a whole company of Plebes dancing together. I really learned nothing new, but it was fun listening to the orchestra and being pushed around by Harris.

This afternoon I went out into town with Jenkins and helped him buy a guitar at a "hock shop". He and his roommates decided that their room lacked "culture", so they decided to learn to play a guitar. None of them know a thing about it. They paid $5.00 for the thing. price included an instruction book and an extra set of strings. I posed as an expert on the things and helped "Ma" (Jenkins) "jew" the guy down. Then we sat in a hamburger joint and "shot the breeze" for hours.

Monday we start taking Analytic Geometry – I wonder how it will be.

We drew our second term books yesterday. Among them was <u>Marks</u>

<u>Handbook</u>, a volume of some 2000 pages, a complete mechanical engineer's guide. It will be our "Bible" for the rest of our lives.

We read Shakespeare next term - "King Lear", "Romeo and Juliet", and "Richard II".

I was measured for my third suit of service this week, and also for white service.

We have had bitter weather here but little snow. The bay is frozen solid. The ferry is not even running. Luckily our room has been warm for a change.

Time for taps, now, good night and

much love to all,
Scottie

I thought George was going to write to me.

Annapolis 2 February 1936

Dear Family,

Half the year is over.

Last night I saw my first boxing meet. Navy boxed Western Maryland. The final score was a draw 4 - 4.

The fights here at the Academy are really something. It's almost as brilliant a function as a first night or an evening at the Metropolitan. All spectators, civilian or otherwise, must wear formal clothes; Midshipmen, full dress; officers, full dress; and civilians either "tails" or dinner clothes - "tails" preferred.

Everybody comes - from the Admiral on down. There was a "hoop" last night, so all the "drags" were there. Beautiful women and lots of gold braid made the affair a splendiferous thing.

The Naval Academy orchestra played between bouts, cheering was allowed only between bouts, and it's a wonder they didn't serve pink tea.

About 5,000 people were there.

Next week - end A.. E....... will be here for the "Masqueraders". Here's our program for the week - end: some sport event in the afternoon of Saturday, either basketball, water polo, wrestling, fencing, or one of the other athletic events that all take place; then dinner at the Cruise Inn (a very nice place); then to the Navy - Syracuse fights; and after that to the play performance (which is, by the way, only incidental); on Sunday, chapel; dinner at Dr. Thomas's, and the afternoon there. The beauty of the thing is that it will cost me just the price of our dinner plus, I suppose, flowers to Mrs. Thomas since I invited myself out after a fashion. Should be a very nice week - end.

The mate just came around with a list for me to initial - I'm on the "sub" squad in swimming!!! Early in the fall, when I took my swimming test, I failed because I kicked the wrong leg back doing the side stroke. Since then, because of football, I haven't had a chance to take the test again. Now I've got to go for instruction every day until I pass - which will be the first day. It greatly amuses me.

I'm awfully glad Georgie had such a nice party. I hope he can have another right soon. Enclosed are his stickers.

ROBERT SCOTT WHITMAN JR.

The weather here is still cold, but today it seems to be
letting up a bit. The sun is shining - I guess the ground hog   .
has been scared back into his hole for another six weeks.

Love to all,

Scottie

Annapolis, 9 February 1936

Dear Mother & Dad,

Sorry my letter is late this week; but you know this week – end was pretty full. Had a grand time. The play was excellently done for an amateur group. I think A.. E....... had a fine time.

My marks are no where near what they should be. I don't know what is wrong. I study more than I have ever studied before in my life – and seem to get less results. For one thing, they (the marks) prove that I have no scientific mind. Compare the "arts" marks with the science marks.

Dad in his last letter speaks of my being on the swimming team. He evidently misconstrued my statement in regard to being on the "sub" squad. This squad is an extra-instruction squad for swimming. I passed my test the first afternoon it met, and am consequently no longer a member.

Speaking of physical work, you might be interested in our Gym periods. Each alternate week we have Gym three times. For the first twenty minutes of the period we (all hands) are drilled in "Swedish exercises". Then we are split up by platoons and get instruction in different sports. One time it is boxing, another, wrestling, a third water polo. Last time it was in life saving. It's really interesting and fun.

This week we have seamanship, next week Gym again. Today our seamanship drill was in semaphore signaling. I'm getting so I can take the stuff fairly rapidly. It is three practical drills which are most interesting.

Notice my new paper – I ran out and decided I'd have a little variety with my new batch. As you can see, Tecumseh is the decoration.

We have had a lot of snow, an awful lot for this part of the country – but it is much warmer.

      Love to all,
        Scottie

ROBERT SCOTT WHITMAN JR.

Annapolis, 15 February 1936

Dear Mother,

Your son has been a bad child – at least the Executive Department says so – and technically they are right. Hence Rhode and I are "swinging in a hammock" for the next thirty days.

Here's the story. Last Sunday, as I told you, A.. E....... and I were supposed to dine with Dr. Thomas. On Sunday morning I called him to find out what time he wanted us. In the course of the conversation, he told me that guests had unexpectedly arrived, that is, extra guests, for he had expected one besides ourselves. He did not tell me not to come, but I was not stupid enough to miss the hint, and, since it had snowed during the night and walking was bad, I told him A.. and I would postpone our call to another time which would suit him better.

Then, like a stupid fool, I went into town anyway and had dinner at the place where A.. was staying. Dining out is not permitted unless with parents, relatives, instructors, or members of Congress. Half the Plebe class went out with faked cousins, aunts etc. – the town was lousy with them. This does not excuse my action at all but helps to convey the circumstances.

Well, Rhode who went with me, and I got caught. We didn't hide our action at all, for several First Classmen in our Battalion said that, although the Executive Department was not allowing the boys to go out, the upper classes were not going to attach any significance to Plebes being in town. So, as I say, most of the Plebes who were "dragging" went out, some under false pretenses; and other, like Rhode and I, just went. It was just our luck to run into a First Classman whose girl was staying at the same place our girls were. It seems he is very much disliked by the Regiment, including his own classmates He came in as we were leaving for the station, made quite a scene, acted in a way unheard of in Midshipmen, especially in front of ladies, and heaved us on the report. (His girl is a classmate and friend (?) of my girl's.)

So, as a consequence, yesterday we were informed that we each had been assigned 75 demerits and should be quarantined on the station ship for 30 days.

The guy had enough decency to come around on Monday morning and admit to us that he did not realize at the time that so many

Plebes were out, but couldn't understand why his classmates had allowed it. (He evidently doesn't get the word.)

The entire First Class in our Batt. – or at least all that know of the incident – were outraged at the man's conduct in front of ladies. This all does not, however, excuse me. I deserve what I got, and perhaps someday I'll learn not to be such a stupid ass.

The offense, while the punishment is heavy, ("Absence Unauthorized from Bancroft Hall") carries a standard punishment of 75 & 30, is not as serious in the eyes of the "Exec." Department as many others with much lighter punishment; i.e.: "Unmilitary Conduct", "Improper Performance of Duty" etc. By this I mean – my "grease" with the Executive Department does not suffer any appreciable loss.

Please do not think that by this rather incoherent explanation I'm in any way trying to excuse myself. I'm not, I was wrong, I'm being punished and next time I'll know better. But I want you to understand that my character is not in the least degraded in the eyes of the officers, upper class, or my own eyes by what happened. Consequently I don't feel humiliated, as must the boy who is here now – leaves tomorrow – been her for copying a magazine article and handing it in as an original – something of that sort is a different story.

As far as punishment is concerned, the ship is far from a hardship. We have more time to ourselves and more time for study. (Of course we go to classes and drills as usual.) We can eat when we like within limits. Have a Philippino mess boy to wait on us. Our own lavatory and showers, ward room, and sleeping quarters. Are treated with respect by all the enlisted men, and generally have a pretty good time of it.

Our only deprivations are not being allowed to go into town on Saturday or anywhere except to classes, eating enlisted men's meals, and sleeping on cots instead of beds. We have mattresses however. And we save money on the food. There is a canteen aboard here with anything we might have need of – and we are thinking of borrowing a radio!!!

Rhode is a fine boy, came from a fine family. Father's a doctor in Reading. Rhode went to Duke for a couple of years and is one of the "star" men in the class. He is in my German class. (He, Harris, and I bum together all the time.) So, I have congenial company. We're hoping and praying for a couple more to make a bridge game. The ship is usually crowded, so we'll have company soon.

He got a huge box from home today, so we'll have plenty of delicacies to last a long time.

Please do not censure A.. E........ in your own mind for this. She had better sense than I, she tried to keep me from coming out.

I know you are going to be provoked at me - you can't be otherwise, but please remember that I have not lost "grace", as you say, with officers or Midshipmen. The demerits are hard to take, but I still have less than a hundred.

The man who popped us has lost more friends, and we have gained more, by the episode than you can imagine. It sounds funny but is none the less true.

As I said, I guess I'm just dumb. It takes a blow like this to knock some sense into some people's heads. I guess I'm one of them.

Now for some good news. My "Gull" final term mark was 3.22. Not so hot, you say, and on the face of just that, possibly not; but, when I tell you that I stood 78 in the class I hope you'll change your mind. The marks for English hit a new low in the history of the Academy.

I'm going to "star" now with all this time to study.

Please don't think too harshly of me. That hurts more than anything they can do to me here.

        Love to all,
         Scottie

P.S. You remember Case, my Second Class friend. His brother died yesterday and he's gone on special leave. I've written him a note. He has all my sympathy. He is such a swell guy.

    R. S. W.

Annapolis, 22 February 1936

Dear Family,

Well, a week of my incarceration has passed, and I seem to have successfully survived.

Since I have not been around Bancroft Hall much, except for classes, there is not much news. Winter is still holding on with an icy grip and the bay is still solid with ice.

We have had a couple of new additions – two Plebes from the Second Battalion.

The enlisted men who are on board ship are a funny lot. We have no direct contact with them; but, from what I can see they act like a bunch of kids – a happy go lucky bunch that seems to enjoy itself in doing practically nothing most of the time.

The "gobs" are a sloppy bunch, but the marines are as clean cut a looking aggregation as I have ever seen. Some of the "leathernecks" are just boys – I swear that two that I have seen are much younger than I.

The gulls are a constant joy to us. They soar around the ship all the time. They are fed scraps from the galley and are veritable chow hounds. I saw one take down three slices of bread whole – one right after another – and only stopped then because there was no more. They soar for minutes on end without so much as a slightest movement of their great powerful wings.

There is no change in my address – all mail is forwarded.

A.. E....... sent me a batch of books. They have arrived at my room but have yet to come over here – probably because of the national holiday.

At noon today we had a holiday dinner – turkey and all that goes with it, a quarter of a pie and ice cream, and a package of cigarettes apiece. They must have been saving up for it, for the meals prior to it for the last two days have been lousy.

The only deprivation we suffer is a lack of exercise; so every day we go up on the quarter deck for a half hour workout.

I've been doing a great deal of reading – have finished two books already. We Who Are About to Die – a story, or rather description, of prison life at San Quentin. I had read about it in the Times and had a chance to pick it up at the library. Thought it would be quite appropriate. It is brand new to our library. I'm the second to have it. Have also read Ann Vickers. Enjoyed both immensely.

Shall start Richard Halliburton's newest tonight, <u>Seven League Boots</u>. That is the one where the fool climbs the Alps into Italy on an elephant – emulating the departed Hannibal.

Navy plays Army in basketball today. I wonder how they are making out. They are at the Point.

I appreciated the letters from my family immensely. Will write again soon.

Love to all,
Scottie.

Annapolis, 27 February 1936

Dear Family,

The box arrived yesterday. My, how pleased I was! I never saw such a grand box of chow. Everything I wanted and just the sort of thing I wanted. Thank you a million times.

Today we had our monthly exam in Chemistry. Tuesday we had "Steam" and tomorrow "Bull", and then we are all through for another month. I think I did passably well on the two I've taken so far.

I really do not know what to write.

We have had several additions to our company since I wrote – all on for a month except three, who are here for forty five days. Most of them are O. K. but there are a couple whom I can't seem to appreciate.

We have a taste of navy life aboard here. A day does not pass but what we have beans for at least one meal. The favorite meal for them seems to be breakfast. I never knew they could do so much with beans. Usually there is no attempt to disguise them, but on occasions we find them made insignificant behind such names as Chili Con Carni, Chop Suey, and, as Manuel our mess boy says, "She is Slalit". He means, I think, salad. Manuel is amusing. He always brings us "Some pitcher Jaba". Translated it means "a pot of coffee".

The cold spell has broken finally, and the bay is clear except when the tide comes in – then the ice floats back up the river.

The aviation squadron had their first flying in a month. They have been forced to go to Washington for land planes to get in their required hours.

In seamanship we have been semaphore signaling. I'm getting so I can take the stuff fairly well.

I wrote Gram about a week ago. Have no fears I made no mention of my escapade.

I got a long letter from Barbara the other day. We no – end surprised as I have not written her for many a moon.

I really have no inspiration, so I guess it would be best if I should end your agony.

Love to all,
Scottie.

ROBERT SCOTT WHITMAN JR.

Annapolis, 21 March 1936

Dear Family,

I guess I've sort of let you down with my letter writing. Please forgive me - It sha'n't happen again.

I've been so busy, and I've had a cumbersome bandage on a smashed finger that has made writing a task. The finger is all right now. I got it in football - tore the nail off and sprained it is all.

Exams are here again and I've had a lot of studying to do - we took the Analyt exam today. I passed easily. Don't know what sort of a mark I got - fairly good, I hope. We start Calculus Monday.

As you have gathered, spring football has started. We played the U. of Maryland today in a driving rain and a sea of mud. It was just a scrimmage with the coaches all over the field finding fault here and there. I played with the third team and got about three quarters of an hour scrimmage. Consequently, since it was my first, I'm dead tired and stiff and sore.

I've been reading the New York Times carefully for news of Binghamton, and the flood, and have found quite a little. It must be much worse than last summer. When you write you must tell me all about it.

Up until yesterday we have been having real spring weather. We have been going to class without reefers and it has been lovely.

Next month we start drilling outside again. The sail boats have already been brought out of the sheds and moved into the bay, and the big patrol planes which are here every summer for 2nd Class aviation are back - moored in the bay.

However, it has been raining steadily up until a short time ago.

White cap covers come back a week from tomorrow!!! Only two months and a half until I'm a Youngster - My! - that one diagonal stripe means more than almost anything to us Plebes.

I'm wondering if Hitler's flare up in Europe is going to cause a change in cruise plans; there is no dope along that line so far.

It seems so nice to be back at the Hall; yet I really enjoyed the ship in many ways.

It's nearly time for taps now and my bed isn't made, so, I'll finish tomorrow. (We tear our beds open Saturday – hence it's not being made.)

After chapel

Dad's letter came just now. I was very interested in his story of the flood. I'm so glad that you are sending some pictures. I'll save them and send them back.

It is again a bright although rather blustery march day.

I'm trying to write in full dress – you can see that it is quite a task.

I shall send a bunch of <u>Logs</u>, George's <u>Reef</u> <u>Points</u> etc. in a few days – as soon as I can get some stamps, for I haven't had stamp money or anything else for some time. I'm trying to save on my requisitions so I'll have some money on the cruise and during September.

Love to all,
Scottie

ROBERT SCOTT WHITMAN JR.

Annapolis, 28 March 1936

Dear Family,

Another week is past, another set of exams is past, and another month shot to pieces - and all is well.

We played Villanova today in a practice game - three hours of it with four teams, each playing a half. I did fairly well, and there is a bare chance I may make the Varsity squad next Fall - my, how I hope so - it would mean so much - some grand trips and all sorts of other nice things.

These practice games are funny. The whole staff of coaches of both schools are on the field all the time and frequently stop the game to criticize the work of the players. We have regular officials though, and everything else is just like a game.

Dad may be interested in this. Harry Stuhldreher, the Villanova coach, was one of the "Four Horsemen" at Notre Dame, and "Rip" Miller was one of the linemen ("Seven Mules") on the same team.

White cap covers come back tomorrow and the Youngsters start their traditional "reign of terror". I suppose I'll be dragged out of bed sometime during the wee, small hours tonight and be treated to a coal shower. Oh, well, - it's only two months and then I'll be a Youngster.

Next week we start outside infantry drills again - how I dread that. Infantry is no fun.

Rumor has it that there will be 1100 Plebes next year. I do know this much at any rate: The battalions are to be split into three rather than the customary two companies, and my roommates are I are in the Second Company; work is to be started on a new wing to Bancroft Hall in the next year or two; voluntary resignations of the graduating class are not to be accepted. It looks as though they really expect to build a Navy.

Calculus is rather interesting. Math. is no fun for me as a rule, so I hope that this will prove an exception. Math. and "Steam" are still my bug-a-boos. I sure have no scientific mind. I sometimes wonder if I have any mind at all - I do such stupid things sometimes.

The pictures of the flood arrived. Thank you so much for them. I wanted so terribly to see some. It is such a tragedy for the poor First Ward people. I don't wonder they are up in arms.

Yesterday we finished off our inside seamanship drills

with company competition in semaphore signaling. As you know, companies compete in almost everything here for the coveted flag which goes to the company amassing the greatest total of points during the year. One of the things the Plebes do is compete in the afore-mentioned signaling. Everybody competes and the company with the best average gets the credit.

I'm sending a bunch of Logs under separate cover.

I had to get another pair of shoes the other day, much as I hated to. Looks as though there is little use in trying to save any money towards leave. I entered so late, most everybody has a couple months' pay up on me. Oh, well, why worry – it does such a great deal of good.

Will write again soon.

      All my love,
       Scottie

ROBERT SCOTT WHITMAN JR.

Annapolis, 1st April 1936

Dear Mother,

Your letter arrived today. You are a bad woman to send me that money. I really can get along quite nicely with what I have – especially since Gram's unexpected gift. Naturally I am awfully grateful for it – and than you a million times. But you mustn't do it again.

Well, for more cheerful things. Today we had our first honest – to – goodness dress parade, uniform full dress etc. It was quite thrilling and not such a task as I supposed it would be. From now on in, we have them every Wednesday. I wish I could see one. I imagine they are quite something to see. It is said that most Midshipmen don't see a dress parade, except in pictures, until years after they graduate from the Academy. Funny – yet not so strange. It really must be a stirring sight. My, how I yearn for the time when you can come down to the Academy and see it all. I shall not be really happy until that time comes. I'm sure it will not be too long.

Football ends Saturday when we play Catholic University of Washington. Monday I go out for track. I don't know whether I'll be able to do anything with the weights but I sure can try.

I've forgotten till now to answer your oft repeated question concerning the Tasmanian paper. It seems we never get our themes back – they are all filed and saved. So I guess I won't be able to send it home. I really did want you to see it.

I'm so happy that George is doing so well at school. I'm thankful that one of your sons is living up to your expectations.

There is really no more news now – I'll write again Sunday.

       Love,
        Scottie

Annapolis, 5 April 1936

Dear Family,

Another week has begun. So far I've spent the day very profitably. Washed three pairs of white gloves and a cap cover, and written a book report. [It Can't Happen Here]

Dad's letter arrived this morning. It was very, very welcome, as all letters from Binghamton are.

Dad asked about numerals. I got my major numerals for football just after Christmas. I'm sure I told you about them at that time when I was home. I knew I was going to get them then.

Football is not over for me. I have to go out with the second section for a couple of weeks. Tommy says I need some more experience. Evidently is planning to keep me on the "A" squad. I hope that is true. It's worth trying for anyway.

The musical club show is next week, and A.. E....... will be down for the week – end. No chicanery this time though. We will obey the rules.\

I had a welcome visitor yesterday. Mr. Bush and his wife were here, and I showed them around the grounds. He sends his best to you, Mother.

I'm enclosing a copy of my book report. It's nothing extraordinary, but, since I was typing it, I thought I might as well make a carbon. It will go over big here. Please don't find too many flaws in it, Mother. I'd like to know your honest opinion though.

I shall send George's Reef Points as soon as I can find time to get to the post office.

We played Catholic University yesterday – same sort of a game – and whipped them. I played another quarter.

       Love to all,
         Scottie

ROBERT SCOTT WHITMAN JR.

Naval Hospital, 14 April 1936

Dear Family,

Calm yourself. I'm not sick. Just a cold in my chest which should be kept out of the wet weather we have been having. Haven't run a temperature since I got here, and am up and around and will go back to the Hall in a day or two. They are breaking up the congestion with radio - thermy and are keeping me here to have me handy. It's a nice rest too.

It was a nasty week - end for Easter bonnets.

A.. E....... was down as you know - we had a fairly nice time, but I was rather miserable with a bad cough. The show as excellent. It was a musical comedy. I never knew that the Midshipmen could make such beautiful women. The chorus was a howl. All the music was written by Midshipmen. I'm going to try my hand sometime at it.

Just finished a long theme for English. It is not so hot. If I don't get an inspiration and get started right, I don't do so well. I'm glad you liked my review. I rather liked it myself. Haven't yet heard what my prof. thought.

The weather is wonderful now, of course, but I guess I'd better stay close till I get rid of the wheeze in my chest - got to get out before the week - end - we're rowing Columbia and I've never seen a crew race before.

I'm enclosing some pictures that I never got developed till now. The other man is Harris. Thought perhaps you might be able to keep them better than I.

Don't worry about me. I feel fit as a fiddle.

> All my love,
> Scottie

Annapolis, 17 April 1936

Dear Mother,

Out again. Feeling fine as fine can be.

I've missed your letters this week - I do hope you are all well.

There is no news. Having been in the hospital I haven't heard anything new. Wednesday, however, we did get a thrill.

A bunch of us got permission from our doctors to walk down on the bluff where we could see the dress parade over on Worden Field. The parade was wonderful and I was very interested to see what one looked like. However, that is not part of the story. Just as it was over we heard a roar in the north which got louder and louder as we listened. Suddenly, a wind storm such as I have never seen before broke. My, how it did blow.

We had seen a small sailing boat on the river and immediately ran to that side of the hill to see how it was faring. We got there just in time to see it go over. One of us ran to the crew shed, which is nearby, and notified the men who were there. There were two very powerful speed boats there, and they were quickly on their way. The man was picked up safely and all turned out well. He never could have swum in. Maybe next time he'll know better than to sail alone. (It was an officer.)

That's about all the news.

There are just five more weeks of academics, and then two of drill and graduation festivities before the cruise. Everybody seems agreed that Plymouth, Cherbourg, and Gottenborg are the principal ports of call. That means London, Paris, and Berlin for sure.

       Love to all,
        Scottie

ROBERT SCOTT WHITMAN JR.

Annapolis, 23 April 1936

Dear Family,

Exams over for another month. I'm sure I did much better on the "Steam" – one more month to go!! and then "sailing, sailing, over the bounding main". It really begins to look as though we really are going on a cruise now. The lists of things required to take are out, and oh, my, what a list!! I honestly believe we don't leave a thing home. And there are a lot of things to get that we don't have, besides stuff to replace that is worn out. More money –

We have had to take our suitcases to be marked with our names and laundry numbers and have drawn our white shoes and socks for white uniforms. It hardly seems possible the year is nearly over, and soon it will be "Tain't no more Plebes".

I'm enclosing a clipping from the Times which you may or may not have seen. The returning dates are not authentic in my case, since the football men return earlier than the rest. (We have only seventeen days leave.) I wonder if it is worth it.

There is one thing I wonder if you could do. I need a camera case very badly. Do you suppose Agfa has any old ones? You know how cumbersome my camera is if it has no carrying case. If Dad can, will he, please, see what he can find out and I'll try to scrape enough money to buy one.

This Saturday should prove to be an interesting day. The German Cruiser Emden is in Baltimore harbor, and it has about 150 Midshipmen aboard. They are to visit the Academy on Saturday. I have been picked with four other Plebes and a bunch of upper classmen to act as a reception committee and to entertain the visitors all day. Should prove to be fun and maybe will give us some practical experience. Rechts ist die Turnhalle.

The other day, we went out in the sub chasers for a drill. It was the first time I had been beyond the harbor since I came here. We Plebes worked the speed cones (cones of some material whose vertical position shows the speed made). It was the best drill I have attended so far. Today, however, it was back to pulling the darned old cutters again.

We're reading Romeo and Juliet now in English. Finishing up Calculus, beginning Organic Chemistry, drawing an outboard coupling in "Steam", and the same old "Dago".

Had a very nice letter from Ced the other day, and from Marsh not long before that.

I've run out of ideas for the present.

Love to all,
Scottie

Annapolis, 6 May 1936

Dear Mother,

All is well here. Dress parade today, and it was awfully hot. My collar was limp after it all.

The visit of the German Seekadeten was very interesting. It was fun showing them around. They all spoke fine English, so I didn't use much German. Once in a while, however, I tried my wares on them and they seemed to understand what I was talking about. They arrived at ten in the morning and left about four. Their uniforms were of the poorest kind of material, which seems to point to Germany's poverty.

It was funny trying to explain that baseball game to them. They had never seen one and had not the slightest idea what it was all about.

The first week of the last month is over. Thirty – four days to graduation. Academics are over for the year on the 22nd. We take our final in "Dago" on Monday of next week.

I guess I told you that we were drawing cruise gear. The itinerary for the cruise has been officially issued in an order, and I see that a copy if sent home, so there is no need to report it here.

My "Steam" was only 2.8, and I had such high hopes. I don't know, I seem to have lost what little mental ability I ever did have. Now I'm frightened, for I don't know when I'm wrong. Had you asked. I would have sworn that I made at least a 3.2 on the exam. The actual mark was 2.8. I don't know yet where I busted, and I've seen the instructors marking drawing. I'm hitting the shoals in Math. again, haven't bilged any tests yet, but am having an awful time: I make silly mistakes in the easiest things in Math. and Chemistry probs and no amount of checking seems to help. Of course I will not bilge any course, but I'm doing so horribly. I've been thinking a good deal lately and have come to the conclusion that the work is no harder here than anywhere else. I'm sure the Chemistry I would have taken at Dickinson would have been far more difficult. I study harder than I ever imagined I would – and look where it is getting me! I've lost every bit of self assurance I ever had – that's what the upper class have succeeded in doing. Time and again I've made a perfect calculation; then, not sure, have checked, fiddled around and ended up in a mess. I swear if somebody told me to mail a letter for them, I'd be scared I'd do it wrong. I don't know what is the matter. I sometimes wonder – am I losing my mind? You will immediately blame it on A.. E....... I doubt very much if she is to blame. We have not seen each other since the Musical Club show the first of May, and one has little time to bother about women here at all.

I even can't write anymore. I wrote an article for the Log the other day (upon request). Today I was stopped in the hall. "Sorry Whitman. We've had to hold over your article. Log pretty well made up this week. Maybe get it in next issue or next fall. Keep up work." The one answer to that is NERTS, for the article was written especially for this issue, "The Cruise Issue" – could not possibly be used in any other – and will not be used in any other. It was good – at least – oh, well, maybe I don't know any more. But I do know that it was much better than most the stuff in this week's Log. I do so want to make the staff. I shall try again, but evidently I have got to do better than I have so far. I feel like a blustering fat fool most of the time and it's not a pleasant feeling. Oh, well – enough of my troubles – I just had to get the steam blown off, and you are the only one to whom I can safely blow it. Don't worry about me. I'm probably just a little crazy. I will be all right in the morning. I'll write a very cheerful letter before the week is out.

The ship assignments are posted and I am on the Wyoming.

Love to all,
Scottie

Congratulations to Georgie on his Math. Dig hard, Kid, and hit 'em with all you got, and try to make a better job of it than your good – for – nothing brother has.

Annapolis, 20 May 1936

Dear Family,

Tomorrow it is all over. Calculus is the last and I'm scared pink over it. The other exams are gone. They were not bad. I'm sure I passed all of them.

Dad asked about next week's work. Next week is devoted to infantry competition - platoon, company, and battalion. There are no more academics after this Saturday.

So my old girl ran off and got married? My, I'm heartbroken! He is quite all right thought, as far as I know - it's time she settled down anyway - she must be 22 or 23 now.

Yesterday afternoon after drill I went sailing. My, it was fun. We had a fine wind once out in the bay and had a grand time.

From now on in, except for tomorrow, it's going to be a country club life. June Week starts a week from Friday; then liberty all the time except for dress parades. I'm standing a man's watch on Monday of June Week for a dollar and a half.

The Wyoming and Arkansas are in. We were going out to the "Wyo" (Mac and I) on Sunday, but the boat was full before we could get there.

In "Steam" now, we are drawing plans for a 35' motor launch. Quite interesting. Had a lecture on gas warfare in Chemistry. Was very, very interesting and quite blood-thirsty - talking about casualty producing efficiency etc.

Mother, I wish you would write me and tell me what's best to do and see in England and France. Dr. Thomas advises me not to go on the regular tours in England. Says I could do much better by myself. Says regular tour spends too much time in London. I don't know anything about it. Got my Baedecker, but now haven't been able to figure out how to use it. What have you to suggest?

Oh, yes; the watch has not gained or lost a minute since I had it - keeps perfect time. Cracked the crystal once but figured that I had better get it fixed, and did immediately.

It has turned cool again. Miracle of Miracles! - and today is dress parade day. Wonders never cease.

If Paul Mitchell is still around, try to get word to him to look me up if he comes down. I'd like to see him. It might mean a free meal during June Week. And it is a good thing to know officers.

I'm writing this during a study period. Quite the country club – windows open – the music of the band floating up (it goes a concert every morning). Dr. Thomas said in class that next time we came, we would be able to get all the dope on the Berlin trip. He is going on the cruise – on the Oklahoma.

No more now.

Love to all,
Scottie

ROBERT SCOTT WHITMAN JR.

Annapolis, 22 May 1936

Dear Family,

Secure!!! It's all over - and I passed the Math. exam. Only six in my section did (less than half) and I was one of them.

The camera case arrived yesterday. It is perfect. Than you a million times. But how on earth did you find it?

Now we can sit back and breathe easy. There is an old custom around here. On Friday night an upper classman can often be heard asking a Plebe, "What's the good word, Mister?" Whereupon the Plebe answers, "Friday night and another week shot to hell, Sir." Well, it's Friday night "and another academic year shot to hell" this time.

Tonight at the table the two First Classmen at whose end I sit "spooned" on me. No more running at the table.

This noon the First Class celebrated "No More Rivers" ("Rivers" being exams). It is a traditional custom that, when the First Class finish their final exam, they celebrate - executing the better known profs. in a mock trial etc. This time they celebrated in front of Tecumseh. They had the old boy rigged up with a loud speaker behind him so it appeared that he sentenced the prisoners as they were hauled up by his warriors (First Class dressed as Indians). Some of the First Class dressed as well known duty officers etc. - really put on a good show as, when asked for a last statement before their death, they got off some characteristic phrase of the man they represented. It was all great fun to watch.

You know they have a very famous song called "No More Rivers" especially for the occasion. We have had to sing it for the First Class for weeks now. First it was "eight more rivers" (8 verses), then seven (7 verses) and now today "No More Rivers". They sure are a happy bunch to have it so nearly all over. Yet I know they will all be sorry to leave.

Yesterday the Youngsters buried Math. After the traditional parade of the anchor sections, dragging their Math books behind them, and all dressed up in weird costumes, they buried them very solemnly (the ones they won't need later). For now the Youngsters are through with Math as an academic subject. Even though, of course, actually if they stay in the Navy - far from it.

This afternoon the First Class "blew up" the ordnance building - another mock disposal of academic subjects distasteful to First Classmen.

Tomorrow I go to my last class, Math - no recitation, no mark, just sit around and "shoot the breeze".

I do so wish you could come down June Week. I know that sooner or later you will be able to and am looking forward so to that time.

In Seamanship drill today, my platoon had sailing - a relief from the darned cutters. It was fine but we had very little wind, since in drills we remain on the river off the bay.

When does George start his exams or has he already? Best o'luck to him when he does. Hit that Alg. with all you've got, Kid.

Barbara wrote me a long letter explaining her marriage, why I haven't the slightest idea. I've written her and her husband the customary congratulations.

The cruise hand book was issued yesterday. My!! all the indecipherable tables of organization and instruction periods, leave, liberty etc. it contains.

Our "Bull" prof. got into a story telling mood today (it being the last recitation of the year) and told some pretty tall ones about midshipmen's cruises in his day at the Academy. He claims the Navy is going to hell - Midshipmen cruising on oil burning ships - going on leave in foreign ports, and all. Says that when he was a Midshipman you had to learn by hard work. As soon as you hear that "when I was a Midshipman", you can just sit back, say to yourself "oh, yeah?" grin and bear it. The Third Class always harp on our easy life as compared to theirs, the Second Class the same, and so on right on up to the Admiral. It's the same old story.

My Math. prof. is assistant to the "Mid. Exec." on the "Wyo" so I've been trying to make a good impression on him. I hope I succeed.

Harris is on my ship. Makes it nice.

Rhode had a birthday day before yesterday. Harris, Shoemaker and I pinned him down, spanked him, and presented him with a box of Hershey chocolate bars. Good choice of present, don't you think? We four get along extremely well. I think it will make a peach of a rooming combination.

    I'm afraid I've about run out of news, and taps will be busting soon. Am sending three <u>Logs</u>. They have been changing the staff from First to Second Class and, therefore, not so many have come out.

        Love to all,
          Scottie

PLEBE TO WWII HERO, MY JOURNEY FROM ANNAPOLIS TO MIDWAY

Annapolis, 25 May 1936

Dear Mother,

Your letter arrived this morning. Thank you, oh, thank you for getting the money for me. It arrive safely and is carefully locked up, I'm sure I acknowledged the other ten dollars, but in writing, I sometimes think I've written something rather than actually done so. I know I thanked you. But - it arrived safely and I am out of debt - a million thanks. It shall all be repaid eventually, and I am so very grateful to have it.

Tonight Commander Wessel, who has charge of the practice cruise, gave us a lecture in Memorial Hall. It was mostly a fight talk; but afterwards we were permitted to ask questions, and in that way I found out a good bit about the leaves and liberties.

As you know, we are to be in each port six days. Out of that six days we have three of leave, that is, we leave the ship to go to London or wherever we have chosen. The other three days we stay aboard ship; but we are allowed liberty ashore from one o'clock to probably eleven in the evening, provided, of course, we have no "watch" to stand. This means that we will have at least two and, in some cases, three days of that sort of liberty. There will be side trips arranged and we can do a lot in that way.

There is one thing I know; if we desire to go to London for our three days, the all expense trip (including every-thing) is only $29.75. Or there are bus tours ending in London. Or tours back from London - quite a choice. We each are furnished (for 50¢ of course) a travel book when we go aboard ship. There are officer representatives of Thos. Cook & Sons on every ship, so it will be easy to get all the information on every-thing.

I'm glad you feel as you do about the museums etc. I feel the same and have been afraid that I was (as you so aptly phrased it) a heretic.

One thing certain - I'll get my money's worth out of the cruise or die in the attempt.

Yesterday Mac and I went out to the <u>Oklahoma</u>. (They are all three here now.) We got to talking to one of the gobs - a very nice chap - and he took us all over the ship from engine room to crow's nest, from powder rooms to turrets. My, such a maze of machinery!!! The hatches into some places in the turrets were so small that I have hopes that I am not too ponderous as I believed, for I actually squeezed through. To think that someday if I have what it takes I'll run one of those things.

This week is rest week. Only a dress p-rade today. Tomorrow platoon drill for competition. Sailed all morning and got a good burn.

      Love to all,
        Scottie

Annapolis, 28 May 1936

Dear Family,

I received a very nice letter from Thos. Cook & Son today. They told me that information booklets were being made up and that we would receive them on board, that tours were being carefully planned, and that they would be glad to help me in any way they could. Thank you very much, Mother, for writing to them.

The grades are all out – so here goes.

Friday morning

Sorry. Rhode just yelled up that we had been challenged to a rubber of bridge. It stretched into two rubbers and a loss by 3100 points – and I thought we were unbeatable – no cards at all.

Our room, since it gives the best view of the waterfront, is being used as a control room for the water carnival, and they made us move out – bag and baggage. So now Mac and I live in 1430, and Joe is down on the third deck.

Our company came in fourth in the competition. Very sad.

My, has this been a "rest week"! Have been sailing twice and am going this morning again in about half an hour. Have been sun bathing, reading, playing bridge, swimming – and drilling now and then.

June Week starts officially at 2:35 this afternoon. Am enclosing a copy of the program – it will tell you much better than I what is happening. A.. E....... will be down tomorrow to the Army – Navy baseball game; and of course, we are going to the June Ball. Really, I wouldn't miss that for the world. It is the high spot in the life of a Plebe.

Going sailing. Finish later.

After chow

Just got Mac's and my clean suits from the tailor shop. All set for our first June Week liberty.

I've been looking for that program and it seems to be misplaced so here's a resume for the time being:

```
Water Carnival Saturday night
Dress Parade on Monday - 5:00
Presentation of Colors to color company
Dress Parade  Tuesday 5:00
Presentation of Awards - Dress Parade - Wednesday 5:00
June Week Ball - Wednesday night
Aquatic events, demonstration "Steam" classes etc.
 on various days
Second Class ring Dance on Monday
Youngsters Hop - Monday
Liberty on every day up till taps
Of course, Graduation on Thursday
```

Millions of visitors etc. Just gives you an idea of what is happening. (I'll find a program later and send it.)

Your letter came while I was writing. What do you mean – "a joke on your"? I think it was wonderful of you to write to Cooks. They evidently have not completed their literatures; said, though, that the tours encompassed the maximum that could be done in the time that was allowed and that we would have definite information during June Week. Thank you again for being so very thoughtful. I felt quite important receiving a letter from them.

I took some pictures out sailing. Shall shoot up this roll, get it developed, and send it before I leave.

When we drew for June Week watches, I drew a supernumerary for tomorrow. Sure hope somebody does not get sick for I want to see that ball game.

My being on the Log staff doesn't mean a whole lot, but it is an opening. Hope I can make something of the opportunity.

Hooray for George! I'm very, very proud of him. Keep up the good work!!

It has been cooler and fair. Beautiful weather!!! Probably will rain all of June Week, though.

Shoemaker I'm sure has been mentioned before. However – he is Rhode's roommate now and is from Elmira, a little young but a fine chap.

A bunch of "tin cans" have arrived in the bay. For your enlightenment, just in case, a "tin can" is a destroyer. They are here ready to pick up a third of the present Youngster class for a month's cruise. During Second Class summer all hands go on a month's cruise to North American ports aboard destroyers. Spend the other two months here. One of them is to be used in the Carnival and is anchored right outside my window.

The Carnival is to depict the burning of the Philadelphia. Remember Stephen Decatur's gallant work during the Tripolitan Wars, how he sneaked up and burned the Philadelphia after it had fallen into the hands of the Corsairs? It is to be very elaborate; paper mache forts, life size, guard the entrance to the basin; in the basin lies the Philadelphia, an old sub chaser transformed by very cleverly built up sides, paint, and spars, into a dead image of the real thing. They are actually going to burn the thing. Field guns concealed behind the forts will add to the realistic touch as they boom forth. Cutters stepped with masts and manned by Corsairs will be in evidence. The tennis courts have been transformed into Tripoli. They are now enclosed by beaver board walls on which oriental or, at least, Tripolitan houses are painted. In this modern Tripoli the first three classes, their drags, and families will have a buffet supper before the Carnival. The musical organizations have been busy for weeks planning entertainment for this upper hour. Then the Philadelphia act, then the Admiral greets Neptune aboard the destroyer, then a First Class hop on the U.S.S. Wyoming, a 2 - 3 hop in Dahlgren. The Plebes rate watching - the meal - the Carnival - and the hop. Just watching. Oh, well, next year. They ought to let Mac and me in for vacating our room to their darn control rooms.

Drew a bunch of engineering books, navigation tables, instructions, etc. yesterday. Really going to get down to the practical side of things. I guess. Such books as "Care, Operation and Repair of Turbines", "Condensers", "Refrigerating Plant", etc.

I go on Engineering duty for the first third. Poor me - 140° in the fire rooms. Four hours watch at a stretch, and before I've got sea legs. My, will I be a sick boy. You see, the cruise is divided into three parts, one Engineering, and two deck and Seamanship hitches for each man.

We of the football squad practice each morning in port (except on leave) and get out of ship's work - a graft, but I think we deserve it.

Our leave starts on August 15, a Saturday, and ends on Sept. 3, a Thursday. Our first game is 3½ weeks from then.

Well, I seem to have raved on and on and said not much of anything. I've tried to catch up on lost news. If I have neglected anything, let me know and I'll try to catch up on all before it becomes stale.

We shove off early Friday morning.

      Love to all,
        Scottie

II
FIRST CRUISE
1936

UNITED STATES NAVAL ACADEMY
Annapolis, Maryland
1 May 1936

————————

SPECIAL ORDER NO. 11-36

SUBJECT: Midshipmen's Practice Cruise-Itinerary.

1. The Midshipmen's Practice Squadron will consist of the U.S.S.
   ARKANSAS (flagship), the U.S.S. WYOMING, and the U.S.S. OKLAHOMA.

2. Midshipmen of the classes of 1937 and 1939 will be prepared to
   embark on the practice cruise on the morning of 5 June 1936.

3. The itinerary for the practice cruise is as follows:

ARRIVAL	PLACE	DEPARTURE
	Annapolis, Md.	5 June 1936
29 June 1936	Portsmouth, England	27 June 1936
3 July 1936	Göteborg, Sweden	9 July 1936
21 July 1936	Cherbourg, France	27 July
10 August 1936	Hampton Roads, Va.	
	(Southern Drill Grounds)	

Period 10 August-19 August
(1) 10-15 August, train for and fire Short Range Battle
    Practice
(2) 16-19 August, at anchor Hampton Roads Area, supply
    and liberty period

Period 20-27 August
(1) 20-26 August-at sea, visit New York City one day and night
(2) 26 August-arrive Annapolis, Md.
(3) 27 August-disembark Midshipmen

4. The Practice Squadron will return to the Naval Academy prior
to
midnight 26 August. Midshipmen will be disembarked to arrive at
the
REINA MERCEDES dock at 0715, 27 August, and (except those under
restriction) will be granted leave until 1000, 25 September 1936.

D.F. SELLERS,
Rear Admiral, U.S. Navy,
Superintendent.

Annapolis, 4 June 1936

Dear Family,

Thank you very much for your <u>Bon</u> <u>Voyage</u> letters.

Right now I'm in the midst of packing and can just grab a minute to dash off a note.

Everything is in a mess. The corridors are full of trash, and so forth.

Now I'm a Youngster. It's all over, and it's now R.S.Whitman 3/c.

I'll have to wait until when I see you to tell you all about it.

The Ball was grand, June Week wonderful, and I'm very happy.

The <u>Log</u> in which an article I wrote is on the way. I'm not particularly proud of it, but it got into the only <u>Log</u> that was on public sale. I'm mad that they didn't use my name.

I'll write soon.

Address is U.S.S. <u>Wyoming</u>

c/o Postmaster, N. Y. C.

Better add "Midsn's Practice Cruise"

Goodby. See you around the middle of August.

    Love to all and lots of it,
      Scottie

We embark at 12:30 P. M.

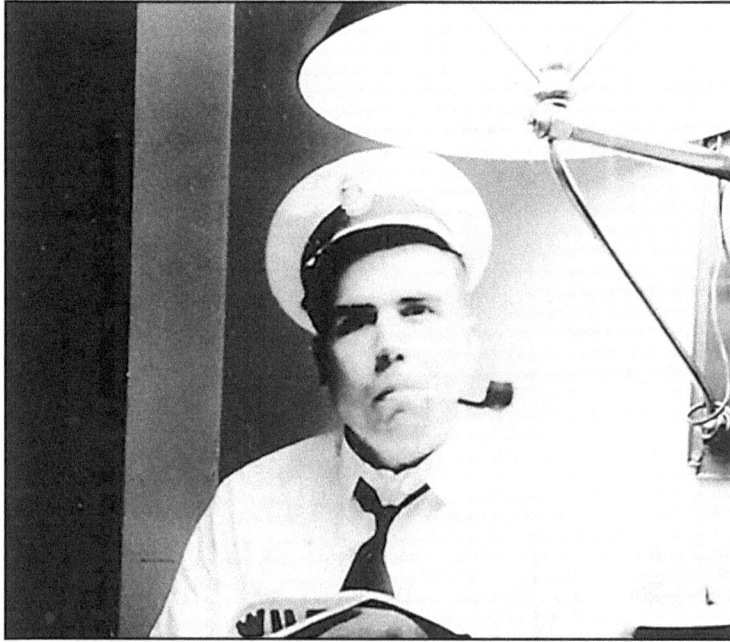

First Cruise, June 1936.

9 June 1936

About 1000 miles out

Dear Family,

Well, here I am on the North Atlantic. All is well, and I'm tired but happy. I'm standing Engineering watches now. I believe, I told you that the cruise is divided into three parts, one Engineering detail and two Deck. The Engineering is the worst for we have to stand our watches at night and go to school during the day. Practically no sleep till I get to England.

While on watch in the different engine rooms, fire rooms, condenser rooms, etc., we have questionnaires to fill out. We stand watches just as would officers in the fleet. Last night, or rather this morning, I was on from 4 to 8. Tonight I have the mid-watch, 12 to 4 in the morning. I have been in the fire room entirely so far. Very comfortable there, about 130° all the time, and such a roar from the blowers that one must shout at the top of his voice to be heard. I went up on top of the boilers last night to see certain valves first hand. It was at least 200° up there. Had to wear heavy cloths on my hands, because everything I touched would have burned me otherwise.

I think I am a pretty good sailor. It has been awfully rough but now has calmed somewhat. I got only a little dizzy. The sea is beautiful, a wonderful blue. Have not seen another ship since we got out to sea, that is, of course, with the exception of the other two in our squadron.

We have movies every evening, sound, of course; but they are pretty old. Did I tell you Harris is aboard?

We get up each morning at 5:30, scrub decks from 6 to 7. At 8:00 we engineers go to a lecture. From 10:30 to 11:30 we all have battle station (gun drill). I am on No. 2 Broadside (5 inch gun). In the afternoon we engineers write up our lectures. At 4:00 we have one hour work out (football players). Eat at 5:30 – movies – bed, – and usually a watch. I have signed up for a tour through the English Country and two days in London, one in Bath.

11 June

Since I wrote this we have covered almost 500 miles. We are nearly half way. The sea has been calm for a long time. Night before last I had the mid-watch again and we were about to gain another hour. We all expected that they would do it at midnight, as they usually do; but no, they would not do that – they waited until about 4:30. So, instead of getting out of an hour's watch, I lost an hour's sleep. My, but I was tired yesterday. I only had a six to eight dog watch last evening, though, so I got a full night's sleep for a change. I'm all through with the fire rooms, and tomorrow morning at four o'clock, I go in the Refrigerator rooms. Talk about contrast!! These next seven watches are included under the head of "auxiliaries" (Steering Engines, Dynamo Pumps, Evaporators and Refrigerators). Then, about seven watches in the Engine Room, and I'm through with the Engineering part of the cruise.

The dope on money available to be drawn is out – sad news. I have $42 coming. Everybody can draw fifty no matter how much they have, so I'll have a hundred dollars – I can do a lot with that if I am careful. The dope is that the First Class were so in debt to tailors etc. when they graduated that, instead of putting the very small amount into reserve pay that they usually do, they took $75 from our funds and put it in reserve pay. Everybody is short about this amount. Don't worry-I'll make out. Probably won't go on all the tours; but you can be sure I'll get $500 worth of experiences out of that $100.

We are due in Portsmouth a day early. The Admiralty has requested our presence for some sort of Naval Celebration. That means that we will arrive on Friday the 19th.

I'm really getting my sea legs now. One hardly notices the roll of the ship now.

Yesterday we had a man-over-board drill. The life boat crews rescued a rubber pneumatic body. They fired the customary gun, flew flags required, and all was just as the real thing. The other ships sheered off to each side. We have all sorts of drills often, "Fire and Rescue", "Fire", "Collision", "Abandon Ship" etc. It is of first importance that we know what to do in each case.

Sat, morning 12:45

The mid-watch again, this time in the Evap rooms. The clocks are due to change at 1:00 again – a three hour watch, I hope. That makes us three hours ahead of New York time. Today is Skipper's inspection, both of ship and personnel, an all morning job. Yesterday was field day, and everybody but the engineers turned out all day long and cleaned up ship. Boy! That is a man sized job, I'll have to do it soon now.

This is sort of a hard way to write a letter. I can't remember what I have told you and what I have not, and I hate to read over everything every time I write a new installment.

Everything seems so commonplace to me now, and it is hard to pick out the things which will interest you.

Every time we have a man-over-board drill, Lieut. Comdr. Wessel has a boat put over the side of whatever ship he happens to be on and transfers to another. He is in charge of the cruise, you know. He came to us four days ago, and today went to the Arky.

Another guy and I have been talking of going bicycling in Sweden. Inexpensive, and we sure could see a lot about the life of the people – which, after all, to my mind, is the most important and interesting thing to see when in Europe. It may develop into something and it may not.

The biggest hardship aboard ship is washing facilities. We have to take our baths, wash our clothes, etc. out of a regular tin bucket. It is inconvenient; but, nevertheless, you would be surprised how good a bath one can get out of a bucket.

Ah, the time orderly just changed the clocks. For once I get away with it.

15 June

Well, we are within 700 miles of England, and we don't arrive until Friday. Evidently we are going to steam in circles until then. Things have been running along quite smoothly. I even got a full night's sleep last night – quite a novelty.

We have been having dummy battle practice on the guns every day. I was a first on the No. 2 five inch gun. I was first shellman, which is the key position in the loading crew, for it is he who throws the shell into the gun. We practiced on the loading machines (just a breech block etc., but no barrel) which are at the stern. The officers in charge were very pleased with my work; for usually a man of my height is not suitable for that position, yet they said I was the best shellman on the cruise that they had yet seen. So now I am no longer a shellman. I have a grand job way up in the forward control tower manning a telephone. They change around all the time so everyone gets a taste of the whole works. Then the final crews are picked, and practice for S. R. B. P. (Short Range Battle Practice) begins in earnest. I hope I keep the job I have now. It is great – you can see all over the ship and see everything that goes on.

The sea up till today has been wonderfully quiet. But now we seem due for another squall. Saw one ship day before yesterday. A Hamburg American Liner came up on us, dipped her flag, and passed about sundown. She was very small, the Iberia. To see another ship is nearly as good as liberty.

I go on leave first in every port. Because all the football men do this, some of the other men had to change their leave times. Harris and I had planned to make our trips together; but, as luck would have it, he was one of the unlucky ones to be forced to change. So now I don't know who I will go with. I am taking a tour through the English Country to London. Most of the bunch are taking this tour so I shall find somebody to tag along with.

These Engineering watches are really awfully interesting. When one thinks of the hundreds whose lives depend on the function of this gigantic "machine shop", one really gets a kick out of learning the whys and wherefores of refrigeration, evaporation, condensers etc. We have finished auxiliaries, and now go into the last stretch – Main Engines, the power which actually drives these 33,000 tons of steel through the water.

18 June 1936 – 5:25 A.M. – in the Engine Room

Five hours ahead of N.Y. I've sort of neglected you all the last couple of days. The note book has piled up so in the last few days that I have had time for little else. Our shift (the first leg of the journey) has less time than the other two to complete the work; and then, to top it off, we are getting in a day early so we have had to do two days work in one each day. We stand watches at night, go to the lectures in the morning, and work all afternoon on note books. Now, however, I am all caught up.

When I went on deck at 3:30 this morning before I came down here, I saw my first glimpse of land, a flashing beacon. We could be in now, but I guess the purpose of this cruise is training rather than sightseeing, so we drop our hook at 11:00 o'clock Friday morning.

I guess I told you that I am taking a tour through Winchester, Salisbury, Stratford etc., and then have two days in London. Leave on the 20th and come back late on the 23rd. We have liberty Friday afternoon in Portsmouth.

I've see all sorts of ships today from tiny fishing trawlers to giant liners. We have been in heavy ground swells for two days now. The sea appears perfectly calm, and yet she has tipped as much as 22° on each side or a total of 45°. I love it.

If George thinks that the control panel of an airplane is complicated, he should see the gage board here in the engine room. I have counted 53 pressure gages, alarm signals etc. on the board itself.

We have had to check our cameras, so I don't know whether I will be able to get any ship board pictures or not.

The nights are better now. You can see that I write these letters when I am dead for rest. It is the only time I get and consequently they are incoherent, disjointed messes. I do hope that you will be able to get some idea of what is happening here. Write me and tell me what you would like to know then I'll have something to work by.

Thursday

We sighted land long ago and have been following along the coast. Tomorrow I go ashore. Probably will have no chance to write anymore on this, so

　　　　　Love to all,
　　　　　　Scottie

Will write about tours.

At Stratford, First Cruise, 1936.

Portsmouth, 25 June 1936

Dear Family,

Well, my stay in England is nearly over. Day after tomorrow we'll be in Göteborg.

This is the second letter I have started to you – I lost the first. I have the guard today so I have lots of time, and I shall try to finish up this and get it off.

We arrived in port and dropped anchor at 11:00 A.M. However, we could not get ashore until about four in the afternoon. There was some difficulty about "clearing" the ship. Of course, we were all so impatient that everybody was very irritable. Finally we were inspected and put in a boat – and then solid ground underfoot again.

My first impression of Portsmouth was not a very complimentary one. It appeared so very sordid; the shops were not like ours; even the best seemed only like our worst; the people were dressed poorly and seemed tawdry. Of course, the actual thing that made this appear so was the fact that I was in a very old city; and that, except for London, England has changed very little in the last 200 years. Many of the streets are of cobblestone. The architecture of the houses, new or old, seems to follow an old pattern.

Another thing that struck all of us, the homliness of the English woman. Most of them are downright homely. With few exceptions they are plain, at any rate. They are all pale faced. The "non-use" of cosmetics may be an exemplary virtue; but if such refraining causes the women to look as though they all were recovering from double pneumonia, I recommend a quick conference with Yardley.

The city of Portsmouth has been awfully decent to us. We ride on all buses, trams, and trolley buses free of charge, are admitted to the municipal beach free, and generally have the run of the town.

The first day in port ashore we spent in riding around the town and trying to become fairly familiar with it.

The streets are narrow and how those drivers keep from killing off dozens is beyond me.

So much for that. Now my leave.

We left by motor bus at about eight Saturday morning. The buses are quite as good as those in the United States. Seats do not recline as ours, but the top rolls back - "a sun tan as you ride". (The tops of all English cars roll back. Funny little cars, like our Austins. Tax is on H.P. the small size.) Immediately as I got out of Portsmouth and into the country, my opinion of England changed. The admittedly bad impression which, as first, should have stuck according to all rules, completely reversed and I fell in love with the English country.

Portsmouth is just an old fashioned city, London a modern metropolis - all right in their place, but not extraordinary; but the English country is beautiful. I would not have missed it for anything in the world. It was when I saw the rolling downs, the tiny towns clustered around their cathedrals, the houses, built before our United States was born and still inhabited, the quiet and peace that I never have seen in America, then it was that I discovered England.

Our first stop was Winchester. We went immediately to the cathedral. I left the party and went by myself to sit in the cool, vast nave and listen to a service which was in progress. It was so cool and quiet. The cathedral was the most completely Gothic of any I saw, with its intricate and beautiful stone tracery, pointed arches etc. I found many evidences of Romanesque architecture, however. Even then, Winchester was the capitol of England before London - from Alfred the Great to William the Conqueror, I believe. I saw the tombs of many bishops and a few kings, Rufus among them. But the history which was continually spouted at us was not of great importance to me. I shall read an English history and get all of that. But to think that that cathedral has been there since 1050, before anyone dreamed there was an America; to see the magnificent architectural achievement - developed without the aid of scaffolding; the giant windows, unparalleled by any modern work; to think of all that, and then to sit and listen to a service, chanted in Latin, much the same service as has been chanted for hundreds of years, in 1936, 900 years after the building was begun.

Anyway, next stop was Stonehenge on the way to Salisbury. We had to go out of our way to get there and, in my opinion, it was an utter waste of time. Very interesting legend connected with it all, but nothing to see or feel that cannot be obtained from a guide book.

We ate in Salisbury at an old inn called the "Red Lion".

Another very old inn, preserved intact with its open court where the coaches used to drive in. The meal was delicious. We were behind schedule and had only a few minutes to go to the cathedral. Much plainer than Winchester, larger, and yet beautiful in its vast plainness itself. It was destroyed in the 14th century and rebuilt- therefore, the lack of stone work.

From Salisbury we went on to Glastonbury. The ruins of the old Abbey are there. It is the seat of the founding of the English Church. All in ruins, it stands for a good deal in the history of England both religious and otherwise. King Arthur and Guinevere are connected with it; and it was here that Joseph of Arimathea came when he brought the Holy Grail to England, and planted the thorn, which even now is claimed to bloom each Christmas.

From Glastonbury to Welles and another cathedral. It was a little interesting in view of the fact that the old cloister of the monastery was still there, the stones worn down by (as I try to believe) the sandaled feet of the monks from generation to generation.

There is an interesting old clock in the cathedral, to the English point of view the greatest pride the cathedral boasts. It tells everything, moon, stars, day, week, year - probably the weather, stock market quotations, and the situation in Abyssinia, and, I suppose, also as most clocks do, the hour and minute. A masterpiece, no doubt. What amuses me is that on each hour a mounted knight chases a templar around the piller on the clock and cuts his head off. On the half hour a fool kicks a bell. That was really interesting.

Outside the cathedral was the market place and a china vender was auctioning off his wares. His ready supply of wit and ability to meet any remark with a "stopper" was really interesting and funny - especially as it was all in the low class English accent.

From Welles, on to Bath for the night. We stayed at the Poultney (our bus load), the finest hotel in what used to be a very fashionable watering place. Still is, as far as I can figure. The royal family was there for six weeks last year. We didn't arrive until late. Had dinner immediately and I ran into what was to be the case from then on: a million knives and forks, seven courses, and a menu printed in French. Oh, my, I tried to remember what was what, started from the outside in, and seemed to come out even. The Englishman uses a knife for everything he eats and never changes his fork from one hand to the other. I see now where Dad got his habit, a throw back from our ancestors, eh? The meal was delicious. While we were drinking coffee in the lounge, a rather distinguished looking gentleman came over to us and started a conversation. He was an interesting old duck and was quite evidently a gentleman of the best class. He did turn out to be a Colonel Cordeaux, a Britisher through and through despite the name, and a retired Army officer. I talked with him quite a bit after the others had left and was rewarded with an invitation to lunch on Tuesday at his club in London, the oldest military club in the world. He wanted me to "pop over and take a look at their extraordinary collection of military and naval portraits". So Tuesday noon in London I "popped over". It was well worth my while. This letter will go forever if I tell in detail all about everything, so we'll let it wait for awhile.

Later in the evening we ran into a middle class manufacturer who took us out to his home, where several of his friends gathered, and we spent a very interesting evening talking about England and the States. The man's home was quite pretentious and quite as much Victorian; but his taste for Victorianism was only evidenced in his interior decoration. It is this sort of experience that really makes such a trip as mine worthwhile, don't you think? The chance to know other people, how they live, what they think, what they do and how they do it; I really think they are the most important things.

Things like this little thing I noticed give one an idea of the sort of country one is in – the man ordered a taxi by phone to take us to his home, which was a couple of miles out of Bath. He asked for "Old Gill" on the phone; and can you imagine? "Old Gill" could not come; he was off duty; they would have to send the other man. In a town of well over a hundred thousand people there was one cab available even though it was raining. He was free to come for us. Where would you find anything like that in the United States?

We could only drive past the old Roman Baths. I wanted so to see them, but we had no time. We arrived at the hotel too late to do any good and left too soon in the morning – one great disadvantage of an organized tour.

I might digress a bit here and make a few comments on the

hotels. The <u>Poultney</u> was luxurious; cuisine perfect; rooms lovely in an old fashioned way; beds like down. Yet, there was no bath - and we had a first floor room, quite as nice as any in the house; no telephone; no radio; horrible lighting; no closets - but wardrobes. But - towels - they were wonderful - thick and easily five feet long. We did have running water - one concession to changing times. But a radio, circulating ice water, and a writing desk would have been out of place in them.

Oh, my, how can I ever get everything I have to say written down; and I've either lost or misplaced my note book which has some of the more peculiar things in it. I know there is a lot I shall forget that I do so want to tell you, and yet I haven't even begun yet - and here I've nearly completed four sheets.

Well, anyway - we left Bath at eight after a bath and a breakfast, the proportion of which was astounding indeed.

We made but one stop in the morning, at a little place called Broadway, a ridiculous name for the place according to New York standards of Broadway. It was a tiny town, a resort, preserved or built in the typical English style of architecture. (I hope it was preserved but have my doubts.) The stop was merely a rest; but I saw a beautiful inn, a quiet place with a dignified paneled dining room as I have always dreamed of for my home, and a gorgeous garden. I have a picture or two which I will show you.

Then on toward Stratford. There was such a large group in the tour (8 buses or about 212 midshipmen) that the plans to feed us at Stratford were out of the question; a lucky thing, for I had my lunch in the walls of Kenilworth castle. That was something I had not reckoned for and, although we had very little time to look around, I hurried through my lunch and went out to the ruins of the castle itself. There was a place with association, the days of chivalry, knighthood, jousts. Oh, I wish I knew my English History a thousand times better than I do. The actual walls have been made into a gift shop and tea room; but the castle in its ruins remains as it was since the days of Richard Coeur De Lion.

From Kenilworth we went back to Stratford. Saw Ann Hathaway's cottage - they wouldn't let us get out, damn them, - Shakespeare's birth place, and Harvard House. The birth place is interesting, of course, - yet - I did not get the thrill I expected. There was one interesting thing: at one time a butcher had his shop in the place and would not let anyone know that his establishment was the birth place of such a famous man. When people paid their bills, however, he took them to the room where Shakespeare was born, let them write their name on the ceiling, and charged them according to the length of the name. The ceiling is covered with names, the last one dating 18__.

Much as I hate to admit it, Stratford on Avon did not thrill me as possibly it should.

On to Oxford. We had only time to see Christ Church. The other colleges were not to be seen for it was getting late - and London 56 miles away. I really did get a kick out of seeing the famous university, talking with some of the students, and seeing their rooms and dining hall. The school is so old in traditions. Their methods of study and instruction seem to be far behind ours, yet we send our finest scholars to Oxford to taper off.

And so off to London. There is much I haven't said about all these places. I shall probably talk your ears off in August.

Now I'm slowly developing writer's cramp. So London shall be reserved for a letter mailed from Göteborg. This goes off today.

Much love to all,
Scottie

Somewhere in the North Sea,

29 June 1936

Dearest Family,

The other letter didn't get off, so you will receive two at once.

And so – o – we came to London Town – tired, dirty, hungry – in a drizzling rain, the only rain we had during our whole stay in England. So, although we cannot say that we had not typical English weather, our entree into London was greeted by the usual novelist's weather.

My first impression was not what I might call pleasant. It appeared quite as any modern American city might at sundown minus the sun. We stayed at the Imperial Hotel in Russel Square. Went there immediately, got our rooms, and went down to dinner, the usual seven course affair with the same galaxy of knives and forks and French menus.

I did not stay with the tour in London. Went independently with a couple of other guys and saw everything they did only in my own way. Monday morning I saw the changing of the guard at Buckingham. Then we grabbed a taxi over to Westminster. Saw the Hall, the only Parliament building open to the public, and the Abbey – a flock of tombs of kings and queens. Did it ever strike you as strange that Elizabeth and Mary of Scots are buried directly opposite each other in identical tombs (chapels)? Then after Westminster we walked up towards Trafalgar and past the Cenotaph and the Horse Guards Parade, along Oxford Street, and back to Piccadilly.

In the afternoon we went to the Tower; and then in the late afternoon back by bus to Hyde Park – quite a ride. In the evening we walked around a while; and then Mike Wallace and I had dates with a school mate of Mike's girl and a friend of hers.

Tuesday morning came the crowning event. It was the King's birthday, and the famous "Trooping of the Colors" was to take place. I got fouled up on my time and, although it would have done no good to go early unless I arrived before breakfast, never-the-less, I could not get near the parade ground. It was lucky for me I think, that I couldn't for instead _____

Well – never a dull moment – at the end of "couldn't" we had an emergency Fire Drill; two words more – and a General Quarters (man battle stations). I wonder what next-----

It is now 8:30 in the evening and the sun will not be down for another hour or more - and we are on day light time.

Anyway to get on -- for, instead of pushing around in a crowd which could not see anything (seats for the better class who had tickets obscured the parade ground), I wangled my way onto the balcony of the German Embassy, which overlooks the Mall, and saw the procession from a wonderful point of vantage - King and all. It was a sight well worth going to London for if that were all that was seen.

At noon I went to the United Service Club for my lunch with Colonel Cordeaux. Had a very interesting time. It was very much like the clubs I had read about, one of those places where no one speaks to anyone else. The lunch was spread out on a huge table, every imaginable sort of meat, fish, vegetable etc. Much like the banquet boards of feudal times. One walks up, inspects, selects, places his order, and then is served at his own table. I let my host order for me; I was lost. Then he showed me over the club and presented me with a history of the darn place and I left. I should have been bored to tears in America; but in England, it turned out as a wonderful chance to get a look at the English people in their own environment.

From the club I wandered back to the hotel, sent some cards, and then went to tea at one of Lyons Tea Shops. Lyons are the "Childs" of England.

At 5:00 we left for Portsmouth again.

Nothing happened in Portsmouth interesting except the Admiral's Reception, a routine affair in every port. I was paired up with as beautiful a woman as I have seen in a long time, a Commander's wife - R. N. not U. S. N.

So England may be summed up more or less by a few impressions; a country clinging to old fashions and ideas, yet striving to keep up with the world; a glorious country side - thatched roofs, rolling downs - a reserved cordiality of all people; the utter indifference to, and ignorance of the majority of the people of their history and historic land marks; the disappointment of Stratford on Avon; the arrogance and conceit of the two Oxford students with whom we talked; left handed traffic; the kindness and courtesy of London bobbies; the lack of ice in any form in anything; warm beer; homely women; the lack of skyscrapers in London; the antiquity of taxis, and antithesis in buses; the wonderful subway system, and horrible trams in London; free speech in Hyde Park; love of pageantry and tradition, yet utter indifference of masses, and ignorance of meaning of same; tiny automobiles; courtesy and thoughtfulness of all drivers; absolute absence of auto horns in London; the Englishman's absolute helplessness when in a tight situation (one of our buses got lost; I'll tell you more); the conspicuous absence of the cockney accent for which I was looking; peaceful cathedrals; Piccadilly; quiet cottages; Buckingham Palace; London Tower and the Mayfair: children beggars after American coins and British coppers; and the Crown jewels – a country of contradictions.

I'd like to live in rural England, but never in London. I had always imagined England as overcrowded; and yet, aside from its cities, which I admit did seem very much so, the countryside was quite otherwise. The farms were pleasant in appearance – not the harsh, ugly buildings which characterize the American farm. The English city is much like our own in one respect; it seems as though the people have crowded into the cities, leaving a country much more inviting than ours.

These incoherent snatches of impressions will undoubtedly leave you with the idea that I derived very little benefit from my short stay in England. However you may rest assured that such is not the case. For the short time I stayed in England, I believe I obtained rather a fine idea of just what sort of a place it is. I saw some of her more famous prides, learned something of her people, and at least learned the monetary system.

This letter has again assumed the form of an installment serial. I try to write it all at once time to save you from translating a series of disconnected ideas; but our life is not conducive to uninterrupted letter writing.

Today is Wednesday. Friday morning we arrive in Göteborg and I go on leave. Mike Wallace, a football player from Mississippi, and a boy named Bush, one of the managers, and I are going off on our own to some little town on the coast – we don't know which yet and spend our time trying to learn how to speak Swedish; rather – in case you should misunderstand me – try to save our money and at the same time become acquainted with the Swedish people. Later this afternoon we are going to get out a map and make our final decision.

We have been steaming on a course 0-0-0, which is due north, and are far above the last city in Norway now - above Bergen, of course - just marking time. We are up where the sun sets at 11:00 P. M. and rises again at about 2:30 A. M. Never gets anywhere near dark. We have been steaming well in sight of land, and what a beautiful sight, all mountains, snow capped, jutting down to the sea. They far surpass anything I have seen - even the Rockies.

We shall turn around soon 180°, head into the Skagerrak and into Göteborg. It is cool all the time, and downright cold at night.

My job now is compartment cleaner. I am one of those detailed to keep my division sleeping quarters clean. It is a fairly good job, a full night's sleep every night, at least. No watches to stand.

I have been shifted back to my old berth on #2 - 5" gun as first shell man.

Oh, yes, there is something I meant to write you about while in England. Now it may be too late to get an answer I want very much to have A.. E........ come up to Binghamton for a couple of days during my leave. The Phi Delt convention is in Syracuse, and there will be a "Grand Ball" one of the nights. It would make a nice thing to do to entertain her if we took that in. If it is out of the question, do not fail to say so definitely. I'll probably not hear before I get to Norfolk. But if it would not be too much trouble (in any way) I should like it.

Now I guess I have about exhausted myself in a literary line.

Shall get this off at Göteborg. I'll mail it aboard ship so it will go off on the pilot boat. Will send a batch of cards with Swedish stamps. That will prove that I have been there anyway.

Love to all from the "Land of the Midnight Sun",
Scottie

Göteborg, 8 July 1936

Dear Mother,

Just a line from Göteborg. I could not find cards when I thought of getting them. Today I have the duty and will not go ashore again. We sail again tomorrow.

We have had a perfectly splendid time in Sweden. Nothing exciting, but all very interesting.

As you know, we went to Allingsäs for our leave. We had no idea where to go. Had very little money. So we picked Allingsäs because it was a small town - had good bathing, and everything reputedly cheap.

We really had a wonderful time - made friends with the entire population, went to a dance, drank coffee, ate cakes with this person and that, swam, bicycled, and took all the beautiful girls from their steady boyfriends. When we left we had half the town at the station to see us off. (mostly feminine).

You see, it was a good place to go because not many Midshipmen came there. I think there were twelve in all.

Sweden is much like New York State. The country looks much the same. Göteborg with English signs instead of Swedish could be almost any American city of the same size. American automobiles almost entirely are used.

It has one thing, however, quite different from the average American city. It is the most surprisingly clean city I have seen in a good while. The parks are different also. Liseberg is sort of Coney Island with the unpleasant parts of Coney left out. Then, there is another park where there is a symphony concert on the terrace of the restaurant - dancing inside. I have been to these two. There are several others, however. Each park has its restaurant. Liseberg has several. There is dancing and entertainment of all sorts. Everybody goes and drinks his coffee or <u>socherdricka</u> or beer as the case may be.

While at Allingsäas we ran into an interesting kid. He was only sixteen years old. Spoke English, German, Swedish, and was thrilled that we stopped to talk to him. He was staying with an uncle at the <u>pensionat</u> outside of town. He was quite evidently one of the better class. We formed quite a friendship with him. Spent an evening with him and his uncle and the other boarders. They all spoke fairly good English.

I've found that if I take English and German, mix the two and slur it all together, the Swedes can get the drift of what I am trying to put across.

The Swedish people are very friendly and could not be nice enough to us. Maybe, however, it was because we bought gallons of coffee and dozens of cakes to feed them.

The Swedish women are by far the nicest looking bunch I have seen. Of course, blond hair and blue eyes is the rule, but there are exceptions. We got to know quite a bunch and they are as nice as they look.

The Swedish food is very good. Every restaurant has its hors d'oeuvres table in the center. One more course is sufficient to appease almost any appetite.

Tomorrow, we are off for twelve more days at sea. Then Paris, and we are on our way home.

I close now. Just a line to let you know I am well, happy, and looking forward to getting home again.

       Love to all,
        Scottie

III
YOUNGSTER YEAR
1936

ROBERT SCOTT WHITMAN JR.

En route - Cherbourg
Now - somewhere along
Coast of Ireland

12 July 1936

Dear Family,

At sea again. A week from tomorrow we arrive at Cherbourg. One short week there, and then we head back across the Atlantic on our way home!!! My, that sounds good. A sea voyage is great fun; visiting foreign lands interesting and thrilling; but I'm homesick for the U. S. A. and home.

Right now we are, I suppose, somewhere near the coast of Ireland or Scotland. We passed through the channel between the Orkney and Shetland Islands about 8:00 P. M. (2000) last night. You see, we are going around the British Isles on our way to France, rather than back through the channel. This is, of course, for the purpose of killing time.

I am on a deck detail now. My watch for the present five days period is on the port revolution indicator and enunciator (Engine Room Telegraph) on the bridge. I was extremely fortunate in being on the bridge when we got under way at Göteborg. I saw the whole thing from the best point of vantage and even played a small part in the business, since it was I who told the Engine Room what to do. (I let the Captain give the orders, though, - he might have felt left out otherwise). It was the smartest piece of seamanship I have ever seen. The channel we were in was no wider than Main Street in places.

I had the mid-watch this morning. Just as I was going off we ran into fog. If you have never had that experience at night before, you have missed a very strange feeling. First the Arkansas's forecastle disappeared; in no time she was complete devoured. Next the Okie vanished, and our visibility was cut from 8 miles to 75 yards in a brief 10 minutes. Now and then we could see a faint glow from the searchlight of the ship ahead. Every two minutes the "moo" of our horn shattered the silence. (On the bridge all conversation except orders is carried on in whispers at all times.) Soon we saw a churning ahead. It was the towing spar, an airplane-shaped gadget, fixed to throw a spray, and towed in thick weather at end of 500 yard line, by each ship in column. Its purpose is obvious.

I lingered as long as I could, and then came below to catch a couple hours of sleep.

The sun broke through in the middle of the morning; now all is clear, but cold.

The watch with the exception of the last half hour was the most miserable I have yet had. Cold (we are still far North), damp, and not much to keep my mind off the two above mentioned hardships. I stood and dreamed of my room at home, that beautiful, comfortable, inviting bed, and of sleeping undisturbed by anything for weeks and months at a time, of hot breakfasts, of newspapers, English speaking civilized civilians, of baths in real bath tubs, and a chance to talk to you and Marsh and Ced and A.. E.. and everybody else. Then I thought of my 1/2" mattress on the hard deck in #5 barbette where the mid-watch sleeps. Ugh!!! It is times like that when this man's Navy takes on a rather blackish hue. But then, the fog came up; things got interesting; and I decided all over again that it's not so bad after all.

Well – as the officer of the deck would say to his relief – Sea calm, Steaming 270° true. Check 286 on master compass. Making nine knots. 135 revolutions. Formation "D" (dog). Arkansas, Oklahoma, ahead. Ark has Div. guide. Land approximately 30 miles to Stbd. Wind direction N. E. Velocity 7 miles. No. 1 gyro in use. No special orders.

So that is just what we are doing. Do you know any more now?

We've left Sweden behind. Half of the boys fell in love in Sweden and were sorry to leave. I was, too, in a way. The Swedes are a fine people. Much more friendly than I expect we will find the French. But, although I had a couple of dates with very nice and very beautiful Swedish girls, I still want to get home.

I didn't do much in Göteborg. Went out to a couple of parks and had two or three good chows.

Had a motor launch duty on the last day and it rained like everything all day long. The reception was on our ship, and the rain rather dampened the spirit of the thing. I got slightly dampened myself. The motor launches are open boats.

Right now I think I shall close temporarily. There is not much more left in my rather sleepy head.

> Love to all,
> Scottie

More tomorrow maybe.

Friday – 17 July

Off Cape Finisterre

My, I've been awfully busy. Now that I am on deck, I work more during the day and sleep more at night. Consequently, I have had less time to write. So now I must try to catch up.

A rather amusing thing happened the other day – I think it is the funniest I have heard of for a long time. We were off Fair Island which, by the way, is one of the Shetland group. Suddenly a hoarse cry of seeming anguish, mixed with excitement – a small boat had hailed us. Orders came from the Flagship to all ships to stop. We veered off in emergency formation and stopped. The boat came along side the Flagship. A man arose in his seat triumphantly waving a huge fish. "Do you want to buy a nice feesh Meester?" We got underway. That, so help me, is a true story. Our log will verify it.

We are now in the Bay of Biscay; and if the weather we are now experiencing is any example of the typical, I have no love for that body of water which I remember so well from 6th grade geography. It is by far the roughest I have ever experienced. The Wyo, being devoid of all her armor, is light enough to be affected by the lightest ground swell. Now that we are really in rough weather, she is rolling from side to side like a barrel. The deck is at an angle of 20° from one side to the other. It is fun for a while; but, after having to lean from one side to the other to keep footing all day long, it gets just a bit monotonous. Everything loose rolls all over the place.

Today was field day. Every Friday we spend the whole day cleaning. My section's cleaning station is up on the boat deck. Working all day on the windward side of a 40 mile gale was no picnic. It was all an experience which helps to make the cruise an instructive and interesting thing.

Right now I am surprising myself by the degree of legibility which I seem to have attained.

Monday morning, we arrive in Cherbourg. I shall go to Paris for a day or two with Mike Wallace, a boy whom I believe I have mentioned before. The biggest attraction of France is, however, the mail which our stop will bring.

I wrote Gram a letter which will be mailed in Cherbourg.

There are so many things I want to see in Paris. I shall not be able to see half of what I would like to.

There is so little that I can think of to say, and yet there of course is such a lot in which you would be interested. I shall probably talk your ears off in August.

Now I shall quit for a while. I will finish up tomorrow or Sunday. Oh! Give me land - land of any sort. No, I'm not seasick; but I am tired of walking on bulkheads - and ceilings, rather than the deck. We have had our baptism. The maximum arc of roll sideways so far is 60°. Tonight, for the first time today, they were able to set up mess tables and we got something more than coffee and sandwiches.

We have had to head out to sea again. The channel is too dangerous for a squadron to maneuver in weather like this - too much traffic.

I guess we'll get in Monday O.K. anyway - at least I hope so.

We fire S. R. B. P. sometime between the 10th and the 15th - the first day weather permits. Arrive in Norfolk on the 8th to drop boats and other gear likely to be damaged by the concussion.

The cruise has been very exciting; but I still will get my biggest thrill when I see the dome of the Chapel from the destroyer coming up the bay.

Sunday

All is calm again - at least comparatively calm. We are due to arrive at about 0200 tomorrow morning. I'm closing up this letter now with a fervent hope that all is well at home, and a wish that the next 27 or 28 days pass like lightening.

        Love to all,
        Scottie

27 July 1936

Dear Family,

I shall not make this a very long letter – just a note to tell you that I am well. Have been to Paris and survived, seen Notre Dame, the Eifel Tower, and all – and now quite ready to come home.

We got back from Paris to find the Oklahoma gone. It was on its way to Spain to stand by to take off refugees. Half of its Midshipmen are now aboard the Wyo. What a mess!!! Rumors of all sorts are running wild. We don't know what will happen. We are, of course, far overcrowded now; and we are standing by now to shove off for Spain tomorrow ourselves to pick up 56 Coast Guard Cadets. The orders read, make tentative plans – so I'm not yet sure whether we will go or not, but the odds are that we will. We certainly are in an awful mess and will be as long as we have 200 odd extra Midshipmen aboard.

Paris was grand. I shall not write about it now – I hope to see you in three weeks – maybe later maybe sooner. These new developments will surely change things one way or the other. We are pretty disgusted right now.

Love to all,
Scottie

10 August 1936

Dear Family,

At 0800 this morning, we had 293 miles to go to Norfolk. We get in sometime during the mid-watch tonight. Tie up at the Navy Yard tomorrow. Load stores all day – and then back out to the Southern Drill Grounds for S. R. B. P. It's not definite as to when we get off, but I think it will be on the 14th. You can expect to see me before Monday. I shall let you know exactly when.

I hope there is train fare waiting for me tomorrow in Norfolk. I have not one red cent, and have not had since we left Cherbourg.

I don't know when I shall be at A.. E........'s. Overnight, at least, on the way home, and I'll probably come back a little early, as at Christmas.

I heard nothing from you about her coming up so I take it for granted that it is inadvisable – I was afraid it would be.

I shall want to spend some time with her naturally but have no fears – home sounds best right now.

I'm hoping for lots of mail in Norfolk. We got only two in Cherbourg, much to my disgust.

I'll have lots to tell you – probably talk so much you'll be sorry I ever came home.

We've been to Spain to the Revolution – taken on a bunch of Coast Guard Cadets from their cutter, which was taking off American refugees. Oh, lots has happened since we left Cherbourg – exactly two weeks yesterday.

No more – no sense in telling the last two weeks news when we are so close to seeing each other again.

Only a week more.

　　　Much love to all,
　　　　Scottie

ROBERT SCOTT WHITMAN JR.

Annapolis, 5 September 1936

Dear Family,

I'm awfully sorry that leave is over in one way, but it does seem good to be back.

I had a perfectly grand time at Cape May. The people were wonderful, the water delightful, and A.. E....... was there.

Had the same nice time in Baltimore. We heard Casa Loma Wednesday night. I never saw such a crowd – it was impossible to even attempt to dance.

Football has been going along quite strenuously and regularly, morning and afternoon. We are not practicing this morning on account of the annual physical exams which we are taking. I just finished mine and am O. K. for another year.

I am on the "A" squad so far, playing guard, if you please. (I have a brand new uniform.) It looks as though, if I keep plugging, I might stay there. I don't know what team I'm on – it has been the third rather consistently. They are mixing them up though, so I have been on the 2nd, 3rd, and 4th at different intervals. We had our first scrimmage yesterday afternoon. There is, of course, little chance I will make a letter this year. I'm not kidding myself on that deal.

The heat has been terrific, and, yesterday in practice, I lost 8 pounds. Gained it all back right away, of course. I weigh about 199 – 200 before practice fairly consistently, and 195 – 194 after, usually. They make us drink a saline solution at practice to keep us from getting heat stroke. It's nasty stuff but does seem to help a lot.

This is an easy life except for football. We are living in the Second Batt. Have no formations, go to meals if and when we want, leave meals when we please, get up when we please, and practice football twice a day. In the morning we wear shorts and skivvie shirts, [athletic shirts], in the afternoon regular uniform.

Sturdevant – you remember he was "unsat" – "bilged" his re-exam and was sent home. I'm sorry. He was a plugger and deserved to stay.

      Love to all,
        Scottie

Annapolis, 11 September 1936

Hello Pop,

Congratulations – Felicitations – Many happy returns of the day – and many of them. I sure wish I could have been with you all tonight to sink my teeth into some of that wonderful birthday cake that I know you had in the double celebration.

Well, I'm moved. As I think I told you, my new room is 1339. I am pretty well settled now.

The Plebes have moved, too, of course. I can't seem to bring myself to shout at them. I still remember last year, I guess.

I think A.. L.. may come down for the William and Mary game. I'll get Harris and Rhode to take her.

We have been having extra instruction periods in Math and "Skinny" (Oct. work), but they will soon be over now. [To make Oct. work for the football squad easier] I'm afraid it is going to be a tough year. The Physics prof made no bones about telling us that their course was tough – very tough. I have an idea what Integral Calculus is about anyway – that's a help.

This is all for now. The Regiment checks in tomorrow. I'm on watch in the Batt Office when they come. Woe is me – it will be an awful mess.

Love to all,
Scottie

Did George get his birthday letter and carton of Luckies?

ROBERT SCOTT WHITMAN JR.

Annapolis, 29 September 1936

Dear Family,

Harris, Rhode and Shoemaker all arrived Friday. It is going to be a grand room. I like all of them a lot.

Of course, academic year has started. I do hope I can make a better record than last year. They say Youngster year is the hardest.

It is remarkable how quickly everything settles down into the regular routine. It is all running as smoothly as though we were through half a year.

I think Integral should be fun. It is only Tuesday and we have already nearly finished the first "Steam" sheet – an assembled drawing of a bench vise.

I'm not doing as well as I might in football – might even hit the "B" squad before I'm through. I'm not worrying too much about it though. It's not important enough. I try, of course, but why worry my head as I once did.

A.. L.. was down for the game. Jud, Tex, and Don took her, so you see she was well escorted. She went home almost directly after but drove down again on Sunday with some friends.

The schedule has been a little changed this year to squeeze in an extra period. We get up a little earlier – classes shortened etc.

It seems awfully good to be a Youngster. Just to carry on in the halls is wonderful.

Well, happy days are here again. Another Ac year started. All is well.

Much love to all,
Scottie

Annapolis, 11 October 1936

Dear Family,

   I received Mother's letter Friday and Dad's today so I feel quite written to. News from home is such an event. I don't mean a rarity, but I do so like to hear from you all.

   The first two weeks of "Ac" year are over and no casualties.

   I suppose I should feel quite downhearted, for the expected has happened. Monday the entire fourth team was dropped to the "B" squad. Tommy said we would get more actual experience playing there. We have a schedule of our own. I, of course, feel badly, but not as much as I feel I should. I had expected it. I'm no world-beater, and (probably the biggest reason why I don't do better) I have no desire to play. It holds no thrill as it once did. It keeps me in condition, however, and there are some compensations. I have to do something anyway. We make a trip to Princeton and get the week-end after the Army game.

   Tonight the mess hall was in the usual Friday night pre-game uproar. The band was there and the whole meal time was so noisy that conversation was impossible.

   I read the article in Forum. Brown has some very good dope in his article. He is right in almost every statement. His paragraphs on discipline are really loaded - very potent. Yet, the Academy does achieve its purpose. True, it does not dispense a cultural education in any sense of the word. It couldn't and still be a four year course. Yet, it does teach the Navy - it trains men to run battleships. The taxpayer is disillusioned about Uncle Sam's hermitage for sea struck laddies. It does not produce gentlemen. The gentlemen produces himself by resisting rather than absorbing a good many of N. A. influences. One does lose touch with social usage and the like. A man slips while he is here. Yet once out, (providing he came from good parentage) he has a greater chance of climbing back up.

   The solution of the problem as far as I can see is a constructive reading program outside of classes. One does not get much time, but I do get a chance to read a good book now and again. I try to fight against that almost inevitable wall of resistance, set up by the majority of Midshipmen, against anything not professional. The more I can get into society of others than Midshipmen, the happier I am. It is the only way to keep a broad outlook. I guess you think this outburst a bit strange. I have had such thoughts for a long time. Dad's mention of the Forum article enables me to set them down.

Don't think I'm dissatisfied for I am definitely not. The Academy, just as we sometimes said, "Ain't what it's cracked up to be". But what is _____?

Did I tell you about my English course? It's a history of the United States Navy. Would be very interesting if it were not, as are all non-professional subjects, a very mediocre memory course. We are nearly half through one of the two books we use.

Well, we play Virginia tomorrow. I shall not be on the bench, and, to celebrate the fact, A.. L.. is coming down and bringing Betty Ruff. Tex and I are taking them to the game and to the informal after.

Next week we go to Baltimore to the Yale game. The "B" squad plays the Yale "B" squad on Friday.

We went to rifle range on Friday. Fired the pistols. They are great fun, but I can't hit anything with them.

Jud went to the hop last night. Came back all pepped up over N. A. hops. He had been rather dubious before he went. I, of course, didn't rate it because of football. Harris, Shoemaker, and I went to the movies in the yard. A fairly good show – entertaining, at any rate.

Well, I have run on and on.

Goodnight and pleasant dreams to all.

     Love,
      Scottie

Annapolis, 18 October 1936

Dear Family,

Well, another week has passed. We've been to Baltimore and seen Navy lose a game, which they no more rated losing than anything. They played magnificent ball and completely wore down the Yale team. The breaks of the game lost the decision.

The "B" squad won 20 - 12. I did not start, mainly because I had not been out much during the week; but I played most of the game - longer than anyone else.

A.. E....... and family were at the game and I saw them between halves and after the game.

I am sending a couple of Logs. In one of them is a rather poor piece I did in reply to Brown's article in Forum. I don't know how it went over with the Regiment. I wrote it only because too many of these kids here were taking too hastily to Brown's questionable ideas. Midshipmen are too hasty in siding with anyone who pans the "system".

I have stated "sat" now for three weeks. Got another good mark in my Physics lab work. Got a 2.9 on a Math quiz in which the average of the entire class was 2.0. And praise be to the gods, I have not yet hit the weekly "tree" in "steam". Only five more weeks of drawing, and I can breathe easy.

I have joined the Glee Club. Don't know why - mainly because Harris talked me into it, I guess. I sort of enjoy the work.

The game yesterday was a crackerjack. I was as limp as a rag when it was over. Navy has a ranking team this year. All we need is a few breaks to bring us through with flying colors. Kelley's kicking the ball was obviously intentional, for he pulled the same stunt later on the blocked punt.

I will wish I could go to law school when I graduate from here.

And so - I guess I'll close for the present.

          Love to all,
          Scottie

ROBERT SCOTT WHITMAN JR.

Annapolis, 25 October 1936

Dear Family,

Your letters arrived yesterday and today. As usual I was overjoyed at getting them.

I got home from Princeton quite late last night, and so did not have a chance to write yesterday.

I suppose you would like to know all about the Princeton game and our trip.

We left at 7:30 Saturday morning in the Navy Team Special, a nine car train. I never travelled in such luxury before in my life, and the way they treated the "A" squad was wonderful to behold. They had two chair cars and two Pullmans – berths made up in the Pullmans in case they wanted to sleep. We had a chair car. We were given all the latest magazines, newspapers etc.

The "B" squad dressed on the train. Got into buses immediately on arrival – (12:00), went to the field, after taking our clothes to the field house, and then went out to the Princeton practice field and played our game, we won very easily 19 – 0 in 12 minute quarters. I started and played most of the game.

We had sideline passes to the big game and sat on the bench. Saw all but the first quarter.

I think the two teams were very nearly matched. Navy played a good game and the score could have been 0 – 0. It was tough to lose. I don't know when we are going to start winning.

I tried to find Gross after the game, but did not succeed – we had only an hour before leaving for Annapolis again.

Had a steak dinner on the train that was a honey – the kind of steak you dream about – fully two inches thick and weighing about two pounds.

I came out of our game with a lovely dislocated finger – painful but of no consequence – hurt some when they put it back in joint. [Finger permanently disfigured.]

You ask me to tell more of my routine. There are no interesting drills now because I do not go to drills – football players are excused.

In "Steam" I am drawing a Liberty airplane engine – sketching each piece, taking dimensions from the actual parts, and then making the finished blueprint. It is our last project in drawing, thank heaven.

I am much more interested in Physics than I expected I should be. The labs are fun, but we do not have enough time - I could enjoy it more if I were not hurried.

Math, as usual, is tough sledding; History a bore; and German incidental.

Dad's and George's projected trip to the Army game thrills me. I do so hope you come. It will be a good game and you will have A#1 seats.

A.. was down today -Rhode was dragging for the week-end and we spent a very pleasant afternoon together. We rate liberty Sunday afternoons now.

I really cannot think of anymore now.

       Much love to all,
        Scottie

ROBERT SCOTT WHITMAN JR.

Annapolis, 10 November 1936

Dear Family,

So the Roosevelts beat the Landons and the Navys beat the Notre Dames. We seem to have come out .500 on the week's major battles.

Evidently Mr. Roosevelt has spent enough money on the P. W. A., P. D. Q. and stuff that enough of the P. W. A.s etc. voted for him. Or maybe we are wrong, and he is America's savior. I certainly hope that he won't let his overwhelming victory go to his head any more than it previously has.

I sure would have liked to have seen the Notre Dame game. It must have been a honey. Navy certainly played a beautiful ball game. The boys in the 3rd and 4th Battalions brought back the goal posts, score board and everything else except the stadium.

I am going to Boston this week after all – the "B" squad game has been canceled. We may play the Harvard "B" squad instead.

My marks are still around a 3.0. I see them every week now because of football. Got a 3.4 in "Steam" last week. The best mark I have ever had in "Steam" – just lucky and got the stuff for a change. We are putting our Liberty Engine together now.

Went to Seamanship yesterday. Had a very cold and uninteresting time catching mooring lines from sub-chasers as the First Class practiced coming alongside dock.

It has been right cool down here for the last few days. We have been wearing reefers.

Mac – you remember MacGregor, my one good wife last year, has become a problem. He is in love and I think it is proving too much for him. He is slowly but surely "bilging" out. Has been "unsat" for weeks now in Math and Physics. I think he has finally awakened and is getting on the ball.

The river right now is full of all sorts of seamanship drills. The cutters are headed across the river in column formation. The Youngsters are sailing all over in the "half raters" and "knockabouts". More Youngsters are working with life boats and life rings; some more are down there on the airplane dock practicing heaving the lead. The sub chasers are practicing docking again, and the destroyers just went out with a bunch of First Class. Oh, yes, and there are some Second Class learning to scull and punt.

It is a beautiful day but quite cold – and I am slowly going mad from the pounding of steam in the radiator pipes.

Christmas leave is only 43 days off now. The Plebes have been responsible for knowing the "score" for a long time. You see just how much Midshipmen look forward to leave.

Congratulations to George for the grand marks Dad spoke of. Keep it up.

Poor Jud and Shoemaker. They are scared stiff that their days as Uncle Sam's protégés are numbered. They both "bilged" the eye exam and it does not look as though Jud will be able to pull his up. (12 - 20 in one eye.) Don is better off-only 18 - 20 in one eye.

There is an amazing number of men with bad eyes in our class. I dare say we will lose more than fifty. The penalty of rushing them through when they entered.

What is the news on Gram's trip East? Is she coming? I wrote to her, you know, but as yet have not heard from her.

Dot is at school in Boston. I am contemplating looking her up Saturday. We arrive there at 7:00 in the morning and have liberty after the game until 11:30 P. M. Quite a nice trip, you see.

No more news now.

        Much love to all,
          Scottie

Annapolis, 15 November 1936

Dear Family,

So I'm back from Boston. Had a very nice trip and a pretty good time.

We left Annapolis in day coaches at six o'clock Friday evening and changed to sleepers in Philly. Arrived in Boston at I don't know when, but got up at seven and had breakfast in the station.

The "B" squad went out to the Varsity Club at Harvard immediately after breakfast. Ate at ten-thirty and played at noon. We won 18 – 0.

I called up Dot Sears in the morning and had a date with her that evening.

Our victory at Harvard makes the "B" squad the champions of the "Ivy League", Yale, Harvard, Princeton, and Pennsylvania have gone down before our assaults. Our season is over; unbeaten and untied, we rest on our laurels. And we played the Harvard game with less than four hours sleep the night before – and in a sleeper at that. Rugged – that's us.

Dottie and I went to the Navy ball at the Copley Plaza. It was a pretty fair dance. Dot had a good time, I guess.

While I was checking our things somebody jumped on me from the rear – it was Ann Titus. Small world.

We had to be back on board the train at 11:30. Shoved off at 12:00 and got back here at noon today. I've been sleeping most of the afternoon trying to catch up.

There is not much news. Bi-monthly exams this week. (Most exams are bi-monthly now). My last drawing exam is tomorrow.

Dad's letter came this morning. I was so glad to get it.

Oh, yes, are, or are not, Dad and George going to the game?

I sure wish they would. But I'd like to know. I do have to make my plans – and we should have reservations somewhere if it isn't too late. I'm afraid it is too late to get anything but just whatever I can get. The point is this. If Dad and George come we will want to be with them. It would be such fun. If he doesn't come, Vera Bergler and Tom Davies 1/c have invited us to be with them and Tom's brother and date.

There is no more now. So now I go but I shall return.

        Very much love to all,

        Scottie

Annapolis, 22 November 1936

Dear Family,

Your two letters arrived today. I am delighted that George is going to come to Philadelphia. I am only sorry because you all can't come.

You will have received the tickets by the time this letter arrives. I hope that they will be satisfactory.

Now as to arrangements: I have forgotten exactly where George's seat is – Section 0 row 64 is it not? After the game, if he will sit tight, I will come up there and get him before I get Ada – then we can go to meet her and the rest of the crowd. We are tentatively planning dinner at the Penn Athletic Club around eight, just six of us – and I think I could arrange for George to be with us there if he would like it – Or we can do something else – just the three of us.

No word has come out as yet but it is expected that the "B" squad will have overnight leave. We go up with the Regiment and come back with the team Sunday afternoon. Stay at the Bellevue Stratford over night.

I am sending a list of traffic regulations. They might be of help.

I have just passed through the most hectic week I think I have ever experienced – exam week, but not the usual run. I should not be surprised if I "bilged" all of them cold, but – only time will tell. "Steam" was a horror – it's all over now though. We start studying basic mechanisms next week – no more drawing!!!!

We have one more exam – the Calculus final – on next Wednesday. Football for me is all over on the same day, so then I can relax.

The usual pre-Army game pep meetings have started. The band was in the mess hall tonight and will be every night from now on.

The "B" squad is still out there playing cannon fodder trying to get the boys in shape for the game. I wonder how many people realize the important part we play in a football season. Just the old martyrs – that's us.

Christmas leave starts at noon on the 23rd this year. We have to be back on the 3rd, I think.

The time has really flown fast, and soon I shall be home.

Much love to all,

Scottie

Annapolis, 2 December 1936

Dear Family,

George's and Dad's letters came today. They made me very happy – fact is I got four letters today. I felt quite popular and important.

My marks are out, and, on the face of things they are the worst I have ever shown – yet I stand better in my class than I did last year in all of them. Youngster year is a hoodoo. With such marks last year, I would have been at the bottom of my class. It's getting more and more technical, and, because of the time I have to spend on the big three my "Bull" (History) has suffered. There are 182 "unsat", so far, for the term in Physics; 102 in "Steam". This is no alibi – merely an explanation. I'm still trying.

In "Steam" now we are studying basic mechanisms – tough but anything is a relief from that darned drawing.

Mechanics in three subjects now – "Steam", Math and Physics; and each department advocates and enforces a different method. What a headache.

Rhode has "bilged" his final eye exam but is staying until mid-year anyway.

The Glee Club and the Orchestra give their joint recital on Saturday. We have been very busy preparing for it.

I am glad that Gram stood the trip as well as you say she did, and hope by the time you receive this that she is well settled. My love to her, and I'll see her soon now.

I expect that I will be home sometime on the 24th. The D.....s expect me to spend the night as usual. I am, however, going to try to get an earlier train that will get me in before midnight on Christmas Eve. I'd like very much to go to the midnight service if somebody will go with me.

Much love to all,
Scottie

Annapolis, 14 December 1936

Dear Family,

Hey, that was the grandest box of chow I have ever seen – marvelous, stupendous, gigantic – super – super – super. The gang has voted you the best in the world and we all thank you a million times. It arrived quite intact – a very superior job of packing, Father.

So we are nearing the last week – my, how it drags. The Physics exam is tomorrow. I've boned till I'm half blind and my head is swimming. No more until tomorrow morning. Will get up early and finish up.

I'm not bringing my tux home. Dot and I are going to the Christmas dance (my only Binghamton frivolity), and I'll wear service.

My Christmas shopping has been finally completed. I spent yesterday afternoon in a drenching rain – shopping – and had a grand time.

Tex and I went to the hop stag last night. I had a fairly good time.

Tuesday

Well, that's over – Technical Tuesday – Physics exam, Math and then an afternoon of "Steam". No prophesys on the exam. Made two insane mistakes – I do that quite regularly. Why I'm not "unsat" is beyond me.

I'm going to close now. Will write soon again.

Thank you again for the chow.

   Love to all,
    Scottie

THE LUCKY BAG 1939, the Annapolis yearbook, was recognized as having been improved over prior years. Congratulations went out to the staff. R. S. Whitman Is noted as Associate Editor.

directly from Baltimore where an accurate mailing list is kept.

It's a hardworking outfit, the *Log* staff, and embraces about one-twentieth of the Regiment, so that plenty of variety results. It's a generally stated and accepted opinion that this year's *Logs* have been a distinct improvement and a real success. That means congratulation to Commander Barringer, the Officer Representative, T. C. Siegmund, Editor-in-Chief, J. C. Lawrence, Business Manager, G. M. K. Baker. Managing Editor, E. L. Schwab, Associate Editor, R. S. Whitman, H. A. Tistadt, M. G. McCormick, R. T. Pratt, H. L. Harty, W. T. Sawyer, C. E. Deterding, J. H Bowell, J. V. Cameron, C. H. Hall, all department editors, and J. F. Splain, F. B. Clarke, H. E. Benham, V. E. Teig, T. R. Weschler, W. L. Savidge, and W. J. Caspari, the Editorial Board.

has been formed within it known as the Trident Staff.

This Trident Staff is the working outfit who are responsible for the quarterly publication of

The men behind the scenes—the great mass who originate and write *The Log*. Such meetings as this let you know you are one in a crowd.

Scottie is seated in the front row on the far right.

Annapolis, 4 January 1937

Dear Mother,

So it is all over and I'm settling down to the long five months grind. My leave was quite the most wonderful so far, and by that token just as hard to forget – but forget I must except for a few odd moments. Got to get down to business now and get to work.

Thank you for the telegram, I wanted that more than anything. I do believe that the time I spent in Binghamton this Christmas was the happiest I have had. My family gave me such a wonderful Christmas and birthday, and I was so happy just to be with them, I know I have the grandest mother and father in the world and I'll stand up against the world to prove it.

My stay in Baltimore was very pleasant. Ada and I spent a relatively quiet time. Got to bed before 3:30 on New Years Eve and that was, by far, our latest hour.

The party was quite a success even though I got the low score as I always do. No cards at all.

We are all back in the old routine. It is not hard when one has to.

I have the guard tomorrow, so no classes; which, however, does not mean no studying – 'cause I have to keep up.

We are to march in the Inaugural parade – Uniform – service, leggings, overcoats, bayonet belts and rifles with fixed bayonets. Woe is us!

Don and Jud will be here until June at least.

  So now I close with lots of love to the bestest family in the world.
  Scottie

Annapolis, 4 January 1936

Dear Dad,

Your grand birthday letter arrived while I was at breakfast on New Years Day. It was such a fine letter and it made me very happy. Thank you for it.

You know, I've been thinking you've let conditions get you down too low, Pop. You're too darn discouraged.

You're having an awful tough time – I know it and you are being very, very brave about it; but, for goodness sakes brace up. Everything is going to be all right. Things will break.

We are all behind you heart and soul – so keep plugging. Sounds funny for me to be writing such a letter doesn't it. I guess maybe you may misunderstand me; but the only thing I want you to know is that I think you are the grandest guy in the world and the world's best father. I don't only think it, I know it. So please cheer up.

I just hope that somehow I can make you as proud of me as I am of you.

> Lots of Love,
> Scottie

Annapolis, 28 January 1937

Dear Mother,

The Inaugural was a horror. We were in the pouring rain for four and a half hours, on our feet all the time, and marched about eight miles. I caught the four-thirty train to Baltimore (Presidential order gave us liberty until one) and spent the evening at the D.....'s Never again do I want to see or hear of an Inaugural.

Thursday I felt so rotten that I went up to sick bay in the afternoon. I was running a little temperature, so they packed me off to the hospital. I thought I had caught the flu along with the rest of the Regiment. Friday I was up and around and was back Monday, so I guess it wasn't flu. Feel fine now. As a result, I missed my "bull" exam.

I suppose you are wondering about the other exams. I passed them all. On the whole, my standing is much better than last year – I got a 3.5 in Aptitude for the last two months. 3.01 average so far.

We have started studying Naval Machinery. Every kind of mechanism used aboard ship will be studied before we get through. This is the first time Youngsters have taken this, consequently the Second Class is studying it the same time we are.

Jud has signed his resignation to be effective in June. We all should have expected it, but it came as sort of a blow. We shall miss him a lot. There are 30 going from our Batt alone, because of physical disability. It is a strange organization, this Navy of ours. They build 'em up to tear 'em down, or so it seems. I prophesy less than 600 in our class when we graduate. My eyes are still doing more than their duty. Let's hope they keep it up.

I'm looking forward to seeing George. I haven't yet heard from him. I'll probably have Ada get in touch with him concerning coming down. She will undoubtedly see him at the dance.

The brownies arrived today – thank you so very much for them – they are the finest thing that comes into the room. The date nut bars were a great success.

Much love to all,
Scottie

ROBERT SCOTT WHITMAN JR.

Annapolis, 12 February 1937

Dear Family,

Greetings to the nicest family I know on Valentines Day. Will you one and all be my Valentine? Or am I being too selfish in asking four such grand people to be my special Valentine.

This week has flown by so quickly. I have been awfully busy, and I find that I am so much more happy when I am that way. The Musical Club show is about to go into rehearsal, Monday, I believe, and we are terrifically busy. I have been trying to write a song and think I have finally hit upon one that may be successful. The music for the show is really good, and the show itself should make a hit. It is nothing pretentious – a show boat business with a lot of slapstick, the kind of thing that will be popular with Midshipmen, and would be booed out of New York.

I took my delayed "Bull" exam Thursday and did fairly well (I hope).

The negro boy has signed his resignation and the song in the First Batt is "By By Blackbird".

The winter term has been really passing much more quickly than I expected it would. All is going well and I feel better than I have for a long time.

I am running for either Editor-in-Chief or Business Manager of the '39 Lucky Bag or, at least, I hope to. We don't know yet when the elections are, or whether I will be nominated; but, in showing an interest, I may be able to get a minor editorship which won't interfere too much with my other activities.

We are thinking of putting on Gilbert and Sullivan's Trial By Jury as a part of the June Week program. Walt Keen wants me to work on it after I am through with the Music Show. So you see I will be pretty busy the rest of the term. And, of course, there is spring football. I just have to start working out – I'm in horrible condition, actually soft.

Mother's letter just arrived, I need not tell you how much I appreciated it. You know just as well as I all about that.

George's visit was very pleasant. We had a right nice time. I do hope he enjoyed himself enough to make it worth while.

My very best love to Gram. I do so hope she is feeling better and is well on the way to recovery.

        Love to all,
        Scottie

Annapolis, 23 February 1937

Dear Family,

I am certainly certain that you feel that I have entirely forgotten that I have a family. My week-end letter is delayed. We had a three day week-end and a hop. Ada E....... came down, and Tex was dragging, and we had the grandest time. I really believe it was the nicest time I have ever had. Tex's girl was grand - a girl from Reading. The girls stayed at an awfully nice place; a new one which we got quite by accident. The company was congenial, and we really had an awfully good time.

We had our "Skinny" monthly exam today. I pulled through all right I think.

Had a nice letter from Marsh the other day. He is all set to graduate from Colgate, of course.

So - life is good. I suppose soon there will be something to spoil it all, but now - all is quite wonderful. A grand week-end just past, and now I'm happy and broke.

The show is coming along slowly. I am awfully interested in it and am afraid that spring football will interfere with it. Well, we can worry about that when it comes.

I am delighted with George's good luck. I am quite proud of him. He is making a good start. He'll get there.

The news of Gram distresses me. I am so sorry she is having so much trouble. I am going to write to her as soon as I finish this letter.

Dad's letter arrived yesterday and the peanuts today. Thank you all so much for being so nice to me. The letter was good and the peanuts - need I say it? They are almost gone already.

Did I tell you that we have shifted around now and I live in the "A" hole. Don who did not want to give up "B" hole because of the radio which he has, has moved out on us into a room vacated by a "bilger." That leaves me all alone in the "A" hole temporarily. Whether we will get somebody to move in I don't know.

It was really cold last night - probably the coldest night we have had; and, to make everything perfect, the power house failed us and our room had a temperature of 42° for half the day. Thank heaven, it has warmed up now.

I was not invited out for the first spring football session - at least the list was initialed today and I am not on it. I am not as sorry as I feel I should be. I do not enjoy football as much as is necessary to make me any good at it; or maybe I'm not good enough to be able to like it after five years of it. Anyway, it would interfere with the show, which has interested me the most of anything I have done to date. I may go out later anyway for the exercise but that will be all.

I have written the lyrics for another song - so I guess I will have two songs in the show.

In general, everything is going along fairly smoothly. I do hope that everything is all right at home.

My best love to all,
Scottie

Annapolis, 8 March 1937

Dear Family,

    Your letters this week were so welcome.

    As I was marching out of chapel Sunday, I saw among the cheering crowds lining the way a familiar face. It was Eleanor Prior. She and a couple of friends had driven over from Trinity. Tex and Eleanor, Ada L.. and I spent the afternoon together. Ada L.. didn't get down until after lunch, so the three of us ate together; and then, when she arrived, we showed Eleanor the Academy and had a very pleasant afternoon.

    There are just four short weeks before the show opens and we are far behind schedule. I really am having grave misgivings as to whether we will ever get it in shape. We are using original music entirely, and the work of arranging and orchestrating alone is to say the least formidable.

    Mother asked what I am doing with the Musical Club show. Well, my job, which carries the glorified title of "Assistant Director," is a varied one. In the show there are, of course, a thousand and one different phases. There are, first of all, the actual speaking principal characters. Then there is what we call the revue – the various musical skits; then the chorus, the Glee Club, Mandolin Club, N.A. Ten, Orchestra, Stage gang, Electrical gang, Business gang, Property gang, Costume gang, and heaven knows what all else – besides, of course, the musical people, writers of songs, lyrics, arrangements etc. each of these groups work separately and I am what I guess you might call, for lack of a better term, a co-ordinator. I keep the departments in touch with each other, work sort of back and forth with Mr. Cristie, the officer advisor, who is working with the principals, and Dick Colbert, who directs the revue. I act as an advisor, believe it or not, on the desirability of this or that. Am a thinker up of ideas, song writer, lyricist and stooge. Keep "Snuffy" (Lt. Cristie) happy; and usually am supposed to be ten places at once. It's fun. I only hope the show is a success. It's jokes and humor are weak but then – most of the music is good.

    Well, in a couple of more weeks white cap covers will be back in style. That's the way one dons his Easter bonnet at the N.A.

       Much love to all and my best especially to Gram,
        Scottie

ROBERT SCOTT WHITMAN JR.

Annapolis, 21 March 1937

Dear Family,

Your letters arrived and I was – as I always am – so awfully glad to get them.

Don Conklin was down here with the Cornell rifle team for the Intercollegiates, and we spent a couple of pleasant hours last night in a bull session. It was nice to talk to somebody from home.

Dad's account of rural England from Mr. Priestley's book was very interesting. His description of Broadway was true – yet it does succeed, even in its exploitation of its age, in presenting a very pretty picture of a rural English town.

Today, we put the show together for the first time. I'm dubious as to the result. Ada was to drive down but I told her not to come, I'll be busy, and besides am not in a financial position to buy even the coca cola which enables me to have a table in the "Greasy Spoon" for our bull session. She is coming down next weekend to a hop and for Easter Sunday, as she always does, anyway, so I didn't feel so badly about putting her off.

I am afraid that the show is interfering with my studies. I took the Physics monthly Friday and am just a little leery as to the result.

I doubt that the score of the Musical Show will be published since there is no continuity in our musical numbers; and they are not good enough anyway. I shall keep it all in my mind and tell you all about it when I am home.

The news about Gram is grand. I am so glad to hear that she is improving so rapidly. Tell her to keep up the good work. I'm proud of her.

I am not doing anything for the Log now – haven't time; and I missed out on the Lucky Bag – just not good enough, I guess.

The news about Bill got me – I didn't really think he would be so foolish. He is a clever boy and could have made something out of himself if he had any punch.

Helen Harding certainly took a step down, didn't she. Or maybe we are all wrong. It is just possible that the standards of society have changed (or should even more than they already have). Be that as it may, I am thankful that, if I have nothing else, I, at least, have nothing but the best of lineage behind me. I need never be ashamed of my family.

Dr. and Mrs. D..... are coming down on Easter Sunday to take us to dinner and then to take Ada L.. home. They are going abroad this summer. Ada is not going. What she will do, I don't know. She is going to wait until she graduates and is going then, or perhaps next summer when I go.

I can't help but be a little glad that night school is over. Perhaps mother will get a little rest now.

Well, so endeth the chapter for the week.

          All my love to all,
               Scottie

Annapolis, 25 March 1937

Dear Family,

Gram's and mother's letters arrived today – and what a surprise. I did not expect any Easter present, and I am so very grateful for it. Thank you – you know just how much it means to me and how I appreciate it.

Thank you, Mother, for getting a wedding present for Bill. I wanted to but just could not. He has, I am afraid, made a mistake; but, as you say, we can do nothing but wish him well.

The exams for this month are over. "Bull", the last, was this morning. Eight more this year. We have been going to class in service for some time now. It has been warm quite consistently.

The show is a mess – it just cannot be ready by a week from Saturday. I only hope that it will be presentable the other two weeks. As I think back I cannot remember whether I told you that Tex has the feminine lead. Anyway, he has, and is quite a charming young lady.

I have been excused from drills for all of this week and will be next week. We are rehearsing some numbers for the second act. The scenery is very nearly all up, and we have nothing to do but put the show together – a job which will take every minute for the next week and a half.

The "Steam" exam was awful. Thank goodness, I have very good daily marks – or I think I have.

So now there is not much to say except,
"A very happy Easter to you all and much love to all from Annapolis."
Scottie

Annapolis, 30 March 1937

Dear Family

Well, the academic month of April has begun and that leaves one more. Also the last week of rehearsals for the show has begun. We worked from 3:30 until 9:00 yesterday without any time out except to grab a sandwich which the commissary department sent over. That will be the program for the rest of the week. Things are beginning to shape up.

It is definitely spring now. All the boats are in the water. The first dress p-rade is Thursday in honor of the Governor General of Canada. I haven't been to a drill for more than a week.

The candy arrived Sunday. My, what a surprise and treat. My family has certainly been good to me. Chow from Binghamton is a treat to the gang always, and you may be sure that they thank you as much as I.

White cap covers are back and the Academy is not so dreary as it was with the somber blue.

Now I have to rush over to rehearsal. I'll be with you again soon with another letter.

        Much love to all,
          Scottie

Annapolis, 4 April 1937

Dear Family,

Well, the show went on according to schedule. It was ragged in spots, but, on the whole, a success. By the time for the next performance we will have everything ironed out and should have a really good show. At any rate, everybody seemed to like it.

Now, I can start studying again. We were at it until after taps every day this last week. My exam marks suffered as a result of the show too. I dropped way down and feel pretty badly about it. Didn't bust in any final mark, of course, but still was not so hot. It has been such fun working on the show, though, I am almost convinced it was worth it.

It has stayed consistently warm here and only at night does it get really uncomfortably cool.

I didn't get to bed until after midnight last night. We had an hour liberty after the show and Tex and I went out and had a coke. Today, I slept most of the afternoon and now feel as chipper as ever.

I've picked up a miserable cold in my head from drafty old Mahan Hall and have been snuffling for the last two or three days.

How is everybody? I have missed hearing from you this week. Hope all is well.

Lots of love to all,
Scottie

Annapolis, 11 April 1937

Dear Family,

Had early chapel today – now I'm free to write a letter or two. My family comes first. First of all comes the good news. I got a 3.7 in aptitude for the last two months. It of course was just luck. They have no rhyme nor reason in the way they mark Youngsters. Put the names on a graph and then throw darts or flip a coin I guess. I'll probably have a 2.5 next time. But anyway 3.7 stood me 49. 3.8 is highest, and 48 men got a 3.8. So I stand 49.

The show went a little smoother this time. It is not a smash hit, but good. I shall send you a program. I meant to get one last night but forgot.

Of all things. There was a flurry of snow this morning. The sun is out now, however.

One of the new gunboats, the Erie is due here soon. We have a drill on her sometime. Should be interesting.

Jud took his final eye exam the other day. He didn't pass and so will be definitely leaving in June. That leaves just Tex and me.

The patrol planes are back and anchored in the river. We will have flight instruction in them this summer.

Very much love to all,
Scottie

ROBERT SCOTT WHITMAN JR.

Annapolis, 16 April 1937

Dear Family,

And so beginnith the umpteenth chapter according to Whitman, and – by matter of contrast – so endeth another week, which according to our calculations should leave just 25 more working days. All praises to what power there be, and may those twenty five days dwindle by just that amount, and darn quick.

For a change, I have a little news. I have to take football leave, whether I want to or not. I'm on the list even tho I did not get out for spring practice, and 'tis said that one has very little chance of getting off. So, I take the first destroyer cruise and the same leave as I had last year. One thing – it will get me home a lot sooner and excuse me from the watches which are such a drudgery.

The football team and the voluntary platoon (those who take early leave and then take charge of the Plebes while the others are gone) form the second company. Tex is also on the athletic list, and so takes the first cruise (he plays tennis), but is unfortunately in the 1st company for the summer, along with the rest of the tennis squad, so we cannot room together.

Mike Wallace and "China" Franks and I are going to team up. You undoubtedly remember my mentioning them to you as cruise cronies. They are both definitely good eggs, and we shall probably have a good time of it.

I went over to the rifle range today for the first time this spring. I had made rather a fine start for a good score on the pistol range when my gun jammed. Before I could fix it up, I had missed out on a whole round of rapid fire at 50 yards, and so, of course, spoiled it. I finally got another automatic, since my first gun continued to act up, and the one was a phonie – I had got a hold of one which had been laid aside because it was fouled up in the sights and persisted in firing low. So the rest of my scores were threes – I couldn't get in the black no matter how hard I tried.

I was more or less astounded when I read that Dad had finally rid us of the "Ark". Good going.

I am sending along a copy of the program of the show.

Much love to all,

Scottie

Annapolis, 25 April 1937

Dear Family,

Congratulations!!! Dad's letter arrived today with news of the new addition to the family. How does it feel to have a car that runs again? My, I'd like to see it. I sure do hope that you can come down after me as Dad said you might.

The projected itinerary for the "Can Cruise" is, as far as I can make out: New York, Newport, R.I., New London (submarine base), Norfolk (Navy Yard), Dahlgren, Va. (Naval gun proving ground), and possibly Philadelphia. What order they are in I don't know. If I can get a 48 hour leave in New York and can afford it, I'll come home for over-night. It won't be a long stay but it will be worth it. It is only a five or six hour ride on the train, is it not? I think those desiring to visit relatives can get 48 hours leave. So let me know what you think of it.

The weather is really bad. A regular gale sprang up last night and has continued unabated all day. Seems as though most of the Atlantic ocean has blown up into the bay and from there on to Farragut Field. The field is entirely under water and the gulls are using it as a haven of refuge from the storm. Storms such as this, nasty as they are, are welcomed by midshipmen simply because it means no infantry.

We've had our first Spherical Trig class - my instructor is the man who wrote the book. Looks like a very easy last month in Math.

Right now, the problem before the house of Whitman and Harris is buying a radio. In less than a month, we are going to rate them, and everybody in the Youngster Class begins to take on a new lease on life. We can get them on requisition, but we don't know what kind to get. It is one expense that I had forgotten. Pray God that my account will stand the burden and still leave me money in September. I'd hate to be broke again this leave.

My Physics grade for last month was only a 2.88. I am not proud of it but not ashamed. The study I could squeeze in during the show was darned little, and we had a rehearsal the day before the exam which kept me over in Mahan Hall until nine o'clock.

Jud is thinking of going to M.I.T. next fall. He couldn't pick a better school.

How is George getting along? I haven't heard a word from him or about him for ages. And Gram - I hope she is getting along better than as of last report.

The thought that possibly you can get down here this summer thrills me. I do so hope you can. It would be the finest thing that could happen to me.

Oh, yes, we are reading a new book in German and it is horrible. <u>Sternstunden der Menschheit</u> - The fateful hours of history - Waterloo etc. Interesting, but far too difficult. It demands more time than it is worth. This is not my opinion, but also that of Dr. Thomas.

No, I never have heard from Bill - the ungrateful wretch. Or maybe he is hurt because I did not write a letter congratulating him. I suppose I shall have to.

It's time for chow so I guess I'll close. This letter is really merely to say that I'm thinking of my family and miss them very much.

   Love to all,
    Scottie

Annapolis, 13 May 1937

Dear Family,

This will be the last you hear of me for more than a week, so I'll try to make it a good letter. If you wonder at my silence from now on, remember that I have an exam week with five tough babies scheduled, and study is the order of the day from now on in.

Well, the first news is my 3.7 in a Math quiz. It is just about time I was getting a few such marks. If I can just do that on the exam now, I'll feel a lot better.

The "Erie", the new gunboat, has just come in after an afternoon drill for the Second Class. She arrived here Saturday last. In trying to dock her, they parted a couple of lines and had a lot of trouble. The next time they tried to dock was on Monday. That time they tore a hole in the dock and in her bow. Today her skipper took no chances – carried lines with a motor launch and snaked her alongside with a winch. The dock here is tricky especially when the tide is coming up the river. We can watch it all from our windows, and have great sport arguing as to how we would handle the situation.

Now a destroyer is coming in. We have quite a fleet here now – a brand new gunboat, a destroyer, an aircraft service tender, and there was a submarine.

Before long, the battleships will be here to take the boys to Europe. I'm certainly thankful that I am not going, even though it should be a good cruise. Athens, Kiel which, of course, means Berlin, and Livorno – Rome. The cruise boxes are starting to appear in the halls, the First Class trunks are being packed, and soon it will be all over. And it is just about time; everybody is getting plenty fed up with the Naval Academy, and I am not any different from the rest.

I have been chosen to take the Assistant Director's job with the Music Show next year, and, against my better judgment, I accepted. I'll probably have full charge of the staging, and, if I can do it in my own way, I can do it a lot easier than it was done this year.

As you noticed probably, I was kept on with four others of the Feature Staff of the Log when it changed hands. I am getting all this year's work cleaned up this week, and then can devote all my energy to exams.

ROBERT SCOTT WHITMAN JR.

It certainly has been hot today. Right now I have four windows wide open, am stripped down to skivvies and am only fairly comfortable.

I'll be sorry to see the First Class leave this year. Some of my best friends are among them, Tom Davies for one. Met him first through Ada L... He drags with a friend of hers, as I have undoubtedly told you. The four of us have become the best of friends, and drag together a lot. Tom is probably the most brilliant man in the Academy. He knows it, which is his one big fault; but, nevertheless, he is not a "greasy grind" or a "brain". He has invented all sorts of range finding equipment and mathematical devices. A vector slide rule is one, and there is a big chance that the Navy will adopt it. His ideas are sound, and he probably will go a long way.

We have bought a radio – a $52 Philco, as I mentioned we might. We got it second hand for $20 – $6.67 apiece. Been used four months and is in perfect condition – a real buy in my estimation. Jud shares the expense. He has been given a reprieve for a year and will stay on.

We had infantry drill today – practiced the battalion drill for competition, which takes place week after next during June Week. Boy, oh boy, was it hot and dusty on that parade ground! They sent us in early – an almost unheard of procedure.

Well, almost two years of my military life are over. Whether they have done me any good remains to be seen. I can't tell whether I have improved or not. I do hope it is making me a better man, and that I am deriving some of the attributes that are so widely advertised as the benefits of a military education.

I certainly haven't learned much; but they claim that no one does here. You forget as quickly as you learn, and it is my opinion that one would sure go crazy if he had to retain everything that is thrown at him here. The Naval Academy is no place for a scientist. We have had approximately four years study pumped into us already – and we are only half through.

Imagine – higher modern Physics in one lesson – Spectroscopy, Rutherford's theory, the quantum theory, Planck's theory – energy level explanation of radiation, and such formulas as

$$r = \frac{2\pi^2 m e^4}{h^3 r}\left[\frac{1}{M^2} - \frac{1}{N^2}\right]$$

OR

$$Ed\lambda = \frac{8\pi r h d\lambda}{\lambda^5(e^{rh/K\lambda T}-1)}$$

Planck's Equation Calculation

which merely gives Planck's equation for the energy per cm associated with the wave length from λ to dλcm - I don't know what it means either, but neither does anyone else.

During exam week we have regular classes with advanced lessons all the week - which is just as it has always been - and such is the life of a student (?).

I have started to review some of the Physics. Will start on "Steam" sometime soon, and probably will not stir from my room this week-end. I have found one thing out here. My retentive memory powers are not as good as they should be - which means, I have to review everything.

And now that I have spilled my academic woes - how is that brother of mine getting along in school? You need not tell me, because I know he is doing famously. Is he sure that he does not want to come to the Naval Academy? He could pass the exams I know, and Mr. Lord might be blackjacked into giving him an appointment. My being here should help persuade him. It would certainly solve his worries; but, yet, I am making no urge because, when one comes to a place like this, it must be on his own head - it's a funny school. I think you understand what I mean.

So now I guess I will close. I've run out of news and gab.

        Much love to all,
         Scottie

ROBERT SCOTT WHITMAN JR.

Annapolis, 23 May 1937

Dear Family,

Secure the Watch!!!! Whew! (or something)! I'm glad that year is behind me. The exams? Oh, so-so. Only mark I know is "Dago" – have a 3.31 for the last two months. "Steam" was O.K., and so was "Skinny". "Bull" was tough – and, as for Math, I couldn't even hazard a guess – anywhere from a 0 to a 4.0. You know how logarithms are – a lot of chances for mistakes, and I had no time to check.

But now it is all over, and I never had such a gloriously relieved feeling. Two down and two to go. And just think, I don't have to pull down my Physics book and bone for tomorrow.

Dad's letter arrived today, and I was awfully glad to get it.

Now comes June Week and then Second Class Summer. As you know, I go on the first cruise. I think I am on the Erie, the new boat, which is very grand luck from many standpoints.

The more I hear of Second Class Summer, the better it sounds. We do a lot of practical work in "Steam" and "Juice". (From now on I shall be studying "Juice" – Electrical Engineering. Started last month and finish when I graduate.) They say that in "Steam" they hand us some tools, provide an old Diesel engine and we go to work and find out what makes it tick. That is the sort of work where one can learn something. We go to the rifle range, and spend ten days learning the intricacies of machine guns. We fly for two weeks and actually handle the controls, getting about four hours apiece of this actual handling. We study Navigation, and our "Nav" work counts as two months academic work. We visit the Naval Proving Grounds at Dahlgren, go through the torpedo factory at Newport. We read about a thousand or so pages of literature in a short English literature course. We have executive duty for about two weeks. And heaven knows what else. So, you see, it is a pretty full summer.

I am told that on the cruise, we actually take charge of the ship when we are standing Officer-of-the-Deck duty.

The cruise shoves off on Monday, the seventh. Comes back about the first of July.

As far as Second Class summer stripes are concerned, I didn't get much – that is, as it appears on the face of things. I am a 1st Petty Officer or as we put it "1 P.O." But that is something, since only about a hundred got anything.

> Much love to all,
> Scottie

Annapolis, 25 May 1937

Dear Family,

Prepare for a shock, sit back in your chairs, take a deep breath and hold tight. Your son got a 3.8 in "grease"[aptitude]. Just call me "handshaker" Whitman. Stands me 1 for the last two months. And what is more to the point, I broke a hundred in "Steam" for the past two months – stood 94. Have all the bi-monthly marks except Math, and one years mark – "Dago"
Here they are –

		Mark	Standing
2 mo.	"Steam" –	3.29	94
2 mo.	"Dago" –	3.31	?
year	"Dago" –	3.40	103
2 mo.	"Skinny"–	3.17	158
2 mo.	"Bull" –	3.08	?
2 mo.	"Grease"–	3.80	1

Just a little better than the last two months, eh?

As I have probably said before, Drill Week is certainly an easy week – two drills a day and that is all – one competition drill and one practice dress parade. Tomorrow we have only a dress parade. I have never felt so completely relaxed. I have, now, a chance to do some reading. Right now I am reading An American Doctor's Odyssey. It is quite fascinating.

Our Company is 3rd in the competition for the flag. We cannot win, but will probably end up second – which is no better than last.

We are still eagerly waiting definite news about the cruise. I do hope I'm on the Erie. Rumor has it that she has air conditioned fire rooms – keeps a steady temperature of 71º. No 136º - 150º as of last summer.

There is no more news now – just wanted to send what marks I had.

       Love to all,
         Scottie

ROBERT SCOTT WHITMAN JR.

Annapolis, 31 May 1937

Dear Family,

Well – finally a lull and time to write a letter to my family.

June Week is wonderful. I'm having such a grand and happy time.

Right now Ada E....... is in Baltimore. She went home Sunday night and will be back tomorrow. She had an exam today and one tomorrow. They were two year comprehensives, and studying for them is impossible – which explains why she could be here at all.

Tonight I am Battalion Officer of the Watch – relief, so the Second Class can go to Ring Dance. I have charge of the whole Batt and am scared stiff I'll do something wrong. I took the watch so one of my friends, whose girl was here, could go to the Youngster hop. You should see me strut round with a sword.

My final class standing for the year, counting everything, was 299.

Saturday morning, I took Ada L.. sailing. Saturday afternoon we saw the lacrosse game with Army, which we lost. Saturday night we went to a hop. Sunday was a lazy day, and we did nothing much until Dr. and Mrs. D..... came at six. We had supper with them at Carvel Hall and then went to the orchestra recital, and saw <u>Trial by Jury</u>. It was well worth while. They all left at about 11:00.

Now I'm sitting in the B.O.O.W's. office writing this letter.

My illegible writing is due to a borrowed pen which is so big around that I practically have to grab it in my fist.

I read the pertinent parts of Mother's last letter to Ada L.. – she was very happy to hear what she had to say.

I'm on the <u>Erie</u> this summer for sure – I saw the list.

Well, I'm off to check the Plebes in from their ten o'clock liberty.

        Love to all,
          Scottie

IV
SECOND CLASS SUMMER
1936 – 1937

ROBERT SCOTT WHITMAN JR.

<u>1937</u>

ITINERARY SECOND CLASS SUMMER PRACTICE

CRUISE OF MIDSHIPMEN from U.S.N.A. ANNAPOLIS.

U.S. SHIPS	ARRIVAL	PLACE	DEPARTURE
ERIE		ANNAPOLIS	June 7
FAIRFAX	June 7	DAHLGREN	June 9
JACOB JONES	June 11	NEWPORT	June 18
MANLEY	June 18	NEW LONDON	June 21
ROPER	June 25	NEW YORK	June 28
CLAXTON	July 2	ANNAPOLIS	

Dahlgren, Va. 12 June 1937

Dear Family,

Well, June Week has gone and here I am aboard the <u>Erie</u> at Dahlgren, Va. I'm a Second Classman, Second Class summer has started; and I'm on the cruise.

So far, the cruise has been a huge success. We are treated as junior officers aboard here. We have spring bunks, real live showers, good food, modern equipment – and so far, not too much to do.

I am on engineers' duty now, and am standing watches in probably the most modern engineering plant in the Navy. My, what a mass of pipes – all jammed into that little engine room. It is really a nightmare to try to trace them out.

Yesterday we went over to the Proving Ground, but saw very little compared with what I expected to see. We did see one of the ammunition dumps with every sort of shell from a 1 pounder to a 16" high explosive projectile. There are rows of giant 16" guns, unmounted and coated with grease and red lead, just waiting until such a time as they will be needed. Every day, year in and year out, these people at the Proving Ground go about their business of testing and firing guns, shells, bombs, torpedoes, etc. – always seeking improvements. Every gun in the Navy must have their mark of approval. No one can say that we are not prepared.

We did see one very interesting thing. They took us over to what they call the "Plate Range" where they test the piercing ability of their guns. They took us right out in front of the several guns; showed us the piece of armor they were going to fire at with a 5" gun (testing fuses), and then herded us into an armored dugout right beside the armor. We watched the plate through a system of mirrors. We could see the shell and hear it burst, and heard the thousand or so fragments rain down on our roof. Then all we had to do was step out of the door and take a look at the gaping hole in the armor. They have fired shells through 14 inches of high test steel armor plate – now that is something.

Today at the Proving Ground was very interesting, that is, interesting for the first half hour, and after that it was an awful bore, for all they did all afternoon was to fire a couple of 5" anti-aircraft guns – round after round – all afternoon.

ROBERT SCOTT WHITMAN JR.

The only break in the monotony was when they fired a couple of hundred rounds from the 1.1" anti-aircraft guns. These are the deadliest of this type of gun. They are loaded by a clip, mounted four together, and can push out a steady stream of high explosive shells. They are actually just a huge machine gun firing explosive shells.

We came back to the ship at about five and immediately got under way for Newport.

Aboard ship here, we are assigned the Admiral's quarters for a work and recreation room. Since we are not carrying any flag now, the quarters are not occupied and make a very nice headquarters for us. I am writing this at the Admiral's desk.

I'm just a little sleepy now. I have been up since 3:30. Had the morning (4-8) watch.

Monday, I believe, we visit the torpedo school and factory, and Tuesday or Wednesday, the War College. Then over to New London for the Submarine Base.

Rumor has it that we are going to Poughkeepsie for the regatta. I certainly hope so. Navy has a good crew and should put up a good battle.

Got a letter from Marsh the other day. He has been accepted into the Naval Air Reserve and goes to Floyd Bennett field for preliminary training sometime in July – then to Pensacola. He will join the fleet at about the same time I do for his two years of service. Well, I guess he knows what he is doing. At any rate we may be shipmates some day.

Right now, I'm run out of news, so I'll close. Mail this tomorrow and will have a long letter for you from Newport.

      Much love to all,
       Scottie

I'm starting a letter to Gram immediately.

18 June 1937

Dear Gram,

Well, and here I am in Newport – and the cruise is just a week old, it is really a very different cruise from the one I took last summer. This year only one class is aboard, which means everyone rates evenly and that, in itself, is a big advantage. Living aboard ship is not the new experience that it was last time – and that, too, goes toward making a more comfortable time of it. All in all, we are having a fine time of it and all of us are enjoying a little respite from the Academy routine.

But the real purpose of this letter is not so much to tell the news of my cruise, but to thank you for your lovely but entirely uncalled-for generosity. It was so very nice of you to send me that money. I really needed it, and it was quite like a gift from the gods. Thank you, Gram. I know that you know just how much I appreciate it.

I'm so happy that you are up and around. I'll bet you feel fit as a fiddle. I'm so glad.

In about an hour, we get out of Newport, and will be in New London sometime this afternoon. I have only been ashore in Newport once – have done nothing. Society is here I guess, but I certainly did not see anything of it.

We did have an interesting day on Wednesday, however. We went out on the station destroyer, the <u>Hamilton</u>, and watched them fire five torpedoes. Every torpedo from the factory must be fired and tested before it can be approved.

We had dinner on the destroyer, and then came back in, and took a tour of the factory. These torpedoes are certainly some machine. They cost about $15,000 apiece and are a complete miniature ship. They run by steam turbine, steer themselves, and are accurate to within 300 feet at 15,000 yards. We saw how they were made from beginning to end.

Yesterday morning, I had the 0000 – 0400 watch on the signal bridge. (I'm through with engineering now.) Since only Midshipmen were on watch on the signal bridge of all ships in the squadron, we had a three and a half hour bull session with the yard arm blinker lights. –

I had to interrupt this for a while to go up to the bridge while we got underway. It has been soupy weather, and it was two hours before it shifted enough to get out of the harbor; but now we are at sea again headed for New London.

In New London we make a tour of the submarine base, and I hear that we go to a planetarium in New York. That will be the most interesting to me.

I hear that we are not going to Poughkeepsie.

It's almost time for chow, so I must stop again.

Lots of love to all,
Scottie

Montauk Bay, L.I., 23 June 1937

Dear Family,

We have been at sea for two days - operating in Long Island Sound and along the coast from Boston on down, exercising in tactics, holding all sorts of drills, and generally getting in some sea duty. At present my duties are as Navigator and tomorrow I am Officer of the Deck. So I am right up on the bridge where I can see and take part in our getting underway tomorrow.

Since my funds have depleted from five to two dollars, I have decided to take Mother's suggestion and call upon the Ridgway's - a free meal away from this ship-board chow (which is unspeakable) will be a decidedly welcome change. I hope I can wangle the invitation.

I had a very pleasant afternoon on Saturday in New London. The Chamber of Commerce, among the other things that it did for us, engineered a very pleasant tea dance at the Mohawk Hotel. I had a much better time than I could have believed possible. New London also let us into their theatres free of charge, and those who wished were admitted to the ball park for nothing. So - I saw a free show, went to a free dance and ate a quarters worth of hamburgers and beer, and checked it off as a good day.

Tomorrow we swing ship to calibrate compass - a long and tedious job. And Friday morning, we moor at pier 73 at the bottom of 33 Street in New York.

I don't know what my stay in New York holds in store for me and I do not much care. I have had a good time on the cruise - far better than I thought I would have. I've learned a lot and will probably learn more before the cruise is over on the 2nd of July.

Among the interesting things we have done is piloting work - navigating in sight of land. We take bearings on different buoys, lights, and other land marks, and from them fix our position.

Tonight, I have no watch - which means my first full night's sleep in a long time. Just as last year, I've become able to exist without any bad effects on about half the sleep I get at the Academy - three hours last night - and I'm rarin' to go.

No more now - this has to get into the mail.

       Much love to all,
       Scottie

ROBERT SCOTT WHITMAN JR.

Montauk Bay, L.I., 23 June 1937

Dear George,

So now you're graduating – and you're graduating well up in your class. Good for you, Kid – I'm proud of you.

Just how good it feels to be through, I know very well. There is only one thing to remember, and that is that, instead of being through, you are just beginning. That sounds as though this letter was to be a sermon, and that is not so; but I just want you to remember that you have a lot more ahead of you. Soon, maybe not this year, but soon, you will be starting the next step, college. And you will start putting a new lot of experience behind you. Which all is a roundabout way of saying that you have finished a definite part of your life, and will be finishing, as the yahrs go by, other parts or stages or what have you. There is just one little morsel of advice to glean from all this stuff. Try to be able to say honestly, at all times, that you have played ball, played it square, and have got your money's worth.

There – no more preaching. I am not so good at this sort of letter writing, so you will have to write off any gross discrepancies to my inexperience.

At the present moment we are steaming along on a glassy ocean. Drills are over for the day and we are all up here on the after gun platform lolling in the sun. This part of the ship we call our bathing beach; the only fallacies being that the water is about 30 feet down, and there is no sand.

Tomorrow, we dock in New York at 0800. I'm going ashore and am going to call on Aunt May Ridgway. I hope she is in New York. I'm in the mood for some city chow.

I don't know whether I have written much dope about the Erie so maybe if I have not you will be interested in hearing about this ship I am on. She is in reality a small battleship. Naturally we have no armor belt and no terrets; but, for her size, she is a formidable war vessel. We carry four 6" 48 caliber guns, and we will have several of the new 1.1" anti-aircraft guns, of which I have already written. Midships, we carry an airplane; the engineering installation is the most modern in the Navy; our range finding equipment is the best. The ship is designed for use in and around Panama, and, at the end of the summer, that is where she goes.

Yesterday, we steamed down the Sound to within sight of New York City, and then turned around and came back to Montauk Pt. for the night. Right now we are about 150 miles from the Ambrose Light Ship which is at the mouth of the lower bay.

Now I must stop. The real purpose of this letter can be very briefly stated – Every sort of congratulations, Old Boy, and the best of luck. I do wish I might be home for the festivities.

      Much love,
        Scottie

29 June 1937

Dear Family,

Having yesterday left New York - if you will pardon the split participle - we are now in the Delaware River - why, neither I or anyone else seems to know.

Just when I will have a chance to mail this letter I do not know, but I have the suspicion that we will anchor tonight somewhere, and there may be a mail posting.

As you have probably gathered, we did not get to the races - something fell through.

In New York - I made good my threat - and visited the Ridgways. They were more than nice to me. Friday Charlie took me along to a dinner party to which he - and I when I arrived - was invited, and from there we went to the Stork Club - my expense in the whole evening being practically nothing.

The clipping which you sent about Ced gave me a brain storm - I got hold of him - and Sunday Aunt May had him and me to their place for dinner; and then Charlie, Ced and I went over into Jersey taking along a perfectly marvelous picnic supper. The Ridgways belong to a sort of a club on Deer Lake. We had a swim and ate - and then came back to New York. Charlie had a date so Ced and I went over to his place and went to bed - both of us being dead tired.

Friday we arrive in Annapolis - I rate week-end leave, and am going to Baltimore, naturally.

This morning we have been doing more piloting - very interesting and instructive. This afternoon, we are scheduled for tactical maneuvering and gunnery drill.

      Much love to all,
        Scottie

Annapolis, 10 July 1937

Dear Family,

This week we spent an hour at radio and three hours in the "Juice" lab each morning; and in the afternoon we spent two and a half hours over in the armory on the bombing trainer. There is no outside studying to do, however, and strange as it may seem, the time hangs heavily on my hands.

Each morning we leave for Sampson Hall at eight. First we go to the radio lab. There we have an hours work on receiving radio, that is, Morse code as it comes by wireless. They have long tables with a regular wireless hookup with an enlisted radio man sending, and individual ear phones for each Midshipman. The tables are graduated as to speed. We move up as we pass each qualifying test. I am taking ten words a minute, a word being five letters. That, so far, is the highest table. In "Juice" the rest of the morning; we see movies of electricity and its various phases, and work on experiments in the lab. The bomb sighting was rather interesting. They have a setup which simulates actual bombing from an altitude of 6500 feet. If you work the machine correctly, you cannot miss. No wonder the Navy has such a fine bombing record.

They are certainly trying to stir up our interest in aviation. We have had several lectures on Navy flying, technical and otherwise. Last night the director of the personnel department of the Bureau of Aeronautics lectured to us about Pensacola. That is where Marsh is going. They quite evidently want as many of us as they can get to go there.

Up till today, I have been an orphan - Mike is in the hospital having his nose straightened, and "China" had been on special leave (his father was seriously ill); but he is back now. (His father is much better.)

The weather here is unbearable - very, very hot and humid. I have been spending my spare time in working out and finishing up with a cool-off in the pool. This afternoon I took a sun bath and "China" and I have just returned from the pool. It seems to be the only cool place around here.

The picture arrived quite safely. It certainly is a marvelous picture of George. Thank you so much for it. It now occupies a very conspicuous spot on my desk.

ROBERT SCOTT WHITMAN JR.

My week-end in Baltimore was uneventful. We went to the movies on Saturday evening – and went dancing for a little while on Sunday evening. Spent Monday at home. We had a lot of fun shooting off some "shootin clackers" as they are called in Baltimore.

Ada L.. goes to Cape May on Wednesday to spend the summer so I guess it will be a womanless world for quite a while.

Well, I have run down.

       Love to all,
        Scottie

Annapolis, 20 July 1937

Dear Family,

This week I have been spending the mornings in the "Juice" lab again, and the afternoons at the rifle range taking the weeks course in aerial gunnery. It is rather interesting. We fire the regular Pensacola ground school course. There are six different practices fired with the machine guns, as well as some work with automatic rifles and heavy Browning ground machine guns.

My wisdom tooth has been bothering me again. I went up to dental quarters a week ago and had another X-ray taken. Went back the next day for the results - which are that I go back next Monday to have the gum split open and the tooth removed - some fun!!!

This afternoon weather permitting, I am going to play golf with Jud. We can play on the Academy course free of charge and Jud has some clubs which we can both use.

I have found no men from Binghamton or vicinity in the new class as yet - I rather doubt if there will be any.

I'm up to twelve a minute in radio.

The news of George is the best I have had in years. I'm so happy for him. It is the first intimation that I had that there was a chance of his getting away at all. I really can't get over it. I have a friend here who went to Michigan before he entered, and he has some dope on rooming etc. that he has promised to give me to send on. When does he leave?

Thursday, we make an all day trip down to Langley Field, for a tour of inspection. We were scheduled to go to Anacostia today, but the rain (which is still falling) cancelled the trip and we got up for only an hour.

I think that, providing we get paid before week-end after next, that I will try to go up to Cape May. I have been invited to come anytime I can, and can get a ride back to Baltimore with Mr. Maxwell, Ada L.. uncle. Second Class day is on that week-end and Ada L.. cannot get down - can't get out of Cape May in fact, her family having left strict orders to the contrary. I guess, being so far away, they feel safer if they know where she is. Since I rate the week-end and it will be hard to stay around here on the big day of the summer, if I am not dragging, I think I shall try to swing it. I think I owe myself one week-end besides that of the glorious Fourth, don't you?

It is just a little more than a month before Sept. leave
starts. I am so anxious to get home and see my family again.
Though what I'll do with Marsh and Ced gone is beyond me.
Write and tell me more of George's plans.

       Much love to all,
        Scottie

Annapolis, 23 July 1937

Dear Family,

Well - another week is shot - and this was a good week. Flight is great - indeed, the most fun I have had in a long time.

Yesterday we flew down to Norfolk for the day - to Langley Field. It was an extremely interesting trip. I am enclosing a program of our tour which will explain better than I just what I did. I piloted the plane today for about fifteen minutes. There is nothing to it, but it is fun and thrilling when you bank or dive. The planes are big old patrol planes which fly themselves better than we Midshipmen, as one pilot put it.

I have written to the Phi Delt rushing chairman at Michigan. It is perfectly cricket for me to do so, and I figured that I had better take what advantage I could of being a Phi Delt. I'm going to see if I can't get my Michigan friend to write to his house too. I believe he was a Deke. Just how much does George know about Michigan? Does he want to get a place with room and board, or just room? In other words does he expect to be eating at a fraternity house after the first few weeks, for he will undoubtedly join a fraternity. This will of course affect his choice of rooming house. George Ghesquiere knows some places of both types which sound plenty good. I haven't been able to get the addresses yet but will have them soon.

So friend Dorothy is stepping off the deep end? - I'm not particularly surprised, but I never heard of the man before.

As far as Sept. leave is concerned, I shall, of course, spend some of my time with Ada E........ in Baltimore. She will not be in Cape May then as you seem to have deduced. She is there only for the time her family are in Europe. They arrive back on the 14th of August. How much time I spend there depends, of course, on how soon you get sick of me at home and how much they want me in Baltimore - and, of course, if I should go out to Michigan with George, we shall have to make plans accordingly.

Ada L.. and I have not talked over any plans yet. All we know is that we are spending a week-end in Carlisle some time after school opens, preferably for the Phi Delt pledge dance. In my next letter I'll ask Ada L.. what she has in her mind for our leave and then maybe we'll have something tangible. With Marsh and Ced gone, I think I'll have time to read "Gone with the Breezes" so am saving it until then.

I have been trying to count up who I want to see in Binghamton and I can count all the people on one hand – Mother, Dad, George, Gram, and Gramma Sheridan – period. Poor family – you are going to get awfully tired of having me under foot.

Much love to all,
Scottie

Annapolis, 29 July 1937

Dear Family,

Sunday was a lonesome day around here. Most of the regiment is away; two companies rate leave, two are on cruise, and the football men are on leave. (They rate every week-end.)

Today I completed my introduction to the field of transportation. At last I can say I've ridden in the air, on the ground, under the ground, on the water, and under the water. Today we had a drill on a submarine and were submerged most of the morning. It is no different from anything else except, when submerged, it gets awfully hot. It was quite an interesting morning, nevertheless, and I earned quite a lot.

Tomorrow we fly again and in the afternoon we do nothing at all. I played bridge this afternoon. It was a pretty even game. I made two little slams.

Sorry to disappoint you again, but the dentist seemed to think that my operation was not necessary. Instead he filled two teeth and made an appointment for me to have them cleaned and I'm through with him for another year.

Next week, we have a sort of "hodge podge" of everything. "Juice", "Steam", and two days of flight, on Friday and Saturday.

I imagine that George will be admitted to the university without much trouble. Your being a graduate etc. should turn the trick.

    Much love to all,
        Scottie

ROBERT SCOTT WHITMAN JR.

Annapolis, 13 August 1937

Dear Family,

The Cape May week-end was very pleasant indeed, and I enjoyed it very much. Saturday evening we went over to Wildwood which is not far from Cape May, and spent the evening on the board walk. It has just about every sort of entertainment, and all sorts of things to ride on and shoot at etc. Sunday we spent our time on the beach.

Everybody is on leave now so I have the deck to myself.

Saturday noon I go on watch, and will probably be on watch for 10 out of the 12 days. There are only 25 of us to stand 18 watches which looks like three out of four days watch to me.

Today's watch is in charge of the main office. I am the only Second Classman in the main office, and as a result, I am kept pretty busy. (The Plebes not knowing about how to do things, knowing no more, have to put up a bold front and make believe that I have everything under control.)

I have passed my final athletic tests in gym and swimming. Now I am through with such tests for good. The swimming test included life saving this time, which, of course, gave me no trouble. In gym we had to climb a 30 foot rope hand over hand, high jump and run the 440 in 6.6 seconds.

I am just a little fella now. I weigh a mere 201. The least I have weighed for years and years. Wasting away to a mere ton, eh.

Oh, yes, I went out to see Dr. Thomas on Sunday, and went sailing with him on Tuesday. We had quite a time sailing – a stay carried away, and we had to come in on the jib, since to leave the mains'l up was courting a broken mast. It seems that the wind was a little strong. We had a good sail nevertheless except for the fact that we were soaked to the skin when we finally got back in.

I saw "Mac" last night. He bilged out you know, and now is re-entering in the class of '41, I think he is a fool but I guess he knows what he wants.

They are making a movie here again. It is Navy Blue and Gold this time. They are paying town boys $8.25 a day to act as extras, I wish I could work at that for a couple of weeks.

The D..... seem to want me to divide my visit with them – that is, if it is convenient with me and you, but I think I want to come home on Friday – staying just Thursday with Ada L.. You would rather that I come straight home, would you not? I am sort of lonesome for my family. Strange, is it not? It has been such a short time since I last saw you (I don't think).

     Love to all,
      Scottie

V
SECOND CLASS YEAR
1937 – 1938

ROBERT SCOTT WHITMAN JR.

Annapolis, 24 September 1937

Dear Family,

It seems that I arrived back at the Academy at ten this morning and went on watch at ten-thirty. Started and ended my leave by standing a watch - or something like that. My room is in an awful mess since I have not even had a chance to make my bed. (The room incidentally is 1131.)

There is, of course, no other news of Annapolis - Tex and Jud are both well and that is all I know.

My stay in Baltimore was a great success. Ada L.. and I worked pretty hard most of the time on the sorority rooms, but it was fun, and kept us busy The rooms certainly are beautiful with their new furniture and new paint, wax, etc. We had a mixed rushing party Tuesday evening and carried it off beautifully. Thursday of last week we went to see <u>Dead</u> <u>End</u> - the stage play, not the movie. It was magnificent. The little boys who were the main characters did a wonderful job.

Oh, yes, the trip to Dickinson. It was a huge success. Saw all our gang - Jake Aschinger, Penny Edwards and the whole crowd. Sunday we went over to the Hershey and saw the model town, had dinner, drove back by the way of Gettysburg and spent the afternoon on the battle fields.

Tex appeared at the D....s yesterday afternoon and spent the night. He had arrived in Annapolis earlier than he had anticipated and so came up to see us.

Isn't it grand that George is enjoying his school - I am very happy for him. Have written to him and expect that he has already received the letter.

We will take Ordnance, "Steam" (thermo dynamics), "Juice, "Bull" (a reading course - Ibsen, Cervantes, Balzac, Tolstoy, and Goethe), and, of course, "Nav" and Dago". I can't tell whether it will be tough or easy.

You were right, Mother, I am not playing football. Concentrating on the <u>Log</u> and a new racket - (Pep Committee). I hope I make it, for it should prove fun First Class year, Overnight leave before each football game to set up card stunts.

> Much love to all,
> Scottie

Annapolis, 7 October 1937

Dear Family,

As I sit here to write, it seems a long time since I have written home, yet I have not been here two weeks and I know I have written twice. For that matter it seems a century since leave ended. The routine here is so unchanging and it has been such a part of my life, that it does not take long to get back in the rut.

This week has been a bad week for me. I haven't done so well as I might, I am afraid. But I did have my "Bull" prof read aloud one of my daily papers (written in class the time before) and tell me that I got a 4.0 for the day.

On Wednesdays, the first two periods in the afternoon, we have what is known as a "Nav P work". It amounts to a monthly examination once a week. Boy, what a beating 1131 took in the last edition.

Tomorrow, I have the guard, and so my school week is practically over. Dr. Thomas is still my German prof, and is as good as ever. We are reading Der Durchbruch der Möwe – a story of a German raider during the World War. It is rather deadly, principally because of the abundance of colloquial German. It was written by one of the seamen on board and he is no scholar.

Sometime before 6:00 a.m.

There being a little time before I go on Watch I shall continue where I left off last night.

The papers yesterday announced that the new Superintendent is to be Admiral Wilson Brown. He is the man who had charge of my Youngster cruise. What sort of man he is, I do not know, and there will be a change of policy when he takes charge, no doubt. I only hope that he does not undo all the good work Admiral Sellers has done in modernizing the school which is still far behind the times in many ways.

The President is to be at the Harvard game. We are doing the Presidential Flag as one of our card stunts. I worked it up the other evening........

Well, I've had my breakfast now, and feel much better than I did a couple of hours ago.

The First Battalion goes to the Harvard game (Baltimore), Princeton, and of course, Army.

I am working hard for the Log. Have written one article

about the <u>Texas</u> and had a lot of fun doing it. The book from which I got my material was very interesting, and I enjoyed it so much that I read all of it. My next will be either about Navy musicians or Naval gunnery. They seem to want more material on professional subjects, and I believe they are right. The <u>Log</u> needs something to tune it up, and articles of this nature which are broad enough to interest the layman are part of the solution to the problem.

No more now, will write again soon.

       Much love to all,
        Scottie

Annapolis, 18 October 1937

Dear Family,

Well, that was a good game Saturday but Navy didn't look so good. I only hope they pull themselves together before the Notre Dame game.

It was a pretty hectic day for me. We got to Baltimore at 8:30 (seven of us) and were busy every minute until the game started, tacking up cards. They tell me that the stunts looked right good, though, so I guess it was worth it. I had no chance to see Ada L.. and, of course, that was a disappointment.

Last week went a little better, but I still didn't' do so well in "Nav". It certainly was hectic – an awful lot of work with the Pep Committee getting ready for Saturday, two articles for the Log, to say nothing of the usual studying.

In "Nav" we are studying Astronomy and it is no fun!!! We have finished Don Quixote and are wading through Faust. Then Old Goriot Anna Karenina and Ibsen's plays, That, I think, carries us through this semester.

I've had a letter from George.

Went out yesterday and watched the 1st Batt beat the 2nd Batt – in football 7 – 0, and then came back and wrote two Log articles.

No more now.

       Much love to all,
        Scottie

ROBERT SCOTT WHITMAN JR.

Annapolis, 5 November 1937

Dear Family,

Friday night and another week gone. This week started off pretty sadly, but ended up with a bang. I got a couple of cold 4.0's in "Steam" to make up for a lousy mark on Monday – a pretty good mark in the "Nav" practical work and another today to make up the complete bust, on Monday and Tuesday – so I'm feeling right good at this point.

The nuts arrived yesterday. Thank you so much for them. They taste <u>so</u> good.

Ada L.. comes down tomorrow – nothing but "Dago" to study – and some good radio programs tonight – so all is well, and I am happy.

Did you hear the broadcast Wednesday of the D.A.R. presentation of state flags? The D.A.R. presented the flags of all the states and territories to the Academy. It rained, so the ceremony was in the Armory. All we Midshipmen got out of it was a bunch of tired feet. I suppose it was a fine thing to do, but I think they could have done much better if they used the money to help some veterans' home or hospital – at any rate, now we have them – even the Philippines' – even though they are no longer such a possession.

"Juice" is really very interesting even though tough. I'm trying to get everything out of it I can.

Do you remember my talking about Tom Davies and Vera Pergler his fiancé? Vera was going out to the west coast to marry Tom at Christmas time. She had her trousseau practically bought and was all set, when she got a telephone call from Tom. He was sailing under sealed orders that evening and did not know where he was going.

Well, the next she heard was a cablegram from China – and such is life in the Navy.

Things go along much as usual here. We have been busy fixing up the card stunts for the game Saturday. I do not make the trip since only one Second Classman rates going each time, and I went last time.

Navy should win easily tomorrow. I don't know whether the game is being broadcast or not. Certainly hope so.

And so – goodnight.

My very best love to all,
Scottie

Annapolis, 18 November 1937

Dear Family,

The Army – Navy tickets have been issued and they are lousy. I have Mr. Murray's four. They are two separate pairs. Two of them in the end zone and the other two not much better. I'm sorry I couldn't do any better for him, but the Athletic Association has done the Regiment wrong this year. We rated only four tickets apiece, and lousy ones at that. 8000 tickets out of 105,000 is certainly not very many to give us, since it is our ball game and we pay just as good money for the tickets as anybody. I want him to realize that I did my level best for him.

Just took time out to listen to the scores, I've been playing the Gillette football pool. Pick seven teams and write fifty words on why you picked one of them. This week I picked 'em right. Of course I won't win anything but it will be fun to listen in and find out.

Next Saturday we go to Princeton. I don't look forward to it much – the train ride on these football trips is not particularly pleasant. I think that Navy should have little trouble in winning. Princeton has not shown much to date.

Dad's quotations from George's letter about the Michigan band was very interesting indeed. They certainly must have a tip-top organization. Michigan has been picking up in the last few weeks as far as football scores are concerned.

The exam week is almost over, and I am far from sorry. It certainly has been a headache from beginning to end. Up until today I had not done badly, but I certainly fear for the results of today's exam in "Steam". It was a horror. In the first place, our instructor had told us that we would be given a sheet with the formulae on it for us in the exam. No sheet appeared. I got most of the formulae finally by deriving them, but as a result did not finish. I'm afraid I bilged the exam. The only saving factor is that very few people did well. Only time can tell the results.

Ada L.. is going up to the Army game as the guest of Sally Coburn – one of Tex's friends. We have until 9:30 only this year. Ada L.. is driving back to Sallie's home that evening with the Coburns, and is then going back to Baltimore on Sunday. I have no idea what we will do during our short liberty in Philly. We will have a car which will prove a big help.

I do so hope that Dad will be able to get down for the game next year, and Mother too. It will be the last chance, and you must not miss it. George has had his turn, and next year must be yours.

There is no more news of any interest so I shall close this off with all my very best love to my wonderful family.
Scottie

Annapolis, 22 November 1937

Dear Family,

Mother's letter arrived today, and I was certainly GLAD to get it. Letters from home and from Baltimore constitute my greatest enjoyment here at the Academy.

The trip to Princeton was very uneventful. The game was a headache - what has happened to that team of ours is a matter of conjecture. One thing is certain: they just did not have what it took. It was the sorriest exhibition of football playing that I have seen in many a moon. Heaven help us next Saturday if they do not snap out of it.

The Pep Committee work is over for this year as far as card stunts are concerned.

Enclosed are some clippings which I am sure will interest you. Personally I think that it is about time that the shack burned down. [Carvel Hall] It is, of course, a pity that such a fine old landmark should be destroyed, - if it were destroyed, but it isn't. It can be rebuilt - the majority of the outside structure will remain the same. The appointments of the bedrooms and the general inside decorations will receive a refurbishing that they have needed for the last fifty years. You may wonder if I was among the Midshipmen who fought the fire - I was not - thank goodness. The Midshipmen did nothing but get in the way anyway, and I was mighty glad that my company was not called upon to go.

The movie that you want to see from all that I have heard is Navy Blue and Gold. The general consensus of opinion ranks it as the best Navy picture ever produced. I am told that it will be shown here in the yard on Wednesday night of this week, so I will have a chance to see it. I read the book and it struck me that it was the kind of a story that would make a good movie.

Dad's pictures of the U.E. football players both old and new were mighty interesting. The resemblance was striking. Do all football players have to look like that?

I received a letter from Paul Evans today. He asked me to look up some Plebe friend of his, I shall of course oblige him. He is a senior at California now, is he not?

No more news, so I shall close off this chapter. A very happy Thanksgiving to all my family.

Much love to all,
Scottie

Annapolis, 25 November 1937

Dear Family,

Here another week has past – almost. One more week and then we have our first exams. This year is the first year that we have four weeks devoted each year entirely to examinations. Previously we kept right on with advanced work and recitations. Now, we have one three hour exam each day and that is all. Whether it is a good thing or not remains to be seen. The exams are an hour longer and probably harder.

Mother asked about "Nav". At present we are studying the calibration of the compass – compass errors due to the variation and deviation caused by the Earth's magnetism. It is not so easy.

This week, we have been making a concentrated effort to get a little spirit into the Regiment – there has been a decided lack of it for the past few weeks. We certainly succeeded. I never saw such a madhouse as the mess hall was last night. Everybody had a big time and it sure was noisy.

I hope Navy wins Saturday. It is about time that ball club stopped making first downs and started making touchdowns. That Penn game was typical – 18 first downs for Navy to 3 for Penn. Yet look at the score.

I heard from Marsh. He is at Pensacola – has been there for about a week and is very enthusiastic.

I had the guard yesterday and got out of the "Nav P – work".

And I guess that is all for now.

Much love to all,
Scottie

PLEBE TO WWII HERO, MY JOURNEY FROM ANNAPOLIS TO MIDWAY

Annapolis, 26 November 1937

Dear Family,

Friday night before the Army game. No classes tomorrow, and so this letter. First off, I want to thank Mother for the chow. The reason that I have not acknowledged it before is that it did not arrive until yesterday. I know that it must have been mailed long ago because the mate who brought it to me had found the box in an old mail bag in a corner. When the First Class were relieving us for exams they were not particularly careful about delivering mail. It is my guess that it arrived on one of those days. Late or no, however, it is being thoroughly enjoyed. Thank you so very, very much.

Tonight in the mess hall there will be a rally to end all rallies. Then of course, a big bonfire. What the outcome of tomorrow's game will be is problematical. From last weeks showing, one would guess a big victory for Army, but you never can tell. Tomorrow night at this time will tell the story.

I have been reading Alexander Wolcott's While Rome Burns for the second time. I certainly wish that I had his style of writing and his great fund of experiences. The fat man certainly enjoys life, if one is to draw any conclusions from his writing.

In "Nav", we started celestial navigation - that is, learning the art of telling where you are when you can see nothing but the ocean and sky. It is rather interesting. In "Steam", we have progressed to the intriguing subject of "non flow processes" - now do you know what we are studying? Take my word for it, it is interesting. Today we had a three hour "Juice" lab. We measured resistances with Wheatstone Bridges, Murray and Varley Loops etc. Are you any wiser? - You see, your son is starting to get his technical education.

I have bet a sweater with some Pointer - friend of Mac's. The Army sweaters are pretty nice. I hope that I will be wearing one soon.

I have a program of the game and will send it up. It might interest you. It is the nicest thing of the sort that I have ever seen. I wish so that you all could be in Philly tomorrow. Next year, however is another year.

What did you think of our fire? Carvel Hall does not appear to be particularly damaged and will probably be open before June Week.

I can think of no more news, so as usual will stop thinking and close.

> Much love to all,
> Scottie

ROBERT SCOTT WHITMAN JR.

Annapolis, 4 December 1937

Dear Family,

You have probably been wondering why you haven't heard from me yet this week. The truth of the matter is that I have not been feeling so chipper. Wednesday noon at lunch, they fed us some pork and sauerkraut. The upshot of the whole thing was that in the wee small hours of Thursday morning I and about 75 other Midshipmen came down with cases of ptomaine poisoning. They were very light cases and we are all O.K. now; but at the time I was as sick as the proverbial pooch. They sent us all over to the hospital Thursday and released us today. I was just sick enough to not care much about letter writing - hence this delay. Have no fears, I am as well as ever now.

So to catch up with the news - here goes. The Army game was a mess - wet - very wet and very, very dull. The Army club had the better team on the field and they won - which was quite as it should be. After the game, Tex, his date, Ada L.. and I went out to the Anchorage, a very nice restaurant in Fairmont Park. We dined and danced and had a very pleasant three hours. From there we went back to the station and rode back to Annapolis. That is about all there is to say about my trip to Philadelphia.

The marks are out and my average is 3.06 - not so hot. At any rate that is how it is, and we will see if we can't improve it for the next two months.

How does everything go at home? I look forward so to your letters and enjoy them so much. This afternoon I went out into town for an hour, and bought the family Christmas present. I am scared stiff that you won't like it one bit, but anyway I done my darndest.

I have decided against George's robe - you are right. I can't afford it. I am giving one to Ada L.. - she has wanted one for a long time, and two on requisition would be too much, and for cash would be impossible. So I am still lost as to what to give him.

This letter is probably an awful mess - two days in bed knocks the devil out of one when he is not used to it, and I am just a little woozey. I will mail this off tonight, and attempt a better offering a little later in the week.

        Much love to all,
        Scottie

Annapolis, 16 December 1937

Dear Family,

Well, I can almost see my way out of the woods now – six more days – and have the days been dragging!!!

I imagine that by the time this arrives, you will have heard all about George's first college experiences. He arrives Saturday morning does he not?

This week we have been making preparations for our Christmas dinner – the Second Class always arranges it for each table – and I have been in charge. We went out into town and bought decorations for the table, 10¢ toys for each etc.

I won an officer's cap in a tailor's contest here in town. We had to write a paragraph of a hundred words on some subject which tied military efficiency and smart tailoring together – I've forgotten the exact title. I'm doing my best to sell it now. I wanted to win the first prize of a suit of clothes – but I came out only second best.

There really is no news to tell. I just wanted to write a few lines to let you know that I was looking forward so very eagerly to getting home and to send my best love to my grand family.

        Much love to all,
          Scottie

Annapolis, 3 January 1938

Dear Family,

And so with the memories of a very happy leave at home and in Baltimore - back to work. We're back in the rut again without a bit of trouble.

Thank you for the telegram and letter on my birthday.

The Baltimore stay was very pleasant. The dance was very nice. There were, of course, very few people that I knew but I got to know them, and we had an awfully good time. Thursday we had a busy day - lunch down town - then an egg nog party - and finally bridge in the evening with a young married couple at their new home. I knew them both from previous visits and we had an enjoyable time.

New Year's Eve, we went to the theatre and saw <u>Moon Over Mulberry Street</u> - It was passing fair. After the theatre, we did a few places and so home.

Ada L.. gave me a desk lighter for my birthday, one of the practical kind which you strike. It is a chromium pelican with the striker in his head. We have christened him "Schnoz".

And of all things - Doctor gave me a Yellow Bole pipe!!! I can't understand it.

Saturday we went to another egg nog party and then came home to play bridge with the family.

Sunday - Grrrh!!! (you see the postmark)

Mrs. D..... told me to tell you that I have been a very, very good boy, and a model guest.

Ada L.. is fine and sends her love to all.

I'll write later in the week. Have written all my "thank you" letters.

Heard from Aunt Julie today.

       Much, much love to all,

         Scottie

Annapolis, 7 January 1938

Dear Family,

We have our new Commandant, Capt. Draemel. He has the reputation of being a holy terror, and has made a good start to bear out his reputation. His first step was to inaugurate Sunday formal room inspections – something that has happened only infrequently for the past years. However, it is not the type of inspection that gets us, but the frequency. We are to have them every Sunday without fail – a thing unheard of formerly. Everything is tightening up proportionately. I am certainly thankful that I will be a First Classman next year.

The new Superintendent arrives on the first of the month. Here is hoping that he is a good guy; two martinets would make an unbearable combination when they sit in the driver's seat.

The next set of exams come up in a couple of weeks. This time Ordnance has us all fearful, the Ordnance department is noted for granting "no quarter", and the stuff we have been studying during the past two months could make an awful tough exam if one set himself to make it that way.

What is hear from George? I hope that he buckles down to work and makes a name for himself. He has so much more ability than I, and at least one of us should shine. Sounds as though I wanted to pass the buck doesn't it, but really am plugging along in the very best way I know how. I am even looking all the time for better ways.

Today, if you are interested in what I did, I went first to a "Steam" class; we had probs on the Diesel cycle, and I think I got a 4.0 (my, don't I pat myself on the back beautifully?). Then I had a study period I which I read the paper, and then boned "Nav". Then "Nav" class and another 4.0 (what is this?). Then a study period in which I vainly tried to read 80 pages of Karenina. Then I ate chow – oyster stew, salmon salad, and lemon sherbet – today is Friday as you see. Then I went to "Bull" and recited on that part of Anna that I had no time to read – and not another 4.0. Another study period, and then a gym class – we went swimming and were instructed in the new resuscitation method which has been devised since we took our life saving exams this summer. Now at 5:10 I am writing this letter. So you see my day, which is just the same as any day.

> So with all my love to the best mother and dad in the world, I guess that I will sign off till next time.
> Scottie

Annapolis, 18 January 1938

Dear Family,

I am just back from an afternoon in the "Juice" lab. We did some more work on a generator – it was not particularly interesting.

The Naval Academy keeps tightening up under the influence of the new Commandant. No longer can I use the cigarette lighter that Ada L.. gave me for my birthday – it is not regulation, and I can't keep it on my desk. There is talk of their putting a soda fountain on the "swabo" [zero] deck under the rotunda – why I can't imagine. It seems to me a waste of money – but then, I am not running the Navy.

"China" Franks, one of the boys with whom I roomed this summer :: remember – has resigned. His father is in very poor health and he needs "China" at home to run the business – whatever it is.

I am scared stiff of the Ordnance exam this time - it is going to be a terror. We have about four hundred pages to review, and I frankly don't even know how to start. The only saving factor is that everyone else seems to be in the same boat. My daily marks are pretty good, so I don't guess there is any real need to worry, but I do so like to get good marks in everything.

We have drawn our books for the second term - $21.50 worth. We are studying the history of American foreign policy in "Bull". I am afraid that it may prove pretty deadly. Not because it necessarily is, but because of the way such courses are attacked here.

We are almost finished with D.C. in "Juice". Then on the A.C. We start torpedo control in Ordnance next week. "Nav" carries on in the same vein as formerly. Our German is to be Naval Phraseology. I have not forgotten that I am to send Anna Karenina as soon as I am through with it; that will be at the end of next week.

I hope Dad is not overdoing. Take it easy Pop – nobody made a million in a day.

Tom Davies was back in Washington for a while and came over to see me. It was nice to see him and learn all the dope – he always has it.

I had to write an article for the <u>Log</u> about mystery ships, and had a grand time reading a very interesting book about them.

The Musical Clubs are afraid that we will have to put on <u>Pinafore</u>. The Executive Department does not want us to put on an original show this year. Personally, I am all for <u>Pinafore</u> – it will certainly be a lot better than any Midshipman's brain-child.

No more news now, so I guess I'll have to stop.

Much love to all,
Scottie

ROBERT SCOTT WHITMAN JR.

Annapolis, 20 January 1938

Dear Gram,

I just received Mother's letter reporting that you had moved out on us to a place where you can have all your meals in bed - such a luxury. Are the nurses pretty? If they are, I shall have to try to arrange a quick trip up to see you - I always was partial to pretty nurses. Then too, I would like to see my Gram - she is such a nice Gram.

Are they taking good care of you? They had better, or I will personally attend to them. There, that's a threat you can hold over the heads of anybody who bothers you.

The semester if almost over. Next week we take our mid-year exams - and that means a lot of studying; but then, by now I am pretty used to studying.

Today we had the first snow of the year - not very much, but enough to make the ground white and stay that way. It has been very, very cold, and I envy you in your nice warm room. And they always feed you so well in hospitals. You see it can't be so bad - once you get used to somebody waiting on you hand and foot all the time. I have a real affection for hospitals, and perhaps one of these days I'll come up and join you.

Today, we got some news - next year there are to be a thousand Plebes, I guess that they are taking this Naval expansion seriously. The Hall will certainly be crowded to overflowing - that is just twice as many Plebes as there are now.

I bought a new pair of shoes today - not a very interesting piece of new perhaps, but I sure hated to do it - but then, think how pretty my dainty feet will look at formations. I find that there is a bright side to almost everything; it is good philosophy even if it is not original.

With the little snow that we had, the Midshipmen who come from snowless regions have been making the most of it, and there have been some battle royals. I of course received a goodly portion of it down my neck.

There is really no more news - I just wanted to write a note to let you know that I was thinking of you and that I love my Gram very much.

Much love,
Scottie

Annapolis, 3 February 1938

Dear Family,

The news of Gram which I received from both Mother and Dad is very, very encouraging – I certainly hope that her improvement continues.

The new admiral took command Tuesday. At noon we formed and were marched to the Armory. The ceremony was very short since we couldn't possibly miss any of our first afternoon class. Since we were packed into the Armory like sardines, and I was in the next to the last row, I saw very little of what happened and hear less. The old admiral made a very pretty little speech, and the new one said nothing at all except to read his orders.

Rumor has it that with the change of command this place is going to become even more of a horror than it already is. Well, I should be one to kick, it has given me an awful lot, and since we are getting paid for what we take, there should be no reason to complain. Thank heaven, however that I am more than half way through.

Enough of my troubles. It has warmed up again, rained a little this morning, and now I suppose that it will get colder again.

This term we are taking six courses – the added one being Seamanship. I missed the first class (today) and so have no idea what it will be like. I think that we study the International Rules of the Road mostly.

Best of luck to you and all my hopes for some more good news.

       Much love to all,

        Scottie

ROBERT SCOTT WHITMAN JR.

Annapolis, 13 February 1938

Dear Family,

The letter is a little later than usual this week. Sorry to have kept you waiting, but I have not been able to write – had my eyes refracted. They are O.K. even though they are giving me periodic headaches. The doctor gave me a prescription for glasses which, if my eyes don't snap out of it, I will have filled. The trouble is the old farsightedness that I have always had; so, when I say O.K., I mean that I can pass the tests for the physical exam.

How is Gram? I have missed hearing from you this week – rather expected a letter from Mother, but I know she is having a pretty hectic time of it, and it is no small wonder that she has no time to write a letter. Please don't overdo, Mother, and take it as easy as you can.

The D..... family was down yesterday for the boxing matches and the Masqueraders. We had a very pleasant evening even though we had to leave the show early in order to get the people off to Baltimore.

The Masqueraders are presenting <u>Whistling in the Dark</u> and are doing by far the best job that I have seen them do.

We are putting on <u>Pinafore</u> this year for the Musical Club Show. It is a departure from the practice of staging an original production, and should, at least, be a little less sloppy than the usual Midshipman's product. The Glee Club is well underway, and there is really nothing much else to do but wait until it is time to put the show together.

Yesterday, I went out to pick out my class ring. I think I have what I want. The finish is called medium Burmese, a slightly darkened finish with a slight oxidization – gives it a sort of antique look. The coast of arms is set in enamel, which sets if off to good advantage. The ring is going to cost me seventy dollars, forty-four for the ring proper, five for the plug, and twenty-one for the engraving. I get sixty-five dollars credit on grad terms. It will make a very, very nice looking ring.

Navy lost the fights last night to Virginia, but they were a darn good bunch of bouts, and I enjoyed them very much.

Next week, all three of us here in 1131 are dragging together. Tex is dragging his Sally, Jud another Sally, and I guess you can surmise, if you concentrate, that Ada L.. will be down.

Will the grandest of family that I know be my valentine?

       Much love to all,

        Scottie

Annapolis, 18 February 1938

Dear Family,

Please, why haven't I heard from Mother in so long? The very last letter, or rather word, I have had from her was the note at the bottom of Dad's letter dated February seventh. Are you sick, Mother, too busy, or what? I am so worried. Just a line is sufficient so that I will know that you are all right. Is Gram home? Worse? Better? I am crazy to know what is wrong at home. Please - just a note.

First, I have received back from Bailey Banks & Biddle a copy of the crest as it will appear in my ring, and it looks darn good - so I shall go out tomorrow and O.K. it.

Second, the authentic dope on the cruise so far has it that we are going to make approximately the same cruise that we made before. The approved itinerary has been seen by several people, so it must be good dope. We go to Cherbourg, Copenhagen, Portsmouth, in that order. So you see that the only change is Copenhagen, rather than Göteborg. Personally, I am very disappointed. I had so hoped that we might get down into the Mediterranean for a change and see some new country. Then, too, Cherbourg is such an awful town to have any liberty in. There is absolutely nothing to do, nothing to see, and not much of any place that you can go to within one-day distance. Portsmouth is little better. I am told that Copenhagen is a fine city; but that is small consolation. We sail on June third, and get back about August twenty-fifth.

I was very much interested in Dad's report that admiral Brown has a brother in Binghamton. I shall have to let him know that I am from the dear old town if I ever have any conversation with him - which is highly doubtful.

What news do you hear from George? He owes me a letter, but I don't expect that I will hear from him, I guess all my family has forsaken me.

Today we woke up to more of that phenomenal spring weather which we have been having. I suppose that tomorrow it will be as cold as it was yesterday. None of us can keep the uniform straight - first we wear reefers with collars turned up, and next we wear service. It is all very confusing and all the fault of this crazy Maryland weather.

Did you receive the book O.K. Mother? I mailed it out last week Wednesday, I believe.

The other day I had a brain storm and wrote to the editor of Colliers suggesting that I write an article about the Naval Academy for him. With this frenzied ship building under way, I thought perhaps his "very timely magazine would see the sagacity of publishing for its delighted readers a little dope about how Uncle Sam builds officers to man these warships he is constructing" – or words to that effect. Did I get even an answer? Of course not but you can't blame me for trying. Next I'll try American. None of these magazines have ever published the traditional N.A. story from a Midshipman's pen. Who is better qualified to write it?

Just prior to writing this letter, I was over in the gym for my daily work-out. I feel right good at the present moment after a good "hot-then-cold" shower and clean clothes. If I just would get a letter from Mother, my cup would be filled to the brim and over-flowing.

There is no more news, and so for the time being – Aufwiedersehen.

        Much love to all,
          Scottie

Annapolis, 21 February 1938

Dear Family,

This is just a note to say hello and to send my love to you all. Tomorrow being a holiday, I have a little free time.

The week-end was very enjoyable, as they all are. Tex's Sally was here, went home with Ada L.. last night, spent the day, and now is back again. The hop was right much fun. It was just for the Second and Third classes this time, and so was not quite so crowded as usual.

Saturday afternoon we went to the basketball game, and then to the wrestling match. We beat Catholic University in basketball, and Harvard in wrestling – so you see it was a very successful afternoon.

Today, I had classes in "Juice", "Nav", and "Steam, and a long drill in "Steam". This time it was an analysis run of an air compressor. Our class room work in "Steam" has been the detailed analysis of turbine operation from the efficiency aspect. We have spent a great deal of time on it as we rightly should, for turbines are the backbone of a ship's engineering plant.

This month we have our morning classes the second and fourth periods, the last ending just before chow formation. It gives us about then minutes to change uniforms and shoes and get brushed off for the noon inspection.

1131 has been in more or less a lethargy for the past two weeks, and as a consequence none of us are breaking any academic records. Whether it is premature spring fever or what, we have no idea. At any rate, it means another hectic preparation for exams when the time comes. Oh, well – all in the happy life at the naval school.

Much, much love to all,
Scottie

Annapolis, 26 February 1938

Dear Family,

Mother's letter arrived today, and I was so glad to get it. And, Dad, I am sorry that I riled you with my query about my lack of news from home. I didn't realize that things were such a mess, and I had not heard from Mother for a long time.

Tonight I go on watch again. I have had the guard every twelve days for a long time. I am on the second section this time, so I will be relieved at 9:30, and will not have to stay on until the hop is over. The first section stands from 9:30 until about 2:00 A.M. on Saturday evenings, so I'm lucky to have it the way it is.

From what mother says, she has the mid-watch every night.

I ordered my sword today. We have to have them for First Class year, you know.

Nick Shields came up to the room to see me this afternoon. He is at Mercersburg, and is here with the wrestling team which meets the Plebes this afternoon.

Just now a funny thing happened. A man came into the room, a civilian. Said he had this room back in 1907, and hadn't been back since. Wanted to take a look at it again. He is a superintendent of schools in Texas.

I am so glad that George came through. I was a bit worried about him myself, but felt sure that he would come through all right – as he did.

I don't know whether to consider the reports on Gram's condition as encouraging or otherwise. I do hope that she isn't too uncomfortable, and that mother is not wearing herself completely out. But, from all indications, that is just what is happening. For heaven's sake take care of yourself, Mother. Relax, and don't worry – it just doesn't do a bit of good. Young squirt that I am, and knowing that it is far easier said than done, it is still darned good advice.

They sure are building up this Navy of ours. There is not a prayer of any of our class getting out after graduation from what reports we have. They are considering increasing the officer strength to about 1200 more than at present, let alone letting anybody out. And for what are they building all these warships? Just a great big game of keeping up with the Jones'. Now I see by the paper that we are going to argue with Great Britain over some of the Pacific Islands. What next - maybe all this talk about policing the world is a lot of bushwa after all.

Sure as shooting, Mr. Hitler and some of his playmates are going to get into a squabble over their marble game, and it looks as if we want to play too. The threat of war in the Pacific certainly is not what it is cracked up to be at least, if there is a serious threat, Japan must have unearthed a gold mine in Fujiyama. Well - I probably don't understand it at all, and so before I show too much ignorance, I had better stop shooting off my mouth.

        Much love to all,
            Scottie

ROBERT SCOTT WHITMAN JR.

Annapolis, 14 March 1938

Dear Family,

Mother's letter arrived and I was indeed delighted to get it. The news of Gram is certainly not very encouraging. She and you are certainly having a pretty tough time of it. I do so wish there was something I could do to help. Keep a stiff upper lip, Mother, and try to take things as easy as you possibly can. How I wish I were home and could carry a little of the burden.

We have spent the last week trying to find a house or apartment for June Week (Tex, Jud, and I), and so far we have been very unsuccessful. The absence of Carvel Hall makes it a big problem, and everyone is hunting. However, we have two or three pretty good leads and will soon have something, I hope.

Exams start next week and I am not the least bit ready for them – looks like some after taps work for the first time this year.

It is nice that Jimmie Wiltsie joined Alpha Sigma Phi – gives George a fraternity brother in the old gang.

If friend Adolph doesn't settle down to normal, it would surprise me not in the least if we did not go to Europe this summer – which does not make me the least bit unhappy. If he runs true to form with his promise breaking, he will be grabbing at Czechoslovakia next and then – "Hold your hats – we're off."

I have been appointed Feature Editor of the Log for next year. I am doing practically nothing on the Musical Club show. Mr. Christie has taken charge, as usual, and there is nothing for Wood or me to do. I am inclined to think that he has a grudge against Wood (who was elected the Director for this year); and, since it was Wood who appointed me Assistant Director, I am suffering along with him. At least, we are in the dog-house for some reason or other.

Seems to me that if we must have our war, it would be the best thing in the world to have it and get it over with. Then perhaps we can all settle down for a while and make a living. If they wait a few years longer until all this projected rearmament is completed, we won't have done until "they ain't no more world" and we'll all be blasted to hell and back.

I had a try-on of my ring Saturday, and it is O.K. I'm going to wear it on my left hand ring finger. I was afraid it would have to be too big to get it over that knuckle; but although it is plenty loose, it will do. [Knuckle enlarged from football injury].

This "Bull" course of ours on American diplomacy is deadly. So I know, at least, that I don't want to be a diplomat.

I wrote to Marsh a month ago and have had no answer. I am wondering if he is still there or has bilged out. It's very easy to do that at Pensacola.

Wasn't that thing of mine in the Log lousy? They wanted a detective story, and all I could do was something ridiculous, and then it wasn't even that. Oh, well, - the Log (as you have seen) will print anything.

All my love to the grandest family in the world,
Scottie

Annapolis, 30 March 1938

Dear Family,

Dad's letter arrived today – thank you very much.

Although it is not yet Easter, we are wearing white cap covers – they were changed Sunday.

On May 15 the new warm weather dress uniform becomes effective for hops. It is quite a change – white mess jackets with vest, gold studs, dress shirt and tie, and one shoulder mark (You only rate one, it seems, until you are commissioned.), which makes it all look lopsided. But, all in all, it is a welcome improvement, aside from the fact (the one universal gripe – no more fervently expressed than by me.) that it means $15 to $20 less money for the cruise or, as will be the case, September leave.

You undoubtedly saw the story about the Soda Fountain in the Log. It is practically finished and is quite fancy – 'tis indeed. But what they want with one is beyond me unless, as it has been persistently rumored, they are going to cut down our liberty next year, and this is a measure to cut short any objections from the boys who like their sundaes of a Sunday afternoon. Time will tell.

I got a letter from Marsh – From all I can gather, he is doing pretty well.

All for now.

Much love to all,
Scottie

POSTAL TELEGRAPH

5

NA151   37   GOVT-ANNAPOLIS MD 3 238P   1938 APR 4 PM 3 16

R S WHITMAN-   -

   7 JOHNSON AVE BINGHAMTON NY

YOUR SON MIDSHIPMAN ROBERT SCOTT WHITMAN JR WAS OPERATED UPON

THIS MORNING FOR ACUTE APPENDICITIS HIS CONDITION IS EXCELLENT

AND AN UNEVENTFUL CONVALESCENCE IS EXPECTED YOU WILL BE KEPT

INFORMED OF ANY MATERIAL CHANGE IN HIS CONDITION-

      COMMANDING OFFICER NAVAL HOSPITAL

Annapolis, 4 April 1938

Dear Family,

     When you get this, I will be without one of my most cherished
possessions, my appendix. I don't know whether the hospital
notified you or not; but, in any case, don't worry - there is
no danger. I had a pain in my side Sunday, a little Saturday;
and today, Monday, they are going to operate. They always do if
there is even a hint of it. It is the best thing - better here
where they do a reputedly cracker jack job than on the deck of a
rolling ship. They do hundreds of them a year. The surgeon who
does the job has a wonderful reputation, and I'll be as good as
new in two weeks. I've had a twinge or two before - and feel
that I couldn't have picked a better time to get the works -
just after exams and all.

     Don't worry, I'm fine.

     Send all my love to my grand family.

     Will write later in the week.

          Scottie

ROBERT SCOTT WHITMAN JR.

POSTAL TELEGRAPH

NA53 6-ANNAPOLIS   MD   1050A 5   1938 APR 5 AM 11 08

ROBERT S WHITMAN

   6 JOHNSON AVE BNGHAMTON NY

SAW SCOTTY THIS MORNING DOING SATISFACTORY

   DR ARTHUR J. D.....

Annapolis, 8 April 1938

Dear Family,

   Well – I'm feeling quite chipper now – am practically as good as new.

   There is no news – I felt awful lousy for the first three days, but now I'm well on the way to recovery.

   Your letters and telegram have been quite cheering – thank you.

   It's hard to write this way and a little painful to sit up, so I won't attempt a long discourse – I'm O.K. – feeling much better, and send my love to my grand family.

   I suppose George is home now – How is he?

        Love to all,
            Scottie

Annapolis, 13 April 1938

Dear Family,

I'm "up and around" now – feeling quite well except for being pretty shaky.

Ada L.. is coming down this afternoon – she has no classes on Wednesdays.

I guess I'll be going back to the Hall next Monday. Will be on the excused squad for a week, and then it's all over.

Now I've got to think about getting caught up with the two weeks work I have missed.

There is no news. Hope everything at home is, at least, no worse than usual.

Your letters have been such a grand event.

> Much love to all,
> Scottie

Annapolis, 17 April 1938

Dear Family,

In a week I'll be out – <u>sans</u> appendix, and today I was up for half an hour in a wheel chair. I'm feeling fit as a fiddle but very weak in the knees.

Also, today, I get my stitches taken out and saw the incision for the first time. A very pretty little thing about 2 inches long.

Mrs. D..... and Ada L.. were down today and brought me some more flowers – they brought some on Tuesday, or rather when Doctor came Tuesday.

There is absolutely no news to tell you.

The operation was no ordeal. I got a spinal anaesthetic, which deadened me from the waist down. A couple of shots of morphine and – before I knew it, it was out.

I'm in the ward now and have been since Wednesday. Have been feeling better and better each day.

It is a real task to write in bed this way, and so I shall attempt no more.

> Much, much love to all,
> Scottie

ROBERT SCOTT WHITMAN JR.

Annapolis, 21 April 1938

Dear Family,

Well, in the rush and hectic struggle to get back into the swing of things here at the Hall, I have been neglecting my family.

At any rate, here is the news such as it is since I got back. I arrived back at 1131 Monday afternoon, and indeed I was glad to get here. Am feeling very fine indeed, and am only anxious that my time of comparative inaction be up so that I can get back into some semblance of condition.

Jud has gone on four days special leave. He is to be discharged at the end of the term because of his eye trouble, and wants to go home to arrange for the future.

Saturday evening at the hospital, I hit the "pap" for strolling in the grounds after hours. I don't know what I will get out of it. It was such an innocent offense that I hardly think that it will be at all serious, but it seems that we are under the same restrictions over there as we are here. So time alone will tell. I was gone from the ward only an hour.

I am on the Wyoming again this year. It has great advantages in some ways. Knowing the ship is the biggest one.

The itinerary is the same as I outlined to you before except that we go to Le Havre instead of Cherbourg. The dope on what tours are available is out, and as soon as I can get a copy of it, I will transcribe it for you, or send it on - I'd like your advice on where to go.

I suppose that George is well back into the school routine by now, I am so glad that he enjoyed his vacation. Wish I could get one. The rest in the hospital after the first week was a help though, but I would like to come home.

Must be off to class now.

                Much love to all,
                Scottie

Annapolis, 1 May 1938

Dear Family,

To plunge right in and get it over with, the "pap" I got over at the hospital back-fired on me – and here I am roosting high and dry on the ship. Please don't let it worry you because, when you hear the circumstances you must agree that my offense was far removed from anything criminal, malicious, or bad.

I was absent from the ward for about an hour on Saturday evening and was so reported; the hospital authorities put me on the "pap". I rated it. It was a class "B" "pap" and I expected nothing more than some extra duty. I knew I didn't rate going out, but never dreamed it was a serious offense. When I got back to the Hall on Monday, the exec called me up and told me that hospital restrictions were the same as Hall restrictions, that he would have to change the "pap" to a class "A" and put me under restriction. I still wasn't worried. It was such an innocent offense. I didn't believe I could get the ship – or a week at the outside. Then bam – last Wednesday the dope came through, 75 demerits and 30 days. Ever since I have so de-winded that it has been impossible to figure out why I got such a crack. Of course, I rated getting "papped", I'd violated a restriction. But 30 days!!!! I can't figure it out. I'm going to go and ask. They didn't ask or tell me a thing. I have talked with two officers of the Executive Department and they say that the only thing I should be sorry about is that I didn't really go out over the wall and have a big time. The "pap" is standard and five minutes or all day makes no difference; so perhaps that is the explanation – I come out of hock on the 27th of May, just in time for June Week.

With all your troubles at home, I contemplated a long while before I decided to even tell you about it, but I think you can see that it was not a dishonorable offense and that – as any officer will tell you – my mistake was in getting caught. It was all very innocent, and I guess, even though I was plenty mad at first, I rate it. It won't spoil my record, so don't worry about that.

So there's the dope. Don't worry.

Lots and lots of love to my grand family,
Scottie

ROBERT SCOTT WHITMAN JR.

Annapolis, 10 May 1938

Dear Family,

For a man who should have plenty of time to repent his sins and dwell upon his wickedness, I have certainly been kept plenty busy. Even Ada L.. has been righteously indignant with the lack of letters.

For some unknown reason the Academic Department has taken the last two weeks of the academic year to really bear down on us, and they can bear. Then too, the <u>Log</u> work has been keeping me pretty busy. My confinement has not interfered with it in the sense of lightening my duties any; but, to the contrary, because of my isolated spot, it has made it even harder. Everything is pretty well in control now, and, as far as that is concerned, I can relax.

There is no news from here except that now that we are almost First Classmen, we are beginning to assimilate First Class rates. The first to come our way are permission to wear rubber heels, and to have side pockets in our "Trou". After June 3rd we rate wearing low shoes.

Naturally, I am looking forward to June Week with a great deal of anticipation. I hope that it turns out as pleasant as is anticipated. Tex's girl, Ada L.., and two other Goucherites are staying together at the Cooper, the same place we had last year. It is just outside the main gate into the Academy, and the finest place in town to stay.

I can't think of another thing to tell you all now, but you will be receiving lots of mail from me between now and June Week, since I will be spending Drill Week down on this tub with nothing in the world to do but read and write letters.

        Much love to all,
        Scottie

Annapolis, 14 May 1938

Dear Family,

The gorgeous chow arrived Thursday – and what I mean is it was, and is, gorgeous for it isn't quite all gone yet. The cookies and brownies and fudge really alleviated by homesickness for a chance at some of Mother's swell cooking to a certain extent.

My time in the brig is more than half up, and two weeks from yesterday, I become once again a free man. I have missed hearing from Dad, but I suppose that he is a pretty busy man this time of year.

I have put in my tour requests, I am taking independent tour in England, and have not fully decided what I will do. I am taking the cheap tour to Paris, principally because I don't know what else to do. I tried to find someone congenial to tour around Normandy with me, but everybody is going to Paris, and, to get away from the ship, I am going too. Le Havre is close to Rouen, Bayeux, and Caen – close enough to get to on liberty, so I shall be able to do them. There are no tours in Copenhagen, so I had nothing to decide for that port. I wanted awfully badly to go to Scotland, but the cost is more than they had first anticipated, forty-five dollars, and I can't afford it.

Next week I have to go over and interview the Admiral and get his blessing upon June Week, in general, and the June Week Log, in particular. May help my "grease" some.

I do so hope that George can do something with his ties for a Naval Academy appointment. If not the Academy, the Point. One is just as good as the other, and even if he can't make it this year or next – the age limit at the Point is considerably higher. It would settle his worries about an education. I realize full well just how lucky I have been – and I hope and pray for the same luck for George. I can't recommend a Naval or Military life for a life's diet, but for a lad in his or my shoes, it is a heaven-sent opportunity if it ever arrives. Is there any chance of getting an appointment if his physical qualifications are up to snuff?

It is a dirty rotten shame that he won't be able to go back next year to Michigan. Has he exhausted fully the opportunities for part time work out there? I only wish that I could do something to help him.

> The best of love to my family,
> Scottie

Annapolis, 21 May 1938

Dear Family,

Today has been quite an exciting one at the Academy. The President and all his family came down for the Adam's cup Crew races (which Harvard won), and the place has been a madhouse. All sorts of guns booming, and everyone from the Admiral on down running around as though they had lost their heads. Then after the President had gone, two of the wagons which are going to make the cruise came in. More salutes and more gunpowder wasted.

My interview with the Admiral was very uneventful. He seems very nice, gave me what I wanted, and I left - that's all there was to it.

Have you seen this week's Colliers? I sent in an item for "Keep Up with the World" about two months ago and they printed it this week and I received a check for five dollars in the mail. How'm I doin'?

Here on the "tub", I am the short termer now. There are four others, as I have mentioned, and they are all here for the rest of the year up until the cruise. I get off on Friday. The food, thank you, is lousy. I feel fine and chipper with absolutely no ill effects from the operation. I have managed to save quite a bit of money.

Jud is staying for June Week, but is dragging for only one night. He is in love, it seems, and his girl can be here for only the Ring Dance which is Monday evening of June Week. Tex and I are rooming together next year - just the two of us. At this late stage in the game it would have been hard to find anyone congenial - everybody is all hooked up with their roommates of former years, and so we decided not to try to find anyone else.

You hit the nail on the head when you said "no more funny business". I've had my fling, and you can rest assured that you have a very, very regulation son in the Naval Academy. My "grease" mark for the last two months was a 3.3, so I must not have suffered too much because of this incarceration.

We get our rings next Friday - the day that I am again free from bondage. I am anxious to see what sort of job they did with mine. There is not much to do down here now that school is over except sun baths, and I am looking forward to getting quite a tan in the next week. Next week is Drill Week as you know, and that is all we do - drill for the company competition. The second company has a chance, but not a very good one, to win the flag this year. I sure hope that we do.

There sure will be a lot of ships around here next week. Three battleships, six destroyers, a submarine, a new light cruiser, and heaven knows that else.

When does George arrive home? I imagine that it won't be so very long now before you will have at least one of your boys under foot again, and it's not an awfully long time before the other big lummax will be tripping you up wherever you turn.

The June Week program is about as follows:

Begins Friday the 27th - liberty starts at noon - I get off the ship first thing in the morning.

Saturday - Army-Navy baseball - 1, 2, 3, hop in the evening.

Nothing Sunday for our class - baccalaureate, of course.

Monday - The Ring Dance

Tuesday - 1, 2, hop - (The First Class are using our
   decorations for their hop so they had to invite us)

Wednesday - Farewell Ball - We don't go - Ada L.. has to go
   back To Baltimore for an exam Thursday Morning.

Thursday - Graduation - your son is a First Classman -
                  Ada L.. gets back this afternoon.

Friday - We sail.

That's the dope in general - they issued programs but I missed mine - it will all be in the Log, and you will have all the full dope in that.

Ther ain't no mo news of any size, shape, or description. If ther war, I wouldn't be a signin off now, but anyhow - as you say I will have lots of time to write in the next week, so don't fall dead from surprise if you hear from your bad-boy son again real soon.

All the best of love to my grand family from their son who is awfully lonesome for them,

      Scottie

ROBERT SCOTT WHITMAN JR.

Annapolis, 24 May 1938

Dear Family,

Here I am writing again. Please don't let the shock take too much of a hold on you. The one reason that I want to write to you is to tell you the dope on the marks for the year – not that they are any too good, but I know that you are anxious to get the dope. I'm not very proud of my record, but here it is.

"Steam"	Term Mark	2.93	Standing	312
"Juice"		2.94		269
"Ordnance"		3.02		162
"Grease"	Year	3.21		289
"Bull"	Term Mark	3.32		22
"Dago"		3.33		108
"Nav"		2.91		362

By figuring out the multiples which I did not bother to give, I figure that I have almost a 3.10 average for the year. If it had not been for the last two months, I would have done a much better job of it, but what with the hospital and other things, I didn't seem to have what it took.

Two of the battle wagons are in, the <u>New York</u> and the <u>Wyoming</u>. I have been spending most of my time at the Hall getting my cruise gear in shape so that I won't have to bother with that during June Week. It has been a powerful lot of work, but everything is under control now.

I have but two more days to put in down here, and then June Week, Ada L.., and freedom. I can tell you that I am looking forward to all three with a lot more anticipation than ever before. I sure hope that June Week turns out as pleasant as I hope that it will be.

Yesterday we had a lecture about the cruise and the leaves by the members of the Bull Department who have been arranging the tours. It seems that in Paris we are going to hit the most gala time of the season. We are invited among other things to the Embassy Ball, which tops of the big week. (I don't know what they call it, but it seems to be a Parisian institution. It is the American Ambassador.)

It will be fun to go just to be able to say that I have been to one of those affairs. I don't imagine that it will really be so very exciting.

Well, there is the dope since I last wrote, and I am going to sign off.

Much love to all, Scottie

VI
SECOND CRUISE
1938

ROBERT SCOTT WHITMAN JR.

UNITED STATES NAVAL ACADEMY

Annapolis, Maryland

28 April 1938

_____

SPECIAL ORDER NO. 12-38

SUBJECT: Summer Practice Cruise Itinerary for Midshipmen
            Practical Instruction, Summer of 1938

1. Upon graduation of the present first class on 2 June 1938, the
present second, third and fourth classes of midshipmen will become the
new first, second and third classes respectively.

2. Practical instruction will be given to midshipmen of the new
first, second and third classes during the summer as follows:

        (a) First and Third Classes - A foreign cruise in a Practice
Squadron consisting of the U.S.S. New York (flagship), U.S.S. TEXAS,
and U.S.S. WYOMING, with the following itinerary:

ARRIVAL	PLACE	DEPARTURE
	Annapolis, Md.	3 June (Midshipmen embark in forenoon)
18 June	Le Havre, France	27 June
5 July	Copenhagen, Denmark	9 July
15 July	Portsmouth, England	23 July
6 August	Hampton Roads, Va.	8 August

   Train for and fire Short Range Practice, conduct scheduled
gunnery training 8 to 12 August; disembark football squad upon
completion.

13 August	New York, N.Y.	17 August
18 August	Hampton Roads, Va. (supplies and fuel)	20 August
20 August	Solomon's Island, Md.	23 August
24 August	Annapolis, Md. (forenoon)	
25 August	Disembark midshipmen (to arrive at Reina Mercedes dock at 0715)	

                              WILSON BROWN
                      Rear Admiral, U.S. Navy,
                            Superintendent.

At sea, 5 June 1938

Dear Family,

Well, here we are, rolling on Europeward, already about 200 miles out at sea, and I have been so busy every minute of the time that I surprise myself that I find time to start this letter.

June Week was grand, no other word can express it. Never have I had such a wonderful time. The Ring Dance was all I had expected it to be and then some.

Then, of course, Friday we sailed. Ada L.. came into the Yard bright and early Friday morning and we had most of the morning together. At about 12:30 we formed and marched down to the boats, embarked, and went out to the wagons. At 3:30 we were under way – in the rain.

It wasn't at all the mess that it was on the Youngster cruise and before long I was all "stowed away" and well settled down. We had no watches for the first day, and so had plenty of time to get the Youngsters squared away.

This time, I am on the "deck" detail first, and my first job is as "boatswain's mate 2/c" Besides standing watches in the communications office, I have charge of the compartment cleaners, the Division laundry, "lucky bag" (stowage of lost articles), and about a million and one other things. So you see it is a twenty-four hour a day job with very little let up.

Friday night 6/3 we anchored somewhere in the bay, but since early Saturday we have been under way and, as I told you, we are well out to sea.

This year, we (the First Class) sleep on canvas cots instead of in hammocks. They are, besides being infinitely more comfortable, a lot less trouble. All in all the condition of living for the First Class is far better than that for the Youngsters – and I am enjoying being one of the "chosen people".

Now we have twelve more days at sea. Then – and I guess we'll all be glad of it – a little respite.

The old tub is rolling – but she always does.

There is just time for me to wash up before lunch, so I shall close the first chapter of the first volume.

       Much, much love to all,
        Scottie

Thursday, 9 June 1938

Dear Family,

It has been a lot longer than I thought it would be since I wrote last, but they have been keeping me humping. Now, however, we have changed details, and I am in the Officer of the Deck group. We stand watches on the bridge as OOD, JOOD, and Quartermaster. I am a Junior Officer of the Deck.

The watches in the Communications office were awfully interesting, and I am going to try to spend some of my spare time down there. Besides being extremely interesting, they were also a lot of fun. For instance, one night I sat there with ear phones on my head banging away at a typewriter – no, not taking messages, but writing a letter to Ada L.., listening – no, not to code but dance music from the States, and eating toast and drinking coffee. What a life!

This new group that I am in is the best detail of the cruise. We live all together in the Junior Officers' bunk room. (There are no J.O.'s on this ship.) Big thick mattresses, real bureaus for our gear, real wash basins, easy chairs, and all the works. Oh, it's wonderful. As I told you, we stand watches on the bridge, and besides that have four lectures a day on tactics, the duties of an Officer of the Deck etc.

I am writing this letter in the Log offices, an empty stateroom in "Officers' Country" that they turned over to us. The typewriter belongs to one of the other boys on the staff. We are putting out a weekly paper in conjunction with the regular ship's paper, or rather, just helping out the regular ship's paper.

The sea has been fairly calm so far, and the weather perfect. I only hope it lasts. Surprisingly few of the Youngsters have been sick.

Even the food seems to be better than we had on the Youngster cruise.

The one big thing that I have minded is the loss of sleep. Standing watches at night, then having to keep going at top speed all day takes it out of a guy. For instance, tonight I have the 0400-0800 (or rather tomorrow morning). Which means that I will have to get up at 0300. At any rate, I should see a marvelous sunrise tomorrow morning. (Here's hoping that the good weather lasts until then, at least.)

On the Communication watches, we had a regular course mapped out for us, reading a lot of dope in "Communications Instructions" etc. and practicing the code. The last half hour of the watch we had a drill message (each watch); the ships would take turns sending it, and Midshipmen would carry out the whole procedure. The big trouble in receiving seemed to be not my own ability which, although not too much, was adequate, but the sloppy sending of the Midshipmen - including myself. But it was fun while it lasted.

There is not a lot more dope for me to give you. The <u>Texas</u> is about 15 miles on our port quarter, and the New York about 15 miles on the other side. Why, I do not know - some sort of extended order no doubt.

I suppose George is home by now. How did he enjoy his first year at college? Muchly, but not too muchly, I hope.

Sunday - 12 June 1938

Hello again,

I didn't get my sunrise. It was soupy and has been so more or less ever since. Now we are heading into what may turn out to be a really heavy sea. The old tub is rolling and pitching around as though it were a row boat instead of a 30,000 ton battleship. But I am a better "sailor" than I used to be and hardly notice it.

Mike Wallace, Tex and another man and I have been playing bridge here in the bunk room. The last couple of days have been a lot easier - lots of sleep. As a result, right now I feel pretty chipper.

At this point we are a good deal better than halfway along on the first leg. By all reckoning we should get in on Friday - a day early, I hope.

My next detail is "Nav", which I shall have at sea from Le Havre to Copenhagen and from Copenhagen to Portsmouth. I'm afraid that it will turn out to be pretty much of a jonah, for we have to get two sets of star sights - one both in the evening twilight and morning twilight. When we get north there will be only about two hours between the two - the first at 11:00 P.M., the next at 0100. Which all points to very, very little sleep.

Yesterday we had the regular Saturday morning "Skippers Inspection," both of personnel and ship. It lasted all morning and got to be just the least bit tiresome. And did this old wagon ever gleam for that inspection; a hospital ward would be a shambles in comparison. Next Saturday we will be in port, so there will be no standing in ranks for an hour and a half anyway.

I had the 2000 - 2400 watch last night and have the 18 - 20 dog watch tonight; so, unless they turn the clocks ahead again (as they probably will), I will get a full night's sleep. Right now we are in zone plus 2, two hours this side of the Greenwich zone. It's now 1000 A.M. here so it is 0700 in Binghamton.

My duties on the bridge have been primarily to keep our correct distance from the other ships with a stadimeter – a small hand range finder. Aside from that there is not much to do.

The cruise so far has not been too bad, but I would much rather be back in "God's Country".

There is not much more to write now except (I just remembered) I am on a five inch gun as gun captain (plug man). I wish I were in a turret, but no soup.

One of the boys came in just now and said that it is raining cats and dogs and the wind is reaching gale proportions. Maybe we will have a real one!!!!!

       Much love to all
       Scottie

Thursday 16 June 1938

Dear Family,

There is only time to write a note. I hope that when we finally get into port I will be able to get caught up and make up for this scrimpy letter.

My duties after the O.O.D. detail were as Division Officer – the head man in my Division – and I have not had time to turn around and think since. There have been a million and one things to do – and then some. And to top it all, getting my whole part of the ship ready for an inspection by the Admiral tomorrow.

It is quite an honor to be picked as a Division Officer – it is the second highest ranking Midshipman job on the ship.

We are in the channel now. Anchor off Le Havre tomorrow at 0900. Dock Saturday.

The mail goes out tomorrow.

Much, much love from your very harassed son,
Scottie

Friday, 17 June 1938

Dear Family,

Having just mailed the other letter, I have suddenly found time to write another and I'll try to get partially caught up.

Last Tuesday, the details shifted and, for some unknown reason, our Commissioned Division Officer picked me to take charge of the Division; and, as a result, it has been rough going for this feller ever since. The paper work entailed in getting everybody squared away for liberty and leave has been enormous, and it's not all over yet, but anyway no casualties so far. Then getting the whole of my part of the ship squared away and spotless for inspection has been quite a task.

At present we are at anchor about five miles off the Le Havre lightship – about 15 miles from Le Havre. We go in tomorrow morning at six; liberty begins at 1300.

No mail has come aboard yet. It is a matter of speculation as to whether we get any until tomorrow, but here's hoping for a speedy delivery.

I think I told you that I was a gun captain – of gun #14, a 5" broadside gun – same thing I was on before. I'm the one who has charge of the entire gun crew and work the breech. It is quite a responsibility, but should be fun.

We had some really rough weather for a while, but the last two or three days have been fine – smooth sea, lots of sun (though I didn't get much of it), and generally excellent cruising weather.

Our Division Officer is Mr. Ross, a "j.g." from the "Bull" department. He is really a fine fellow, especially in letting us take entire charge of things. I only hope that my work has satisfied him. I go on second leave and so will probably have lots of time during the first four days to write letters. So I'll quit for the present to continue this later.

Same day

The lull has continued and all goes well.

My next detail is "Nav". I hope I can do well with it; at least I shall try.

Don't know whether you know the ship's routine or not, so here it is:

0530 – reveille

```
0600 - turn to (work, cleaning etc.
0730 - breakfast
0800 - turn to
0945 - lecture
1030 - general quarters (gunnery drill)
1130 - knock off work
1200 - chow
1300 - turn to
1430 - lecture
1530 - knock off
1530 - 1730 - recreation
1730 - chow
1900 - "hammocks" (set up beds etc.)
---- - movies
---- - taps (immediately after movies)
```
This applies to general deck force. O.O.D. detail has a lot more lectures. The lectures are on Seamanship and Ordnance.

Saturday

The lull did not last. If it's not one thing, it's half a dozen others. Now it's six o'clock Saturday morning. I've been up since four-thirty. We get under way to go in, in about a minute and a half, according to schedule. Reveille was at four-thirty this morning, French "summer time." They set the clocks ahead again last night. Five hours sleep and at that it's a lot better than I did the first two-thirds of the cruise. Now we are six hours ahead of Eastern Standard time. I "dropped the sack" this morning hence my ability to write this early. Have had no breakfast yet. Don't know what time it is scheduled for.

I go on liberty at one o'clock this afternoon. Have the "duty" tomorrow - on watch.

Mail today for sure!!!!!!

I'm going to mail this ashore. The others, as you see, were mailed on board. I think they go out quicker with less delay.

Mike and I are going ashore together today. Tex has the guard. I think I told you that Tex and I are going to Paris together. We're staying at the Hotel Jena. The cost of our transportation, three nights at a hotel, and breakfast each day (though as you know a continental breakfast is pretty scrimpy) is $8.25. Not bad, I say. The franc is worth .27875 at present; so, if there is no corresponding rise in prices, we will get three times as much for our money.

Right now, I'm too sleepy to think, so I'll close this and write again tomorrow.

Much, much love to all my grand family.

Scottie

Sunday, 20 June 1938

Dear Family,

And how is everything today? Mail came aboard yesterday, but it was a very, very scrimpy one. For me, one letter from Ada L.., none from home. But the <u>Aquitania</u> docks tomorrow and the <u>Normandie</u> Tuesday, so I expect there will be a letter or two for me pretty soon.

As you know, we are in now. I had liberty yesterday and have the "duty" today. There is nothing in Le Havre – I found that out. But tomorrow should prove a good day. About eight of us are going to Rouen. We have special permission to leave the ship early in the morning, and are going to make a day of it. It's only about an hour and a quarter by train and very inexpensive. We get the "military rates" on the train – 25% of the regular far. 75% off!!!

Yesterday all we did was walk around the town, drink a bit of beer, wander some more, and then ate a splendiferous steak at Le Gross Tunnel, really a fine restaurant – said to be the best in Le Havre. It is a low ceilinged, hewn-beamed place and very, very fine. The only trouble last night was that there were too many Midshipmen and officers there – it was packed.

We are tied up at the French Line piers and, as a result (of being docked) the ship is overrun with Frenchmen all the time during visiting hours. They are generally a poor looking lot and all of them so very small in stature – hump shouldered, beaten down people. But then, the poorest part of the city lies adjacent to the dock yards.

There is a Loyalist destroyer, the one that sank that big Italian cruiser, lying here at one of the government docks. She had been bombed and is here for repair and reconditioning. Leaves very little doubt as to which way the French Government leans in the Spanish fracas.

France, for an American, is cheap this year. The franc is worth 2.78¾ and we are getting 35.5 for a dollar. Looks as though Ada L.. might get some perfume after all.

We go to Paris on Thursday morning. I'm taking enough money to eat on and not much more. Going to do some extended wandering.

Did I tell you about the Embassy Ball in Paris on the night of the 23rd? Well, I'm going, and to a dinner party before that, given by a Mrs. Dounes for Admiral and Mrs. Johnson. Ten Midshipmen are going and, by a stroke of good luck, I am one of them. It will probably be an experience well worth while.

Last night at dinner we had chateaubriand - which seemed to me to be just very, very delicious tenderloin - French fries that were really good, and bread and butter. Cost F11 33 centimes. But tomorrow we are going to gorge ourselves. There is a place in Rouen, so I'm told, that puts out one of the finest chows in Europe - fairly expensive but well worth it. We're going to try it. It is called the Hotel de la Couronne. I'm looking forward to the trip with a great deal of anticipation, for they say Rouen is the best in Normandy. I'm takin two rolls of film along.

Not being able to speak the language has turned out to be pretty much of a handicap, but we get along. There is little more to write now so I'll put this up and continue at a later time.

Wednesday

Hello, again,

Well, we went to Rouen as scheduled, and had a grand day. I suppose you would like to hear all about it. Ten of us went together, and we left the ship at about eight o'clock. The walk out to the station was pretty much of a chore, and we only just made the train. The dock yards in Le Havre are so extensive and they are full of tidal basins - which must be bridged. The bridges are not any two on the same street. Consequently our hike to the station resembled a series of figure S's. but we made the train and rode to Rouen. The country along the way was beautiful - much as nice as anything I've seen at home - fields covered with acres of poppies - growing wild of course - strange poplar trees growing straight and tall with no branching out.

The ride lasted about an hour and fifteen minutes. We had picked up a folder about Rouen and in it was mapped out an itinerary for seeing the town, so we split up and started out to follow the guide book. First came the Tour Jeanne d'Arc, which was not very impressive to look at, merely a tall old stone tower. We went in and climbed to the top. There was nothing in it of any sort - just a couple of bare stone-walled rooms with the "wall name writers" of a couple of centuries well represented. Here was where Jeanne d'Arc was tortured and held prisoner awaiting trial. We left there and went on down the Rue Jeanne d'Arc till we came to the Palais de Justice. It's an old, old building which has been there since the 15th century and is still used as a court house. For the usual franc we got one of the charwoman to open up the court rooms for us. We saw both the criminal court chambers and those of the civil court. They both were really worth seeing. They had beautiful oak ceilings – very ornate but, nevertheless, very, very nice. The medallions on the wall were of Louis XVI – dating from his time. The outside of the building was almost as interesting as the inside – 'twas studded with the queerest gargoyles, and around the eaves hovered a band of angels.

From there we headed toward Le Grosse Horloge, and under it to the cathedral – very lovely but not outstanding. From there we headed back to the other side of the main business district to find the Hotel Bourgetherould, which is now a bank, and to try to find La Couronne. We found them both. Bourgetherould is an old, old building with a very quaint inner court. You could almost see the spectres of the past as you stood in that little court yard; but, in reality, all we saw were very modern bank clerks hurrying about their business. Then we went to La Couronne to make reservations for dinner. From there, next door to a restaurant called the something-or-other for lunch. Had an omelette and it was so good that we had another; still being hungry, and not wanting to spend any more of our good French francs on rather expensive omelettes, we hiked back to the market and bought about a ton of cheese and ate that. My, but it was good. Then to a pastry shop for some pastry. My, but that was good. The market is on the spot of Jeanne's execution. From there we wandered back and into Saint Maclou, a very lovely church. Then to Saint Ouen, which is all they say it is and more – truly magnificent. From Saint Ouen, we took a street car up some hill that overlooked the city. Got a very good view, then started walking down a road looking for strawberries and cream. Why? I don't know; but we decided we must have some and thought we might find it fun to get them at some French farm house. We didn't find any – there were no farm houses. After walking what seemed miles, we gave up, walked back to the car line, and rode back to the city – tired – dead tired. The ride rested us some so we wandered down to the Seine leisurely, window shopping on the way, and stood for a while on a bridge watching the city of barges along the banks. Back to town for dinner. Ate in a little restaurant in the shadow of the Horloge. As you must have surmised, we did not go to La Couronne. It was far too expensive even when we had expected it to be fairly so. I would have liked to have gone but the other boys voted it down. I wanted to experience one of those culinary masterpieces the French are so famous for - but then I guess it was a silly idea.

So back to the station, and back to Le Havre, a long hike to the ship - and mail - two grand letters from mother, but none from Dad. S'matter Pop? Won't talk, eh?

So come yesterday. In the morning I was paged and told that my services were requested with the N.A. 10 at the Consul's Ball that evening. Their regular piano player was not available. I had the guard but was excused and went over to the New York to rehearse with them. In the afternoon went ashore with Tex and a boy name Williamson. Spent most of the afternoon looking over tweed at the Jardine establishment. Harris Tweed - the real stuff costs $13.12 for enough for a suit - I'm getting enough for a suit and am having them make me a top coat, I think. Oh, yes, and we went aboard the Normandy - my, what a ship!!!

I got along fairly well at the Ball, and had a right good time. It was quite a party.

All this has been sketchy but I'm trying to keep a note book with all the details and will have many a story to tell when I get home. I'm going to close this off now in hopes of catching the Normandy mail before it closes. I go to Paris tomorrow.

Much, much love to all,
Scottie

Hotel du Louvre

Paris, Sunday, 26 June 1938

Dear Family,

So our Paris excursion is practically over, and tonight we go back to the ship. Tomorrow we sail.

It has been a grand leave but pretty strenuous. At the party which, by the way, was pretty fine, I met an American girl living here in Paris. She took me under her wing, so to speak, and with a bunch of other Midshipmen and her friends, we had quite a fine time at the Embassy, and yesterday swimming at the Racing Club, at cocktail parties, etc.

There have been a lot of parties and consequently it has been a very cheap and very enjoyable leave.

I'm just back from four hours at the Louvre and am dead tired. There is really so much that I wanted to see and so little that I could in that great big place; but I saw all my favorites again - renewed acquaintances, so to speak, and made a few new ones.

How goes everything at home? It's just a little more than two months before I shall be seeing my family again, and the time is passing so slowly.

I wish I had a thousand dollars to spend in the Parisian stores - everything is so lovely. I saw a hand-done lace (I guess) blouse that was the most magnificent thing of its kind I have ever seen. Went into an art store and looked at etchings. My, but some of them made my fingers itch to grab them and run. And, of course, perfume and gloves are grand.

Tex has come to get me to go for a stroll - I wanted to get a note off because it will probably be the last until Copenhagen, since we are sailing early in the morning.

Love to all,
Scottie

Friday, 1 July 1938

Dear Family,

I've been a long time starting this letter, and heaven only knows how long it will be before I'll have to stop again. You see, this part of the cruise for me is devoted to Navigation, and it seems that the navigator (at least the student) is a busy person day and night.

I knew – I got just this far and we had a fire drill, not navigating that time certainly, but just as much an interruption. Right now we are at anchor somewhere near the entrance to the Kattegat – exactly (if you're interested), in Lat. 57-37.5 N. and Long. 1043.5 E. We anchored here last night, went for a bit of a jaunt this morning to give the Midshipmen O.O.D's. a workout, and are now back and at anchor until Sunday at least. We go into Copenhagen on Tuesday.

So much has happened since I last wrote, that it is going to be difficult to know where to start – that is, so much has happened in the way of work, and I've been in such a fog that I don't know what I've told you and what I have not. Nothing exciting has happened since we left Le Havre.

So, let's see. In Paris – we arrived at about noon on Thursday, a week ago yesterday – took a special train up from Le Havre, transferred to hotel by bus, the Hotel du Louvre, as you know, directly at the opposite end of the Avenue de Opera from the Opera, and right across from the Louvre Gardens and the Palace. That afternoon Tex, Mark Lowe, and I went out to the "The Cite Universital" – Tex and Mark were looking for dates for the Embassy Ball that evening. We had quite a time finding what we were looking for, the United States House, where the American students at the Sorbonne live, and in the process saw most of Paris which lies on the left bank of the Seine. First we went out to the Sorbonne which is almost at the exactly wrong end of Paris, but finally we got to where we wanted to go, and Tex and Mark got themselves a couple of American girls. We went all through the buildings out there. They have houses for thirty-nine different nations, and it is quite something to see. I left the boys and got back to town to get dressed for the dinner party. Then John Harper and I taxied out to Mrs. Dounes – way up past the Etoile. The dinner party was grand. We all had dates, and, for some unknown reason, I got hooked up with the "Queen of the Ball", so to speak, an American girl, living in Paris and quite definitely a "stunner". She was a good sort although a little reserved, but after she warmed up a bit and got rid of her shell, she became a right good sort. We went to the Embassy Ball, which was right much fun. It lasted until about four-thirty, from all accounts; but six of us left about two-thirty, got a bite to eat, took the girls home, and then went back to the hotel.

The next day, we went over to Notre Dame and wandered around a bit. After we got back we went window shopping. Then, out to the home of the girl of the previous evening for cocktails, and from there on to a party at Le Triomph, the largest café on the Champs Elysee. It was given by the owner for First Class Midshipmen. Then to the Follies, and to bed. On Saturday we spent most of the day swimming at the Racing Club, the most exclusive in Paris, if you please. Then back to wander around, see the sights, and eat. In the evening we went slumming down by the Bastille – then out to Montmartre. The week, as I told you, was a festival week in Paris, and in Montmartre they were having a regular Mardi Gras – dancing in the streets, blocking traffic for miles and generally having a big time. We just circulated from one street to another, watching. My, but it was fun.

Sunday we spent most of our time at the Louvre. I enjoyed it immensely – getting a lot more out of it than I did two years ago. Sunday evening we returned to the ship after a good leave, and Monday we sailed. My impression of France has done an about-face. Everyone in France seemed to want to go out of his way to be helpful; no one tried to take us in when we went shopping (or rather "window shopping"). As a whole, the stay in Paris was a great success.

There is much more to tell, but let's let it wait until September.

Now for what has happened at sea since we left Le Havre. As you have already been told, this middle third of the cruise, I am a Navigator. One third of the First Class take Navigation, each for a third of the cruise. Two of the barbettes (dismantled turret rooms) are given over to the "Nav" detail. In the barbettes are desks etc. where we can work, and in them we sleep and practically live.

The "Nav" started out to be pretty much of a hectic time but now there is practically nothing to do. Since we are anchored there are no positions to compute, and, since the weather has been mainly overcast, there is practically nothing to do except to listen to lectures and keep up our notebooks as best we can, taking an occasional sun sight and making computation for practice.

At sea, however, it is an entirely different proposition. We have star sights both evening and morning, a morning sun line, a noon sight, and an afternoon sight, computation of time of sunrise and sunset, compass errors to calculate, three position reports to hand in, and lectures to boot. Average about three scattered hours of sleep out of twenty-four.

From now on, however, no matter what they throw at us, it won't be so bad because now we all know the ropes and have become accustomed to the work. That is half the battle won.

Today, a German pocket battleship (I haven't yet been able to find out it's name) hove into sight and there was much bustle and storm while we exchanged honors – much firing of guns and playing of bands and the like. It all seems just a little silly to me, but it's been done for centuries and probably will continue for many more.

The mail delivery in Le Havre was poor, and for the last six days no mail came aboard. As a result only two letters arrived. I sure was mighty glad to get them, and am keeping my fingers crossed for a big mail when we go into Copenhagen on Tuesday.

More Later

Not much has happened today except that we got under way about nine this morning and steamed down the Kattegat to about 35 miles from Copenhagen. Now we are at anchor again until early Tuesday morning.

There was quite a flurry aboard this afternoon when it was reported that King Christian of Denmark was to pass by in his yacht – all sorts of preparations to render honors – and then – no King.

I don't know of much dope to give you. The sea around us is full of those funny fishing boats – power boats, all with the inevitable ineffectual sail. We've seen several war vessels of different nationalities, some in the distance, a German and two English close aboard. It is cool here where we are all the time, and at night downright cold. At the movies it is uncomfortable even with a sweater.

I've no idea what I'll do in Copenhagen – probably spend most of the time swimming. There are some nice beaches not far from the city, and one can kill two birds with one stone – see a little of the Danish country side and get in a swim at the same time.

The possibility that some mail may be sent out tomorrow makes me inclined to close this letter now. I'll start a fresh tomorrow if Navigation continues in a lull – it has been so easy for the last couple of days.

        Much, much love to all of my grand family,
          Scottie

Monday, 11 July 1938

Dear Family,

Time slips by, and day after day goes past without my having a chance to even start a letter. Now I'm grabbing a lull in the routine and will try to make a dent in what I have to tell since last I wrote. Now, by the way, we are somewhere near the mouth of the English Channel on our way to Portsmouth. We have been under way since Saturday. Where did I leave off in the last letter? Somewhere in the Kattegat was it not? At anchor off Helsingør? Well, the next day, I think it was, or, at any rate, on Tuesday, we got under way in the rain – and a mighty cold rain – and went in to Copenhagen. I had the piloting watch from 3:00 A.M. (the time we got underway) until 6:00, so you see I didn't have a whole lot of sleep before the first days of liberty. I had signed up for a local forenoon tour of the city, and Tex and I were among those who were allotted to make it the first day. It was supposed to start at eight o'clock, and at eight o'clock we were still steaming merrily down the bay. We finally came to anchor about nine, and it was eleven o'clock before we finally got ashore. Since the tour ended at one, regardless of what time it started, you can see that we were gypped out of the dollar we paid. However, we did get some idea of the city – saw the various royal homes, the Houses of Parliament etc. – and finally ended up in the Karlsburg Brewery, which seems to account for half of Copenhagen's biggest industry; the other half is the Tuberg Brewery. They took us through the plant, let us sample the wares, and then took us back to town and dropped us. We spent the rest of the day wandering around, eating a big juicy steak, and then going to the Tivoli, an amusement park right smack in the center of Copenhagen and really a beautiful place. As I think I told you [on postcard], it is Coney Island without any of the unpleasantness of Coney – a huge park full of trees, peaceful and yet busy and gay. It has several restaurants, beer gardens, concessions of all sorts – roller coaster and all the other rides which you might expect. The best way to express it is to say that it is a combination of Coney Island, the Steel Pier at Atlantic City (as I imagine it) and Recreation Park in Binghamton. There is a free pantomime theater (open air), a free symphony concert, a free movie, free vaudeville, each following the other in succession. As one show is over, all you have to do is move on to the next and you spend a very, very cheap and interesting evening.

The next day I stayed aboard ship until time to go out to Klampenborg to the Danish Minister's Garden Party. We went out on a special train, 435 of us. My, but it was a crowded party. The Minister's wife had provided for two sandwiches apiece for each Midshipman. What she planned on for her other guests, I do not know. Naturally the chow ran out in half an hour and she was frantically telephoning all over town for sandwiches.

At the party, I met a Mr. Reames, the American Consul. Tex and I spent most of the afternoon talking to him. He was an awfully interesting chap. Had just been transferred from Johannesburg. Had a charming wife whom we met at the party and saw again when we went out to his place later in the evening.

The next day George Ghesquiere and I went ashore, sent some post cards, drank a bottle of beer, window shopped, stopped at the "strawberry celler" for a huge dish of strawberries topped with a big hunk of vanilla ice cream, and came back to the ship. The last day, I had the guard. Tex and I were the Night Midshipman Shore Patrol Officers, our duties being to patrol the Tivoli and see to it that no Midshipman got into trouble. Naturally we found no trouble except for ourselves. Almost as soon as we hit shore, it started to rain; and let me tell you, when it rains in Denmark, it really rains. It was as though someone had just upended Boulder Dam, and it continued without stopping except for brief intervals until one o'clock in the morning. It was a couple of wet Midshipmen that came aboard the Wyo about two Saturday morning.

Copenhagen is a fine city. I'd like to spend a month there sometime if I had lots of money, for it is expensive. However, I spent three liberties in it and five dollars, which is not bad. Everything in the stores, however, is expensive, much more so than the equivalent in the States. I suppose the reason for that is that almost everything is imported. Consequently I didn't buy anything and saved my money.

Do you know, I spent four days in the town and heard only one or two auto horns in all that time, and those because I was listening for them; saw only a couple policemen, and I was looking for them; saw a million and one bicycles, and was trying not to see them. Everybody rides a bicycle – from the Mayor on down. Copenhagen has a population of something like 900,000 and I think it has 700,000 bikes registered. The city was full of the same blond hair and blue eyes that we saw in Sweden. One would almost think that it was typical of the Scandinavian countries, wouldn't one?

There was a British cruiser and a division of destroyers in while we were. Tex and I went aboard the cruiser for a little while. It was a fairly nice ship, and had some really mean looking anti-aircraft guns.

The "Nav" has been tough since we left Copenhagen. To make up for the inactivity of the last two or three days before we got in, we had star sights on Saturday night. Got to bed at about two. Up at six - morning sun sight. Local apparent noon sight for latitude, and then just as we had turned in our 1200 position, we were handed a "P-Work" which lasted until three. Then afternoon sights, 2000 position to figure out, lectures, and finally secured about ten in the evening. Nice day, eh?

Tuesday

Hello, again,

We are very much in the channel now. In fact, almost out of it on the other side. It has been an easy day today - cloudy all day, and not a chance for a sight. We had another "P-Work", but it was easy and I got a 3.8 out of it. I spent most of the afternoon translating the instructions for the use of a Zeiss camera which Mr. Cowe, one of our "Nav" instructor's, bought. It is all done now. My lecture for tomorrow is prepared - each of us has to deliver a lecture to the rest of the class sometime during the period we are taking "Nav". Mine is scheduled for tomorrow and is re the Naval Observatory.

Wednesday

Since yesterday, the Navigators have had another bad day. The weather suddenly took a turn for the worse, which, actually, in the ordinary sense, means it decided to clear up. As a result we had evening and morning star sights again. It sure is funny how much one can learn to like cloudy weather - even rain, snow, hail. Now, however, we are anchored somewhere down the English coast from Portsmouth. We go in Friday. Whether we stay here until then is highly problematical.

The next leg of the cruise I have Engineering. We leave Portsmouth on the 23rd, I believe, and get into Norfolk on the 6th. Then Short Range Battle Practice, New York, and finally Annapolis. They are starting to intensify the gun drills already. Today, for instance, we had drill in the morning and afternoon. Later this afternoon we held an Athletic Field Day with all sorts of three-legged, one-legged potato races etc. The navigators didn't have much of a chance to take part, but I saw some of the fun. I'm looking forward to the mail in Portsmouth. It has been so good to hear from home. I know my letters have not been up to Youngster cruise par, but I have been a whole lot busier on this cruise. I'm glad I have, for it makes the time pass so much faster. But I haven't had the chance to write as much as I'd like.

Much love to all,
Scottie

On Westminster Bridge, Second Cruise, 1938.

Tuesday, 19 July 1938

Dear Family,

Since I last wrote I have been to London and returned. My leave is not up until this evening, but Tex and I decided to come back yesterday. We had a good time in London, but were tired and the ship seemed pretty good to us, so here I am.

We left on Saturday - got into Portsmouth Friday. When we got into Waterloo Station, we had no idea where we were going to stay or what we were going to do, but luckily a man stopped us inquiring after a couple of Midshipmen whom he was trying to find, and, since he couldn't find them, he took us under his wing, taxied us all over London looking for a cheap but good hotel, and finally ended up by taking us to the Park Lane - probably the most exclusive of all in London. He took us around to the back to the Annex and got us rooms for about two dollars a night. So we stayed at the famous Park Lane for as cheap a price as we could anywhere.

Nothing really exciting happened during our stay in London, but we did meet up with some funny characters, and had a wonderful evening in Hyde Park - it really was a scream. Some old man was speaking on something or other on one of the soap boxes, and he had a larger crowd than any of the others, principally because he took their riding better than any of the others. Well, to make a long story short, we got involved in a discussion with a cockney Londoner, a Jew, and the son of one of the Royal Air Force stationed in India. What it started out about, I really don't remember, but the main point of argument was the class and race distinction in the United States, and the treatment of the Jews by Hitler, and the attitude toward Jews in England and the United States. In no time at all we had a bigger crowd than any of the others, and I think I can safely say that we (Tex and I) won a fine verbal victory.

On Sunday we saw a part of the afternoon service at St. Pauls.

Aside from that, I really cannot think of a thing that we did definitely. We walked and walked and saw an awful lot of London, got a much broader and more intelligent impression of the city than last time, but did very, very little sightseeing as such. We did see a huge mass meeting in Trafalger Square on Sunday afternoon. I think I mentioned it on George's card. Our favorite stunt was to get on a bus, pay the man two-pence, and ride as far as we could go, take another bus and come back a different way. They all end up in Picadilly or Trafalger Square. Yesterday afternoon we sat in Green Park for a couple of hours, just watching the English men and women go by. Then it was that we decided that we had spent as much money as we cared to and that we would hop a train and come home. One thing, I think that we know every Lyons Tea Shop within a radius of two miles of the hotel – they are the cheapest restaurants in England and were our exclusive eating places.

Saturday, we start back to the States. I think we get into Norfolk a couple of days early, but it may just be bad dope. Your letters have been grand, and I was so glad to get them. I shall write again before we leave, but the next mail for the States closes this afternoon, and I'm going to close this now.

Much love to all,
Scottie

The typing, spelling and grammar are horrible I know – You'll forgive me I hope.

Thursday, 21 July 1938

Dear Family,

Yesterday, I received Mother's last letter and was very, very glad to get it. You are right, it came in the last mail before we get back to the States. We sail Saturday morning bright and early, and will arrive in Norfolk on the fourth (two days early).

Nothing has happened since I last wrote – have not even been ashore. However, there is this one thing of interest. Tomorrow the <u>Wyoming</u> is giving a reception, and great have been the preparations therefor. It is to be just about the biggest thing of its kind ever given aboard a Navy ship and you should see how this wagon has been transformed. There are veritably thousands of dollars worth of flowers aboard her. The top of the number two barbette has been made into a huge pond with a moss-and-flowers-covered island in the center. Water runs from a waterfall into it on one side, and out into a "wishing well" on the other. Way forward in the bow of the ship is a miniature Niagara Falls, and a little further aft a replica of Tower Bridge. On one side of the forward turret is painted the American Eagle, on the other the British Arms. The whole ship is awninged over and Flag draped. You can't believe what indignities this poor old battleship has been subjected to to make it into as purty a garden as you will ever see. I have been helping with the decorations and am on the reception committee. I can't begin to describe it all, so will keep it until I see you.

Got a letter from Ada L.. at the same time I received Mother's last. She and her father and mother, an aunt and uncle, and Jean Riley, A.E.'s best friend, are sailing from Montreal on the 25th for one of those 10 day Nova Scotia, Labrador cruises. I suppose it is all right – but Labrador!!! They get back to Montreal on the 5th and are going to do a bit of auto touring before coming home. Had hoped for Ada L.. to meet me in New York, but now I don't know. I'll have fun anyway. Felice and Jud will be there, and probably Charlie Ridgway, who, for all his trouble, still seems a pretty good egg and was awfully nice to me.

This letter is the last from European waters – the last mail closes tomorrow and will arrive in New York on the 1st of

August. You will get it on the 2nd, two days before I get into
Norfolk. Once back in the States and Battle Practice out of the
way, the time will pass quickly enough for me. The cruise now is
just a little over a month from finis.

       Much, much love to all,
        Scottie

Friday, 29 July 1938

Dear Family,

It's been a long time since I've written a letter home, and there has really been no reason to, since we are still at sea even though we were scheduled to arrive in Norfolk yesterday.

Four days out of Portsmouth, the New York broke her port shaft putting the entire port engine room out of commission until she can go into drydock. As a result, we had to cut our speed almost in half - from 14 knots to about seven and a half. We limped along at that slow speed for days, and finally on Tuesday we were detached from the squadron - left the New York and the Texas, and speeded up. Now we are about 800 miles out of Norfolk and expect to go into the Navy Yard about five o'clock Sunday morning.

Sunday we fuel, load stores, and pick up mail for the three ships - go back out to the Southern Drill Grounds on Monday - rendezvous with the Texas, which will have also left the New York. Tuesday the Wyoming fires battle practice, Wednesday, the Texas, and Thursday the New York - if she gets there by that time. Then the Wyo and Texas leave immediately from the Roads for New York City. The New York goes into drydock. We'll be in New York as scheduled. Leave the 17th, go back to Norfolk. We stay there five days, and then back to Annapolis. The Admiral shifts his flag to the Wyo when we rendezvous with the New York off the capes - and that's the dope.

Since leaving Portsmouth I've been Engineering. Right now I am standing my last watch - "Juice" watch in the Gyro room. The quizzes and questionnaires are over and there is nothing to do - for the first time since I left England.

Tomorrow, all of us who took "Nav" the second set shift back to "Nav" because we got so little of it the first time - so they claim. Personally, I had plenty.

I stood 21 in "Nav" for my set which was not so hot. The Engineering standings are not computed yet but I stood 3 for the quiz with a 3.40. The quiz has the heaviest weight in the final standing. There are about 75 in a group. It's not so much that I'm proud of the standing, but I worked like the dickens, and it is gratifying to know that hard work does sometimes bring results.

It must be really hot on shore, for out here it's not at all comfortable. We have had glorious weather all the way over, but for the last week it has been hot as blazes. I've been sleeping top side on the boat deck, and every night we have run into rain squalls – and every night I've got wet. It only rains for a few minutes though and all the time it's raining you can see the stars behind you and ahead of you. During the day there has been no rain – just cloudless sky and a blazing sun.

There is not much more dope to put out. I'm pretty sick of seeing nothing but water everywhere – haven't even seen another ship though they say we have passed some.

We have been having gun drill twice a day now since leaving England, and my crew, I hope, is just about set – I do so hope for an "E". To get it, we have to put out eight shots in an aggregate time of 44 seconds. My loading crew can load fast enough and with time to spare, if my pointers and trainers can only make the hits – for all eight shots must be hits. Well, Tuesday will tell the story.

No more now – will wire when we arrive in Norfolk.

       Much love to all,
         Scottie

Sunday, 31 July 1938

Dear Family,

Well, it won't be long now before I can bid this old crate goodby – and will be with my family once again.

The New York trip proved very successful – principally because I did decide to go to Baltimore and got out of New York. I went back out to Aunt May's after I called home, to leave a note – for lack of anything else to do, and found her there. She had been out when I called. She was all alone, the boys being out of town and Barbara in Santo Domingo. I spent the day with her, went down town to a movie all alone when she had some callers, and then went back about nine for some supper and to say goodby.

Ada L.. was fine – as usual, and of course I had a grand time in Baltimore. I expect that I shall be home on Sunday – a week from today, or at the latest Monday. I'll wire you exactly when.

Norfolk has been outdoing itself showing the Midshipmen a good time. Day before yesterday, we all went to private dinner parties – every blasted Midshipman on the ship except the duty section. We have free access to all the bathing beaches at Virginia Beach, and generally have the run of the town. Yesterday two other boys and I went out to the Surf Club and spent the day swimming – had a grand time and then came into town and went to a movie.

There is no other news except that I am anxious to get off the cruise. I'm told that I stood 22 on the ship for the cruise, and will be virtually assured of two stripes this year. I hope it is good dope.

> Lots of love to all,
> Scottie

VII
FIRST CLASS YEAR
1938 – 1939

ROBERT SCOTT WHITMAN JR.

Annapolis, 26 September 1938

Dear Family,

And so beings the last year at the Naval Academy – with no excitement and only feelings of relief that it is to be the last. The first news is that I am very sorry to say that I am sporting only one stripe instead of the two that I was sure that I was going to get. Evidently the officer that told me that I was getting two didn't know what he was talking about. It was quite a disappointment to me, but I'm sure that I will survive. [Hospital escapade was to blame.]

Tex has his three, as was predicted, and is our Company Commander. I am assistant Platoon Commander of the First Platoon – not a very exciting nor important job.

The room number is 1317, as I thought. It is rather a nice room, looking out over the bay. Tex and I each have a Plebe, and one utility man for the two of us. Mine is from Kingston, New York – his name is Turvo. I call him "Topsy".

Everything is squared away and has been for some time. It's not hard to get back into the swing after doing it so many times. Classes start tomorrow and the grind of the last stretch begins.

Tex and Sally were in Baltimore at the D..... over Thursday night. I knew that Tex was coming and, evidently, so did Sally for she called us and asked if we had room for her. We made it although it rather filled the house to overflowing. So Thursday evening we had a big time doing the town.

Tex bought a car to go home in – a 1932 Lincoln, a big seven passenger limousine. What an ark – about as long as a city block, and really a nice car except that, of course, it eats all sorts of gas. So we rode around in it and felt like a bunch of gangsters.

Sally and Ada L.. came down for the game yesterday; Sally stayed on and is still here; Ada L.. went home about nine last evening.

The game was very, very dull – the weather was more suited for swimming than watching a football game. The papers call the victory very satisfactory. Personally, I was not very impressed with the team's showing. I suppose that the heat took a lot out of them, but they will have to play a lot better ball to get by some of the big teams we play.

There is no longer a Pep Committee. It's title now is the "Stunt Committee" – a part of a larger committee known as the Regimental Activities Committee. I think that I am to be the chairman of the big committee, but am not sure, since the confirmation of the appointment by the Class President has not yet come through from the Executive Department.

That is about all the news for now, and I shall close with lots of love,

        Scottie

ROBERT SCOTT WHITMAN JR.

Annapolis, 3 October 1938

Dear Family,

Both of your grand letters arrived, and it is needless to say that I was overjoyed to receive them. I'm glad that Mother has the chance to get out, and that Dad is able to take care of Gram. Good for you, Pop. I'm proud of you.

The first week passed uneventfully. The academics have not proved overtasking as yet, and I have had time to get things squared away and the ball rolling on the Log and with the Pep work. We held a rally last Friday evening before the V.M.I. game, and the consensus of opinion is that it was the best rally that has taken place in Bancroft since we have been here. Maybe it did some good, for the V.M.I. club was supposed to be really hot, and I guess you have read in the papers about the result of the game. I am the Editor of the Log which comes out on the 21st. We are planning to feature the new construction in the Yard. I guess I told you that they are spending seven and a half million dollars building a new laundry building, and a dispensary, are doubling the officer housing on the reservation, rebuilding the mess hall – sound proofing it etc. – building a new museum, and enlarging the chapel.

The first out-of-town trip with the Pep Committee is on the 15th when we go to New Haven for the Yale game. We leave Friday night, as far as I can make out, and come back with the Regiment on Saturday evening.

Sunday Tex and I went out to Mr. Ford's for coffee and cake (as it turned out). He is one of the few really nice Naval officers I know, has a lovely wife and two very pretty little girls, the nicest mannered little tikes I have ever seen. We had a right good time chewing the fat, and I am in hopes that I can go out there again.

The first Log comes out on the fifteenth, and your subscription has already gone in. So you may expect it from now on. Don't know whether you received the Plebe Log or not – came out published by the Plebes last Friday evening, and was not particularly good.

In "Bull", we are studying modern European history, just as everybody in the world is, except that we have a text besides the newspapers. Starts with the French Revolution, as usual, and carried up to the present. In Seamanship we are hard at it trying to get the rudiments of Military Law – and it is extremely interesting to me. Everything is much the same as last year with these two exceptions.

I am the sixth ranking one striper in the Regiment, which means if I had stood six numbers higher, I should have had two instead of one, so I feel a little better than I did.

I am glad that George is comfortably settled, and hope that he will find time, now that he is well started, to drop me a line. Got a letter from Jud. He is at M.I.T. and seems very well satisfied – is studying Chemical Engineering, the logical choice, of course, since he had two years of pre-med at Duke.

I am delighted that Dad has fully decided to come to the Army-Navy game this year. I only hope that we can win for him. Shouldn't be surprised if we had a good team, but some of the opposition looks awfully strong.

Ada E........ is in the middle of rushing just now and naturally has very little time for the Naval Academy, but that will be over in a little while, I hope.

So that's the news. Thank you for your letters, and the best of luck to you.

Much, much love
Scottie

ROBERT SCOTT WHITMAN JR.

Annapolis, 22 October 1938

Dear Family,

I guess by this time you have given up all hope of ever getting a letter from me, but it has been a hectic two weeks, and the times that I usually have for letter writing have been filled up with Log, card stunts, and pep rallies. Please forgive my laxity, and chalk it up to the busiest two weeks I believe I have ever put in.

I'm just back from Baltimore. The game was very exciting, and quite a disappointment, all in one. Navy should have won by a fairly large score but, as usual, did not. I don't know what is wrong with Navy football teams, but they sure don't win the ball games.

The stunts went off in fine style, and got quite a large round of applause.

Since it has been so long since I have written, I suppose it is in order to start at the beginning, and tell you about the Yale game. We left for Yale about noon on Friday – the Stunt Committee that is. The cards were delivered to us in Baltimore and we sorted them out on the train, bradded them together, and were all set to tack them up by the time we got to New York. Got to New Haven about six in the evening, and went to the Taft hotel. Did absolutely nothing that evening but walk around. Went out to the stadium in the morning, tacked up the cards, and waited for game time. The stunts went off quite as well as they did last week. We came back with the Regiment.

The past week, I have been busy getting out my issue of the Log which you will have seen by the time you get this. I'm not entirely satisfied with it, but, at that, it turned out better than I thought it would. How's to write your candid opinion? Naturally, I have little or no time to study, and will be very interested to see what has happened. I guess I'm getting along all right, but I really couldn't be sure.

Saw Ada E....... for the first time in more than two weeks for about an hour today. Haven't any idea when she will be down, probably another month.

We go to Philadelphia next week; maybe this time Navy can win a game. Here's hoping at least.

This is a very sketchy and poorly constructed letter – I'm dead tired, and should have put it off until tomorrow, but there is no telling what would have come up had I waited, so please make allowances.

        Much, much love to all,
           Scottie

Annapolis, 23 October 1938

Dear Family,

The Army-Navy applications are out, and the closing date for tickets is Saturday of this week.

I'm too flat to swing $4.40 apiece for tickets at this point, and will have to have money to get them. The reason they have rushed so is that in past years Midshipmen have tried to make a racket out of the tickets. This year they are not giving them time. I got my application about three minutes ago.

That's the dope. Much love to all,
Scottie

Taps has sounded.

"Up on the Gun, Down on the Whistle"
as Chairman of the Activities (Pep) Committee, 1938.

ROBERT SCOTT WHITMAN JR.

Annapolis, 25 October 1938

Dear Family,

Mother's letter arrived today with a very worthy reproach in it. I have already written (on Saturday) and there is little enough news now, but since I am on watch and have a little time, it might be in order to "write while I can".

It's off to Philadelphia this weekend, and Baltimore the following. Then the card stunts for this year are finished.

I hope you received my hurried Sunday night note. I have talked with Commander Gilmore, the Treasurer of the Athletic Association, and he has promised me good tickets for Dad. The only draw back is getting the money to pay for them before Saturday. Commander Gilmore, who is retired now, is definitely a good egg. I naturally have had a lot to do with him with the stunt work, and we are the best of friends. So I expect that he will make his promise good and give me really good tickets.

Right now, we are working on an idea for a pep meeting to end all pep meetings for the Army game. It probably will turn out a dud, so I'm not going to say any more about it now - the papers will be full of it if it works out.

George hasn't written yet, and I have no idea where to write him - his address has been lost somewhere in the mess of stuff in my belongings. I probably wouldn't have time to write even if I did know it, but it would help for future reference.

I wonder what became of Mr. Murray's letter to G.E.. you would think that it would at least be acknowledged. I have no real hopes that it will be lucrative at all, but I had hoped that it might prove a wedge by which I could get a head start on some of the rest of the college boys who will be yammering for jobs.

We are getting some good stunts lined up for the Army game - no card stunts, but there will be a good show. I sure hope that Dad's arrangements turn out O.K.

This year, since Armistice Day is a national holiday, I have the day free from after breakfast until supper formation, and will probably go to Baltimore for the day. Thanksgiving we get the same liberty, and, if I'm invited, I may get a home-cooked Thanksgiving dinner for a change at the D..... .

Once this stunt business is over, I'm going to have to buckle down and get my Log staff to work. I've been letting that slide since I got the issue out, and am badly in need of copy.

How is George getting along in his work? Does he enjoy his rooming arrangements? Will he be home on Thanksgiving and, if so, for how long?

It's been two hours since I wrote the last paragraph, and I've completely lost the drift of what I was saying. I write lousy letters, and I know it, so I'll stop.

Much, much love to all,
Scottie

ROBERT SCOTT WHITMAN JR.

Annapolis, 6 November 1938

Dear Family,

Again, I have relapsed into silence for too long a time, and I am afraid that my lack of verbosity has you wondering. It is the old story, more to do than I can take care of, but now the worst is over. The last of the card stunts for this year have been performed – in the rain at Baltimore yesterday. That they were a success seems to be assured since I have had a lot of favorable comments on them already.

You asked how we do them. The stunts are plotted out to scale on cross-section paper, and then the instruction cards are made out from these plans. The cards are then sorted out. There are four cards, or eight colors, for each seat in the section; the "gouge" cards are bradded to them and the cards tacked up in the stadium. We always have what we call a "set-up" showing before the Regiment take their seats. This week it was a shield with a block "N" imposed on it. At the half all hands unfasten their cards, take off their caps, get the first color for their seat ready, and bend down. On the gun they come up showing the first stunt. They go down again on the whistle, and come up on the gun for the second etc.

The game yesterday turned out much as everyone expected. Notre Dame has a better team, and the better team won. The rain didn't make things any too comfortable during the second half, and Ada E......., for one, left at the start of the fourth quarter, soaked to the skin.

The first two months of the academic year are almost over, and exams start next Monday afternoon. I am not afraid of them, principally because, although I do not expect that I will make any too fine a showing, there will be no disaster, I am sure. What with trying to run about three things at once and still keep studying, it has been a tough grind.

Dad's money order arrived and the tickets were ordered. I only hope that Commander Gilmore comes through with good tickets, as he said he would. I'm sure that he will though, for he is the sort that usually does what he says he will.

I shall be in Philadelphia on Friday night, and am thinking seriously of taking my fall week-end then and going out to Birdboro with Tex, Sally, and Ada E....... . As soon as you know your plans, Dad, let me know, so I'll know where and when to meet you.

This week is to be a gala and an easy week. In the first place, I have the guard on Thursday. On Friday we have a holiday and all day liberty to leave Annapolis – a First Class rate. I am going to Baltimore and go to school with Ada L.. in the morning – play in the afternoon. On Saturday Ada L.. is coming down for the week-end, her first this year. So you see we are having a big week.

From all indications the Army-Navy game should be one of the best in years, and, quite appropriately, Dad will be there. It makes me very happy to know that.

Mother, in answer to your query about the sweater – if you are sure that you can't use it, I know that Ada L.. would be tickled to death to have it. But I am awfully sorry that I busted so on the size. At least you know I would much rather you had it, but if it is really too small, it might as well be put to use.

Now that Tri Delt is through rushing and pledging its freshmen, maybe I will get a chance to see Ada L.. a little more frequently. Last night they finally slapped the button on nine girls, the pick of the campus I have no doubt, and now we can settle to a more ordered life once more. Darned if I didn't feel like a clubwoman's bachelor husband for a while.

I see that Syracuse finally broke the jinx. Bet that they are still celebrating the victory. And what will happen in New York day after tomorrow? From what we can tell down here, Mr. Dewey has an outside chance to win, and is coming closer to the inside every day. Certainly the New Deal is being set back everywhere and, from the looks of things, 1940 may mark the death of the "noble experiment".

I still have yet to hear from George. Hope that all is going smoothly for him.

There is no more news now, so I close with best of love to you, and the hope that life and luck, if not smiling, at least holds a promise or two.

       Your recalcitrant son,
       Scottie

ROBERT SCOTT WHITMAN JR.

Annapolis, 14 November 1938

Dear Family,

The first exam is over and I pray to all the powers above that the rest not be quite so strenuous nor, I'm afraid so disastrous. I did not do well. In fact, I did very poorly. That the rest of the class seem to have done just about as badly makes very little difference since I have had very, very poor daily marks to average in with the exam – 3.3 for 1st month, but a sad second month. It was "Nav" – the sort of exam which contains nothing that you do not know, but if you are hurried, you can make a million and one mistakes and all disastrous to your mark.

Tomorrow we have "Steam" which promises to be just as bad. It is a bad week in the offing, and I am spending every minute that I can on the books. The only reason that you are getting this letter is because I have to do something to clear my mind.

I am anxious to hear Dad's plans for the Army game. Is Mr. Conrad coming to the game with him? When are you coming, and what are all the plans and all the dope? I shall, as I said, be in Philadelphia Friday night. Ada L.. is coming up Friday night also.

Of course right in the middle of the hurry to get ready for exams and the fluster attendant upon taking them, we also have to put the Army-Navy <u>Log</u> together. It is to be a sixty page mag. this time – the largest ever published at the Naval Academy.

What did you think about the election results? Or did we discuss them in my last letter? By the way, as I remember, I signed my last letter "Your recalcitrant son". May I correct the closing words of that letter, ignoramus that I am? I guess I didn't know the meaning of recalcitrant. At any rate, I meant to imply that I was a very, very poor correspondent, that I knew it, and that I was sorry for it. What was it that I meant to say?

Life here has been much of the sameness for the last two months. Lots of work – busy all the time – and all pretty hectic. On Armistice Day, I went up to Baltimore and spent the day with Ada E........ . One very interesting thing happened. Chump that I am, I let Ada L.. inveigle me into going to class with her – she had two in the morning. So off we trapsed to a Political Science and an International Law class. Me and the other girls - seems, however, that it is done quite often, so I wasn't breaking precedent. As a matter of fact, it was fairly interesting and we had quite a time. Both of the professors were men, and I think that I was like an oasis in the desert for them after their having to face an all-woman class day after day; at least the International Law prof seemed to be lecturing to me and me alone.

In the afternoon we played around with Jean Lowe and her man, a graduate of Maryland University and, of all things, a Pro Ball player - baseball. He was very much O.K., and we had a lot of fun, the four of us.

I can't help but feel that you are cross with me because I have been so remiss in writing, and in a way I can't blame you, but if you could see how busy I have been this year, you would not censure me too strongly. Now that the football season is almost over, perhaps I will have a little more time to myself, and you can be sure that the letters will flow more freely.

Since it had been many, many weeks since Ada L.. had been down to the Academy, and it was quite an occasion - her coming down - I had five Plebes write to her and tell her how glad they were that she was coming. She immediately had five freshmen answer the Plebes' letters, and now she is all for fostering a romance or two - some fun. So I guess that next Sunday I am going to have to round up the Plebes; Ada L.. will bring down the freshmen, and perhaps the romances will blossom.

There is no more now, so I will say Auf Wiedersehen and close with hope that sometime soon I may hear from the grandest family in the world.

Lots of love
        Scottie

Annapolis, 17 November 1938

Dear Family,

Both letters arrived, and I sure was glad to get them. It has been a hectic week so far; but since the Navigation exam, I think I've more than held my own. Naturally I won't know until the marks are posted, but feel that I did fairly well on "Steam", Ordnance and "Juice".

Dad's plans for the Army game sound wonderful. Only one thing puzzles me. Did you realize that I won't be in Annapolis on Sunday? I'm sure that I wrote you that Tex and I are taking our week-end then – going to stay in Philly. I guess, until sometime in the wee small hours, and then drive out to Birdsboro. If Dad had planned to come to the Academy to see me specifically, I can try to cancel the week-end request and the plans and see if I can't come back with the Regiment – although I would have a comparatively short time to see him, since Sunday morning, I am not free, and I would imagine he would have to start back fairly early in the afternoon. Please straighten me out on this,

As far as plans for after the game, I hardly know what to say. I think Sally (Tex's girl) is making reservations for us somewhere and, if so, we can always make room for two more. If not – Tex just came in and said that Sal is not making reservations, so we are free to go and do what we want. I don't know where we can go for dinner, but there ought to be some places – in fact lots of places, I guess probably the best plan is to just have me see you at the game which I can do very easily since I will not be marching, and then make what plans that are to be made. The six of us will find some place to have dinner and chin and celebrate the victory.

Doctor and Mrs. D.... are going to the game – a last minute plan, Sally had a ticket for Ada E........, so it left the two I got for her free, I have an idea that they will be sitting with you two.

Are your tickets in a box? I don't know where the D..... tickets are since I had them sent to A.E., but I do know that they are on the field in a box. So that may mean that there will be eight of us at dinner – in fact I imagine, on second thought, that there will be. See what a muddle I'm in – wonder I'm not in the bug house.

Perhaps, if the D..... are not driving, you and Uncle Charlie can drive them back to Baltimore. That's all I know. If it seems feasible, I will get Sally to make reservations for us somewhere and then there will be no doubt as to where we will eat.

Drop me a line and tell me when and where you will be in Philadelphia, if at all, before you go to the stadium. I shall have my hands full probably before the game but will have a little time if I have to make it.

Oh, heck – this is certainly a poor excuse for coherency and I guess you don't know any more now than you did before you started reading. Blame it on the exams, my stupidity, or anything else. The main thing is that the knowledge that Dad is going to see the game brings me a big thrill, and I am looking forward to seeing him an awful lot.

> Much, much love to all,
> Scottie

Seamanship tomorrow
"Bull" Saturday

Annapolis, 29 November 1938

Dear Family,

Well, it was grand to see Dad, I hope he enjoyed the game. Ada L.. is nuts about him.

I'm sorry about our foul up at Kuglers - serves me right for believing them when they said that there would be plenty of room for all.

How was the trip home? My, how it did snow that night. I was pretty worried about you all driving far. Hope you didn't.

My only regret is that Mother could not come. I missed you Mom, and was thinking about you.

The marks are out - they are awful, I feel very, very badly about them, but not so much so as I would if I had had time to study and hadn't.

So begins the second two months. I'm hoping that I'll be able to do a better job this time.

It is still cold down here, but is beginning to warm up. Hope the freeze lasts tomorrow at least; then there will be no parade.

There is a new book out, Annapolis Today by Kendall Banning. If Dad will be a good boy I'll give it to him for Christmas. It's about the best of its kind I have seen.

There is no news. Of course Tex, Sally, Ada L.., and I had a grand time in Philly and got back tired and very happy after a fine week-end.

Much, much love to all,
Scottie

Annapolis, 4 December 1938

Dear Family,

Another week begins – and that means two and a half until Christmas. The time so far has gone pretty fast, but it sure is starting to lag now. No more Stunt Committee to worry about – no more pep rallies.

Mother's letter arrived day before yesterday, or was it yesterday? Yesterday, I believe. Dad sure did have a time on the way home. Was afraid he would. Only hope that the trip with all its difficulties was worth it.

Ada L.. says that her mother is talking so much about how grand Dad is that she and Doctor have been kidding her. Ada L.. sure fell like a ton of bricks too – what is the power, Pappy?

The other day in "Bull" class, they passed out mimeographed sheets with about 250 suggested topics for our First Class thesis. There is certainly a wide choice of material to pick from, and I am at a loss as to what to pick. The paper is due in the middle of January, and is the big project for this year as far as English is concerned.

Tomorrow I have Seamanship the second period, Ordnance the fourth, and a long "Steam" drill, all afternoon. In Ordnance we are studying fire control. In "Seamo", the fleet – organization, battle tactics etc. In "Steam" metallurgy, in "Bull" still the same History, in "Juice" finishing up AC, and Navigation is the same as ever.

Ada L.. and I are invited to a debut and dinner following at the Shoreham, Washington on the 23rd, and I think that Ada L.. and I will stay over in Washington at Jean Lowe's that night. I'll take the train from Washington and be home in the evening of the 24th.

When does George arrive home? And what do you suppose he would like for Christmas?

It has warmed up considerably down here since the cold spell in the middle of the week, and today, it has been a thick soup, one of the worst fogs I have seen here.

Everybody feels pretty low at this point – the Army game over, and Christmas, although just around the corner, still far enough off so that to the convicts on the Severn it seems years away. It is funny – First Class year, which should be the easiest to take as far as restrictions are concerned, seems to

be the hardest. You would think that we could resign ourselves
to almost anything when we know that we are getting out in six
months, but everybody seems to be more discontented than ever –
funny human nature – yes?

I am afraid of what you will think when you see my marks.
They are terrible and I am ashamed of them – very ashamed, but
it just goes to prove that extra-curricular activities and
scholarship don't mix for this lad. Now there will be a big
improvement – that I promise. When I arrive, put a white light
in the window, and, if all is forgiven, I will come in – two
white lights, and I will stick my hat in first on the end of a
stick to catch the volley.

Last night Tex and I went to the movies in the Yard and
enjoyed them hugely. It was a western picture with some very fine
music in it.

      Much, much love to all,
        Scottie

Annapolis, 8 December 1938

Dear Family,

Heigh Ho – and another week is almost gone. Mother's and Dad's letters arrived, and were received midst great rejoicing upon the part of your son.

The Whitmans and the D..... have evidently turned themselves into a mutual admiration society – all of which makes me very happy indeed. The D..... rave about Fawther, and Fawther raves about the D....., and Scottie sits by and beams. Hooray for us. I knew it would be so, so you see I can doubly beam – the I – told – you – so kind.

Great has been the furor down here in the past week. I think I told you that we were getting a series of inoculations that are intended to immunize us for life from the dangers of tetanus – something that is supposed to do away with such difficult times as I had that time – (remember?). About two months ago, we had our first of three shots, and day before yesterday, I had my second. To make a long story short, the shots have kicked back at about 85% of the Regiment with a vengeance, but at some much worse than others – the hospital is full to overflowing. Sick Bay is full, and some of us hardier souls who are not quite so sick are struggling along without turning in, with very, very sore arms and varying degrees of fever. Tex is in the hospital along with the rest; and things are so bad that they are turning them out as soon as they see whether they are dangerously ill – fever or no fever. Personally, aside from a little headache and a very tender arm, I feel swell, so there is no need to worry about me. The story out now is that one of the worst cases is that of the lad who got lockjaw from the shot, and has now passed on to a better land all of which I doubt very strongly. If I were sick, I would not tell this story, so don't think I am; but you see what a mess regimented medicine can make sometimes. Perhaps it is a good argument against socialized medicine, I wouldn't know.

Since the slack off after the Army game, I have had time to write to George and have. No answer yet, but there has hardly been time for a letter to get here anyway.

I have invited Dr. D..... down for Christmas dinner. This year is the year that I rate a guest, you know. I do so wish that it could be Dad instead – but next to the grandest Dad in the world, the Doctor will have to do.

Mother, you had better start thinking about how you and I are going to be able to get away this Christmas, because we have a date for dinner and a show. It will be just about time for a real good movie I have heard about to be in Bingo, so get set – we're stepping out at least one evening.

At this point everybody is looking forward to Christmas, and counting the seconds until it rolls around. It is less than two weeks now until leave – we passed that mark at noon today.

Had a letter from Marsh telling about his assignment. He does not seem overly anxious to go to Hawaii. He's crazy – every officer to whom I've talked says that it is the only duty – best pace in the world to live. He is going to fly the "big boats", the patrol planes. It will be the best kind of training for him in case he wants to take a crack at a piloting job for one of the airlines after he gets out of the Navy.

Much, Much love to all and then some.
Scottie

Annapolis, 11 December 1938

Dear Family,

It now being in the proximity of one o'clock, and since I have just sated myself on a splendiferous repast consisting of chipped dried beef and a lettuce and tomato sandwich, prepared only as the chef de cuisine, U.S.N.A. can prepare them, I am now ready to sit back contentedly and tap out a few nonentities to BINGHAM(NY).

This week, I have splurged myself and ordered evening dress, the whole kit and kaboodle - Tux and Tails. I figgered since I will have to have them soon enough anyway, I might as well get them at this time and be able to present myself properly accoutered during leave, no matter what the occasion demands in the way of fawncy dress. I have no doubt but what when the time comes, there will be nothing to which my attentions and presence will be directed more exciting than a church supper or masquerade ball where overalls will be not only as apropos but even far more desirable. But then, no one will be able to say that I am not well heeled.

George's letter sounded happy, expectant of getting home, and as though he has been really hitting the books. For heaven's sake, don't tell him what an awful mess my marks were - he would be only too disillusioned.

I am in great hopes of seeing Marsh at Christmas time, and expect that he will be home. It seems only right that he would be allowed to get home for Christmas, as he is to be sent to the far ends of the universe, immediately following.

I have been reading a fascinating book this morning. You have probably heard of it, With Malice Towards Some. It is as delightful a creation as I have run across in some time. If you haven't read it, please tell me, and I will see if I can't get a hold of a copy to bring home with me.

This week also, I ordered my graduation outfit. Naturally no takkee if I don't have to take a commission, but at this point the outlook is not bright for anything but that. Ordering at this time saves some money, if it is necessary to get the outfit at all - hence the plunge.

I rather expected a letter from home this morning, but now I know it will arrive tomorrow. So my pleasure is to be prolonged - the anticipation, and then the realization.

All this foolishness must stop - finis.

       Much, much love to all,
        Scottie

ROBERT SCOTT WHITMAN JR.

Annapolis, 4 January 1939

Dear Family,

Mother's letter arrived quite promptly on Sunday morning. Thank you for the good wishes and all.

The stay in Baltimore was very pleasant aside from the fact that my bad wisdom tooth began kicking up and became infected – face swelled up and I was a very purty mess. Two trips to a Baltimore dentist and considerable doping before I felt O.K. At present, I'm in Sick Bay (not hospital) principally so that I can keep using hot mouth washes and get the thing cleaned out so it can be pulled. Feeling very chipper, so don't worry.

We had a grand time New Year's Eve and had all sorts of parties to go to before the dance. Then three parties on Sunday – very gala and very much fun.

I am hard at work on the term paper. For a while, I was stymied by lack of material to work with. By the time I could get there everything in the library was taken. So smart Scottie calls Baltimore, and has Ada E....... send down everything in the Goucher and Public libraries.

The paper, to all intents and purposes is now finished. I am dubious as to its worth, and probably will start all over again before the time for handing in comes.

We had gym today, and had a lecture on how to play golf. It sounded like good dope, and perhaps I'll get a chance to try it out this spring.

Aside from the above, there is no news whatsoever. Exams begin in a week and a half, and this kid is going to be a busy one for a while now. We had our first lesson in radio today. I have qualms.

       Much love to all,
        Scottie

Annapolis, 22 January 1939

Dear Family,

Another Sunday, another week, this time exam week. Mother's letter arrived yesterday and I was so glad to hear from home. Mail is the bright spot in our lives down here. The exams are over, the term is over, and the last lap has begun.

You are probably anxious or at least interested to know about the exams. It was a vicious week, and Tex and I had quite a job battling very runny noses and academics at the same time, but we both came through O.K. - passed exams and purged colds. Average using coefficients for weighting - 3.1413. This is the straight dope using the coefficients as given in the academic calendar. My marks were somewhat better this two months than last, but still could stand a lot of improvement.

Yesterday Tex and I went to the basketball game in the afternoon. We played North Carolina and came from behind to win. It looked for a while as though we would be badly beaten, and the game, ending as it did, was very exciting.

In the evening, I went to the boxing match. We fought Cornell and won 5 to 3. A couple of fights were right good, but, as a whole, the match was very tame. It was fun though, and something to do.

We have drawn preference numbers for ship assignments, and I have number 155, which is a lot better than average, but still not as good as I had hoped for. I have definitely decided to stay on the East Coast by hook or crook. The consensus of opinion seems to be that I won't need too much luck to get an East Coast ship. At any rate, I am going to bust trying. What ship it will be I have no idea, but in all probability, it will be a light cruiser of the Brooklyn class.

I sure hope that everything is at least hanging on as usual at home, and am thinking of you all constantly and hoping for a turn of luck.

There is no more news now except that the book is not in the N.A. library, and so I won't get to read it but it does sound really good.

Much, much love to all,
Scottie

ROBERT SCOTT WHITMAN JR.

Annapolis, 14 February 1939

Dear Family,

Another week is well started – and today was not such a good one academically. I hit a rough slip in Seamanship and just got by.

Today there are 106 days until graduation. It might well be 106 years, the way time is dragging, but February is always the longest month relatively, and the shortest actually.

This term we are taking the same old subjects plus a course in Hygiene and another in Personal Finance. The Hygiene is a little of Physiology, first aid etc. We have been having public speaking in "Bull" and it is a welcome change from the history of last semester. Next week we start advanced composition which I won't mind either.

Wednesdays during the winter we have no drill, and consequently are free at 3:00. It is a welcome respite in the middle of the week.

As I said, this month is the hard one and tempers are short and nerves on edge. When it gets warmer and spring takes hold all will be changed again.

My physical exam comes up Thursday. I expect I will be O.K. in everything except of course for color – how I make out on that depends on how rigorous the exam is. They say they are making it tough.

An awful lot of First Classmen are "unsat" in straight vision this year. Guess maybe our class has studied harder than the others.

Tomorrow is the easy day in every way. A "Steam" class, a Hygiene lecture, and a Personal Finance Lecture.

I read the <u>Yearling</u> last week and agree with Mother that it is a really good book. Right know I'm reading the <u>The Strike</u> a very readable but not particularly classic story of a strike in a shoe factory.

Every Friday night we have an outside lecturer (First Class only). Later in the spring Felix Frankfurter is to speak. It really should be good and I'm looking forward to it.

Dr. D..... and Ada E....... were down last Saturday evening for the boxing matches; and Tom Davies – you remember my speaking of him – arrived Saturday afternoon for the week-end. Tom is stationed in Philadelphia now – attached to the <u>Wichita</u>, a new heavy cruiser.

There is no more news now. Happy Valentines Day.

      Much, much love,
        Scottie

Annapolis, 19 February 1939

Dear Family,

The physical exam is passed, and successfully, so come June we'll be in the Navy for better or for worse. I imagine that my ship will be either the Tuscaloosa or the Quincy – heavy cruisers to be stationed on the East Coast.

There are now 101 days until graduation. It seems such a long time but of course it will pass.

I was much interested in the news of George. I cannot imagine what Mr. Lord meant by his giving him a recommendation to take the entrance exams. I think I shall write to him – it won't do any harm – perhaps I can help the thing along some.

Spring seems to be well on the way here, and today has been almost balmy – hope it remains so.

Wednesday of this week is a holiday, and I expect the Tex and I will go to Baltimore. Ada L.. is coming down for the Masqueraders on Tuesday evening. The show this year is "Room Service".

I am reading The Ramparts We Watch now. I think the man is fairly authoritative but am not sure.

I can't think of another thing to say now so will close.

Much, much love to all,
Scottie

ROBERT SCOTT WHITMAN JR.

Annapolis, 27 February 1939

Dear Family,

A day late this time – but with a good reason. I took my second term week-end. Naturally I visited the D..... Ada L.. and I had a swell time, very quiet which was what I wanted. In the afternoon we went to the "Outdoor Life" show, a very elaborate show of all sorts of things, in the 5th Regiment Armory. It was very interesting and I'm glad I saw it. In the evening we saw a movie and played and danced a bit thereafter.

Barring a war, Ada L.. is going to Europe this summer. She has a grand 7-week tour planned which covers almost all of Europe that draws tourists. I hope, for her sake, along with the rest of the world's, that we don't go at it.

So George has a 3rd alternate – all we can do is wish for the best. I was a 2nd alternate.

There is no news from here, that is, as far as the school itself is concerned. Things go on much the same as always. We now have 93 days to go until graduation. Our Plebes have made us a calendar-days to go until graduation. It shows the day of the week, month date, number of days to graduation, number of working days, and number of holidays. Very clever eh?

The Masqueraders were excellent, and we had a good time Tuesday evening and Wednesday.

Friday afternoon last, my English instructor had our section out to his house for tea. Another lad and I were almost the first to arrive, and I made great friends with his little girl, a lassy far from the "shrinking violet" type, of about five years. The guests arrived in droves, many officers and wives and, of course, Midshipmen. The place was full and suddenly there was one of those inexplicable complete silences. My friend, the precocious youngster, piped up in a voice that must have been herd in Baltimore, "Gee – you've got an awful big hole in your stocking". She was talking – and pointing to me. I've read about that sort of thing before, now it has happened. Yes, when I could safely inspect, there was a B I G one. Woe is me.

So much for now.

Love to all,
Scottie

Annapolis, 7 March 1939

Dear Family,

Time marches on – and since my last letter very little has happened that is worth repeating.

The next to the last set of exams come up week after next, and soon I'll have to get ready for them.

The work this term has been sort of tough. Radio is a mystery to all of us. I don't know what it's all about, but neither do any of the others so far as I can make out – and that including instructors.

We are, as I think I have told you, studying warship construction in "Steam", and it is full of my old bugaboo, Math and Mechanics. But then, I'm getting by and so why worry.

Ada L.. was down for the week-end. There was a hop and boxing matches on Saturday evening and we had a very nice time.

No dope has come out as yet about ship assignments, and I am waiting impatiently to find out where I'll be sent. God grant it is the East Coast.

This afternoon, Dr. Warner a friend of the D.... came down, bringing with him some lad in whom he has taken an interest. He, the Doctor, was here during the war for a while. I showed them around the Yard, and had a very pleasant time doing it.

For a while, it looked as though spring were really setting in, but it has turned cold again now. But it won't be too long.

Infantry starts in a couple of weeks.

The first third of the mess hall is almost finished exteriorly. I don't expect, however, that I will get to eat in it, W.P.A. work is so slow. They have done most of the work with the pre-fabricated steel etc. though, and watching the progress has been a real education in modern construction methods.

Much, much love,
Scottie

ROBERT SCOTT WHITMAN JR.

Annapolis, 20 March 1939

Dear Family,

Two letters in one day!!! My, but I'm a popular lad. My telephone conversation Saturday evening certainly was not lucrative of news was it? But there was none. I just wanted to say hello.

I'm proud of George. He seems to be coming through in fine style. Hooray for his Calculus grade – the lad must be good. I only hope that something may come of his Academy bid.

Ada L.. and her father are sailing Friday for Florida for a spring vacation. Pretty soft eh? Friday, by the way, is the gal's birthday.

I am planning at present to take out ten thousand dollars 20 year paid insurance (Gov't). It will cost me $18.50 a month and can be paid by allotment. The Actuary from the Metropolitan Life was down talking to us the other day and he urged us all to take the maximum allowed amount of Government insurance, ($10,000). We are advised to take $25.00 a month for insurance.

The first exam is over, "Nav"; it was much as the other "Nav" exams. I made an average mark, I expect.

Last Saturday we saw the ashes of Saito off. You probably saw something about the ceremony in the papers, but, risking a repetition, here is what happened. The Regiment was formed all along the line of march in two solid lines. It made quite a sight and will undoubtedly impress the Jap theater goers when they see it in the news reels. When the cortege entered the gate, it was met by a detachment of blue jackets and a marine guard under arms, the band, and the honorary pall bearers, plus about a hundred officers in full dress who marched in the procession. The saluting guns started the first of the nineteen one minute guns due a dead ambassador. The band struck up the funeral march and away they go. It wound around the roads of the Academy and down to the docks. The ashes were put aboard the Admiral's barge, and taken out to the Astoria which is now on its way to Japan. It was a very impressive sight, and very interesting to watch – that is, except for the fact that we had to stand at attention for the better part of an hour.

Saturday afternoon four of us who are going to the Quincy went out to visit an officer who is to go to her in June. He gave us some very good dope, the best of which is that she is to make reserve cruises out of New York this summer. That is, she will take reserve officers and enlisted men for two weeks' cruises. We will be in New York for a week between each of the three cruises. After that I don't know what we'll do or where we shall go. The officer that we visited seemed very nice, and was very cordial.

It has been very cold over the week-end, but now has begun to warm up.

Much, much love to all,
Scottie

Annapolis, 27 March 1939

Dear Family,

Dad's letter arrived a few days ago, and Mother's today. Needless to say, I was awfully glad to receive them. The exams are over, and now it is just seven more before I can be done with exams for three years – until I take my promotion exams for "J.G."

Right now I am about to put out my second issue of the Log. It is to be just a general issue, and will probably exude a very definite and unmistakable odor. But a Log has to come out that week, and Whitman is it.

It is grand that George will be able to get home. The rat owes me a letter, but if I can get the time now that things have let down a little, I will write again anyway. As far as the Fair goes, of course George will get to see it. He must come when I am in New York so that we will be able to do it together. It will be fun to show him the ship and all. I expect that I will see quite a bit of the Ridgways while I am in New York – they had better be around so I can cadge a free meal now and then.

The excitement of getting out is finally beginning to take a hold of the First Class. They don't look forward to graduation or June Week or anything but just getting away from the Naval Academy. It has been a long four years – done me lots of good too, I know but it WILL be good to get away.

Today, we made a destroyer cruise. Out in the bay and around and around for a couple of hours. It was very warm and raining a little, but the rain which was very definitely a spring rain, felt good. Over the week-end, the temperature hit 88.

The first baseball game is this Wednesday, so spring must really be here.

After her week-end in New York last week, Ada L.. is coming down this week-end for the First Class hop. She and her pal Jean went up to visit with one of Ada's Goucher chums. The Florida trip fell through, as you may surmise. She will be down for Easter week-end. That is one day we have never missed.

I have been trying to think of some other news to pass on but am at a loss.

So with the best of love to you both, I close this poor excuse for a letter.

Scottie

Annapolis, 3 April 1939

Dear Family,

First off this week comes a report of the marks for the last set of exams. Average 3.166. So that is the story, and the next report that you get will be the final for four years. I think that I am assured of graduating "With Credit" – it is a 3.0 average that is required, I think.

In Seamanship this month we have a good guy for an instructor. He "runs" us unmercifully, but is so good natured about it that you like it rather than mind. He will hear a recitation at the board, and then will ask the reciter before he has taken his seat some outlandish question in seamanship relative to the meaning of terms. As for example, he asked me today what was meant by "Belay the dog's ear in the shark's mouth". Naval or rather sea language is still pretty much a mystery to me and probably to all the rest of us, so I guess he has the right idea.

We had our first dress parade last Wednesday and everybody was pretty rusty. It won't take long for us to get back in the swing again though. We changed back into white cap covers last Saturday.

I got a long letter from Marsh today. He seems very happy, and very interested in his work. He has found out evidently, however, that he can't set the Navy on fire. The cadets are made second pilots on the "big boats" under a commissioned officer, I think that Marsh would like to have his own plane - naturally.

Things have certainly been moving fast in Europe of late, haven't they? No one knows from one day to the next what will develop. My guess is that, if things don't blow up this month, they won't for some time. April is always the month, is it not?

Concerning the insurance and Mother's very wise suggestion about health and accident – The Government policy carries with it for about two dollars extra a month a total disability clause. It all amounts to a double indemnity in case of total permanent disability. In case of temporary disability, it pays after the first four months, I believe. All Government policies carry, at no extra cost, a total permanent disability clause. That is, at any date after the taking of the policy they will pay, in case of permanent total disability, $57.50 a month for twenty years. Until the face value of the policy is expended.

With the extra premium, payments for temporary disability are not deducted from the face value, and in case of permanent disability the payments are doubled for twenty years. You all know so much more about such things than I that it is foolish to explain them except that it helps this unfamiliar finance straight in my mind.

I have been fooling around with figures trying to work out tentative budgets, and have arrived practically nowhere. It is so hard to tell how much I can save until I get at it. Of course we are given figures from the past experience of our officers, but theirs are not quite so thrifty as I want to be for a while.

Another problem which I am toying with is that of the exact type of insurance that I want to take. I would think that it would be swell to take twenty payment, and have then thousand insurance paid up when I am forty-three. At the same time, by that time I should be able to pay the premium without much trouble — so what to do? Then again, I need more insurance when I take a leap into matrimony, and is it wise to get in when the price is lower? It is all such a problem, but I will work it out. There will be much of this to mull over then I see you.

The Pennsylvania will be here next week-end for quite a stay. Tex and I are planning to go out and see what a battleship looks like. We haven't seen a line battleship yet, and the Pennsy is the fleet flag. It is a funny thing, but in my four years here, I haven't been aboard but one first line fighting ship, and that the Erie which is a special type and an experiment.

There doesn't seem to be much more of interest (if the above proved work reading), so I guess I'll close for now. I missed your letters this week.

> Much, much love to all,
> Scottie

P.S.

How many graduation announcements will I need and to whom do I send them and when? This is something about which I know nothing and will have to be guided entirely by Mother. In the first check to get an estimate on how many to be ordered for the class, I played along with the majority and said 25. I don't know what I would do with 25, but perhaps there are that many who would be interested.

Annapolis, 11 April 1939

Dear Family,

Mother's letter arrived on Sunday, and I was as usual very, very glad to get it. I expect that George arrived safe and sound.

The week-end was very pleasant indeed although it was too cold on Sunday to go sailing as we had planned. Naturally, on Monday the weather was really springy, and it has been so ever since. Right now it looks as though a real thunder storm is blowing up.

I might tell you about the drill on Saturday. Our company went out on the "Y-P" boats – they are a little smaller than the Sub-Chasers. I think I have told you how we operate out in the bay, just like a squadron of destroyers – go through all the maneuvers by flag signal, and get a lot of good practice handling ships in miniature. Each drill we take turns as Officer of the Deck, and this time it was my turn. My group happened to be the "flagship", and so we took charge of the whole squadron. The officer in charge let me run everything, and it was sure fun. We went through about every maneuver that a group of ships can go through, and for two hours we played around in the bay.

Today we had our first combined fire control drill. In the armory they have the entire set up for a ship's battery, control towers, plotting rooms, four six inch guns to represent turrets, spotting towers, directors, and the whole works – all hooked up just as it would be aboard ship, electrically, mechanically etc., all the telephone circuits and all. They even have a miniature ship set up on a shelf; and from the spotting platform at the other end of the armory it looks just as a battleship would at twenty-thousand yards. There are electrically operated flaps on this ledge which are operated from a remote station and represent the shell splashes. The method of conducting a problem is very complicated, but it is exactly like it would be in an actual shipboard firing practice. We get only the data that would be available in battle, and then set up the computing mechanisms, transmitters, etc., and fire our practice. It is scored just like an actual practice, and the battalions have a competition which is part of the competition for the flag. Each Batt. Has four competitive drills and, as I said, we had our first today. I don't know how we made out, but I do understand that we didn't get many hits.

The "Y-P" drills are also competitive by the way.

Tomorrow, there is a drill that is not so much fun – dress parade. They started two weeks ago, and will continue from now on in.

I ordered a trunk and a new suitcase from the store the other day. My uniforms have all been given a first try on, and slowly but surely the work of getting squared away to leave is progressing. Fifty more days now.

There doesn't seem to be much more news, so I will close with every best wish and lots of love.

Scottie

Annapolis, 17 April 1939

Dear Family,

Mother's letter arrived today, and glad I was to get it. I'm glad George had so little trouble in getting home. It must have been grand to see him. Now it won't be so long before we can be home together.

Right now, there are but a little more than six weeks until I shall be a free man again. It is funny how we look forward so to getting through with the Naval Academy. I suppose that in a few years we will be wishing that we were back.

Before I forget it, there are some things that I want to ask about. In the first place, is my white palm beach suit home; and, if so, is it in good condition? To answer your question, no, I don't want it sent, I'll get it while I am home, and have it altered there. (I thought there was something else that I wanted to ask, but it slips my mind now).

I am thinking seriously of buying a used car to use this summer. If I am going to be in New York all summer it will be a great pleasure and material aid in that I shall be able to get home and to Baltimore much easier. During the month of June, it will make the only big leave that I will have for a good many years to come a lot pleasanter. My plan is to get one as inexpensively as possible, and then when I go south in the winter get rid of it for as much as I can get, or trade it in for a credit slip on the car that I will someday get. Doctor D..... has some patients who are agents, and it is possible that he can get a lead on a bargain for me. At least I am going to look around.

The dope is that we will be in and out of Norfolk and New York until after Christmas, but nothing official has come out yet. The Navy is the hardest thing in the world to predict.

Tomorrow I have the guard, hence my being able to write tonight.

It has come to my mind, that if George gets out of school after I do, I might be able to go out and get him.

So far I don't know the plans for Ada L..'s graduation. All I know is that she gets her diploma on the thirteenth.

Today we got a little pamphlet with hints to the new Ensigns in it. It gave us quite a thrill.

How do you like the <u>Esquire Log</u>? My issue was a stinkeroo, and I didn't much care. We were putting all our energies to the big issue, and just "put out" a <u>Log</u> the week before.

It has been raining for three days straight. Miserable weather, and our spirits have corresponded. I have become quite a cross word puzzle fiend in my spare time, and now know all the unusual words that one finds only in cross word puzzles.

Best love to the grandest family in the world.

All of it and then some,

Scottie

Annapolis, 24 April 1939

Dear Family,

My calendar has just suffered defacing for another week. That leaves three more weeks before the final set of exams. Your letters arrived on schedule, and I was as usual awfully glad to get them.

George certainly did make time on his return to Corning - but then a kid with his appearance shouldn't have any trouble.

Lambie's kittens interest me. I hope that they are not full grown before I get home. I like kittens, but abhor cats.

This week we start a series of four airplane flights. They are just a continuation of the indoctrinal flights that we had during second class summer. However, this time the emphasis is placed on serial navigation. When I have made the first flight, I will write you all about it.

Ada E....... was down Sunday. We had a very pleasant time. Had dinner together and then went to the show in the yard (which was pretty awful, but entertaining enough). Then we came in to the canteen and had a coke. A very quiet time but fun.

Mother said that she had made out a tentative list of people to whom I should send announcements. There most certainly is no hurry about getting it, but please remember to send it sometime in the next month. And when do I send them?

Now that the Log has changed hands and everything in the way of extra-curricular activities has passed on to the Second Class, time begins to be more my own. Now I spend my time out in town getting fittings from the tailor for my uniforms, and sitting in the Greasy Spoon drinking coca-cola and shooting the breeze. The year is almost over, and everything is beginning to sluff off. Today we had the shortest assignment in the history of our dealings with the Ordnance Department. Most of the instructors spend most of the class time talking about the fleet and fleet activities. It is all very interesting, and I am getting quite excited about getting into it.

Tex took his week-end last week. He and his Sally went to New York, and then drove back down here in Sal's car. They gauged their time wrong, and the wonderful weather brought out everybody onto the road. As a result, friend Tex arrived an hour and forty-five minutes late. He is now under restriction, and will probably reap a few demerits from it.

It hardly seems possible that after four years of restriction and cloistered life I shall be finally out on my own more or less. Although as long as I stay in the Navy my life will not be my own, at least I shall no longer be treated as a child. The only thing that worries me is that I do not know, now that I have been so well nursed for these long years, whether I am capable of taking care of myself. It is funny, but we are not very worldly wise – ludicrous but very true.

If you think of it, Dad, will you stop in and ask Dick Fuller if it is possible to license an automobile with New York tags when the care is bought and is in Maryland. I haven't bought a car yet and am not sure that I am going to; but, if I do, I want to tag it with New York plates, since my driver's license is a New York permit.

I am completely exhausted of news now, so I guess the smart thing to do is to close.

My very best love to the best Mother and Dad in the world.

      Scottie

Annapolis, 1 May 1939

Dear Family,

And so begins the third week before the end of academics, and I start it out by having the watch today.

It is an old Naval Academy custom to celebrate May Day by the Youngsters stealing out into Smoke Park in the dead of night or early morning, and decorating one of the trees with toilet paper from head to foot – a sort of May Pole effect, you know. Last year someone took a picture of the result and sent it to the Washington Post, with the result that it was spread all over the country. This year the Executive Department swore to uphold the good name of the Naval Academy and have no such pictures. One First Classman of the watch squad was to get up before light and see that there was no disturbance, and if there were any decorations in Smoke Park to have them removed. We shook around for it here and, of course, I lost. So I have been up since four-fifteen this morning. Now at six in the afternoon, I'm just a little tired.

Today our trunks have started to appear in the halls, and soon, I suppose, mine will show up. We have what is called a Naval Academy Special. It is a rather large steamer, very heavily constructed, and is sold for fourteen dollars. A pretty good buy, I think.

Tex goes to the West Virginia – a battlewagon.

The weather over the week-end was horrible, but now it is lovely again. It is a Maryland surety – rain on the week-ends.

Mother's letter arrived on schedule, and I was sure glad to hear from home. I'm thinking seriously of shipping my trunk home rather than directly to the ship, so that you will be able to see my uniforms.

The flight drills are very unexciting. It is almost as thrilling as riding around in an automobile for two hours, and a lot less comfortable. Space is limited, and we are cramped for room. Can't even see out unless you want to risk a crick in your neck.

Friday evening William Lyons Phelps lectured to us in the last lecture of the year. He was most certainly the best that we have had, too. His subject was the "Art of living", and he said very little that we didn't already have in the back of our minds. However, he said it all so cleverly that he held me, at least, spellbound.

In talking about his many, many interests, he said that he was interested in everything in the world except higher mathematics. He spoke of being on the Princeton campus and running into Einstein. Said that he was thrilled every time he saw the man just thinking of the exciting life that he must lead – all alone out where no other man has trod, on the farthest frontiers of mathematics. He likened it to living in a house on the top of a mountain eternally covered with snow – it was "cold but antiseptic."

He also put me in my place. In speaking of the movies, he mentioned several that he considered as excellent, and one that was the worst he had ever seen – it was one of the few movies that I have seen that I really thought was good.

I was talking with Mr. Ford, a Lieutenant who is to be on the staff of the Commander of the Atlantic Squadron. He seems to think that I will meet the Quincy in New York. I hope he is right.

There is no more news now, so I will close with the very best love to you all.

Scottie

Annapolis, 8 May 1939

Dear Family,

There is so little news to tell you that if it were not for one thing, there would be no sense in even writing.

Mother's letter telling of Mrs. D.....' invitation was not a surprise. I learned on Saturday of it. I was so hoping that it would make it possible for you both to get here, but evidently that is out of the question. If it is absolutely impossible for Mother to come, can't Dad come? It would make me the happiest guy in the world if you both could come, and just half as happy if one of you can. It would be just about the grandest graduation present that I could get if you would come, Dad.

I'm pretty sure that I will have a car, and we can drive home together. If you could come on Tuesday evening, we would then have Wednesday and Thursday, and could drive home on Friday. There is no sense in my waxing eloquent over this, because you know just how much it would mean to me if you could come. Everything worth seeing and doing can be done in just that time, and we could have such a grand time. The D..... are really very anxious to have you, and they are not one thousandth as anxious as I am. So, please, if it is at all possible to do it, say that you will come.

I know just how disappointed Mother is, and I am just as disappointed. My heart aches for her, but I know just how brave and wonderful she is, and know that since it is impossible for her to come, she wants Dad to come just as badly as I do.

There is just that to say, and perhaps I have not done it very well. Anyway it would be about the grandest thing that could happen if I would have a least a part of my family here for graduation.

Will write later in the week.

       Much love to all,
        Scottie

Annapolis, 14 May 1939

Dear Family,

And so the last week of Naval Academy academics begins. Six exams and then it's all over. Tomorrow we start off with Nav.

Nothing much of interest has happened this week. However – on Monday we staged a dress parade for Crown Prince Frederick of Denmark. It was entirely uneventful and very much a pain in the neck, since we had to stand out on the field for almost an hour waiting for him to arrive.

Wednesday there was a little excitement. Somebody tossed a cigarette out of a Second Batt. Window into some rubbish around the mess hall construction and started a fire. It was put out before it had got well under way, and no damage was done.

One third of the mess hall is completed, by the way, and we are using it. It is very nice and much, much quieter.

Ad L.. was down for the afternoon and we went to a movie. Not very exciting, but fun.

Aside from the above there is absolutely nothing to tell. I haven't a car yet but have almost definitely decided to get one. Dr. D..... is looking around for me.

The information from the license people arrived, and many thanks to Dad for getting it for me.

I've completely run out of news, so I guess the smart thing to do is to close.

Much, much love to all,

Scottie

Annapolis, 21 May 1939

Dear Family,

It's all over. I'm through going to school, at least for a while. The exams are over.

They weren't so tough, Ordnance excluded. I don't know any marks yet, but they should be coming out soon.

Yesterday noon we had our "No More Rivers" ceremony. In it, the various "characters" so inevitable in any department are lampooned, and we generally take a last crack at the profs and the Executive Department. It was good this year and we all howled in great glee at some of the caricatured profs, I'll tell you all about it when I get home; it makes too long a story for a letter.

I received Mother's letter with the list for announcements, and for it I send a million thanks - I've started to address them, and got quite a thrill when I put the first card in.

This next week is drill week and, as you know, it's then that we have our drills for the company competition. The Second Company has little or no chance of winning - though it would be nice for Tex's sake.

June Week begins on Friday of this week. Our plans at present are thusly. We have got a cottage about five miles out of Annapolis for Tex's Mother and Brother and Sally and Ada L.. However, it now seems doubtful whether the Harris family can come and we may have to change our plans. At any rate, Ada L.. arrives Friday at about noon - that's all I know.

Talk about putting it on thick. Ada L.. was down for this week-end too. One of her chums came down and dragged with Tex and we had a perfectly grand time. There was a First Class hop, which was very nice indeed, and we went sailing all of today. It was beautiful on the bay, and the breeze was just right. We went way, way out and got back just in time for the girls to pack, change their clothes, and catch the 6:15 trolley back to Baltimore.

I think that the car that I'm going to buy will be a '33 Plymouth. A mechanic friend of Dr. D..... has it. Will guarantee it, put it in tip top shape - it's a one owner car with about 30,000 miles on it, has never been wrecked - wants $125, and will buy it back at the end of June for $100 if I want to sell it. Don't see how I could do better.

It seems funny not to be thinking about Monday's lessons at this point. I haven't yet been able to convince myself that it is now all over but the shouting. But so 'tis indeed.

Lots and lots of love,

Scottie

ROBERT SCOTT WHITMAN JR.

Annapolis, 26 May 1939

Dear Family,

This is the letter that I promised earlier in the week, and then just didn't find time to write.

June Week commences officially today at 1510, when liberty begins. Tex and I are all set to go, and now I am just waiting for Ada L.. to get down from school. She is driving my car down - the car which I bought yesterday.

And that deserves a paragraph by itself. It is not the '33 Plymouth that I told you about - something fell through about that, and Dr. D.....'s man couldn't get it. Tuesday the D..... called me, and told me of the car that the man had very contritely brought around in penance for his earlier failure. (Dr. D..... had already made a deposit on the '33). It was a '36 Plymouth in perfect condition. Practically new tires, 22,000 miles on it, one owner - oh, a dream of a car to hear them talk. I took it all with a grain of salt, and told them to have the man bring it down. So down it came, and they were not only right in their praise but had under-extolled it. It is a beauty, and the man gave it to me for $285 - exactly $150 under the lowest market price (perfect finish). Buying it crimps the bank roll no end, but, instead of getting rid of it in the fall, I'll keep it and any time I want to sell it. I know that I can get rid of it for more than I paid for it. I don't know how the man could sell it so cheap, but I trust him implicitly - he has been dealing with the Doctor for twenty years and is the sort that you can tell is honest the minute you talk to him. He only did it as a favor to the D..... So that is the end of my hunt for a car. You'll be crazy about it, I know.

Tex's Mother arrived this morning <u>sans</u> brother. There is a chance, however, that his brother may arrive later if he gets out of school soon enough. He graduates later in June from the University of Texas as a Petroleum Engineer.

The nuts arrived on schedule, and have as yet been unopened, because I know just how long they will last once opened with me around - I nuts about nuts (as you well know). Thank you very, very much.

The exam and term marks are all out, and frankly, I didn't even bother to copy them down - all marks are above a 3.0 for the term, I am sure. The four year marks are the ones that count, and as soon as I get them, I'll either send or bring them with me when I come home.

The exams, by the way, were sheer fruit with the exception of perhaps Ordnance.

We have more or less started to pack, but there is so much truck that we will need this week that it is really a pretty futile task. Much diversion has been created by the filling out of umpteen million forms incident to getting commissioned.

This morning, we had a rehearsal for "Sob Sunday", and that is all that we have had to do today. Yesterday there was a dress parade and that was all. Our Company did not win the competition nor did we come close. The First Company won.

The Lucky Bags are out, and they are not as nice, in my estimation, as the last ones. However, they will pass inspection and you shall see one soon.

The weather has been as hot as the hinges of hades, but today it is a little cooler. Here is a great big hope that it remains so from now on in.

Just as I wrote that, Tex called my attention to the tin-cans that are now steaming in. They are coming in preparation for the Second Class cruises this summer. The battleships are already in.

Admiral Leahy is to give out the diplomas this year. I guess that the President will call at West Point, since he was here last year.

I have most of my uniforms now and am just waiting to get my whites and a couple of pairs of trou to have all complete. We have set up a wardrobe here in the room; and as I look at it now, it makes quite an array.

There seems little or no other news worth passing on, and I shall see you in a short time to gather up the loose threads. Most of all I wanted to write to tell you that I am thinking of my family, and to send them all the love in the world.

Scottie

ROBERT SCOTT WHITMAN JR.

FIRST CLASS

UNITED STATES NAVAL ACADEMY
Annapolis, Maryland

Relative Standing and Marks for Term, ending 25 May, 1939

MIDSHIPMAN R. S. WHITMAN, JR.

Total membership of Class 1939 is   581

Mr. R. S. Whitman, Sr.
7 Johnson Ave.
Binghamton, N.Y.

Scale of Marks	Character of Work Indicated by Mark
4.00 to 3.40	Distinction
3.39 to 3.00	With Credit
2.99 to 2.50	Fair and Passing
2.49 and less	Unsatisfactory

For the information of those accustomed to considering marks on the scale of 100 – a mark of 4.00 equals 100%; a mark of 3.00 equals 75%; and a mark of 2.50 equals 62½% which is the lowest satisfactory mark. All marks below 2.50 show that academic work is deficient and not up to the required standard.

DEPARTMENTS		Mark For Term	Relative Standing (1)
Seamanship & Navigation	Seamanship..........	3.18	151
	Navigation..........	3.04	272
Ordnance & Gunnery............................		2.99	290
Marine Engineering............................		3.26	184
Electrical Engineering........................		3.13	221
English, History & Government.................		3.30	55
Hygiene.......................................		3.16	455
		Mark for Year	
NON ACADEMIC			
Aptitude for the Service..........		3.36	1.89
Executive Conduct..........................		3.94	102

Demerits for year................   6

Order of General Merit: For Year 204....; for four years' course 243

[General average for First Class year (without coefficients)   3.26]

[General average for four years course (without coefficients)   3.136]

(1) A relative standing of 1 is the highest obtainable

WILSON BROWN
Rear Admiral U.S. Navy

```
                    WESTERN UNION

P85  28 DL-ANNAPOLIS MD  31 922A

R. S. WHITMAN-                    1939 MAY 31 AM 10 14

 422 PARK ST YORK PA

 CARE E. E. WHITMAN

GRADUATION AT 1030. MEET ME AT MAIN OFFICE AT 1000 HAVE
TICKETS FOR UNCLE BERT AND WIFE. TRAFFIC IS AWFUL SO ALLOW
TIME SWELL THAT YOUR COMING LOVE-
                    SCOTTIE

1030 1000
```

USNA Graduation Diploma.

VIII
U.S.S. QUINCY
JUNE 1939 – MARCH 1941

Ensign Appointment by Franklin D. Roosevelt, June 1939.

CA39/

U. S. S. QUINCY

Wednesday 28 June 1939

Dear Family,

At last I have a chance to write a too long postponed letter, and much there is to relate.

To begin chronologically, the trip to Baltimore via New York was very uneventful and we arrived there about six - spending about two hours in New York, as expected. Of the stay in Baltimore there is very little to say. I had a very nice albeit quiet time and enjoyed myself much as usual. On Sunday I took the boat down, as we had prophesied, and arrived in Norfolk at six in the morning. There were four others on the boat headed for the Quincy and so the trip was very enjoyable and congenial. We reported at about ten, and had just an hour to shift into white service, gloves, and sword, and report to the Exec. (The Captain is on leave.)

The rest of the day was spent in getting unpacked and squared away, as was the next day, Tuesday. However, today we have received our assignments to duty. I am in the Engineers - and on top of that have the day's duty, since my section is the duty section for today. In the Engineers that amounts to almost nothing since the officers do not stand watch in port but are just on call in case of emergency, and make periodical inspections of the engineering spaces. Naturally there is an experienced officer standing the duty with me. It seems that we are just in the Engineers for instruction purposes and will always stand our watches with another officer. It looks as though we will be Engineers (there are three of us) for about six months. Then, if we are lucky, they will qualify us as watch standers, and then we shift to another department to start learning all over again.

As far as the living quarters aboard are concerned, they are so much different from anything I have had any experience with before in the Navy that there is no comparison. Bill Sawyer and I are rooming together. We have a stateroom with regular stateroom bunks, two closets, a raft of drawers, two desks, a washbowl, bookcases, two combination safes, and a waste basket. We have a colored boy to keep the room clean, make the beds, shine our shoes, stow our laundry, run errands, and generally help us. Right now, I am going to punch the button and have him bring me a coke.

We are staying here in Portsmouth across the bay from Norfolk until the sixth, when we leave for New York. We arrive in New York on the 7th and sail off again with the first reserve cruise on the 8th. Not a lot of time in New York for the first time, but we will be back again on the 22nd for about ten days.

Naturally as soon as we got aboard ship the older officers started to fill us with the latest hot dope, most of which is probably very bad. The best is that this fall or next spring we are going to escort the President across the Atlantic to Europe to return the royal visit just completed - I will believe that when we sail. I do know that we come into the Navy Yard here in Portsmouth for about six weeks beginning the first of September.

There is little more to write now without getting into great detail, so I will close with the best of love to all.

Scottie

UNITED STATES SHIP QUINCY

4 July 1939

Dear Family,

   Mother's letter postmarked June 24 arrived yesterday – where it has been since it started on its way is beyond me. At any rate it finally arrived and glad I was to get it.

   So far I have found out practically nothing about my job – have just been trying to find my way around the Engineering Department, learn the names of the men in my division, and generally get acclimated. So far I feel in almost as much a storm as I was when I first reported on board. Nevertheless, things are beginning to settle down a bit and as soon as we get underway there will not be quite so much of a mess as there is now. You see, we have been here in the Portsmouth Navy Yard for repairs and the Engineering Department has been in such a mess that they have had very little time for brand new fresh Ensigns.

   The "bug", when I last saw it, was behaving beautifully. It is now in Baltimore. Just a few minutes ago I got a wire from A.E. saying that she was arriving in New York on Thursday. Perhaps she is driving it up, I don't know.

   We sail for New York Thursday morning and arrive early Friday. We leave again on the first cruise on Saturday. So I won't have much time with the gal. This week has been mostly holidays – Saturday, Sunday, Monday, and today. I've been out to Virginia Beach twice and have played golf once, and that is all the "extra-curricular" work so far.

   The officers have courtesy cards to two beach clubs, and as a result we can swim for practically nothing any time.

   I am in the auxiliary ("A") Division in Engineering, and we have charge of all auxiliary machinery such as evaporators, auxiliary Diesels, ice machines, boat engines, etc.

   I can see how the Navy can make lazy men out of officers. Everything is done for us – shoes shined, clothes kept in order, and all. Living in "Ward Room Country" is like living in a club – just punch the button and the boy does the rest – and no tips.

   A million rumors are flying around concerning our employment schedule after the cruises. They even had us going to Charleston, S.C. between the first and second cruises; but I think that is bad dope now.

Most of the officers aboard here seem very nice. They are almost all new (new to this ship), since this is the year for changes on the <u>Quincy</u> (She went into commission three years ago).

I can't think of any more news now, so I'll close with lots and lots of love to all.

Scottie

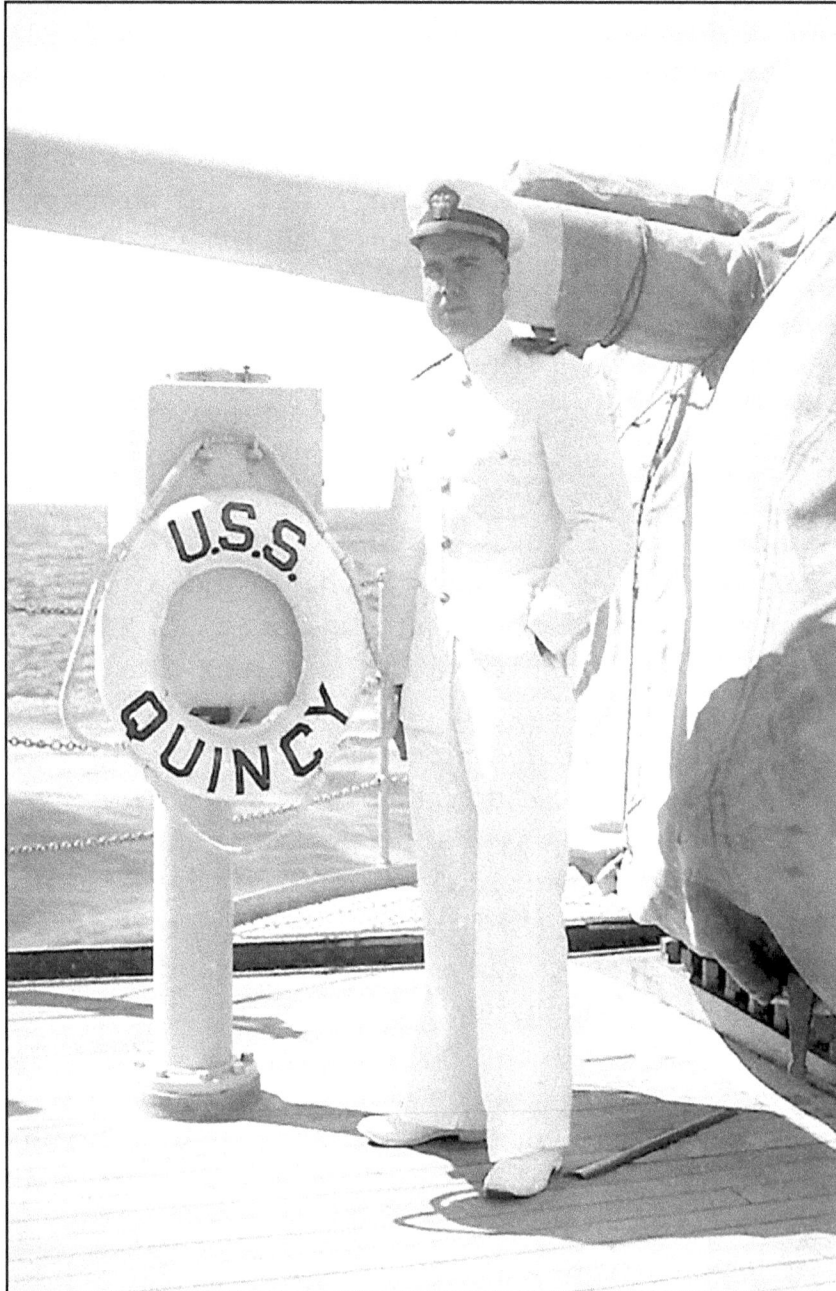

Aboard the U.S.S. Quincy.

Thursday at sea, 13 July 1939

Dear Family,

Since we go into Norfolk tomorrow I guess I'd better get this letter written and in the mail.

We have been at sea since Saturday, as you know. Nothing happened much during the first part of the week. Just regular routine watches etc. Yesterday, however, we fired a rehearsal run for the Reserves' battle practice. Each gun fired three salvos (6 guns). Then today we fired the practice – ten salvos from each gun.

I was "safety officer" for three of the guns (they fired separately) and had to stand by to be sure that they observed all safety precautions and obeyed the rules. It went off without a hitch.

This evening we fired a night illumination practice (star shells), and now we are through firing for two weeks, when we get the next batch aboard.

There are a flock of reserve officers under foot in the wardroom now, and things are pretty crowded.

We stay in N.O.B. until Monday, and then put out to sea until Friday, when we are due back in New York.

We were in New York for only 24 hours last time. A.E. was there to see the fair and I saw her for a while.

We have been anchoring every night and, as a result, the watches have not been so tough.

Slowly but surely I'm learning the engineering plant – the sooner the better for me, since the sooner I learn, the sooner I qualify and can stand a watch by myself.

I really can't think of any other news now, so I'll close and post this in the mail.

       Much, Much love to all,
        Scottie

Wednesday, 26 July 1939

Dear Family,

I've been a long time in writing this letter, mainly because I have been pretty busy. Over the week-end I had the duty and had to stand beach patrol on the dock during most of both days; and since then, since the Division Officer is gone, I have had my hands full trying to fill his job and my own at the same time.

I so hoped that I could get home this last week-end, but a series of circumstances arose that just made everything work against it, and I couldn't get out of the duty.

Everything has happened so fast lately for you, that I expect that you are pretty much in a fog. Grandmother's going was, of course, a blessing, and she is so much better off now that you can be nothing but thankful. I'm afraid of the "let down" for Mother though; and you, George and Dad, must be very good to her and make her rest lots and lots and forget all the horrible mess of the last two years. If I could only have come along this week-end to do my little bit to help – but so it goes in the Navy.

As for George's disappointment, I don't know what to say. The only thing that I could possibly suggest is that he write to the Surgeon General's office, explain just what happened and cite my case, perhaps get a civilian doctor's opinion to include, and ask if there is anything to be done. The appointment is probably still open. This all if it was just the color that got him. I talked with the doctor aboard here, and he seemed to think that there was little chance, but at the same time didn't think that it could do any harm to try.

I've been out to the fair twice, and have enjoyed it immensely both times. It took an hour for me to get into the G.M. exhibit and out again, thirty-five minutes waiting in line, and fifteen minutes riding around the world of 1960 (where the rest of the time went I don't know). It was worth waiting several hours to see – the best exhibit of any sort that I have ever seen. I saw a three-dimensional movie at the Chrysler exhibit. It is one where you are given polarized glasses to watch the movie with, and you can then see depth also on the screen. An automobile driven toward you on the screen makes you actually duck and want to run for fear it will run right over you. Then, too, I saw a television broadcast, and a lot of other interesting things in the industrial exhibits. They and a few of the foreign exhibits are the only really worth while parts of the fair. The fire-works at night are magnificent, and the "aquacade" is the only really good amusement in the Midway.

Today I have the duty again (this being the week of the month that is bad for me). No beach patrol though, and I have been correcting examination papers all afternoon. Exams, that is, that were taken by enlisted personnel for promotion to a higher rate. (Enlisted men have rates, Officers have ranks.)

Whitman Ridgway is coming out for dinner tonight. I was at the Ridgway's for dinner Monday night, and invited him then. Ced was out Sunday evening. He seems to be getting along all right at the bank. I went down town to Jardine's bank Monday to pay them off, and stopped in at the Stock Exchange on the way back to see what the floor looked like. What a mad house!!!

We sail with a new bunch of reserves on Saturday, and then it will be off on the bounding main for another two weeks. The Tuscaloosa has left us to go to Norfolk to get an escalator and a bath tub for el Presidento; and maybe there is some truth to the rumor that he is going to Europe. Who knows - certainly not the Navy - we always get the dope last.

   Much, much love to all,
    Scottie

Thursday, 3 August 1939

Dear Family,

Mother's letter arrived just before we sailed, and was I glad to get it!!!

I suppose by now all the storm of moving is over, and you are all settled on St. John Avenue. Perhaps a change of address will bring us a change of fortune - who knows, and here is hoping. I have thought of you constantly, and so wish that I could have been home to help out.

The first week of the second reserve cruise is almost over, and tomorrow we go into Norfolk for the week-end.

Today we fired the battle practice, and after tonight's star shell firings, the gunnery for this cruise will be over. I am getting quite used to the five inch guns now, and they don't bother anywhere near as much as they used to. I had the same job as safety officer this time that I had last time.

This week we in the Engineers have had little time for engineering since we have been topside most of the time coaching the pointers and trainers on the guns. It was nice to be up in the fresh air and sunshine all day, and I have no kick coming except that it got awfully monotonous looking through the "check-sight" hour after hour and coaching the reserve crew.

The crew on one of my guns this morning was very, very inexperienced, and they tried their darndest to run away after the first salvo, but we kept them passing up ammunition almost by force, and there were no casualties; for which I am certainly thankful.

You are quite correct when you say that life aboard ship is monotonous. It is not boring, but there is very little to write about. But let's see what else might be interesting to you.

I told you what the cigar mess was, didn't I, when I was home? That is the profit sharing enterprise run by the officers for the sale of coca-cola, root beer, candy, cigarettes, cigars, etc., razor blades, tooth brushes, shaving cream, etc., etc. to themselves and non-member officers. It is not compulsory to buy a share, but if you don't, anything bought from the mess costs ten percent excess. I bought in for $13.65 when I got aboard, and the share is now worth about $15. Of course, when an officer is detached the mess buys back his share at the prevailing price, so you always make some money even though it is in part your own money that you make, if you see what I mean. Every evening after dinner the cigar mess boy comes around the table with his box and everybody who wants to gets his cigar, or piece of candy, or pack of mints. Most items cost four cents. Then we shake poker dice to see who pays for the lot. Dad, at least, probably knows what poker dice are. If, by the freak of chance, any person shakes five natural aces all at once, he pays not only for his own table but must "set up" the whole wardroom. It is lots of fun and not at all expensive since everything is so cheap, and you don't lose too often. (No one has had five aces since I've been aboard. If you get them you rate also putting your name on the dice box.)

The laundry on board is very cheap – mine costs about a dollar and a half a week with white service, since we have been wearing that all the time.

The reserves this time are from Jersey City, and are almost entirely (the officers, that is) Naval Academy graduates. That was not the case on the last cruise, where a lot of them were R.O.T.C. people etc.

The schedule this week has been the same as that for the last cruise. Anchor every night. We are anchored now and are about to get underway to do our illumination practice. I have the duty today and must be down below to help get going, so will close. It is just as well anyway because I have just about run out of dope.

> Lots and lots of love to the grandest family on earth,
> Scottie

Sunday, at sea, 20 August 1939

Dear Family,

Today we'll at least start that long letter that I promised. I'm sure that I have no idea what I will say, for absolutely nothing has happened since I last wrote, long ago as it was.

I guess that I told you that for the first week in New York I didn't leave the ship. The regular "A" Division Office went on leave again, and I took over. The fact that I was broke also had a little to do with my hermitizing, but I found an awful lot to do and kept very busy. Then Wednesday night I had a date with the older sister of one of my classmates drags. The older sister turned out to be eighteen years old, and the other girl sixteen. We went out to the fair and those gals certainly did lead us a merry chase. I have never walked so much in my life – twenty miles if it was an inch, and on our feet from four in the afternoon until one-thirty in the morning. They were from Auburn, by the way, and very nice, but still sixteen and eighteen respectively.

Friday afternoon I went out to the Ridgways and visited for about an hour, and then went on down town to do a couple of errands, returning to the ship about eight. I think that Aunt May was a little peeved because I didn't come out more, but I didn't want to take the chance of getting caught without any money at all, and decided that it was best not to show up.

The Engineering Ensigns have been shifted around again, and now I am with the "M" division, which has charge of the main engines. In another month and a half we will shift again.

Directly following this cruise we go to Norfolk, and will be in and out of there until the first of the year – probably out every week and in on the week-ends. We start our own gunnery almost immediately and will fire our first practice in the middle of September.

The reserve units this time are from Rochester and Oswego. They are mostly young fellows and very nice.

Oh, yes, Ada L.., and Jean Riley are coming to New York this next week-end. They arrive on Friday and will stay through Sunday.

Yesterday we had some dirty weather, but today it has cleared and is beautiful. We are still steaming for Hampton Roads and expect to anchor at about five this afternoon. We go back to New

York for the week-end, and then go out again until Friday.

This afternoon we had emergency drills for the benefit of the reserves. They are always an awful task, taking such a long time, and are monotonous. By emergence drills is meant fire drill, collision, abandon ship, fire and rescue, and man overboard. All very necessary but a bore.

I can't think of another thing to say except that I miss my family pretty much, and enjoy your letters more than anything that happens aboard here.

Lots and lots of love to all,
Scottie

ROBERT SCOTT WHITMAN JR.

Monday, 4 September 1939

Dear Family,

Well, it has happened. We all have been waiting for this war for a good many years, have expected it, and known that it was coming, and yet it was somewhat of a shock when it finally came.

As far as it effects the Navy in general, and me in particular which, I suppose is what you are most interested in, nobody yet knows. Right now we are taking on capacity fuel and provisions, and are standing by on twenty-four hours notice. All of which, I think, is merely a precautionary measure.

There are so many differences of opinion aboard ship here that I couldn't even make a good guess. The possibilities seem to be one of the following:

1. (and most probable) Continue regular schedule.
2. (next probable) Be distributed at principal cities as patrol for belligerent vessels and a reassurance to the citizenry.
3. Be sent to the Caribbean as a patrol, the Caribbean being the most strategical point for a concentration of American ships.
4. Be sent over to act as convoy for evacuating merchant vessels.
5. Be sent over to aid in evacuation ourselves.

Aside from that, your guess is as good as mine. Right now we're lying at anchor at N.O.B. and, as I said, standing by to stand by.

If the Neutrality Bill forbids American travel on ships of belligerent nations, there is going to be a helluva rush of American shipping from Europe. What that means, I don't know. We were scheduled to go out for short range this week, but it has been cancelled indefinitely, although, personally, I think that as soon as the President makes his proclamations we will go about our business as usual.

This is not a very newsy letter, but please don't think it too awful. I'll write as soon as I get any new dope. All the news is the war, and you know as much as I.

All the love in the world to the grandest people I know,

Scottie

Tuesday, at sea, 12 September 1939

Dear Family,

The voice of the dead speaks – and how are you all?

The first question, I suppose, is "where am I?" And here is the answer. We are at sea on Neutrality patrol, steaming back and forth along the coast – 120 miles up and 120 miles back – the northern point being 150 miles from Nantucket Light bearing 140 degrees. We have been here since the morning after I wrote to you, and we will continue here until the 23rd when we go into Norfolk for a rest, being relieved by another ship.

After that I don't know – maybe we'll come back out here, and if we don't, we will go down into the Caribbean where the rest of the Division is now. It is all a matter of conjecture, and your guess is as good as mine. I suppose that patrol in one way or another will be our job for the rest of the war.

A destroyer is coming out tomorrow with mail and will take ours in to Newport, so I am getting a chance to write to you and tell you the news.

They are keeping us very busy and in that way hope to fight off inevitable boredom. Drills of all sorts all day long – damage control, gunnery, emergency etc. But still the time passes very slowly, and it seems that we have been at sea for a long, long time. However, it gives us a chance to learn and study a lot which is certainly not amiss.

Today we had a drill which we didn't expect. A man fell overboard, and the man-overboard drill was in real earnest. It turned out O.K. and we got him safely.

We are right on the steamer lanes, and every once in a while we see a British or French vessel all camouflaged and zig-zagging to fool potential submarines. It is the only thing that we have seen of the war. How long that we will stay in Norfolk or where we will go is, as I said, unknown; but as soon as I know anything definite, I'll let you know.

There is, of course, no cause for worry. It is just a case of our staying out here and warning American shipping of the presence of any belligerent craft – a thing which we have not and will not see.

One of our class has already been transferred to a destroyer, and I'm hoping that I may be the next. But since I want it very badly, there probably is no chance.

I think that I shall sell the car if I can as soon as I get back to Norfolk. It is doing me no good and certainly shouldn't sit idle.

Aside from the news that I have given you, there is no other.

A very happy birthday to both Dad and George again – now a little late for Georgie.

       Much, much love to all,
        Scottie

Saturday, 30 September 1939

Dear Family,

Well, here we are in Norfolk, and here we stay for another week.

I'm qualified in Engineering now and take charge of the Engineering Plant underway by myself. It is quite a feat to do it in so short a time, so I'm told.

After that horrible example of a letter which you must have just received, I can imagine with what trepidation you peruse this one. The truth of the matter was that I was in a very, very sour mood, and as a result did not feel like writing, or doing anything but sit around and gripe. However, as it is with such things, the prodigal has snapped out of it, and today feels quite chipper again.

First of all, we are going to sea Monday for about three weeks. The first week we train for and then fire short range practice – the same thing that we did on the Midshipman cruises, with newer and different guns, of course (different as to type, I mean). My job as battery officer is probably the least important gunnery job on the ship as far as work is concerned. All I do is stand around with a pair of headphones on and a telephone strapped to my chest, and listen in on all orders being sent to the guns and make sure that the various gun captains carry them out. It is a sort of safety factor and, of course, very necessary since I am the only commissioned officer in the vicinity of the guns – however, it is very, very dull. The reason that I have such a job is because I am an Engineer, and that is supposed to take all of my time.

After we have fired the practice on Thursday, we go on out to sea and relieve a patrol vessel for an indefinite time. It is rumored though that we will be in in two weeks – also that we won't be in for a month – also that we won't be in for two months – and your guess is as good as mine.

This afternoon the Quincy officers are giving a cocktail party at the club over in the yard. I am dragging a school teacher to it – very nice and a lot of fun. Graduate of William and Mary. I have a ride in my car – since it is technically mine until I have the title changed. I was sorry to let the "bug" go, but, under the circumstances, I am well rid of it though it would come in handy while we are in port.

We are all talking football here on board and speculating on our chances to see the Army – Navy game. They look mighty small right now, but here is hoping, AND HOW.

As for the war, I know no more and probably less about it all than you all do. Being at sea as we are such a great amount of the time, and the news broadcasts being so sketchy, it is hard to keep up with it all. So, as Mother said, who knows, but I am sure that there is little cause for worry for a long, long time to come.

I guess that I told you that I am standing top watches in Engineering now, and it makes things a little more interesting.

Hooray for George and his job – he'll be back to Michigan before he knows it. I am busting with pride for my brother. He is O.K.

We had a change of Admirals yesterday. Admiral Ellis replaced Admiral Johnson as Commander of the Atlantic Squadron. We did not see the ceremony, but I understand it was quite sumpin.

Mother's letter that arrived yesterday was very, very welcome. Letters from home are such a treat to me, and I do so wish that I could write as nice ones as I receive. However, nothing has happened, so help me Hannah, and so what can you do about it?

My very, very best love to all my family,
Scottie

At sea, 12 October 1939

Dear Family,

Tonight we found out that a plane is going to be sent in with our mail in the morning, so now I make haste to get a few lines out at least before the mail closes.

At present we are out on the Southern Drill Grounds and will fire short range practice tomorrow. As soon as we are finished we will go out on the line for patrol for the next two weeks. We are to get in on the 27th if the present schedule holds good.

There is very little news from here except that I have been given the "A" division permanently as long as I am in engineering. The regular Division Officer went to the hospital and will be gone for a long time, so they turned the custody of all material and the entire responsibility to me. I hope that I make good at it because it is a wonderful chance.

I got a free plane ride up to New York last week-end, and took it. It sort of looks as though Ada L.. has outgrown me, although, of course, I can't be sure. At any rate, don't be too surprised if you hear that that little episode is all over. There is no reason to feel badly about it because I have expected it for some time and even then I may just be imagining things. I don't know whether it is my fault or hers or a combination of both – at least only time can tell. So what the heck.

As for our plans for the next few months, all that is definite is that we expect to get into Norfolk for a couple of weeks on the 27th – even the two weeks in is merely a matter of conjecture. The Tuscaloosa and the San Francisco have been in the Caribbean for the last two months and are aching for relief. Here's hoping that we are not it.

The war seems very, very remote to us out here now. I have not had time to listen to the news or to do much of anything but keep going for eighteen hours a day, and try to get my work done.

There is really little else to tell you as you well know. Life aboard ship is not the exciting thing that the story books would have you think – it is just a job like anything else, as I expected it would be; a very pleasant job in some respects and a very, very dull one in others. Everything is like that, isn't it.

I guess that isn't the pleasantest letter in the world and certainly not the best typed, but it should suffice to tell my family that I think of them so very often, and send them my very best love,

Scottie

30 October 1939

Dear Family,

After my phone call last night this letter seems a little superfluous since there is no news except what little I told Mother yesterday. However, I'll start out, and perhaps a divine revelation will reveal some little tidbit that I overlooked.

In the first place, as you must know, the Quincy is a sea going packet if there ever was one. We have just come in from three weeks of watching the ocean, and now tomorrow morning we are off again. However, we will be in for the week-ends for the next three weeks, and then in for about two weeks altogether. That will keep us in port for Thanksgiving, no matter which one the Navy decides to celebrate if at all, and for the Army game.

Oh, yes.. As for tickets for the Army game, I can get only two, which I have ordered. I want very much to go to the game with Ada E......., and have had the tickets sent to her since the Navy mails and plans are so indefinite. However, as things stand now there doesn't seem an awful lot of chance of my going with her, and if that is the case Dad certainly can have the tickets. When and if I do hear from her in regards to the game, I'll have her get the tickets to you if she can't go with me.

Next week we go out for gunnery, and this time I have no duties in connection with that. I have been relieved of all but engineering duties, and thank the powers that be for that. It is a full time job. As I told you last night. However, I like to be kept busy. It is the quickest way in the world to snap back into battery as we would say in the Navy.

Then, too, I am learning a lot of things that will be valuable to me no matter where I am or what I am doing, and have started to get a lot of practical engineering experience. I am told that I could get a Chief Engineer's ticket in the unlimited class right now in the merchant service. Not that I would ever do that and go to sea with the merchantmen - God forbid!!! But it is an indication at least. In fact, there are so many things that I want to read up on and check on, plus so many personal things that I would like to get done that I am way behind on my schedule with little or no likelihood of catching up in prospect.

When I will get home before Christmas, if at all, I do not know. All I can do is to watch for a break and hope for the best. I thought I was going to be able to make it a couple of weeks ago, and finally decided that it was impossible.

     My very, very best love to all my family,
      Scottie

11 November 1939

Dear Family,

It is rather ironical that we should be celebrating Armistice Day today, is it not? But, nevertheless, it is a Navy holiday, and, of course, I have the week-end duty.

We arrived here in N.O.B. late yesterday afternoon, and expect to be in for two or three weeks. That is a break, since we have been at sea for so long. Naturally, plans are subject to change without notice, so it will not surprise any of us if we get underway again Monday morning.

Perhaps, Allah willing, I can get free for a couple of days and get home sometime around Thanksgiving, but don't count on it. The Navy has been clamping down on leave more than ever, and the week-ends are just about all anyone can get. As soon as I have any definite dope, I will try to make some plans.

We are tied up at the dock this time, which also is a pleasant change. It does away with boat schedules and waiting on the dock for a ride back home etc. Norfolk is such a horrible place to get to from the base here that waiting for boats made just about the straw that broke the father's back. I swear that perhaps I will buy a jalopy again. It is admitted shamefully that selling the "bug" was the biggest mistake I have made in a long, long time.

Last Sunday a reserve Ensign (not flyer) reported aboard. It is the first that I knew of their taking reserves into the Line. He is to be on active duty for a year, or until the limited national emergency is over should that be less than a year.

There is a lot of talk of our going into the Navy Yard in Portsmouth in January for three months instead of waiting until March. In fact, I think that is just about decided on. Personally, I'd rather wait until March and have some warm weather, but anyway it will be nice to have good dry land around for a long time.

Last week we fired local control battle practice, and then calibrated radio direction finders. Since we did both in one week instead of spreading it out, we got in for a stretch ahead of time. Our next assignment is damage control practice. That is the time when observers from another ship which has made up a battle problem for us come over and go to sea with us. When all is ready they start the problem. Only the observers know where the various shells are going to hit us and what the damage will be. At stated times the hit and damage is announced, and we have to so adjust and repair to keep the ship under maximum efficiency. If a steam line is supposed to be shot away, all valves are closed and the line made inoperative even if it means stopping the main engines. I am in charge of the after engine room and it means a lot of work for me. Have to know every valve and line in the room by heart so I can make a snap judgment as to what is to be done when the various damages are announced, and can get to work.

Did you receive my letter mailed on board ship this week?

Please write soon and give me the dope on the grandest family in all the world.

> Much, much love,
> Scottie

CA39/   (70) - ss
U.S.S. QUINCY

NOB, Norfolk, Va.
14 November, 1939

From: Ensign R.S. Whitman, Jr., U.S. Navy
To: .   Commanding Officer, U.S.S. QUINCY.

Subject: Leave - request for

1.   It is requested that I be granted four (4) days
         leave commencing on or about 17 November, 1939.

2.   I have had four days leave this fiscal year.

3.   I am not a member of any court or board.

4.   If this request is granted, my address while
         on leave will be:

         51 St. John Avenue,
         Binghamton, New York.

                              (signed) R.S. Whitman, Jr.

FIRST ENDORSEMENT   U.S.S. QUINCY   (70) - ss
                                   14 November, 1939

From: Commanding Officer,
To: Ensign R.S. Whitman, Jr., U.S. Navy

1.   Returned, granted.
                              (signed) Paul Bastedo.

```
W E S T E R N

U N I O N
_____

NF 141   17 NT-Norfolk VIR 14              1939 NOV 14 PM 10 41

MRS R S WHITMAN-

  51 ST JOHN AVE BINGHAMTON NY-

  WILL BE HOME EITHER EARLY FRIDAY MORNING OR LATE FRIDAY
  EVENING IF ALL GOES WELL MUCH LOVE
       SCOTTIE
```

Tuesday, 28 November 1939

Dear Family,

This is just a note to tell you the glad news, and that I arrived safely back here after a rather nasty day.

The first thing that I heard was that we are to be at sea not only for the Army game, but also on Christmas Day. Since we are due to go into the yard in January, when all the rest of the ships go south, they are giving us the dirty work. Please try not to be too disappointed. I am, and find that the Navy has at least taught a measure of resignation.

I have written to Ada L.. telling her about the change in plans, and have told her that if she is free on that Saturday, and could use the tickets, she is to do so. If not, then turn them over to Dad for him to get rid of for me. Get the best price you can, but I will be satisfied with $4.40 which is the established price.

The man whose division I had is back, but I think that they are going to keep me on in the same job. I rather hope so since it is very good experience. Tonight I am awfully tired and so will not try to write a long letter. However, we will be in after Christmas on the 27th, and perhaps I can wangle a little leave then. At least there is a very good chance of it. I know better than to say anything definite any more.

It was grand being home with you all again, and now all I look forward to is the next time - may it be soon.

> Much, much love to all,
> Scottie

ROBERT SCOTT WHITMAN JR.

Monday, 4 December 1939

Dear Family,

So much has changed, and so much happened since I last wrote to you that I hardly know where to start. However, if you will bear with me, I'll struggle onward and try to keep the unity, coherence, and emphasis well under control.

In the first place, I am now in New London, Connecticut, still with the Quincy, of course. We are up here for this week to act as a target for submarine torpedo practices. Now, Now – don't be alarmed. They fire torpedoes without any charge in them, and at a depth that passes well under the ship.

Typically after the Navy tradition, our plans were changed at the last moment after we had put out to sea, and we were in for the week-end here. All of which was very nice since I had already got rid of the Army game tickets. I only hope that Dad gets a chance to sell them. A bunch of us accepted the invitation of the Officer's Club at the Sub. Base and went over there to hear and watch the game on a playograph. It certainly did turn out beautifully, did it not? That evening a young officer and his wife got us dates, and we went out dancing.

The last boat was at midnight, and Bill Walker and I just did make it. We had no desire to stay ashore over night, and so were even more glad that we were successful in the attempt, since that boat was the last until this morning at seven. A 45 knot wind sprang up, and kept all boats either on the beach or at the ship; and, as a result, about half the ships company were stranded on the beach. The Paymaster, Lt. Commander Duffy, had ten guests out to see the ship, seven men and three women, and they were all stranded out here over night. Quite a lark for his two nieces, I imagine.

The next piece of news concerns more changes in plans. At sea last Thursday, we received word that the Quincy would go into the Norfolk Navy Yard in Portsmouth, Va. for three months overhaul on December 18th, which means that we will be in port from then until the 18th of March, 1940.

So, you see, instead of being at sea for the Army game and for Christmas, we were in for one, and will be in for the other. Perhaps there is a chance to be home Christmas after all. Now it is the same lash-up as I explained while at home. Of course, the plans can be changed at least a half a dozen times more before we finally do get into the Yard and get the machinery torn down so that we can't move.

Ever since we got word we have been in a veritable storm of activity trying to get all the work requests out and plan for the Board of Inspection and Survey, which inspects the ship and decides on what work is to be done and what is to be deferred. On top of all that, we have had another set of examinations for promotion of enlisted men, and I have had the burden of marking all of the engineering papers.

Mother's letter was most welcome. It had seemed such a long time since I had heard from home. As for her query, which I am sure that she remembers – sure – I'll match Georgie.

The car functioned quite satisfactorily and I am well satisfied with it. [Bought while home.]

We are due back in Norfolk the 9th, and from then on I'll be in Portsmouth, Va., (NNYd). As soon as the holiday watches are arranged I'll let you know when to next expect me. As you know, I have the duty Christmas day, but may be able to get out of it – at least here is hoping. At any rate, if not then, certainly New Years.

The weather was so bad last night that there was great fear that we would drag anchor and land with our stern dragging the beach. So we got the engineering plant ready to get underway and stood by for ten hours to answer any emergency bells. I have been at it all day now and, as a consequence, with two hours sleep out of the last thirty-six, it is just about time to turn in.

       Much, much love to all,
        Scottie

Thursday, 14 December 1939

Dear Family,

Here the week has almost passed, and I have yet to get my letter off. However, it has been a busy time what with getting ready for the Board of Inspection and Survey, and there has been little time for letter writing.

The biggest news to date is the dope on leave over the holidays. Much as I expected, I have to stand the duty on Christmas Day, and for that matter for five straight days before Christmas. However, I can have leave from the 26th to the 2nd. I almost made it for Christmas, but they suddenly decided to change the method of standing watches, and I couldn't get anybody to take my duty on Christmas Day (small wonder). So – I'll be home sometime Tuesday a week, and will stay until the next Tuesday.

We are in the Yard now, and start our overhaul on Monday. All this week we have been tearing down machinery for the Board. The Board of Inspection and Survey is a group of experts who inspect each ship in the Navy once each two years for conditions of preservation etc. We had the final day of inspection today.

Saturday we get a new skipper, a Capt. Wickham, who is said to be a very, very fine man and officer. Time will test the statement.

Tonight I am going to a dance on the Texas which the Admiral is giving for his daughter. Eight of us bachelors are going from the Quincy. Uniform – full dress, railroad trou and all. It will probably be a bore but, what the heck, it might be fun.

There is probably a lot more news, but it is time for chow, and I'll be seeing you before so very long.

It sure looks like the controversy over the efficacy of the "pocket battleship" has been finally decided. It looks as though they're not so hot.

Anyhow – much, much love to all, and I'll see you soon.

      Scottie

Monday, 18 December 1939

Dear Family,

    This is just a note to tell you that the plans for leave have been changed in such a way that it will be possible for me to get free on this Friday and to return on the 2nd of January. What you will do with me for all of that time will be a problem, but, at any rate, I can get home for Christmas. The reason for the change is so complicated that I couldn't begin to explain it — so I'll attempt it when I see you.

    You can expect me home either on Friday night, or Saturday night, depending upon whether I can see Ada E........ in Baltimore. Doctor D..... is very, very seriously ill with an embolism (sp).

    The Navy Yard overhaul began today, and already things are pretty much in a storm.

    This is all for now, but I thought that I had better pass on the good news. See you all soon.

        Much, much love to all,
           Scottie

W E S T E R N

24

U N I O N

_____

NAA355   7-Norfolk Vir 22 1245P   1939 DEC 22 PM 1 29

MRS R. S. WHITMAN-

    51 ST JOHN AVE BINGHAMTON NY-

SEE YOU LATE TOMORROW SATURDAY MUCH LOVE-
                    SCOTTIE

5 January 1940

Dear Family,

The holidays are over, and now we are back to work again with some changes in the offing. I have meant to get this letter off before, but, as you can gather, have put it off and put it off until finally my desires and my conscience brook no further procrastination.

The trip down was highly satisfactory albeit very uneventful. The roads were not so good north of Baltimore, but from there on they were excellent. I stopped in Baltimore as planned, but did not see Ada E........ she was out, and rather than spend money uselessly in waiting over, I drove on down to Norfolk arriving early in the morning.

New Years Eve I took Louise Outland out. Quite a crowd of us on the ship went out together to the Country Club and had a grand time. I wore my tails and was quite the belle of the ball. New Years day, Winky Wilcox, a girl who drags Quincy quite a bit, had a cocktail party, and we went to that. So it was a gala New Years celebration.

The biggest news so far is that Bill and I have been shifted from Engineering to Deck duty, as I told you I expected we should. I go to the 4th Division and Bill to the 1st. The 4th Division is the Anti-aircraft Division, and so I'm back with the five inch guns again. We are to start standing top deck watches immediately, which is a break for us. The other lads stood J.O. watches for five months before they were qualified. We are both sorry to go, and the Chief Engineer is sorry to lose us, but it is best for us to get deck experience while we can. At least, it will mean a new environment and new things to learn. (Not that there is not a lot to learn left down below).

My stay home was by far the most enjoyable all around that I can remember for a long time. I enjoyed every minute of it, and was pretty blue for a while after I got back wishing that I had not left. However, perhaps with the change of duty, I will be able to get home again for a short while before we finish our overhaul. The deck divisions do not have a lot to do during this period, and it is a time for leave.

This week-end I have the duty, my last as an Engineer and as a Division Officer. I'll have to go back to asking the boss every time something in my division comes up. At least I drop a lot of responsibility. In June one of us goes back to engineering permanently, and the other of us will undoubtedly go to a destroyer. The engineering duty was fine, I got along with everybody, and got good marks so I am satisfied that my first tour of instruction duty was a definite success. I only hope that the rest will be as successful. If it is humanly possible to make it so, it will be.

It was awfully cold down here for a while, but it has warmed up considerably now, thank goodness. For the first two days back I had to spend all my time getting the ship warm. We had the devil of a time getting enough steam from the yard power house, but I finally traced down the trouble, and yesterday I got a lot of very pretty compliments from the warm room officers who were warm for the first time in two weeks.

I played touch football with a bunch of the boys yesterday, and am as stiff as a board. However, the exercise was most welcome.

That is all for now. Please write to me soon.

Much, much love to all and thank you for the wire,

Scottie

Monday, 15 January 1940

Dear Family,

I am just barely sticking my head out of the dog house to draw it back in when you lop it off for not getting my letter off on time. You see, four of us went up to Annapolis this last week-end, and thereby hangs the reason for my tardiness.

Bill Walker, his date, Betty Roberts, and Louise and I drove up Saturday for the boxing matches and a hop. The girls stayed with Louise's aunt, and we, after much hunting, at Carvel Hall. It was a very nice week-end, and we all enjoyed it thoroughly although it did rain all the time we were there. The worst part was the drive back. We left on Sunday afternoon about three and arrived here at two in the morning. There was a horrible fog all the way, and my windshield wipers went on the fritz. However, we had fun even on the long ride.

Mother's package with the laundry and the pajamas arrived safely. Thank you muchly, Mother dear. I guess you know how I needed another pair of not so flossy pajamas. Now I am all set.

There is not much news here. The deck duties are not particularly arduous, and so far I have had no trouble getting along in the new work. Most of the work topside here in the yard is chipping and scraping and repainting. The Fourth Division has more of the ship to take care of than any other, but it has more men and officers, a Lieutenant and two Ensigns.

The weather has changed constantly down here. One minute it is cold and the next warm – the only consistency is the constant rain, today being the first day that we have seen the sun in more than a week.

We have been having a sort of gunnery school for officers aboard here with lectures three times a week. A lot of good dope is put out, and it is quite interesting. There is so much to learn that I feel as though I shall ever remain stupid. Here is a hope that I am not too correct in my feeling.

According to the present schedule, we go south immediately after overhaul, around the 20th of March, for patrol duty, and then stay for gunnery. We have an awful lot of gunnery practices to fire to catch up with the other ships of the division.

I have given up lunches in the hope that I can pare down some of the excess avoirdupois – a futile gesture I am afraid. I guess I will always be a fat man. There is so little opportunity for any exercise, and that is what I need most. The fresh air on deck is making me a rosy cheeked little dumpling again.

I expect that I'll take a little leave in February and come home – if I can get it.

        Much, much love to all,
          Scottie

Sunday, 21 January 1940

Dear Family,

Mother's letter arrived yesterday, and Dad's earlier in the week. Naturally I was very sorry to receive them. You know how I hate mail.

The work is progressing favorably, and I guess that we shall be through with our overhaul on schedule. Cruisers of the Atlantic Squadron are to remain on this coast for another year according to the dope that we have received. I expect that we shall make reserve cruises again this summer.

Friday night we had what turned into quite a party. There was a dance at the Club here in the Yard, and it turned out that all of the J.O's. were dragging. So we decided to have all our dates aboard for dinner, and then go in a mass to the dance. We arranged to have the dinner hour set a half hour late and all met at the Club first for a cocktail. Then we had dinner, and went on to the dance. It was highly successful, and we are thinking of making it a regular bi-monthly affair. The dance is free to members of the Club, and so it is an inexpensive way to have a grand time.

Bill Sawyer, my roommate announced his engagement today, or rather yesterday for it appeared in the Washington papers today.

As soon as it gets warm, I am going to overhaul the Chevvy. I can get about $75 worth of work done for the cost of material alone by doing it myself with the help of the motor boat engine repair gang.

As soon as I can get a minute, I am going to write to George. I owe him a letter, and have been meaning to get it off much before this. However, there is so little time to do anything – or there seems to be but little.

       Much, much love to all,
        Scottie

Saturday, 27 January 1940

Dear Family,

Another week has blown by, and comes time for my letter home. Mother's letter arrived betimes, for which I am thankful.

We have just finished with Captain's Inspection below decks, and the Fourth Division came through without any defects - for once. There was to have been an inspection of personnel, but the weather, rather than breaking for the warm side, got even colder, and now it is about ten above with no prospect of relief for the next couple of days. So there was no topside inspection.

As usual, there is no news worthy of mention. All the work topside that concerns me is chipping and repainting surfaces - which is not particularly exciting. I have been made Catapult Officer, though, and that entails a good bit of reading and study since I have never even watched at close hand the firing of the catapults.

This morning I had the watch from four to eight, and believe you me, it was cold. I have never been so thoroughly frozen before in my life even though I did spend most of the time in the OOD Shack in front of two electric heaters. However, I have now thawed out the two ice cakes that were my feet, and feel normally normal again.

At present the speculation is concerned with who will be transferred in June, and who will get whose job. I have a sort of a hankering for a turret but think that the possibilities are small indeed. Either that or a new destroyer. The way it shapes up now, I'll probably go back to engineering since the Chief Engineer liked my work - and I don't think that it is best for me that I do. Gunnery, although as yet I don't like it particularly, is still the best sort of specialization for the officer that wants to get ahead. All of the officers of flag rank were gunners. That in itself is indicative of a lot.

They are going to lay down one of the new battleships, the Alabama, here in the Yard on the first of February. I suppose that there will be some sort of a ceremony, and think that I will go just to see what it is like. Then I can chalk that off the list of experiences.

Tonight there is a dance at the Club, and I think that I'll go. We have a pretty good time, and there is not an awful lot else to do.

For some reason or other, I don't seem to have the good time that I used to have. Maybe I'm getting old – although God forbid that!!! The other night, however, we did have a nice party. A friend of Bill Walker had a house guest from South Carolina, and we got her a date with Tom Bennett. We all went over to the Portsmouth Club and it turned out that this gal was studying music at some little school down there. Boy, could that girl play the piano! I guess we kept her going for three hours.

And that is about the news for this time.

      Much, much love to all,
       Scottie

Tuesday, 6 February 1940

Dear Family,

Another letter late, and this time with fair excuse. I had the week-end duty, and having the duty on deck is quite the opposite from having it in Engineering. We stand four hours on watch, and eight hours off, which is bad in itself, and I had the 12 - 4 watches. All I did was to eat and sleep and stand watch, with never a thought to writing letters or anything else.

The time seems to be flying by, and in less than two months we will be at sea again. The overhaul period is beginning to wear from its original novelty, and I think that there are quite a few of us who would not mind a little sea duty for a change. Not because we love the sea, or want to get away from land, but because Norfolk in the winter time is not the pleasantest place in the world in which to live.

This last week I have been instructing my gang in the use of the gas mask, and tomorrow I will take them all up to the gas chamber and let them try their masks out with a little shot of tear gas. Not having known anything about gas masks myself, I had to do quite a bit of studying before I felt qualified to tell any of the rest of them how to use one, but it was fairly interesting.

Got a letter from Marsh yesterday. He seems to be quite happy and contented with his wife and his airplanes. I suppose that there is a good chance that he may stay permanently in the Navy if the limited emergency remains in effect.

Tonight I am going to see Gone With The Wind. It is going to have to be plenty good to keep me interested for three and a half hours. However, those reports that I have had on it point to its being really worth while.

As for my letter to Aunt Julie. I wrote once and got the letter back. I had mailed it to Sonoma Avenue, Binghamton, N.Y. So I shall write again. Should have long before this, since it came back a week ago.

Something else. Will Dad please get me an application blank for license tags. I have been trying to remember to ask him now for the last three letters. The car is being driven illegally at this point, as are all the rest of the N.Y. cars down here.

You will have to excuse the poor typing. I am trying to learn to type by touch, and it is not working out too well as yet. If and when I come home, I think that I'll get my old typewriter overhauled, and bring it back with me. I need one badly.

As for coming home, weather and work progress on board will determine when if. As soon as I know definitely, I'll let you know.

No more now, it's time to go back to work.

Much, much love to all,
Scottie

Monday, 12 February 1940

Dear Family,

Another Monday evening, another week begun – perhaps before it is over I'll see you and perhaps I won't. Dick Phillips and I are planning very tentatively as yet to drive up either on Thursday or Friday, so stand by for a wire.

Right now the car is all torn down ready to have the valves ground and new rings. I'm doing the job myself with the help of a couple of mechanics off the ship, and it should run like a top when I'm through.

There is not an awful lot of news – nothing much has happened except one thing. Mr. Schieke, the former Senior Assistant Engineer officer, has been transferred with no immediate relief, and so a j.g. has stepped up into his job. That leaves "M" Division, the senior division open. I have been requested to fill the job, and it now remains to be seen whether the Captain will approve the request. It is quite an honor, but I would rather stay on deck. At least I have qualified as a top watch stander underway. I have also heard that I am to stay on the Quincy next year, and I know that the Quincy stays on the east coast for another year.

Saturday night we had a party for the new Captain and his wife. It was a dinner preceding the regular Saturday night dance at the Club and was a very nice affair.

Dad's letter arrived and was very much appreciated. The clipping concerning Hyde Park was very interesting. I think I remember seeing the negro "prince".

I'm getting pretty sick of Norfolk, and am just about ready for a little sea duty.

Hope to see you, but don't get the hopes too high.

Lots of love to all,
Scottie

Wednesday, 28 February 1940

Dear Family,

It has been a long week so far, and it promises to be a longer one before it ends. And not a very fortunate one.

To begin with, I started out to come home on Wednesday. Mr. Andrews had told me that I had better take my leave then since it was the only time that they could spare me. Why, I do not know since I am far from an invaluable sort of person to have around. At any rate, I started out about four o'clock with the thought of surprising you all with a visit. All progressed fairly well with the exception of a flat tire and a blown gasket until I arrived in Washington or on the Maryland outskirts of Washington.

And before I go on, I should explain to you that I was using '39 N.Y. tags. The Virginia tags for '40 are not sold until 15 March, and '39 tags sold only by half and whole year rates. The upshot of all that being that to buy '39 tags would have been the height of foolishness - $8 for six weeks of driving. The Virginia authorities realized this, and had let me and several other people with N.Y. and Calif. tags get away with it.

About ten miles out of Washington I was stopped, hauled before a J.P., fined $12.50, and the car impounded. I didn't have enough cash, and had to wait around until Mrs. D..... had wired the money to the Judge. Then took the bus to Baltimore and got a room at the Emerson. Thursday was a holiday, of course, and had to wait until Friday to get plates in order to be able to get my car. The police, however, had promised not to have it hauled away (at my expense) until Friday night.

Friday morning after straightening out a few minor details such as my lack of notarized bill of sale (a necessity in licensing an out-of-state care in Md.) I bought Md. tags, paid a 2% sales tax on the full purchase price of a car bought in N.Y., took out a learner's permit, took a driving test, and bought a Md. driver's license – then I could take the bus back to Savage, or wherever it was, and change the plates, and with my $50 license plates good for six weeks only, I could drive back very broke and very chagrined to the Quincy from which I have not since stirred.

It was a very, very disastrous and unpleasant trip.

However, my neck was out, and I should not have thought that it was O.K. to use the dead tags in one state just as much as another. So I have no one to blame but myself for the little jolt, and anyway am sure that I'll recover.

The only thing that I am really sorry about is that my chances both financially and otherwise of taking any leave for a while are sorely shot. However, we are due to be in these waters rather than go south for a couple of more months, and all may change then.

Right now the Quincy is in drydock. Yesterday and today the entire ship's force has been turning to scraping and painting the bottom. Now it is all ready for us to go back to our regular pier in another part of the Yard. All of us have had to turn to and help supervise the men, both for workmanship, and especially for safety. Of course, I have had the duty and stood night watches on top of it all, and today as soon as I got through in the drydock, I started taking roller path data for the guns, which lasted until a few minutes ago. Two 20 hour days make one ready for a little sleep.

At any rate, I walked under the Quincy yesterday – something which I have been promising myself. It has a pretty bottom.

The overhaul is almost over, and then to sea for gunnery practices – AA and machine gun, I believe. It will really be grand to get to sea again and away from Norfolk. I do almost wish that we would go West, but not really so, I guess. There has been no more said about my going back to the Engineers, but I'm expecting it almost any time now, and would rather not go.

Although I shall not be able to send any money until the middle of next month now, tell George not to worry about that which I owe him, and that I will replay him an even hundred because I want to. Eighty before time for school, and twenty later on. He is going back and that is all there is to that. Mother's repayment will be along in full next month.

I still owe George a letter especially so after his swell birthday present. It is coming tomorrow. My not writing sooner is no indication, as you well know, of the pride I have in a kid brother who has the "intestinal fortitude" that mine has. I use the case every day, and it is the finest thing of its kind that I know of.

The snow that you all must have wallowed through was certainly sumpin'. I don't ever remember seeing anything like it.

Oh, yes – the car. I overhauled the engine completely. New rings, new valves where needed, new ignition wiring, a new windshield wiper, motor overhauled, generator and starter, and everything else that I could think of. It runs like a charm. I'll probably sell the darned thing, but it was fun doing about a hundred dollars worth of repairs for ten dollars.

The typing, the spelling, and the continuity are horrible I know, but I'm awfully tired. Please excuse, and know that one awfully poohed-out lad sends all his love to the swellest three people in the world.

        Scottie

Thursday, 7 March 1940

Dear George,

At long last there seems time to at least start a letter to you. They have been busy days, these last, and there just hasn't seemed time during the day, or energy at night to write.

In the first place, Old Sport, thank you for the cigarette case. There was no need of your sending it, but it is sure a handy thing to have. I use it constantly, and now just can't seem to get along without it.

Of course you know all about my two false starts home, so there is no need to tell you my tale of woe. However, we got news today that the Quincy has been granted an extension here in the Yard until the 5th of April, and after the 15th there is just a wee possibility that I'll try it again.

The reason for the extension lies in the Engineering Department. It seems that they are having some trouble that was not foreseen. On deck we are well finished with our work, and expect to start gunnery drills to indoctrinate the new people next week. About three quarters of the crew have never been to sea before, and so you can see what a problem we are up against.

The Navy Yard is overfull with ships, building and overhauling. Right at or own dock there are six destroyers nested in pairs, a transport, and the Quincy; while opposite us on one side on the next pier are three tankers, and on the other side are eight more destroyers. Besides that, there is a battleship (Alabama) building, and two other cruisers overhauling, plus I don't know how many destroyers and a couple more transports. So, you see that there is a lot of business for the navy yards.

My Division Officer has gone on leave, and I am left here holding the sack. It has kept me busy, since up until today I have had 105 to handle. Now, however, we have transferred about 30, and the allowance is back to normal.

It won't be so very long before you will be back to Michigan learning how to build airplanes for the Navy and the Army. You certainly have done a swell job of buckling to and plugging, and you know the big brother, who ain't so big, is mighty proud of you. Keep plugging, Old Sport, and don't let anything get you down. You're due to go a long way and nothing can stop you.

Dad's letter arrived for which I am very grateful. I hope you are all well, and hope to see you sooner than you or I expect. Thank you again for the case, and lots of love to all.

        Scottie

Dad's fall worries me, do hope he is O.K. Let me know please.

Tuesday, 12 March 1940

Dear Family,

Mother's letter arrived today and 'twas indeed welcome. It had seemed ages since I last heard from home, but I don't suppose it actually was so long.

Every time I sit down to write a letter to you, the same problem arises – what can I tell you that will be interesting enough to warrant writing? Each time I'm stumped for those things that happen have happened a hundred times before and seem quite commonplace.

This week has, however, been the busiest for a long time since now we are in the midst of getting the "green" crew whipped into shape to go to sea. Mornings are devoted to gunnery and afternoons to emergency drills and damage control. Naturally we have to start from scratch, since most of the men are raw recruits and so there is a lot of work cut out for all of us.

Perhaps you will be interested to know how I spent today.

I got up at 0715, had a glass of orange juice and a cup of coffee for breakfast and finished just in time to go to "quarters" for muster of the crew at five till eight. From eight till 8:45 I worked getting the finishing touches on the crew's assignments for emergencies (drills), and then listened to the 2nd of three lectures on "thyratron control" given by a G.E. Engineer, who is aboard doing some work on range finders. From 10 till 11:30 I was up in the after A.A. director for gunnery drill (my new gunnery station). Then lunch, and at 12:30 a conference of all officers. 1300 collision drill instruction and then the drill itself. 1400 inspection of all 4th seaman's clothing outfit for completeness, marking and condition ("bag inspection". Finished at 1530 – 73 men). Now writing letter after reading Time for about half an hour. 1830 dinner, then the movie if it's any good and so ends a normal day. Except, of course, for routine inspections and "overseeings" of work, etc., etc., etc., which goes on every day.

I've given up trying to go out in the evenings at all during the week even if I could afford the money. I cannot afford the loss of sleep entailed.

We are due to leave the Yard on 5 April but expect to operate out of Norfolk indefinitely, so sometime before long when they will let me and when I have enough money to get me there, I'll be home – and as for me the sooner the better.

No more now except lots and lots of love to all,

        Scottie

Friday, 29 March 1940

Dear Family,

The trip down was very uneventful, and we arrived just as we suspected, at about three Monday morning. It was awfully cold all the way, and just as we got to Richmond we ran into a snow storm. When we arrived here there was about four inches of snow on the ground. The first white Easter in the history of Norfolk.

Between Binghamton and Owego we saw quite a few cars parked along side the road with the people standing gazing up on the hillside. What do you suppose was there but a herd of deer grazing very nonchalantly along side the road. They had evidently been driven out of the hills by the deep snow.

We are very, very busy with drills now, as I told you. However, the Engineers found another valve that was leaking, and when they took pictures of it they found that there was a stress crack about half way round the circumference. About half the ship was torn apart to get the thing out and up to the yard shop for repair, or so it seems; and we are to be delayed for a while again - just how long no one seems to know.

Our schedule from now until the first of June calls for gunnery and more gunnery; and the sooner we get out for the necessary training the better. I have been trying to feel out the bigwigs as to what job I'll have after June, but can't seem to get any word - I guess that they just don't know. Time will tell, and I guess that there is no use in worrying about that.

I yanked the battery out of my car and am having the ships electricians charge it for me. That is one advantage of the Navy. You can get little things like that done free of charge if you know the right people.

It was certainly swell being home even if for just a little while. I only hope that the next time will be soon. You never can tell about those things, and I'm keeping my fingers crossed.

Every bit of the best love to the grandest family in all the world,

      Scottie

P.S.

MOTHER - Thank you sweetie pie - but I guess that you don't need to have me say that to know how I liked my Easter present.

Sunday, 14 April 1940

Dear Family,

I guess you must think that I have forgotten you completely, for I know that I have not written for a long time. However, when you hear the tale, I think that perhaps you will forgive me. A week ago last Friday I got an invitation to take a blind date to the Portsmouth Assembly, Portsmouth's most social dance. I did, and ate their midnight supper of chicken salad etc. with great gusto – the salad turned out poisoned and I have been laid up with ptomain almost the whole time since. Now, however, I am up and around and feeling pretty close to normal again. If I can find the clipping which showed me what was wrong two days after the doctor turned me in with ptomain, I will enclose it. So you see, I really have not been able to get a letter off any sooner.

The Quincy is at sea again or rather operating. We went out on Wednesday – I still in bed and sick as a dog – came in Saturday for the week-end. The address from now on should be NOB, Norfolk.

Friday we fired an antiaircraft practice. I got up and controlled one run – my first, and as a result of being up, was down with a temperature that night. Now, however, I am up and should be back on duty tomorrow when we go out. I am writing with my own typewriter this time – it works fairly well don't you think?

Our schedule takes us out every week for a while and brings us in for the week-ends. We have several machine gun practices to fire, and later three practices with the turrets, plus that damage control problem that we were to have had last fall.

This will have to be all for now, but during the week I'll get out a really long letter.

        Much, much love to all,
          Scottie

Tuesday, April 9, 1940

MANY ARE ILL
AFTER DANCE

Ptomaine Suspected By
Portsmouth Doctors

About 35 Portsmouth people who attended the Portsmouth Assembly dance Friday night were today recovering from what was described as a mass attack of ptomaine poisoning.

Dr. Julian T. Miller, director of public welfare, said today that the city health department had made no effort to ascertain what had caused the illnesses because at this late date the food which was contaminated had in all probability been destroyed.

The only method left, Dr. Miller said, to trace the source of the poison would be to interview the people who have fallen ill and by a process of elimination as to what they ate, arrive at a conclusion.

One physician is reported to have hospitalized eight of his patients who had become violently ill.

ROBERT SCOTT WHITMAN JR.

Sunday, 21 April 1940

Dear Family,

Mother's letters all arrived but in inverse order. The first one last, and the last one first. However, the mixed-up arrivals detracted none from the pleasure of receiving and reading them.

Next week the Quincy has the busiest week that it or any ship has ever had - that is, if the present tentative schedule is adhered to. We are due for the damage control problem on Tuesday, to fire Day Spotting practice on Thursday and Day Battle on Friday, and to sandwich in some AA machine gun drills in between. Day Battle practice is the most important of the gunnery year, since it is fired at long range under what most nearly approximates battle conditions. It is a turret practice only, so I am not directly affected.

Last Wednesday and Thursday there was wild excitement. All of a sudden the Quincy started hightailing it for port at twenty-five knots, when we had all known that we were to stay out until Friday. We had orders to fuel and provision to capacity immediately and to stand by for further orders. Rumors of all sorts flew back and forth - we were going to Iceland to take the new Minister - we were going to Greenland, to Europe, to South America. Thursday the rush was called off and apparently the emergency no longer exists. Nobody except the Navy Department, and the Captain probably, knows what it was all about; but we imagine that we were actually about to start on some very important and secret mission, and then the State Department got cold feet. Perhaps some day the truth will out, but until then conjecture will have to take the place of fact.

Right now, although no official word has come out, we expect to head south two weeks from Monday and to be gone for from six weeks to two months. We go down to relieve the Omaha which has been down there.

I have finally recovered from the effects of the ptomaine, and have been off the sick list since Tuesday. However, I have not felt any too chipper, and had been staying aboard and taking it very easy.

We had our annual Military Inspection on Friday, and the Admiral and all his staff plus most of the officers from the Wichita snooped and probed around the whole morning. I guess we did all right considering how little time we have had to clean up since we got out of the Navy Yard.

Tommy Bennett, the other JO in the Fourth Division has been transferred to the <u>Gleaves</u>, a new destroyer; so all the work he did has devolved upon me to augment my own jobs. It keeps me pretty busy, but I guess that that is the way to be.

The weather has turned cold and it is drizzling out - more typical of Norfolk than the fine spring weather they had all the time that I was laid up.

I understand that the <u>Quincy</u> is going to hold the gunnery school this year which will mean that we shall have to arrive back north around the first of July at the latest.

Much, much love to all,
Scottie

Sunday, 28 April 1940

Dear Family,

Dad's letter arrived yesterday, and I do believe that it was the nicest letter that I have had from him in a long, long time. That is saying a lot because all of Dad's letters are swell.

Well, we are finally going south just as the weather here starts to become livable. We start out on Saturday and go down to Guantanamo to relieve the Omaha. We expect to stay for about a month and a half, and then to come back here and hold gunnery school aboard the Quincy. Well, it will be all new to me, and, although I am told that the part of Cuba that we will see will not be particularly exciting, at least I am looking forward to it. Mother can expect some more perfume - I hope.

We have been in since Wednesday taking on fuel, stores, and small caliber ammunition. While down there, we are all required to fire the Navy rifle and pistol course. That will be fun and good experience for all of us.

We have been operating out and in and doing not much of anything. But next week, we fire the two long range practices, and that ought to be interesting and instructive.

I have the week-end duty, and so have not been ashore for some time. I hope to get ashore when we come in to load stores on Thursday or Friday and find a place to put my car, and buy a pair of white shoes. It will be white uniforms for us for some time to come.

Dad's description of the Evan's book sounds fascinating and I hope to be able to read it some time soon. I believe that Capt. Evans is some relation of the D..... but I am not sure. At least, there is a Capt. Evans that is.

I have seen Tom Davies a couple of times. He was over with the umpire party for our damage control drills, and I have seen him ashore a couple of times.

Got a letter from Jud Rhode yesterday. He is graduating from M.I.T this June and is going to continue on and get his Master's degree in Chem Engineering. Says that he is going to be married to the gal that he dragged at the NA in December.

If we are going to be here for gunnery school this summer, we shall have an awful lot of time in port, and I should be able to spend quite a bit of time at the beach; and there is a possibility that I might get home some time during the summer after the '41 comes aboard.

We are to get six new Ensigns, and I know three of them slightly. The three that I know are good eggs, and they should be a welcome addition to the ships company.

Until you hear from me again with the dope on the new address, you had better send all of my mail through New York.

I hear that we are going to San Juan, and if we do I have a flock of addresses from Barbara Ridgway that should prove helpful.

      Much, much love to all,
        Scottie

IX
GUANTANAMO
MAY 1940

ROBERT SCOTT WHITMAN JR.

Guantanamo, Cuba

Saturday, 11 May 1940

Dear Family,

We arrived here last Wednesday, and have been at anchor ever since. Next week we are to go out and start training for night battle practice.

The weather down here is wonderful even though it is as hot as the proverbial hinges. The sun has shone steadily except for two ten minute rain squalls, the sky is a blue that one never sees in the north, and the sea the really true ultramarine. I am now burned to a crisp, and before I get back expect to be as black as a native.

There is nothing here at all except the naval and marine stations. The bay is a closed port. The only town within striking distance is a filthy dirty village called Caimanera. We went up one evening, and that was enough of that.

There are lots of tennis courts, and baseball diamonds, and, of course, the inevitable club. We go swimming off the ship (over the side) once a day at five o'clock, and liberty begins at three in the afternoon and expires for the enlisted personnel before supper. I have started to learn to play tennis, and to try to get in some sort of good physical shape – knock off the excess avoirdupois.

Last evening, we gave a cocktail party for the other ships that are in here and for the officers stationed at the Base. It was quite an affair. Tomorrow we JOs are playing the older officers in softball in the morning, and if that game does not materialize, I am going out with the Patrol Plane (Big Boat) patrol and take a look at Uncle Charlie Ridgway's Santo Domingo – from the air, of course, since we would not be able to land.

As for the war, I really know absolutely nothing except the bare fact that Hitler has started his big push. Whether he is being successful or whether he is not, I don't know; and we only get a radio press news once a day, and that sketchy.

Bill Sawyer and I are going to sleep out on deck tonight since it is as hot as blazes here in our room.

This afternoon Pete Peterson, a reserve aviator, Bill and I bummed one of the motor whaleboats and went out to try to catch a barracuda. We didn't.

Next week should be a busy week, since we are planning to fire on Thursday and Friday nights. It will be just like the Fourth of July with star shells bursting, searchlights playing around, and, of course, the guns booming.

I am to control the spotting practice on Thursday, since it does not go on the record and will give me just as good experience as record run on Friday, which will be controlled by a more experienced officer.

        Much, much love to all,
            Scottie

ROBERT SCOTT WHITMAN JR.

Monday, 20 May 1940

Dear Family,

Since we arrived here and spent the first few days loafing, I have had less time to sit down and do anything at all that I wanted to than ever before. It seems that there is more work to do each day and I seem never to get caught up.

We went out and fired Night Spotting practice, and things did not go so well. As a result, we have had drills morning, noon, and night. All that in addition to the regular ships work. Saturday and Sunday, however, we took time off, and nine of us started for Santiago.

When we got as far as Guantanamo City, a typical filthy dirty Cuban city, we found that we could not make train connections, and so we decided that instead of going back to the ship, we would spend the week-end there. There was a fairly decent hotel that was at least clean, and so we all got rooms.

There was absolutely nothing to do there except watch the Cubans, and duck automobiles, bicycles, ox-carts, and horsemen, all of whom with the exception of the cowboys honked continuously on airhorns. Some one must have imported a carload of the darned things and sold them to the sucker population.

I took some pictures and will send them to you as soon as I have them developed. One thing at least! I had heard about cock fights and wanted out of curiosity to see one. Sunday I did. They certainly are a bloodthirsty proposition and I don't want to see another. However, now there is another thing that I will not have to take hearsay about.

We hired a car (five passenger Ford) to drive the eight of us - nine with the driver - from Caimanera to G-City. He charged us, after much haggling, a paltry six dollars. We were outraged at the exorbitant price when the train is only 40 cents round trip, but after we had made the ride we were all calling him the world's biggest fool and sucker. I wouldn't drive myself alone over that road for a hundred dollars, let alone an overloaded car like that. That man must have done at least fifty dollars worth of damage to his car alone and taken ten years off his life. No words can describe it except to say that the average depth of the mud, which lasted the whole way, was about a foot, and the ruts and bumps at least five or so, it seemed. The ride of about ten miles took almost two hours. We drove because we missed the last train – Cuban railways being very uncooperative with us.

There is little else to tell about the week-end. We wandered around and soaked in atmosphere and the smell and the dust, and got a good idea of why the United States gave Cuba back to the Cubans. At that, it was better than going to even Havana, since now we know what typical Cuba is. The ride over there could easily have been through the wilds of Africa.

At this point I am going to sign off and go to bed since it is well on toward midnight, and there is a hard day ahead. More tomorrow when I can get a minute.

Day after tomorrow

Not a thing has happened since I left off. We are having gun drills morning, noon, and night and that is all I have had time to do.

    Much, much love to all,
        Scottie

Tuesday, 28 May 1940

Dear Family,

Mail arrived today with a letter from Dad, and a package from Mother. To say that both were welcome would be underestimating the situation, and to say thank you would be gross understatement. But thank you both very much, and my you know that mere words are insufficient.

We are at sea again steaming around in circles while a board made up of constructors, doctors, and engineers studies the effects on personnel of wartime cruising conditions in the tropics. To be brief, they shut the ship up as they would under battle conditions and then study the physiological reactions of the officers and crew in various places. Their recommendations, I presume, are sent to the Department, and the changes made on the new ships and, I suppose, perhaps the older ones. Wartime cruising in the tropics is no fun.

We are to arrive eventually in Key West to drop off the observers and then turn around and come back. The latest dope has it that we arrive back in Norfolk the middle of June.

Nothing of note has happened since we went to Guantanamo City. It has steadily become hotter, and as a result it is a relief to get to sea where it is a little, although not much, cooler.

Hooray for George and his trip to Boston. I am sure that if George likes the gal she must be tops - however, there is not a woman in the world with one very, very glaring exception that is worth the powder to blow her to hell. Experience is the only teacher in that respect though, and then again perhaps I am wrong. More power to you, kiddo, anyway.

I have been playing - or rather trying to play - tennis and find it great fun. More and more I regret the lack of knowledge of the more gentle sports that I have. The only solution is to learn and learn fast, which is what I am trying to do. I don't seem to lose any weight, and yet all my clothes are looser. Perhaps it is just a reapportioning of the avoirdupois (which is in itself quite a weighty sentence).

Of course I have sunburned and peeled, and am now in the process of getting somewhat of a tan. Gunnery drills every day and night, and lots of other drills keep us more than busy. This week also, I am acting as Assistant Navigator. That takes me off the watch list, but also gets me up at four every morning to take the morning stars. We all have to do it to qualify in Navigation (part of the two-year job), and I am glad that I am getting it over with now.

Time for the afternoon volley ball (we play every afternoon at four) so now I'll quit temporarily.

Friday

My, such a lot has happened since the above. We are back in Guantanamo after turning back two hundred miles from Key West. We were all the way to the western tip of Cuba and ready to go around and into Key West when we suddenly changed course and steamed with every bit of speed that we could make back here. Arrived this morning and started to fuel and provision to capacity. Now no one knows where we are going – if we are going, which in my mind is highly improbable. It is all very secret, and those few people who, because of their duties, must know are not putting out any dope. However, it seems to be the consensus of opinion that we are just going through another one of those false alarms as we did that time in Norfolk. It is well known that the Navy Department had us turn back to stand by to go to a definite place that is also known to the chosen few. Where that place is, I personally don't know.

It is also known that we are to be ready by midnight. However, the Exec. has given us permission to attend a party on the beach with no orders as to when we get back, so it looks as though the Department either has found out that the phantom emergency was a phantom or that the emergency was not an emergency after all. I have seen the navigator plotting courses to South America (yesterday) if that means anything. At any rate, we have been definitely told that it is not Europe, so you may rest easy.

I do believe that the Quincy steamed more miles in less time this last week than it ever has before. Rarely did we go below twenty-five knots, and it was much, much higher a lot of the time.

If you should not hear from me for a while you will know that we are underway for the mystery port and that mail is not being mailed.

The reason for all the secrecy is easily explained. The

dispatch giving us our orders was sent in a secret code that would be compromised if the gist of the message was known by interested foreign powers. All of our radio is intercepted and copied by the espionage systems of other countries, just as we intercept theirs. I would appreciate that you keep even the little that I know within the family.

       Much, much love to all,
        Scottie

X
SOUTH AMERICA
JUNE 1940

Saturday, 1 June 1940

Dear Family,

Well, the news is out, and you have undoubtedly either read it in the papers or heard it over the radio. As a matter of fact, you probably knew all about our cruise before we did, since it was not announced over the ship's loud speaker system until this morning; and it was only by chance that one of the officers heard the dope on the ten o'clock news broadcast last night (Esso) and told me when I got back aboard ship at about twelve.

Just in case you do not know, and are champing at the bit to get the dope we are getting underway this afternoon at two o'clock for Rio de Janeiro and for other South American ports. What ones, I do not know except that we probably will go to Montevideo. It is to be a good will tour as pinch hitters for the Midshipmen's Cruise, which has been cancelled as far as South America is concerned.

When you next see me I will no longer be a weak little Pollywog, but a mighty Shellback – we shall cross the line, of course.

It will be a perfectly swell cruise as far as any of us can figure, and, since it is a good will tour, the entertainment will not be lacking. It is funny that the Quincy should be picked to make the same cruise twice, since it went around the horn last year. This year I don't believe that we will go around to the western side at all – however, who can tell.

I suspect that the words "good will tour" cover a multitude of things, and that there is probably more to the cruise than meets the eye. However, be that as it may, I think that I am plenty lucky.

How long we are to be gone I do not know. It will take us twelve days to get to Rio, which will get us in there the twelfth of the month.

Address my mail to the U.S.S. Quincy for the next twelve days or so in care of Rio (such English). You can tell I am in a hurry.

Well – so be it. I will write as soon as we arrive.

   Much, much love to all,

    Scottie

Enroute Rio

8 June 1940

Dear Family,

In three days we are due to arrive in Rio de Janeiro, and very glad indeed shall we all be to get there. It has been a long and very uneventful trip on the whole, and everybody is anxious for a change in the monotony of shipboard life.

With the exception of the ceremonies in crossing the line, nothing has happened. However, the metamorphosis of your son from a slimy Pollywog into a full grown Shellback might be interesting to relate.

We crossed the equator on Friday, the 6th, and the horseplay started on Thursday. Davy Jones came aboard on Thursday afternoon as ambassador from King Neptune, Lord of the Sea. All the Ensigns who were not Shellbacks were members of the guard of honor which greeted him. The uniform being; brightly colored sarong, (one of the large alphabet signal flags), mess jacket, Turkish towel turban with a whisk broom fez, black shoes and leggings (the sarong being knee length), coca-cola bottle binoculars, undress sword belts, grey gloves and brooms. Thursday we paraded and maneuvered and had the time of our lives making darned fools of ourselves, and Thursday night the Kangaroo Court was held. Here all the officer Pollywogs and some of the enlisted men were charged with various nefarious crimes and sentenced to various horrible punishments by the Royal Judges. Five of us who had similar charges relating to the use of automobiles among our others were sentenced to be driver, engine, and four tires of a car, and to perform as terribly as possible. I was the right rear tire for having: 1. Made the "A" Division act like a bunch of garagemen (when they helped me overhaul) and 2. Failing to arrive home when I started out in a perfectly good car (my little affair with the Maryland State Constabulary).

We performed to the delight of the crew, and had a whale of a good time doing it. Naturally the officers took most of the beating because there were so many Pollywogs in the crew that they couldn't possibly hail them all before the Court or make them members of the Guard etc. - also this was the one time when all rates were passed by the board and the crew loved to get in their licks.

Friday morning the entire Court of the gracious and all powerful monarch of the deep came aboard. Neptune, the Royal Queen, the Royal Baby, Dentist, Doctor, Chaplain, Torturer, Devil, and a million others along with the Royal Bears and Royal Police. On the well deck the tank was set up, and on the platform that was beside and above the tank were all the instruments of torture – the Royal coffins, the Royal electric chair, the Royal barber chair, the Royal stocks etc. In order of divisions the Pollywogs were taken up to the Royal platform and given the Royal double works. The Royal Devil had a pitchfork charged with a small shot of electricity, and the Royal Executioner a scimitar charged the same, as was the Royal electric chair. The Doctor fed each one a horrible tasting dose, and the Dentist a worse mouth wash (every kind of spice etc. that you can imagine, diluted with vinegar); the Executioner electrocuted each, the Barber lathered each face with wallpaper paste; my mustache (now gone) was painted with shellac; and then each was seated in the barber chair, whose back faced the tank below. Over we went turning usually a complete flip in the air and landing in about six feet of water. The Royal Bears in the tank pounced on us and kept ducking us until we shouted Shellback (I finally had to say it though I swore I would not), and then out of the tank head first on the other side and through the mill of Royal Police with shellalies (canvas stuffed with rags). Once through the mill we were Shellbacks. It was grand fun and helped a lot to keep up the spirits of the crew.

From Rio we go to Montevideo, and from there we do not know. All sorts of guesses are running around, but nobody but the Captain, if he does, knows the dope and he is not putting it out. It is all very mysterious and secret. Now, as I suppose you know, the Wichita is also coming down, and is to arrive in Rio just after we leave for Uruguay. Does that sound logical if it were just a good will tour? However, they keep harping to us (a little too forcefully for me to believe that something is not being covered up) that we are just on a friendly visit.

The favorite joke is that we are going down to the Antarctic to pick up Bird's snowmobile, arm it, and then pull a blitzkrieg on Greenland.

Speaking of Blitzkriegs, Hitler's little party certainly must be terrible. Of course you know a lot more about what is going on than we, since we have been away from any steady news except the barest reports for more than a month. However, we hear enough to know that it is certainly a horrible, horrible mess.

Tuesday

Well, we are now within twenty-four hours of our destination, and we are getting ready to enter Rio. The dope now is that we will stay five days, and then on to Montevideo. Still no word further than that. If I find that we are going to be down here for a long time, I shall either send my keys to the car home or to Norfolk and work some plan out to get rid of it. It is nothing but a liability now which I would like very much to get rid of.

What with Italy's little play for glory, the European War has become universal. Roosevelt's speech last night certainly left no doubt in anybody's mind as to how he feels about the whole thing. I can't say that I do not agree with him; but still the head of a government should be a little circumspect in what he says. Now we are fearing all sorts of attempts at sabotage to try to break good will between the United States and Latin America. The security watches aboard ship here while we are in port are almost on a war time basis.

That for the time being is all the news, and I shall close this and mail it via airmail as soon as I get ashore.

Much, much love to all,

Scottie

ROBERT SCOTT WHITMAN JR.

17 June 1940

Dear Family,

Once more we are at sea and on the way to Montevideo. It was hard to leave lovely Rio, and I certainly hope that someday I may get back there again for a long visit. However, new land and new sights lie ahead, and that is always exciting.

We arrived in Rio in the morning of Wednesday, the 12th, and the first sight was a good sample of what was to come. First Corcavado, the Hunchback, loomed up out of the morning haze with the huge statue of Christ surrounding it. Then the familiar (even to me) Sugar Loaf appeared; and soon we were steaming into the most beautiful harbor in the world, and firing our twenty-one gun salute to the Brazilian nation. Airplanes zoomed over the ship, and the Naval Attaché came aboard with a Brazilian liaison officer from the pilot boat to greet us. Soon we were tied up to one of the municipal piers right in the center of the city.

On Wednesday I had the duty and so did not get ashore until Thursday. And on Thursday, I was detailed to go to the Brazilian Air Station (Naval) with three other officers to inspect the base, and to have lunch with the Commandante of the Air Station. The visit was very interesting, and we saw a lot of the German and English airplanes that are being used by the Brazilian Navy. It is much cheaper for them to buy from Germany than it is from us, and you may be sure that the Germans are doing their level best to get a foothold with the Navy. I understand that the Army is already pro-Nazi. All of the shops are patterned after German models, and all of the machinery is German. A force of German mechanics could walk in and never know that it was not home in Wilhelmshaven. However, we were told that American planes and material were far superior in everything but price. (All of which may or may not be true.) The lunch was elaborate and the food lousy, and generally the day was ill-spent up to the time that we left the Base to go back to the ship and change into blues for the Ambassador's reception.

The Honorable Mr. Caffery, who is, I am told, the American Ambassador to Brazil, entertained at a large and rather stuffy reception at his residence from five until seven o'clock on Thursday evening. All officers had to attend. All such parties are almost as deadly as they are necessary, but they do serve one purpose, and that is they serve as a medium for one to get acquainted with the right people. The right people in my case turned out to be a girl (American) who works in the Embassy and who has lived here all her life except for four years at William and Mary.

From the reception she took me on to a smaller cocktail party, which was much nicer and to which most of the other Quincy officers seemed to have drifted. From there we went out to the Casino Urrca, which is the largest of Rio's three large combined night club and gambling casinos. The grill, as it is called, is quite as splendiferous as any night club in New York, and has among other attractions four orchestras, which between them keep the music going incessantly (terrible American dance music and wonderful Brazilian music). The most inviting thing about these places is their inexpensiveness. I decided to lose a dollar at roulette, and instead won two, which paid for my evening. I like that sort of a system.

On Friday after very little sleep the night before, I marched with several other officers, and about two hundred enlisted men to the statue of Almirante Barrossa, who beat the Paraguayan Navy back in umpty-ump. If it wasn't ten miles each way I am a monkey (one of the cute little ones we saw running around wild out in the woods outside of Rio on Sunday). Friday afternoon I walked around a bit and shopped a bit and slept a bit, and then we all went gadding again to the Urrca. And on Saturday I had the duty.

Saturday afternoon there was a sample Brazilian riot, or so the police called it. Some organization held a pro-ally meeting, and the police broke it up with great gusto and much tear gas. For a while it looked as if we would all have to go out into town and herd the Quincy sailors back to the ship, but it was only a tempest in the teapot, and the alarm was all false. That afternoon was about the longest I have ever spent, what with little sleep previous to the watch and all the excitement.

Sunday, four of us hired a car and went really sightseeing. We drove all through the city of Rio and then up Corcavado for the finest and most beautiful view in the world (or so I firmly believe). From high up on the great rocky mountain, one can look down at Rio stretched out at his feet. Beyond the harbor, as it is shown in the picture post card that I sent you, lies the sea, and all around the harbor lies the city. At the back is a rocky range of mountains; at the front the white expanse of the incomparable beaches. It is truly hard to describe. After driving back down the very, very steep switchback roads, we continued on over the hills that surround Rio along what is known as the Tijuica Road, which leads through what I guess would be called the jungle. Here it was that we saw the monkeys and heard many, many parrots although we saw none. We stopped at a very lovely waterfall, and then at some natural caves for a moment; then headed back toward the sea drive to the south of the city. We stopped for a glass of beer at a restaurant called Joa, which overlooks the sea from a high cliff. It is set into a recess blasted out from the face of one of the tall rocks (mountains, I guess they would have to be called). The road makes a wide curve right in front of it; the mountain is casting its shadow over it; and a thousand feet below on the other side of the road lies the sea. For once the beer got scant attention.

From there we drove on down to the sea level, and then along the sea road back along the beaches and through the Copacabana District (American residence district of beautiful homes and apartments fronting the ocean) back to the ship. A five hour ride that was by far the most worthwhile that I have ever taken.

Monday morning, we sailed, and now, since it has taken three days to progress this far in the letter, we are about to arrive in Montevideo.

As for Brazil, I like it. But then, who would not who has seen only Rio. The native language is, of course, Portuguese, and the natives are the same. The exchange is 22 to 1 which is not hard to take, and everything is as a result very inexpensive. I have a lovely Bahian doll for Miss Thurston, and a butterfly tray for Mother, and aside from that, since I had not contemplated coming to Rio and had paid off fifty dollars worth of debts just before leaving, very, very little in the way of souvenirs.

Vargas seems to have everything well under control although I did hear rumors that the Army was all pro-Nazi. The only demonstration that took place while we were there was the one that I mentioned, and that was stopped in short order by the police, who have orders to bust up everything and ask questions later. It is against the law to have any sort of demonstration in Brazil. Vargas dictates with an iron hand. The Brazilians seemed very friendly indeed, and, on the whole, those that I met were definitely pro-Ally. However, there are an awful lot of

Italians in Sao Paulo, and Germans in Santa Catharina. It is now against the law for anything but Portuguese to be spoken in any of the schools, and there are many other Vargas decrees of a similar nature.

In Montevideo, perhaps we shall find something different again. I see by the radio press that there is a good deal of trouble coming to a head. I doubt, however, that we were sent down here to suppress any fifth column movements. We couldn't very well without encroaching upon territory that is not ours. However, it is still a moot question as to why we are where we are. Most of the officers believe that we shall not return to the States for a long time to come, and yet there are others who think that we will sail for the States when we leave Uruguay on the 25th. Argentina has not invited us, and by her silence has indicated that she desires no part of us. I don't think that anybody really knows what our next move will be. The Wichita arrives in Rio day after tomorrow on a purely "unofficial" visit. Why? Certainly not for good will. There have been at least ten American warships in Rio, Montevideo, and Buenos Aires, to say nothing of all the other principal South American ports in the last six months. All of our new ships make their shakedown cruises to South America. There is certainly no need to send two cruisers down just to promote good will.

We have been very definitely invited to Montevideo for five days and no longer, and where do we go from there? I suppose that we shall know more before the week is out. We had better, because my car is sitting on the end of a dock at Norfolk, and is costing me a lot of money for no return. If we are to stay here, I must figure some way to salvage a little of my investment.

Tomorrow, I hope, there will be mail, and tomorrow I'll mail this. There is a lot more to tell you, I know but at present I cannot think of it. So, until next time –

       Much, much love to all,
        Scottie

Thursday, 27 June 1940

Dear Family,

I am wondering how long it has been since you have heard from me. I have had not mail since leaving Guantanamo on the first of June, and I expect that you have not done much better. However, since they have been holding our mail pending definite word as to where we could get it, and you are in one definite place, perhaps you have received my letter and cards from Rio. I am going to start a weekly airmail letter and then you will know that your erstwhile son has not disappeared from the face of the earth.

There is a long, long letter in the regular mail which you should receive about the middle of July, and I will try not to repeat myself too much in order that you may enjoy that when it comes.

Briefly, we are still in Montevideo although until eight o'clock on Tuesday evening we were scheduled to sail for parts unknown - perhaps Norfolk, perhaps not. However, we are still here and expect to be here at least until the <u>Wichita</u> arrives from Rio on Saturday. Of course the consensus of opinion is that we will be in South American waters for some time to come, but if anyone aboard ship knows, he is keeping it very, very dark, and we really know less of what happens than you do in the States by reading the papers. We, for instance, heard last night that the Tuscaloosa was coming down to join us, over the news broadcast short wave. That was the first that we had heard. My biggest worry is my car which is sitting on the dock and costing me plenty every day that it sits there, <u>C'est le guerre--</u>.

Montevideo is a very nice place, and the people of Uruguay have been exceptionally cordial - with good reason, I am sure. They are scared stiff of fifth column activities and are at present in the midst of an investigation of sech which was held off until the long arm of Bro. Unc. Sam could arrive to back them up. It is rumored that there will be five U.S. warships in here before another two weeks. Maybe yes, maybe no - I wouldn't know. The first five days of our stay were hectic with official parties, and I didn't get ashore once except in uniform. I attended a couple of the really flossy ones with all the bigwigs in the Uruguayan cabinet, and it was quite a new experience. I heard the speech of Mr. Wilson, which so boldly stated American policy of direct intervention if necessary, and it was received very well indeed. The Uruguayans are certainly glad to have us around now that they need us.

I have started to study Spanish and am hoping that I'll be able to pick it up rather rapidly. They speak a dialect down here that is not pure Castilian, but it is good enough so I am told.

It is winter down here, of course, now, and the weather is lousy – about like Norfolk winters only with a lot more rain. We have had just one day that it has not rained continuously since we have been here.

More than anything else I should like to see an American (excuse me North American paper). The only news that we can get is that which is published by the controlled press down here, and even the Spanish language papers are all pro-Ally. The British speaking paper is, of course, published by the British, and all it has in it are official British wireless reports. We don't know what is happening.

So far I have been to a luncheon given by the Jockey Club for officers, a luncheon by the Minister of Defense, a cocktail party at the Jockey Club during the Sunday meeting at the track, and a cocktail party given by the English club and a cocktail party given by the American Minister, and have done what little sightseeing that there is to do. I have been to two movies (American with Spanish subtitles for the local gentry), and tomorrow night I am going, of all places, to the Epworth League with the girl that I am running around with down here. (A Uruguayan-born American who is visiting her parents for the summer before finishing her last year at the University of Iowa.) Monday morning, I went flying in one of the ship's planes and took a look at Uruguay from the air.

Air mail in care of the postmaster N.Y.C. will reach me faster than regular mail, since they will forward that.

Will write again for the next plane.

      Much, much love to all,
        Scottie

Rio Grande do Sul

Sunday, 6 July 1940

Dear Family,

    Comes your next word from south of the border, and it from the garden spot of Brazil – Rio Grande do Sul. We sailed from Montevideo on the 3rd and arrived here on the 5th. Why we are here, nobody seems to know, and nobody cares except that we get out as soon as possible.

    Rio Grande is in the state of the same name, and is almost as out of the way as Guantanamo City. There is absolutely nothing here, nothing to do, nothing to see, nothing nohow. There is a large German population in the state and in the one just north, Santa Cathalina; and perhaps we are here to put the fear of God into the fifth columnists. The Swift Company has a big packing plant here, and I had an introduction to the Superintendent, a Mr. Herren, who has been very nice to me and the rest of the officers. They had a couple of us to lunch and tea, and I, in turn had them to the ship for dinner and a movie. Today the Swift people held an Asada for the crew to which most of the officers went. An Asada is just a barbecue, South American style, and I must admit that this particular one was not particularly good. We had fun, but most of the beef was tough, and the lamb underdone. Southern Brazil is mostly all cattle country, as is Uruguay and the Argentine, and the Asada is quite an institution. For the same reason, since beef costs about seven cents a pound, the wardroom has been stocking up, and at the same time eating a lot of it. I fully expect that we shall all come down with high blood pressure before long. (Incidentally I had my introduction to the Herrens from my friends the Conards in Montevideo.)

    After the barbecue we went to a football game (American Soccer) and after having my fill of that, I came home.

    The Wichita is with us now, having arrived on the 29th of June in Montevideo. Where we go from here is a mystery right now, but the consensus of the scuttlebutt is that we go from here to Santos on the 10th, and arrive in Rio from Santos on the 19th. From Rio there isn't even scuttlebutt, and, since the real dope is changing faster than rumor, there is really no sense in trying to even guess.

My Spanish progress, which was practically nil anyway, has completely stopped, since in this country, Portuguese is the vernacular. It is a strange thing about the two languages. One who can speak and understand Portuguese can understand Spanish and make himself understood, but the reverse is not true. Don't ask me why because I don't know.

We still have not received any mail since before we left Guantanamo, that is except air mail, but I am told that regular three cent mail from the Postmaster arrives on the 12th in Rio, and will be forwarded from there to wherever we may be at that time – probably Santos.

Oh yes – one thing that I wish that you would do for me is this. Will you save all the copies of <u>Life</u> that you get since I may not be able to get ahold of all the copies; and, if you can, start buying <u>Time</u> for me, for which I will reimburse you. Then perhaps sometime, I can catch up on all that has happened during the time that I am down here.

I have been wondering and wondering what the war has done to Dad's business, and I am afraid that things may be pretty tough. Gosh, I hope not, and I hope that all is well in every way with my folks that I have not heard from in so very, very long. Soon perhaps I will hear from you.

I suppose that there is a lot to tell you, but I'm darned if I can think of anything now. However, I am trying to keep notes of the various things that happen, and then I won't forget everything before I get back.

For the present now, I'll sign off, and get this in the morning air mail so that you will have some word from me within a week.

                    Much, much love to all,
                         Scottie

Santos, Brazil

13 July, 1940

Dear Family,

Mail finally arrived, and so far there are two letters from Mother and one from Dad. To say that they were welcome is gross understatement especially after being so long without any mail whatsoever. I am sure that there will be more to come since a total of twenty-five bags were brought aboard this morning when we arrived here. I am told that so far they have gone through just two bags of it.

We arrived here in Santos, as you must gather from the above, this morning. We were at sea for about two days, and it was a rough trip up. The sea was nasty, and a lot of the lads were queezy. However, I have yet to be bothered to any extent by rough weather. Naturally, I have been uncomfortable. Anyone who says that he is not that when the old tub is dancing around like a berserk rubber ball is either inhuman or a damned liar - I am convinced of the latter.

It is summer again after a lot of nasty cold and wet weather. Santos is far enough north so that we can change back into whites - as we have. The sun is shining and it is quite hot.

Today, as is usual for the first day in port, I have the duty and will not get a chance to see what the coffee capital of the world looks like until tomorrow. I understand that it is quite a city, with almost two hundred thousand of population. (Another letter just arrived dated May 28th. The others were dated June 8th, 12th and 14th.)

The advance dope is the same - nil. We are to arrive in Rio on the 18th, and from there your guess is as good as the next one. Our Marine complement is to be increased by fifty when we arrive in Rio. The men are coming down on one of the new destroyers on shakedown cruise. We are also going to get our 1940 Ensigns when we get there.

Well, the total is two from Dad and five from Mother. My, but it was good to hear from home.

Thank you, Mother for sending a present for me to Ced. Now I guess that I am all alone as the only bachelor of the triumvirate - a state which will undoubtedly exist for some time to come.

I have not yet gone ashore here, so there is very, very

little that I can tell you about Santos. I am going a little later however, and think that I will postpone finishing this until after I have picked up some news.

July 16

Santos is rather a nice town. There is nothing to see particularly, but it is, at least, a city which has some nice homes, a casino, a good hotel, and a fine beach. We rode around on a street car, then along the beaches, and then stopped at the Parque Hotel and I squandered my usual dollar on the roulette table. So far, for the cruise I am three dollars ahead. The one thing that impresses one about the homes, except, of course, for the Spanish architecture, is the utter lack except in a few cases of any front yard. The houses front right on the street. There are magnificent royal palms in profusion here, some of them a good two hundred feet tall. The beaches stretch for miles and seem to be very good. There is little or no swimming now, since it is fairly cool, and the water is icy. I know that I told you that it was hot, and it is comparatively, but evidently not hot enough for the Latins to swim much.

The streets of most of these Latin American cities are of cobblestone and rough. The cars are mostly of American make in Brazil, and of foreign make in Uruguay. Whereas the cars are mostly new and good, the street cars are all "toonerville trolleys" - open and old.

The food here is cheap as dirt, and a good steak and fried potatoes costs about a quarter. We have eaten a good many steaks and I expect to eat more. Right now I have the duty and should be busy topside supervising the men getting ready for the reception that we are going to hold tomorrow.

All of these cities in Brazil are much alike with the exception of Rio. The shops all seem small - there is a complete lack of showiness, and they reflect the poverty of the average native. On my salary I could live like a king down here and have a home with any number of servants. They say that living in South America spoils any woman for life in the States, since she never has to do a stroke of work of her own. I suppose that they must be very bored.

       Much, much love to all,
        Scottie

ROBERT SCOTT WHITMAN JR.

Enroute Bahia

Friday, 26 July 1940

Dear Family,

    While we were in Rio two letters arrived from Mother which were grand to get.

    Right now, we are on our way to Bahia for a stay of, I suppose, five days. Thence to Pernambuco and another stay of five days, and then to Montevideo again. For a while it looked as though we were heading home, but now it certainly does not. The stay in Santos was very pleasant and quiet, the stay in Rio pleasant and hectic. I did meet a very, very swell girl this time but too late to do much "courting". This time in Rio there were no official parties, and I went to only one - a cocktail party to which I was invited in order to entertain a young friend of Commander and Mrs. Harper's (the hosts). She was quite nice but spoiled and too rich for her own good. However, I took her out again to one of the casinos and let it go at that. Wednesday, however, I had a grand time - took a girl named Virginia Woolman - 19, beautiful, sweet, smart, fun, and also too rich, up Sugar Loaf to watch the lights turned on in the city. Then to dinner at the Pan Air Restaurant, and then, after meeting the Brazil, on which she had some friends arriving, out to the Copacabana Palace for dancing.

    It is really quite a sight to see Rio lit up. Millions of lights wink on like so many jewels catching the sun - and these winding in and out like a million glistening serpents among the rocky hills of the city. Such is Rio at night. Way off in the distance just peeping from behind the "Two Brothers" is Gavea, then coming in, is Copacabana, then Botofozo, then Flamengo, and finally the business section (All the above are various parts of the city which literally spreads in every direction for miles.) Truly it is a beautiful city.

    Our doctor has been seriously sick with infected tonsils. Finally, since he got no better, we put him off in Rio and another doctor reported aboard after flying down from Philadelphia on the Clipper. The 1940 Ensigns reported aboard in Rio along with fifty extra Marines. They came down on the Wainright and the Wolke - two new cans that are on a shakedown cruise. Consequently, I have two J.O.'s - and I'm so used to doing the work myself that I don't know what to do with them.

They all seem like mere lads, but there is no one among them that is a mutual acquaintance of someone in Binghamton (in answer to your question of a previous letter).

Some of the officers have sent for their wives and they, at least, must think that we shall be staying for quite a while.

Saturday.

Tomorrow we are stopping to explore a deserted island called Icke Trinidade, which at one time was used as a political prison. Reports have it that it has been uninhabited since 1925. It should prove interesting, and I plan to go ashore with the party.

There is not much more space so I guess it's time to quit.

        Much, much love to all,

         Scottie

ROBERT SCOTT WHITMAN JR.

Recife

12 August 1940

Dear Family,

   This will be a very hurried and poorly typed letter because
the mail closes in less than an hour, and I want to get it off
if at all possible. So bear with me and try to translate. Things
have been so hectic that I've really forgotten when I last
wrote, so if I repeat or skip, that also will have to be excused
until such time as I can make up.

   We are now in Recife, as you must gather, and have been here
for the last four days. We arrived from Bahia, and from here we
go to Montevideo spending ten days en route. We sail at two this
afternoon.

   First off, our schedule should be of interest to you. We sit
in Montevideo from the 23rd until the 28th. Then we go to B.A.
from the 28th until the 3rd. Then to Rio from the 6th until the
10th, and then HOME. Present approved schedule calls for our
arrival in Norfolk on the 23rd of September - HOORAY! HOORAY!
Now for a little of what I've seen and done.

   As far as Rio is concerned, I don't remember what I told you
about that last stop. Principally of interest is the fact that
I almost fell in love - got out just in time. Bahia - Bahia is
a typical Brazilian city. It is built on two levels, the port
part of the city being connected with the upper city by a road
causeway, funiculars, and an elevator. The population is about
150,000 people, and ninety per cent of them are (as the business
men would say) without buying power. Again the extreme poverty
of the country becomes all too evident.

   In Bahia we found that the Yacht Club had a very swell salt
water pool, which we used often and long, that the beaches are
not so good, but that Pete Peterson and I could have a swell
afternoon by walking way out of town and along the beach for
about a mile until we found a spot free from reefs and rocks,
and then to fight the surf for four hours and lie in the sun
alternately. That the English people are as near human as any
Englishman could be, and that it takes thirty inspectos - one
each three blocks to keep the conducto of one tram honest
throughout his run. It was not hot. It rained every evening at
eight sharp, and I spent a total of three dollars during the
stay. I went to one dinner party given by an Englishman, who

is the NORWEGIAN consul (sort of strange), and went to a dance given by the English afterwards. It was fun, but there were only four English speaking women that were single and presentable in the whole city.

Recife, or Pernambuco, is a city of about 350,000 with about the same percentages as before. Here we have been busy every minute going to official parties – going ashore on duty in other words. The Consul had a reception, the American colony (17 families) a dance, the Mayor a sightseeing trip, the Quincy a reception, various and sundry citizens swimming parties. We all had to go to all of them. I'm tired and sick of all parties and have wanted nothing more than to be able to stay aboard ship and rest and do some of the things that I really must and want to do. The beaches here are the best I have ever seen, and we spent a pleasant Sunday morning swimming. The only other thing of interest that I have found here is that all you need to get a driver's license is a doctor's certificate that you are both insane and blind, and then you are all set. The taxi drivers are the craziest I have ever run across. Our tour of the city yesterday morning (taken after exactly one hours sleep the night before) proved that. Our driver honked his horn on 77 occasions – about two hundred times – in two kilometers (1.2 miles). Our motorcade killed one dog and wounded two pedestrians in the course of our trip – and with all that honking, I had the most splitting headache I have ever known.

Much, much love to all,
Scottie

28 August 1940

Dear Family,

Received George's and Mother's letters two days ago, and Dad's fine long letter today. I have answered George's, and now for another start on a letter to you all.

Let's see – the last letter was written in Recife, and now we are about to leave Montevideo for the second and last time and are going to Buenos Aires tonight. Arrive there tomorrow morning, since it is just a hundred miles up the river.

Our stay in Montevideo has been just as pleasant as before. One would think that the ciudadanos would get tired of seeing us around and at least take us for granted, but no – still party after party until all of us are getting rather tired of keeping on the go every minute. And, I suppose you would like to know what I have done this time in Montevideo.

We arrived on Friday, and on Friday I did nothing except to call briefly on the young lady with whom I ran around last time. Saturday afternoon I went to the races as the guest of the President of the Jockey Club; from there to the home of a man by the name of Tate for cocktails. (He being the manager of Eastman here and having a red headed German wife, who in turn has four cats.) From there to the English Club to another cocktail party, and then back to the ship into full dress and to the Yacht Club with this girl and three other couples for dinner at ten and a dance from midnight until five. Got home at quarter to seven. Sunday I had the duty – slept until three and then stood an eight to twelve watch. On Monday, I did nothing and on Tuesday, which was yesterday, I went to the Naval Club for cocktails, to the Whitmans for more, and finally out to dinner with the Niesson and Mills, the Goodrich people down here. Right now we are on our way to B.A. (there being somewhat of an interval between start and now).

I am just off watch, and on my watch we passed the Hawkins, flagship of the British South American Squadron. She has been in the B.A. for the last two days, and now is on her way down the river to sea again. Didn't see much of her since it was dark, but she passed close aboard. The channel is only a few hundred yards wide, and we need a pilot all the way.

There was very little evidence of fifth columns in Montevideo this time, and I think that the trouble and scare has abated. However, we are being relieved down here by two other ships – the names of which I am not sure of, and could not say if I was.

Montevideo is by far the most friendly port that we have been in. All of the people are swell, and the Uruguayan is so far superior to the Brazilian, that there is really no comparison. It must be the climate that makes them so much more robust and healthy. All the Brazilians are little men, but not so here. Talking of climate, it is really cold now, and the temperature has dropped almost to freezing during the early morning hours. Either my imagination was running away with me, or I saw a flicker of snow in the air the other day.

The ten days that we spent at sea prior to our arrival in Montevideo were uneventful, and were a more than welcome respite even though we did spend most of our time drilling. The training of personnel is the largest problem ahead of the Navy. We have a very inexperienced crew, and just as soon as we get back to the States, we are sure to lose even those few old-timers that we have. We shall get another batch of boots, get them broken in and started, and then they will go and we shall start again. It is an endless and very discouraging cycle, but I suppose really necessary with all the new construction.

The dope is that we leave Norfolk on the 29th, or if not Norfolk, New York, with 250 of the new Reserve Midshipmen to be. They come aboard as seamen 2nd class for a month of indoctrination into shipboard life – no pay. They are observed objectively and critically, and those who are so picked and so desire are then ordered for three months' instruction ashore. The ones who measure up during that time, are given commissions as Reserve Ensigns – and what a mess that will be! I'm not much good after five years – what will they be after four months.

The radio reports that the Conscription Bill has been passed, I don't know the details yet, but am wondering how it will affect George. It is a shame that he did not take R.O.T.C. at school. It would certainly stand him in good stead now.

I have a single room now, and a swell one. It is much better than I actually rate for my rank, but imagine that I will keep it for the duration of my stay on board. It is so much nicer to be able to do as I please, go to bed when I want without fear of disturbance, or to stay up as late as I want without fear of disturbing.

We arrive the 23rd, and I will phone from Norfolk as soon as I can.

Much, much love to all,
Scottie

XI
BACK IN NORFOLK
SEPTEMBER 1940 – JANUARY 1941

Tuesday, 24 September 1940

Dear Family,

Dick being a communicator could get leave and I'm sending a few things up with him.

The blankets are to use as you choose – they are really steamer rugs, as you see. The dolls are for Miss Thurston, the trays for Mother. I've just a few other odds and ends but I'd wait to bring them up when I can so as not to burden Dick too much.

        Much love to both of you,
           Scottie

Sunday, 6 October 1940

Dear Family,

I expect that you think me a perfect heel for not writing a whole lot sooner than this, and you might well think so. We have been up to our ears with work though, and since there has been so very little to write, I have sort of neglected you, I guess.

Now we are in Norfolk, but will sail again tomorrow for where I know not. Just out and around to make gunnery runs, and to give our reserves a little taste of the sea.

We went up to New York last Sunday, and stayed through Monday night (arrived Monday morning and sailed Tuesday). I finally got ashore about seven in the evening after bore sighting all eight AA guns, and Bill Walker and I stopped around at the Ridgways. Aunt May was to return from the hospital that evening (what was wrong I know not except that she had an operation), and Barbara and I went to get her. After we had brought her home and talked a while, Bill and I took Barbara out and we did the town. Had a very nice time, and we all finally got home about five. Barbara is certainly a swell girl, and the lad that catches her has something. Spencer is to be married on the 16th of October. Whit is to be married soon, too, to some girl from Chicago.

We have two hundred some of these special reserves, and everything is quite crowded aboard ship. They live and work as seamen, and probably a lot of them are not particularly comfortable. However, if they want to get into the Navy, they had better work, and I have no sympathy for them. If the Navy Department thinks that it can turn out a Naval officer after four months training, they are sadly mistaken; and that is not just idle prattle. They have a regular short term Naval Academy organization on the U.S.S. Illinois at New York with Midshipman stripers, etc., etc. I saw a lot of the Midshipmen, and they are a fine looking bunch. However, they will never become an efficient part of the officer personnel of the Navy with that little training.

The base is really empty now, but last week there were about thirty destroyers, five cruisers, four battleships, two air-craft carriers, I don't know how many smaller craft in. Now most of them have gone south, and the Quincy, Wichita, and Tuscaloosa are just about alone here except for a few auxiliary craft.

After we get through this month, I think that we go into

the Yard for about five weeks. We shall probably stay around here until after the first of the year and then head down for Guantanamo to finish up our gunnery.

We fired short range last Friday, and did fairly well. My four guns did all right, but I had hoped for a little better. However, it is said of short range practice that it is the year's annual disappointment. This practice is not practicable, but just a means toward arousing interest and training gun pointers and trainers. An engagement would never be fought at such close quarters.

We have all sorts of new officers now, and a lot of the old crowd have left for other ships and stations. That is the way of the Navy. Just as you get so that everybody knows everybody and is congenial or has found out that it is best to stay away from various ones, then flooey, and all is shaken up and you have to start over again. The bunch is very nice though, and we always have a congenial crowd in the wardroom. We now have a piano in the wardroom which makes for a little practice for Scottie.

Now I must close, but you may rest assured that the next letter will not be so slow in arriving.

   Much, much love to all,
    Scottie

Tuesday, 15 October 1940

Dear Family,

At sea again after a week-end in Norfolk. At present anchored in the Southern Drill Grounds. This last week-end I had the duty and was ashore only on Friday.

We are now in the middle of training for another gunnery practice and most of the day is spent at drill. Each night we anchor, and get underway each morning to make runs back and forth using the Tuscaloosa as a target. It becomes extremely monotonous at times, but is necessary – oh, so necessary, and therefore is bearable. We shoot on Friday.

As you know, we have 250 reserves aboard. They are a nice bunch of boys as a whole. Average education is 3.6 years of college and most of them are willing and ambitious. I expect that the way of life of the common seaman is a bit rough for a lot of them, and there are a few who can't take it; but as a whole, they are O.K. However, it is wishful thinking and little else if the Navy Department thinks that it can turn out a Naval officer in four months.

The first cruise is over on the 25th of this month, and we lie in New York from the 25th to the 29th. (Hold your fingers crossed, I might get home.) Then we pick up a new bunch for another month. Where we go with them is problematical. We undoubtedly shall have more gunnery on the schedule and spend our time in this area, but if no gunnery is planned we'll take them to Guantanamo and Panama, as was originally scheduled for the first cruise.

I have had my gunnery station changed, and am now in the main battery. It is a much more important job in many respects, and less in others. My year in the AA battery was far from wasted, and I have a wonderful ground-work for any kind of firing now.

My life has settled back into the all too familiar pattern of ordinary operation. Out for the week and in over the week-ends. I told you, I think, that I am now qualified in all respects to be a naval officer and stand "top" watches both underway and in port. We four '39 Ensigns stand only day watches underway, and as a consequence I get a full night's sleep every night.

I have a new Division Officer, whom I have yet to entirely understand. However, he is a good guy, I guess, and we get along. I'm hoping to be transferred to the Fire Control

Division, since it is that phase of gunnery which particularly appeals to me. The ship now is lousy with officers - more than we have ever had before. What will we do with them all is beyond me, but they will be put to work I'm sure.

We are speculating and wondering just what will happen in the next few days, weeks or months. Something is brewing, I'm convinced - something more than just defense hysteria and newspaper ballyhoo. It's an intangible thing, hard to explain, but whether it be hunch, or what-ever, there is something in the air.

I hope I'll be able to get home from New York over the week-end. No promises however.

> Much, much love,
> Scottie

Monday, 4 November 1940

Dear Family,

Well, we are back in Norfolk and will be here for the rest of the week, and then we go out to fire some AA practices - which, needless to say, do not interest me as they used to. Nothing eventful has happened since I was home for the swell but too short visit except for the Quincy party Saturday night, and the letter from Ada telling me that she is engaged and will be married next June to some lad from Pittsburg - evidently one of the I.B.M. people.

Uncle Charlie Ridgway was not in New York on Monday, so I have still to meet him. Took Barbara out that evening with a bunch from the ship - Uncle Charlie, young Charlie, and she had been out to the ship the day before and stayed to dinner as Bill Walker's guests, so that phase of it was all O.K.

How about the Penn game? I guess that Dad was right in fact of teams, even if I was right about the score. I only hope that I am not so right about tomorrow's game, and that our team comes through with a bang and a million electoral points.

There is a rumor around now that we shall be promoted on the 1st of June - how good it is is a question of doubt. It is a bit more authentic, though, than the vague rumors that I told you all about. At any rate, we are all hoping that it will come, and with it the increase in pay.

I tied a Tux tie for the first time (for keeps) last Saturday night, and Dad's instruction was perfect - at least the finished job followed his instructions and more than did justice to the pupil. It was a good party and I had a grand time - the only thing that worried me was the fact that my best gal couldn't go with me - you, Mom.

The jalop has a new set of tires, so now I can jump home whenever I can get free - I'm striking for some time the last week in November. And, if that gal in Rochester breaks a leg, then Mother and I go on down to Philly to the game. We'd be sure to go anyway, and I was all set to write to her and break the date, when I got a letter telling me that she had already made plans to visit people in New York so that she would have a place to stay, and now I haven't the guts since I do want to see her again. However, let's hope for a broken leg or at least at attack of grippe.

Right now I am just marking time with not much to do. Perhaps I can get some time to write a few more letters, and study a little. And certainly since I am so useless around here, the "old man" should favorably gaze on the leave request that he is going to get. I gotta come home again soon - this last visit was too, too short.

All my love to my best pal and my best girl,
            Scottie

Thursday, 21 November 1940

Dear Family,

Well, here we are somewhere off Bermuda in the nicest balmiest weather that we have seen since we left South America. We have been down here patrolling the route that a bunch of patrol planes are following on a flight to Bermuda; and now, since they have passed over us and have landed, we are on our way back to Norfolk. We were rather mad at the aviators that they had to be so coddled for a 600 mile flight, but at the same time it should prove comforting "mas o menus".

The reason that you received no letter from me last week-end was that Bill Walker and I went up the Washington, and then onto Baltimore to see the Notre Dame game. Our principal purpose in going up was to go to the "home office" and find out when we would go to Pensacola, [He broke the news while home that he had made application to the Navy Department for transfer to Pensacola for training as a Navy flyer.] and the game was incidental, since we didn't know if we could get tickets. The first chance that we have to go to Pensacola will be in March and probably not then – more likely in April, May, or June. At least, the people aboard ship here can relax and depend on having us around for a while now.

The game was swell, and the Navy team should have won. It was the same old story – no oomph when they got into scoring territory. Notre Dame was lucky to win. We didn't stay around after the game but drove straight back to Norfolk and bed. Quite a strenuous day, but very pleasant, and we accomplished our mission. I got tickets by calling up Commander Gilmore, the treasurer of the Athletic Association, Saturday morning, and he left them for me at the reservation booth. The game had been a sell-out for several days, and how we got them is beyond me.

There is a lot of talk of our making a third reserve cruise down into the Gulf; and, if that is true, there is not much chance of our getting to see the Army-Navy game after all. A lot of us will be disappointed, but that is part of being in the Navy, and there is really nothing that one can do about it except relax and forget it. It is not definitely decided as far as I know, and maybe all the screaming is un-called for – here's hoping. Friend Ginger will be disappointed, I expect; but that will be just too bad - if the Navy sends me off, there is not an awful lot I can do about it.

I've been busy for the last two days interviewing the reserves trying to make an estimate of them and decide whether they should be recommended for further training or not. It is a tough job and I hate to turn anyone down, especially since I have had very little chance to see them and get to know them.

Got a letter from George last week - an almost unheard of thing. It shall be answered promptly in hope that another one will come. He says that he will be hitting the Aero courses hard next semester.

Monday I had the first touch of seasickness I have ever had. It was not positive, but I sure felt terrible for a couple of hours. I believe in the theory that it is a matter of physical condition and fully believe that I got my touch because of the rather exhausting week-end. Now, at least, I know somewhat of what people must go through.

We are all quite excited aboard here by the little job that the British pulled on the Italian Fleet. They certainly cannot be accused of not being courageous. It was a beautiful piece of work, and the Limeys deserve a world of credit.

I am now wardroom mess treasurer - a job that I have been trying to dodge for a long time. Now it has caught up with me, and I shall have served out my term and gotten it over with. It is not a hard job and is, as a matter of fact, rather interesting to me, since I've never had anything to do with bookkeeping before.

The Quincy is due to be even more overrun with officers. We were told at the Bureau that we shall receive four, at least, of the new reserves (those who took the first cruise and have now been through their first period of training ashore). They will be dead weight for a long time to come; but, at least, they have made a start toward being of some use to the Navy. What the Navy is going to do with all of these people right now is beyond me. Later, of course, as the building program progresses and some ships start to come off the ways, they will be needed.

I can't think of much else to say right now, and so will close with all the love in the world for the swellest people in the world.

Scottie

Monday, 25 November 1940

Dear Family,

I'm sorry – I guess I have just turned into one of those creatures I used to so abhor – the lousy correspondent. But this time I have been waiting to see if I could give you any good news. Right now I've given up hope. We are making another reserve cruise, getting underway tomorrow and not coming into Norfolk until late Thursday. (The Navy celebrates the Pres's Thanksgiving of course, and Thursday is just another day.) We get underway Monday morning for Charleston, S.C., and so I have from Friday to Monday at 0000, not enough time to get home by any stretch of the imagination. I am so disappointed and was so looking forward to a real good old fashioned Thanksgiving with the people without whom Thanksgiving just "ain't".

I'm going to drive up to New York on Friday IF I can get off, and meet Ginger. I'll stay at the Ridgways, drive to Philly Saturday, and back to Norfolk Sunday, staying with Aunt May and taking three other guys with me to share the gas and oil. I can make it O.K., I guess.

As you can gather, the Navy Yard period was postponed until December 23rd, so now it looks like Christmas or New Years at home. Then, at least, George will be there and we can have a real get together. I know you are disappointed, but no more so than I, and, if there were any way in the world that I could make it, I would.

I have done practically nothing here in New York this time except to treat myself to a $1.65 worth of pro – football at the Polo Grounds Sunday afternoon. Giants and Redskins played and it was a thrill to watch the best brand of football the country has to offer. The Ridgways were out on Saturday when I got ashore after our arrival late in the morning. I got the telephone switchboard man to let me in and spent the afternoon all by myself listening to that amazing Penn-Cornell game. Called Don Jackson in the evening and saw him for a while, but went nowhere – no inclination to spend any money.

Have the watch now and, since it is 11:45 P.M., it is time to go on up into 29° weather for my mid-watch – what fun! If it is not too cold in the O.O.D. shack, I'll continue there.

It's too darned cold, as you can see from this scrawl.

Lots and lots of love,

Scottie

Friday, 13 December 1940

Dear Family,

    George has his watch — an Elgin bought and paid for. He'll
love it and it is a good watch.
    No more now but love to all,
            Scottie

Sunday, 5 January 1941

Dear Family,

    Well, it's Sunday and I have the duty — a good time for
letter writing. Mother's letters all arrived, the pajamas and
the toilet case arrived and George's wire also arrived. Thank
you all for your birthday wishes — it was so swell to hear from
you.

    We are now, of course, in the Yard, and the inevitable
chipping hammers and riveting hammers are pounding almost
constantly — even today. The schedule calls for us to leave
the Yard on the 24th for Guantanamo for gunnery practices and
training. How long we shall be there is at this point only a
matter of conjecture, and I wouldn't even hazard a guess.

    Yesterday the America, the newest liner to be built in the
United States, came into the yard for a five day overhaul period,
and is now tied up just ahead of us. I am told that it is a
magnificent ship, but have not yet had the chance to go over to
verify the fact. The funnels are sure purty — red, white, and
blue.

    The car (new) now is working O.K., but there are a lot of
minor things that have to be ironed out. I am going to take it
into the Chevrolet place for a thousand mile check tomorrow
or the next day and get it all set. I received the dope from
Botnick, but they have not yet sent me a certified bill of sale,
without which I cannot license the car — I wonder if Dad would
call them up and ask them to hurry it up. After all, I am
driving with illegal tags at this point.

    There is no dope about Pensacola — all of us are wondering
and waiting for some definite word. We shall hear in time, I

suppose, and until then I'll just carry on aboard here and get everything out of the job that I can. That, after all, is the thing to do, isn't it?

Six more new Ensigns have reported aboard, and the wardroom is filled to capacity and over – now some of them are sleeping on cots. However, there are quite a few that are here only for further transfer to other ships when we meet up with them, and the congestion will be relieved soon, I hope.

My two months as mess treasurer were up this month, and I asked for and received relief. It was interesting and instructive, since I had never done any bookkeeping before, but I'm glad that it is over.

I suppose George is back in the harness again, and the apartment seems just a little empty and pleasantly quiet again.

I sent Mother's picture a couple of days ago – I hope that you like it and that it is received intact.

Much, much love to all or both of you or something, but at least lots and lots of love,

       Scottie

Monday, 20 January 1941

Dear Family,

A very, very belated letter from a very, very apologetic son. I've been pretty busy and have let it slide far too long.

<u>First</u>. Mother asked about the money – of course it arrived and I did acknowledge and thank both you and Aunt Jule for it. The toilet kit arrived O.K. and thank you very, very much for sending it.

<u>Second</u>. It's funny that Dad should have asked about the picture of the <u>Quincy</u>. I am negotiating now for an enlargement, and will send it to you as soon as I get it. I do not have the negative, since the ship's photographer took the picture.

We are still in the Yard and will leave on Friday for N.O.B. Sail from N.O.B. on Monday for Guantanamo. How long we shall be there is a problem that nobody can solve as yet. I expect that it will be some little time.

There is no news from here that is the least interesting. We have been living in a bedlam of noise 24 hours a day. Riveting hammers, chipping hammers, etc., have been keeping up a constant din. It is a relief to get off the ship once in a while. We left dry-dock today and are now alongside a pier again. In dry-dock we have no plumbing facilities at all and it is a relief to be able to take a shower without having to walk out on the dock with all attendant difficulties. However, the ship's bottom is all pretty again and ready for another year in the water.

As it stands now, we three expect to go to Pensacola in March, but have heard nothing.

All of us aboard ship have bad colds, but mine was light for a change, and I was in bed for only one day. Possibly because the Sunday that it came on Betty and Donnie made me take a hot bath, fed me a stiff dose of hot whiskey, and put me in bed with a million blankets out at their place. I was as weak as a kitten next morn, but after a day in bed here aboard I was a new man.

No more now. Will try to write again soon. Excuse pencil it's easier than a pen and the typer needs a new ribbon.

        Lots of love to all,
         Scottie

XII
PENSACOLA
MARCH 1941 – OCTOBER 1941

ROBERT SCOTT WHITMAN JR.

Navy Department
Bureau of Navigation
Nav-310-ACK   Washington, D.C.

8021

From: The Chief of the Bureau of Navigation:
To: Ensign Robert S. Whitman, Jr., U.S.N., USS, QUINCY

Via: Commanding Officer.

Subject: Change of Duty.

1.   When directed by your commanding officer in February of March, 1941, you will regard yourself detached from duty on board the U.S.S. Quincy and from such other duty as may have been assigned you: will proceed to Pensacola, Fla., and report to the Commandant, Naval Air Station, for temporary duty under instruction in heavier-than-air craft.

2.   Report also by letter to the Commandant, Eighth Naval District for this duty.

3.   The Secretary of the Navy has determined that this employment on shore duty is required by the public interests.

4.   You are hereby authorized to delay until March 24, 1941, in reporting in obedience to these orders.

5.   Keep the Bureau of Navigation and your new station advised of your address.

6.   This delay will count as leave. Upon the commencement of the leave you will immediately inform this bureau of the exact date and upon the expiration thereof, you will return the attached form, giving the dates of commencement and expiration.

7.   You are hereby designated as student naval aviator and detailed to duty involving flying effective upon reporting obedience to these orders.

Copy to:
C.O., USS QUINCY.
Cdr., Cru. Div. 7.
Cdr., Patrol Force.
Comdt., Naval Air Station,
  Pensacola, Fla.
Comdt., 8th Nav. Dist.
Navy Mutual Aid.
Bu. Aero.

Training Div.

FIRST ENDORSEMENT to:
BuNav. Ltr. Nav-310-ACK   U.S.S. QUINCY
82661-4 8021 of 24 February, 1941   Culebra, Puerto Rico

From: Commanding Officer.   Feb-1 1941
To: Ensign Robert S. Whitman, Jr., USN, USS QUINCY.

Subject: Change of Duty.

    1.   Delivered
    2.   Detached this date.
    3.   You will report to the Commanding Officer, U.S.S. YUKON for
transportation to Norfolk, Virginia. Upon arrival at Norfolk, Virginia carry out
your basic orders.

                                                  W.C. Wickham.

Certified to be a true copy:

ROBERT SCOTT WHITMAN JR.

```
U.S. Naval Air Station
Pensacola, Florida
Ground School
18 March 1941
Dear Family,
```

    With two weeks passed and 5000 more miles on "Honeymoon", you are just about due for this letter. So I shall start off with my visit to Ann Arbor. I arrived about seven in the evening after an uneventful trip. George was out and his roommate and I went over to that beeyoutiful library to look for him. He wasn't there but arrived back shortly after we did. There was a dance that evening and George had a date. I took him to get the girl but refused with thanks the invitation to get a date for me. The girl seemed very nice – not, however, the one he took to the J. Hop. The next day we walked all over the campus and what a place it is, and what a walk! We climbed to the top of the Union tower among other things and got a good view of the campus from there. Went to a track meet in the evening. Sunday I took George out to dinner and we went to a movie in the evening. Monday nothing in particular happened and I left Tuesday. George seems to be getting along well. He screamed a good deal about how tough the problems were in some of his courses, but I noticed that he got them done O.K. I like the boys in the fraternity and think he likes them, and vice versa.

    From Ann Arbor I went to Shelbyville – couldn't find Chase and so on to Norfolk. The stay there was very pleasant and very quiet. Drove through from Norfolk Sunday and arrived here yesterday about noon.

    Everything is so new here and confusing that I haven't yet quite gathered my thoughts together. I am living in Bachelor Officers' quarters – not, however, the big smooth one, but in a wooden building. It is comfortable and O.K. now, but won't be in summer because of the heat. My room has a bed, chiffonnier, desk, bed table, desk chair and a big cane chair with leather seat and back. All furniture with the one exception is metal.

    There are eight of my classmates here in the same building – those that entered the March 10th class. I'm the first to arrive of my gang, and from the fog in my mind I don't envy them not arriving early. Since arriving I have done the following things all of them in widely different buildings.

1. Reported to Aide to Commandant.
2. Reported to Aide to Exec
3. Filled out a million forms at central office.
4. Reported to Head of Training School.
5. Reported to Public Works office (why I don't know even now).
6. Reported to Log Room (Got Flight Log Book which will show number of hours etc.).
7. Got Yard tag for car.
8. Got movie pass.
9. Left address at Comm. Office and Post office.
10. Been photographed twice.
11. Reported to officer in charge of Ground School.
12. Got commissary card.
13. Seen Supply Officer about trunk.
14. Checked in at Ship Service Store.
15. Drawn flight gear.
16. Had physical exam (dental only-rest comes when the rest of the gang arrive).
17. Checked in with Mess Treasurer.
18. Opened pay accounts.
19. Bought khakis etc.

Whew!!!

Class starts Monday, but everybody else was due to report on Thursday. It's good that I decided to come early – mine, being the first orders for this class, probably didn't get the modification. I am in the "Right Wing of Squadron 164-0". You tell me what that means. My best address is U.S. Naval Air Station – Ground School.

We go to Ground School for a month before we do any flying at all, so I won't get into the air until the middle of April. Flight pay starts now, however.

It is a huge establishment and I can't find my way around worth a darn now – but in time all will clear up.

I'm quitting for now – more later.

     Lots of love,
      Scottie

ROBERT SCOTT WHITMAN JR.

Wednesday, 26 March 1941

Dear Family,

Time has slipped by rapidly and it is time for another letter. Since I last wrote to you I have spent four lonely days in the hospital with cat fever - a very nice cold; but I am out and have been going to school for the last two days - I missed just the first day and lost nothing.

Mother's two and Dad's one letter have arrived and you can bet it is certainly grand to hear from home.

Our first class in the morning starts at 0630 - rifle range this week. There we fire machine guns and pistols - fired the pistol course today. Then at 0930 we go to radio code for 45 minutes. From 10:15 until 11:30 we get lunch and are free. 11:30 - 3:15 we are in class at the Ground School Bldg., and then are free until the next morning. We have two courses in engines now - one in theory and the other in construction. It does not seem very hard as yet, but will probably get tougher. There are 15 officers and an indeterminate number of cadets and enlisted men in my class. This is a huge plant, and there must be at least 1500 cadets here alone.

I never saw so many airplanes all over the sky all the time in my life. They skitter here and there with no appearance of order, and yet there are no accidents and all is, of course, in the highest of order.

Last night I went to call on a Lt. Koivisto and his wife. They are great friends of Donnie's and have taken me in. They seem very, very nice.

We wear khaki all the time - with a flight jacket when cool enough for one. It is comfortable and cool, and quite satisfactory all around.

Oh, yes, did George find the five dollars I left him in his carton of cigarettes in his bureau drawer? I only hope nothing happened to it. And, Mother, how much is it that I owe you? I've forgotten, but will send a check as soon as you let me know.

No more now - lots and lots of love to all,

Scottie

Tuesday, 1 April 1941

Dear Family,

Mother's letter arrived today and I sure was glad to get it. It is a sort of a lonely life down here even though a lot of my friends are here, and mail means a lot.

We are well into our second week of Ground School now, and I'm more or less shaking down into the routine. We start work at 0630. (Or did I tell you?) This week we are studying Engine accessories (2 hrs per day) and carburation and ignition (2 hrs), plus 3 hours of gunnery and 45 minutes of radio code per day. I have progressed to where I can get just about 12 words a minute of the code.

Isn't it grand that Aunt Julie will be there. I can imagine just how much Mother is looking forward to her visit. I'd like to see her and get to know her a little better.

Last Saturday three of us bowled and had a grand time. They have some very good alleys here on the Station and three games cost only 20¢. I rolled 155 as my top score, which is not so hot, but I was right proud of it, since it was the first time I had ever bowled with ten pins instead of ducks.

Sunday we played 18 holes of golf, and 9 again today after classes quit at 3:15. I used borrowed clubs, of course, but am going to start to save my pennies for some of my own.

Friday afternoon there was a formal inspection of personnel and Friday evening I was invited out to Myrt and Mart Koivisto's for dinner. They have a little fellow jut turned three, and he and I are the best of pals. Went out there again yesterday afternoon and ended up staying for dinner. Mart is not an aviator, but is stationed here in connection with training the cadets, of which there are 1600.

There is a constant roar of airplanes here even at night – as now at ten till nine.

It's time to turn in, since the alarm goes off awfully early.

Lots and lots of love to all,

Scottie

Wednesday, 9 April 1941

Dear Family,

    I suppose Aunt Julie has come and gone. I'll bet you had a great old gab-fest and a grand re-union.

    Life here has settled down into a quite familiar pattern. The schedule is the same as far as time goes; but, of course, we have changed the subjects under cursory study (for that is all it can be). Now it is Aerology (Meteorology) Aerodynamics, Engine operation, Aircraft construction, and, of course, radio code. The best course is "operation" – we go out to the test stand for two hours each day and actually operate various types of engines. Same instruments and engine controls are used as in a plane.

    During the week, I usually go to the movie here on the Station, and then turn in. The theater in the Ground School building is brand new and is as large and as modern as any in Binghamton. Of course, the show is free.

    George Ghesquiere has been here for some time – he is in the class ahead of me. The late appearance of his orders is due to the fact that his first orders were via dispatch, and these are "confirmation" (orders by letter).

    By the time you receive this George will be home. Wish I could see him. I know a couple of people who will be glad to.

    The courses are quite elementary, and so far have not required much study. However, the more one knows about this business the better, and I am trying to get everything out of it that I can. Marks run around a 3.5, which is just average for the officers.

    I got a long Clipper letter from Marsh today. He seemed to get quite a kick out of my being here, and also seems quite unhappy about his forced separation from Helen [his wife]. I have an idea that he will be back in the States soon now, though, since his squadron is due for overhaul.

    I am enclosing a check to pay up my debt to you, Mother, thanks for the credit. I'll have to be sending George some money come pay day. I hope he doesn't need it before.

        Much, much love to all,

          Scottie

Sunday, 20 April 1941

Dear Family,

It's high time I was writing a letter, don't you think. The time is so full and the days slip past so quickly that one really does lose track. It seems only yesterday was Monday and now it is almost Monday again and my flying starts.

First off, I want to thank Mother for the grand Easter tie. It is a beauty and is fast getting an awful lot of wear. Mother has such impeccable taste for ties. You are hereby commissioned to pick out all of mine for me.

This week finished up the fourth week of Ground School and leaves nine more weeks of that. Tomorrow morning the actual flight training commences and thence onward until Ground School is over. We fly alternately mornings and afternoons with Ground School the other half of the day. Until we solo we get an hour and a half instruction each day, and from then on an hour and a half instruction and the same of solo each day. I have been assigned to Corry Field, which is one of the two outlying big fields. We get ten hours instruction before solo, and then a check. If the check is O.K., we solo. Only about three from the class ahead passed their first check - that is, of the officers - and it looks as though ten hours is not enough. However, all I can do is to wait and see.

Last Friday night our officer class had a party out at Gulf Beach. We built a fire and roasted hot dogs, had a half barrel of beer, and a swell time. I had a blind date from Mobile who was swell. Have been out to the Koivisto's for dinner a couple of times since I last wrote. It is nice to have some place like that to go.

I have one "leg" on checking out of radio and expect to check out on test day come Thursday. (14 words plain code - 11 mixed - letters & numerals) That will be a boon because then I won't have to go to code again any more.

There is really no other news, but I'll write soon again and tell you all the dope.

Much, much love to all,
Scottie

ROBERT SCOTT WHITMAN JR.

Ground School

Naval Air Station

Pensacola, Florida

April 27, 1941

Dear Family,

Another week has flown past, and my how it has flown. Now I have six hours time in the air, and have been crazy about every minute of it.

This flying stuff isn't anywhere near as easy as it looks from the ground, and I don't know whether I am going to be able to do it or not. So far I have been completely bewildered and am not doing any too well. The only comforting thing is that nobody else seems to be doing much better, and I have hopes that the fog will clear before so very long. If I fly Monday and Tuesday, I'll get my solo check Wednesday next week. Right now I could no more solo with confidence than anything in the world; but perhaps the next four hours will change the story. They give us a half hour check with an instructor (other than our regular instructor) and, if he considers us safe, we solo.

It is the most fun that I have ever had, and is about the hardest thing that I have ever had to do. There are so many things to remember, and I haven't yet got the knack of thinking of about five things at the same time. My instructor is a swell guy - a j.g. reserve, who screams at me from the time we go up until the time we come down, and then laughs at me. I asked him if he thought I would ever learn to fly, and he said he guessed so - I hope so, cause it is such grand, grand stuff.

Mother's and Dad's letters arrived O.K. I am quite distressed about George's bad news about the draft. I am convinced that the thing for him to do is to either get into the Army Aero proposition or to take a defense engineering job. There is no use in his wasting his talent as a buck private. Much better that he keep on in his same line and benefit by the added experience that he will get.

I have checked out in radio now, which means no more radio code periods. Next week the period for code is from 6:30 to 8:30 - two more hours sleep for me - that is a break.

The only thing that we have in Ground School now is Nav. It should not be hard, and in eight more weeks no more Ground

School if I am still here then – and by gosh I'd better be. The weather has, of course, been very warm, and is getting more so all the time. They say that the heat here in the summer time is terrific. I don't doubt it.

Each day, the paramount thing in our minds is whether the weather will be good enough for flying. So far I have been held up just one day.

I am learning in an N-2-S (Stearman) trainer. They are very, very stable and safe – won't spin unless you make them, and will fly themselves if you will let them. My biggest trouble is, I think, trying too hard. It is absolutely necessary that one stay relaxed and fly naturally instead of mechanically. I don't do that as yet.

There is little or no news except of the flying and I have given you all that. I'll let you know how I make out on the check. Keep your fingers crossed for me.

       Much, much love to all,
        Scottie

Pensacola,"The Flying W's," training on a Stearman Biplane.

ROBERT SCOTT WHITMAN JR.

Monday, 5 May 1941

Dear Family,

Your son has soloed. I passed my first check O.K., they considered my flying safe, and up I went on Saturday. Nothing happened. It flew just like it did when there was an instructor in the front seat, and after an hour and a half I came home. Now I really start to work, and they say that the next twenty hours are the toughest to learn. We work on small field procedure and precision landings for the twenty hour check.

Today I didn't go up since the wind was so heavy that all planes were grounded. I hope that by tomorrow the weather will have changed enough so that I can get in my other hour and half, and an hour and a half instruction.

Your letters arrived on schedule. I was particularly pleased to have you send me the magazine with Marsh's article in it. It was very thoughtful and swell of you.

There is such little news to tell except of the flying, that I really don't know what to say. When I was up solo, I got so interested in what I was going that I sort of got lost – not that I didn't find my way back by myself, but it took some time. Which was all right, since I needed air work, and I just climbed and spiraled and glided up and down between two and four thousand feet while heading back in the right direction.

I have sent George twenty-five dollars as a start on our debt. There was a foul up on our getting credited for flying time, and as a result flight pay has been held up. I do hope that I won't be stymying him by not sending the full amount.

It was a pretty swell feeling to be up in the air all by myself – I was a little scared before I started out, but made myself come right back down and land after circling the field; and then I was O.K. and went on my merry way.

There really isn't any other news to tell now and so till there is I'll sign off.

Much, much love to all,
Scottie

Sunday, 18 May 1941

Dear Family,

It's high time for me to write home again, don't you think? The time does fly past so and we are so busy all of the time that one really loses track sometimes.

Everything seems to be going along swimmingly so far. Next week Tuesday I'll have my next check - the twenty-hour check. In it I must demonstrate my ability to make precision landings in a hundred foot circle, and to make emergency landings in small fields. If I fly as I did for my instructor yesterday on my last instruction hop, I won't pass the check, and so I'm hoping that I'll do better. They say that this one is the toughest of the bunch, but I expect they are all tough or easy depending on ones readiness for them.

I have just come back from the beach where I got a very warm coat of sunburn. The beach here on the Station is swell, and there is an extension of the Officers' Club there. The water was grand and the sun hot, and, all in all, it was a nice morning.

Saturday morning we had no Ground School for a change, and since we didn't fly till eleven I went to Mobile with another boy in my class. We had a right nice time, went dancing and came home about one. Maybe that was the reason I didn't fly so well for my instructor that afternoon.

We are now in the midst of Navigation in Ground School, and since all of the officer students have had so much of it, we are not following the regular course, but are each writing one chapter of the new Nav. manual for Ground School. It is not a particularly enticing task, but at least saves the boredom of repeating all the stuff we learned in our first semester of Nav at the Academy.

A lot of my classmates are getting married soon now, since the restriction is lifted come 1 June. I, of course, have no prospects or any particular desire for any.

I certainly hope that George can swing something for deferment. I am so sorry that his plans for the Engineering Corps went awry. It does seem awfully silly that color would keep him out, and especially since it is not blindness.

There is so little news to tell of and I am quite at a loss as to what else to write. We go to school and then fly - three hours a day now, and that is about all.

No dinner is served in BOQ on Saturday evenings, and last night we went out to eat at a place that serves nothing but fried chicken dinners. The man started by just serving at his farm when someone made arrangements ahead of time; and now his business is enormous and with good reason. It was a swell chow.

Much, much love to all,
Scottie

Sunday, 25 May 1941

Dear Family,

Another week has passed by and there is darned little news that I can pass on to you.

About the only thing that has happened is my getting two downs on my twenty hour check and starting on my extra time. I have four and a half hours extra coming, and then check again. It makes me sort of mad because I know that I can do everything that I am supposed to for the twenty hour; and yet, when I went up with the check pilots, I didn't produce. About fifty per cent have to take extra time so I don't feel as badly as if it were unusual; but at the same time it is sort of provoking when you know that you can do a thing and then don't do it.

I wish that there were other news of interest but really nothing happens. We fly half the day, and go to school the other half. We are still navigating at Ground School, and that is about all that we will have until we finish a month from now. If I get by my checks next week, I should have about three more weeks in Squadron One - then I go to Squadron Two, which is formation flying. From there to Three, which is instrument work, and then either to Miami for carrier planes, or stay here for either Cruiser (observation) or for the Big-Boats (Patrol planes).

Last night I went to the dance at Mustin Beach. They have one every Saturday night, and they are right much fun. I have been going down to the beach almost every day, and have started to accumulate quite a bit of tan. It is a good way to get exercise, and that is something that one needs around here.

Today I spent at the beach and then working and finishing my part of the new Nav text. This evening I went to the movies here in the Base, and now am about to turn in. I can get up an hour later than usual tomorrow, since I have checked out in radio and the first hour is devoted to that this week. That is quite a break, and five-thirty has been rather early to get up.

The Latin American naval big-wigs were here this week; but, of course, I saw nothing of them.

An interesting thing happened last night. I ran across a girl at the dance that I had met in Rio. She is up here visiting her sister, who is married to an officer stationed on the Base.

No more now, but will write as soon as there is any news.

Much, much love to all,

Scottie

ROBERT SCOTT WHITMAN JR.

Friday, 6 June 1941

Dear Family,

This letter has waited and waited until I could write to you and tell you how I made out on my checks after squadron time. I just finished the second one, and it was an "up" as was the one yesterday. So I am all set to start in on the next phase. (We have to fly two out three checks up after extra time.)

The pilot told me I gave him one of the best rides that he has had lately, and so I feel much better about the whole thing. Now three more instruction periods and about ten hours solo, and I check thirty-three hours. This time it will be stunts, pylons, more small fields, wingovers, and precision slips to a circle. After I had finished my check today and we were heading home, the pilot all of a sudden said, "Do a loop". I surprised him a bit by going right ahead and trying to do one although I had never done anything like it or ever tried. As a matter of fact, he said it was a good one, and then he threw the book at me, and did all the acrobatics for me - most fun I've had in a long time. He, the check pilot, by the way, is a very interesting person. He spent a lot of time in Finland teaching the Finns to fly during their war, and has written a couple of books.

About all I've done since I last wrote was to worry about these checks, and lie on the beach when not flying. You see, although there are only four and half hours in the extra time given out, I waited almost three weeks before I got the checks. First, it was weather, then my instructor got sick, then he went on leave, and then my new instructor got sick. Finally I'm over the hump though. I'm going to have to get another instructor again though. The new one is being detached tomorrow.

Mother's swell letter arrived a couple of days ago. I'm so glad that you had a nice trip. Only wish that you and Dad could come down here for a stay. We could have such a good time seeing the sights, and I know that you would enjoy it. Couldn't you talk Helen Thurston into coming down? It gets mighty lonely down here a lot of the time - the one saving factor is the flying.

Two more weeks of Ground School, and then only a half day's work until I get out of Squadron One - unless I am out, of course, before the two weeks are out. I doubt that that will happen though. After the thirty-three, there is about a week of formation, and then about three more days before the final check, which takes into account all the works - a sort of comprehensive.

We are in the middle of strategy and tactics now - very elementary stuff, and not much work for me.

I expect that I shall be assigned to Big-Boats. I hope so. We get assigned as soon as we leave Squadron One. My weight will probably be a deciding factor although I'm not sure. I don't guess I'd mind going back to cruisers as an aviator, though, even if I don't get to the big fellas.

This flying stuff is wonderful, and just wait until I get home, if I get my wings. We will go rent a plane and go riding. You'll love it, I know.

You can tell that I am happy today, I guess. Well, it is nice to get a little praise now and then, and that guy evidently liked his ride. Probably I'll go out tomorrow and smell - that is the way it goes.

Two of my classmates have stepped off into matrimony already now that the ban is lifted as of one June. Both Curt Vossler and Howard Ady are married and living out in town now.

Of course, I am going to take some pictures - right soon now too. Wanted to wait and see how the checks came out first - not that I am through the course yet, but there is a lot lighter feeling in my mind right right now, at least.

I can't think of anything more to say at present. Will send this off special so that you will get it Sunday and not be kept waiting too long for this week's letter.

   Much, much love to all,
    Scottie

ROBERT SCOTT WHITMAN JR.

Friday, 13 June 1941

Dear Dad,

Howdy-do, Pop, and how are things? Bet it isn't as hot up thar as it is down here. If it is you have my sympathy.

They tell me that Sunday is Pop's day - which is sort of silly isn't it, because every day is Pop's day as far as I am concerned. As if a special day had to be set aside so a guy would remember his Dad. But maybe there are some guys who have to be reminded, and if there are, well, then I guess maybe it is a good thing. Funny thing though, I don't think that I am one of those guys. Because I think about home an awful lot, and that means thinking about my grand Pop and how swell a guy he is.

I think about you and how well you have stood up under a pretty bad beating - the kind of beating that sends weaklings straight to the dogs. And you have just plugged along never complaining and never griping and never letting it get you down. Life ain't been so much fun for you these last few years, I know. It's been tough, and I'm proud of you for the way you have taken it.

You have said how unhappy it makes you to think that you have been able to do so little for George and me. Good heavens, man, you have done everything for us. You have given us a boost every time we needed it, you have given us faith, and courage, and love and the feeling that you not only trust us but in us. What more could any two sons want - now I ask you. You have given us the most wonderful example in the world of sheer guts in the face of adversity. You don't need to feel the least bit unhappy, but rather wonder whether we are worth it.

There isn't any way to say it, I guess, except to say that the grandest guy I know is my Dad, and I wouldn't have anybody else for my Pop but my Pop. Just keep on plugging, Old Sport, and don't ever get blue - like I know you do - it doesn't pay.

Well, that's a bit of sentiment from a guy that claims to have none; but it is true, and I guess I sort of wanted to be sure you knew that I was for you all the way, and always have been and always will be.

I haven't started work on my thirty-three yet, there is some sort of a pile up of students on another phase, and they want to get it ironed out before we start on the next part. It is sort of boring sitting around the squadron and not flying much, but I do get a warm-up every other day or so. I have an idea that I will start out on instruction again this afternoon. We have one more week of Ground School and then are through with that. There are three more officer classes scheduled so far. The first one starts in July. Quite a few of my classmates are coming out – but Dick and Bill are not on any of the slates that I have seen.

I have heard form Donna Ovrom a couple of times, and the Quincy is evidently out in the Atlantic on patrol. She has not heard from Bob for several weeks.

I should know in about a month now what my assignment will be. Really haven't decided what I want to put in for, but expect that it will be Big Boats.

Will you please send me George's address in Ann Arbor. I should like to write him and send him some money.

All the love in the world to the grandest guy I know,
     Scottie

ROBERT SCOTT WHITMAN JR.

Sunday 22 June 1941

Dear Family,

Comes a Sunday again, and time, high time, to write a letter home. Nothing really has happened since I last wrote, and so that is the reason perhaps why a letter has not come sooner.

Last night, however, we had a little excitement. Doc Abbott, one of my classmates here was married, and we all went over to Mobile to get him launched successfully. It was a very nice wedding, and we had quite a nice party thereafter. It was a military wedding with all the trimmings, and very "pretty", if that is the established word to use.

I am still working on my thirty-three hour, and expect to check next Tuesday – providing that we have good weather from now till then. I don't feel any too confident about the whole thing so keep your fingers crossed for me.

It has been as hot as blazes down here for so long that cool weather is a thing of which I have little remembrance. However, I'm getting used to it now and it is not so bad. The way I figure it out, I have about three and a half to four months left before I get my wings. That is, of course, if the normal course of weather continues.

The lads are getting married right and left now, and as far as I can figure it, I am just about the only one who has no prospects nor any prospects of prospects. Well, perhaps someday.

Stunting is a lot of fun, but they are so simple and there are so many other things that must be mastered for this check, that I have little time left to kick the plane around in loops and immelmans and the like. After the thirty-three comes formation, and then a final check – then to Squadron Two for primary work in military planes.

I am much interested and concerned about George's situation. I wish that you would send me his address to that I might write to him. I do so hope that he has come through with flying colors in his year's work. I'll bet he has done himself proud.

This is a skimpy letter, but there is nothing else to tell.

        Much, much love to all,

         Scottie

Saturday 28 June 1941

Dear Family,

Dad's & Mother's letters arrived. They were grand letters and you know how much I enjoy and look forward to news from home.

Today we had an inspection out at the squadron, and then secured for the day. So here I am at 9:30 with the whole day ahead of me.

I checked "up" on my 33 hour check a couple of days ago and am now in primary three-plane formations. Formation work is a lot of fun, and I guess it is a good thing that I find it that way, because most of my Navy flying will be in formation. After seven more hours of formations I get one more instruction, three hours solo, and a final check - a sort of comprehensive on the work in Squadron One. If successful, I "sandbag" - move up to the front seat of the trainor with a sandbag in the back seat for ballast - after a short hop move over to Squadron Two - over the hump.

We are in the middle of the thunder storm period down here now and are losing quite a bit of time because of bad weather. Next week, however, we fly in the morning - the storms form generally in the afternoon.

SAY!!! Weren't George's marks grand! I'm as proud as punch of him - he is a smart laddie and is doing himself proud. What is the dope on his draft? The Navy is taking in engineers on the same proposition as the Army. I wonder if he could make it. I know he could except for the physical. I was talking with a couple of them yesterday and think I'll go talk to the Repair Officer here at the station. I'll bet we could get that color business waived - that is, of course, if he is not to be deferred, which I bet he is.

The dope most prevalent now is that all officers go to carrier squadrons. They are very short of regular officers in these units and need them badly. It really doesn't matter to me what kind of duty I get as long as it is flying. If I go to carriers, I'll spend a couple of months in Miami prior to getting my wings. There is, of course, the chance that I might be sent to VOS - observation - scouting on a cruiser or battleship. I dunno and neither does anyone else, as far as that goes.

It's cloudy now, but I'm hoping the sun will come out so I

can get to the beach – that is a nice and an inexpensive way to spend the day.

I really have been doing very little; going to the movies here at the base, swimming, and flying, that's about all. I intend to get some golf clubs when I get George paid off. It's funny how the money goes. Little expenses arise all the time, and it is pretty expensive just to live here. However, I'm getting along fine.

Will write soon again.

> Much, much love to all,
> Scottie

Wednesday, 2 July 1941

Dear George,

    So you beat the draft - and that is a weight off all our minds. Good stuff; now you are set - and those grades for last semester: Say, boy!!! You really did a swell job of it and I'm proud of you - proud as all git out, old fella. You'll be a big man in the aircraft industry some day, and you can bet you'll be a big help to some company when you get out of school. Keep up the good work and keep pitching.

    I suppose you have started summer school by now. It's a lot of shop work, isn't it? Should be darned interesting. Don't slack off now, though. Have fun, but keep the old grades up thar - it'll pay off big dividends.

    Well, I'm just about through the primary squadron now. I have just four and a half hours more and then a final check. That takes in everything we have had so far, air work, stunts, precision spins, precision landings to a circle, small fields, wing overs, pylons, etc., etc. I had a little trouble with my twenty hour check, but that is all so far. Just finished ten hours of primary formation work. That is a lot of fun. When I get through Squadron One, I go to some more formation in heavier planes. Then on to instruments, and then either to scouting sea planes, Big Boats, or to carrier planes. I shall ask for Big Boats, but expect I'll get one of the other two.

    We don't do much down here except fly and go to the beach. There is a right nice beach here on the station and a couple more close by. Am getting pretty brown at this point.

    A lot of my classmates are married now, but I'm free and with no prospects. It's a good way to have it, since there is no telling where I'll go when I get out of here.

    Write me, guy, and tell me all about yourself. Best o' luck to you and again GOOD WORK!!!

        Scottie

Sunday, 6 July 1941

Dear Family,

Your welcome letters arrived. Hooray for George — I'm so glad he got his deferment. That, at least, settles one problem. I have written to him.

We had a long week-end this week and have spent it very quietly — back to work tomorrow and I'm glad of it.

Three more future officer flight classes have been announced and Tex is in one of them. He arrives down here sometime in September. I may see him and I may not — hope so though.

Well, I'm through formations now and should check final Tuesday if the weather is good. It has been raining a lot lately and as a result I was held up a couple of days. I'm ready to leave Squadron One and get on to something else. Keep your fingers crossed for me on that final check.

I wonder whether Russia is really holding up the Germans as they claim. If Germany gets itself involved in a first class war in Russia it would seem a propitious moment for England to counter-invade and make a pass at the continent. Wonder if they will. I suppose it is highly possible — only trouble is that the English have lacked always the dash that such a move calls for. They are always so darned conservative, and as a result often lose out.

Oh, well, it is a crazy world and I guess we are a crazy bunch that live in it.

No more now. Will write again soon.

Much love to all,
Scottie

Friday, 11 July 1941

Dear Family,

How the time does seem to fly, and I have found that my letter home is late again. Well, I wanted to wait until I could give you the dope on my final check, and now I can tell you that I am through with Squadron One. I did it the hard way with one down and then two ups, but did not need to take extra time, and today I'll sandbag in the front seat and then go over to Squadron Two and check in.

It is a good feeling because now I am over the hump, and if I keep my nose clean, I am assured of my wings. The weather has been so finicky that we have had a hard time getting flying time in, but finally I got the checks over with.

Larry Pierce, one of the lads in my flight class, is getting married tomorrow, and I am one of his ushers. He is no particular friend, but being down here, he can't get the people he would really want, and so has asked four of us to usher for him. It will be a military wedding with the sword arch and all, and should be an interesting experience since it is the first wedding in which I have taken part. There have been a couple of nice parties connected with the pre-nuptial gaiety, and it has been fun – of a sort.

Hot as Hades as usual down here and getting hotter by the day. I wonder if it will ever cool off. (Doc Abbott has just yelled for me to come on and play bridge so I'll send this off special delivery a little later so that you will get it.)

Saturday, 12 July 1941

Sorry that it took so long to get back to this, but, as usual, a million and one little interruptions have played hob with my letter writing.

Just now, I am waiting until time to go over to the chapel for the wedding. Just got back from Squadron Two. Have already had my indoctrination flight – two hours this afternoon – and expect to get a check out in the first type plane on Monday. That plane is the O-3-U – a very old observation type, now long obsolete.

I expect to be in Two about three weeks, and then on to the Instrument Squadron – Three. At this point I am supposed to be able to fly, and the rest of the work is military in character.

I really can't think of anything else to say now so until next time, which will be soon – hasta la vista.

Scottie

Friday, 18 July 1941

Dear Family,

Another week is almost gone. My, how they do fly. It's been four months since I arrived here, and it doesn't seem anywhere near that long. Mother's letter arrived a couple of days ago, and was certainly a most welcome sight. I don't get much mail, and mail from home is a real treat.

I have finished a check-out in O3U-1 – a very, very old scouting type – or did I tell you about that? At any rate now I am waiting around for a check-out in either an SU or SBU – one of two other types. Then after four hours of solo in that, I will start formation work – nine hours of three-plane formations, and six hours of nine planes. And then on to Squadron Three.

Each day seems to make the flying more fun and more fascinating. I don't know what it is, but it certainly is both absorbing and fascinating. Perhaps it is the spirit of competition against the laws of gravity and the plane, or just the complete concentration that flying demands. Anyway, I like it. Now I am supposed to be able to fly, and the rest of the work is strictly military in character. Of course there are an awful lot of hours ahead of me before I can even begin to think I am a good aviator – but, at least, I have the start.

I'm glad that Mother has the students for the summer if she is glad, but she must not overdo. I sure do hope that business gets good and stays good. You two certainly deserve a big, big break, and if it were in my power to send good luck your way, you would be showered under with it.

As far as George's last year at school is concerned, you needn't worry. I can help him and help him a lot. So don't worry; he'll make it O.K. You are to tell me just what he needs, and I will see to it that it is provided. However, we can talk that over when I get home on leave, which I expect I will have sometime in October. No promise, mind you, but they have always given fifteen days up to now.

We got Larry married quite successfully, and he is now back from a short honeymoon and working again. It was a nice wedding – very small but very satisfactory, and I think that he can feel that he had a good send off into matrimony.

I am enclosing some pictures – there are more forthcoming

but this is a start for you. I'll send the others as soon as developed. The explanation is on the back of them so that you will know what's what.

It has rained every day at one time or another for the last month at least – usually not badly enough or hard enough to entirely ruin the flying for the day, but it has held up things. I am sort of anxious to get out of here – although heaven knows why. The next station can't be as soft as this and may be off in some god-forsaken part of the world. But I have the itch to get going again, and Pensacola is not a very good town in lots of ways. In the first place there is a definite lack of feminine company – too many men around and not enough girls – and no way that I know of to get to know any. As a result I have a date just about once a month, if that often. We work too late to swim now or do much of anything else and there is nothing to do at night except go to the movie and then to bed. And the rooms are too hot to stay in except for sleep. I have read a lot and am toying with the idea of trying to write something – what I dunno, but it would at least keep me occupied. If it only were not so hot – oh, well, never satisfied – ought to know when I'm well off, I guess. From all the stories that I hear, things are pretty fierce out in the fleet. Donnie has gone home from Norfolk to California because Bob is never there and hasn't been for a long time – since I left the <u>Quincy</u>, I guess.

No more now except lots and lots of love to the best Mom and Dad in the world.

Scottie

Friday, 25 July 1941

Dear Family,

Comes the end of another week and letter time again – Dad's letter arrived a couple of days ago – sure and 'twas very welcome.

I'm still in Squadron Two and should be there for about another week. I think that I'll start three-plane formation work tomorrow. I get nine hours of that and six hours of nine plane and then go on my merry way to Squadron Three.

The big news this week is that I have moved and am now living in the regular B.O.Q. Bob Wood, a classmate, and I have a suite together – two bedrooms, a living room and bath. It is so much more comfortable than my old quarters that there is no comparison. Over-stuffed furniture, double beds, rugs, curtains – quite a homelike place.

The new officer classes have started to arrive. One came yesterday and they will continue to come every two weeks for quite a while. There are only a couple of my class in this first gang, but most of the rest of the classes are made up entirely of '39. It should prove a lot of fun what with re-unions and all.

Some 150 British boys have arrived here for flight instruction. I have not seen any of them as yet but somebody said they are very young.

Mother asked if I have any tan? Yes, sure. Lost weight? A very few pounds – am in best of health and spirits – no colds or anything else since that little bout when I first arrived.

Lots and lots of love to my Mom and Dad,
Scottie

Friday, 1 August 1941

Dear Family,

Another week passed and letter writing time again. Your letters arrived OK and were certainly grand. Got a long awaited letter from George today and so now this week has had a 100% turnout from the people who mean most to me.

Today I finished 9 plane formation work and after a "check out" or familiarization flight in an SBU in the morning, I'll be through Squadron Two.

The SBU is a much faster and heavier plane than any so far and they check us in them so we can get some solo time in over in "Three". I have been assigned to carrier duty – put in for patrol planes but they are over quota so I got second choice. So I'll be shoving off for Miami in about three weeks. The stay there is from 6-8 weeks and then I'll be sent either to Norfolk or San Diego after a little leave, there to get preliminary training prior to "checking out" in carrier landings on whatever ship to which I am assigned.

I have ordered my new uniforms; there seems to be no place to get them in Miami – another $100 expense. Such fun – I don't think.

The formation work was fun, but I'm glad it is over. It is the least safe of any flying down here. Too many inexperienced pilots, too close. I reckon I have 130 or 140 hours now and am beginning to learn to fly.

The work in Three is instruments, as I guess I have told you. I get 18 hours in the Link Trainer and 18 in the air under a hood (with a safety pilot up front of course). We learn to fly on instruments and to ride the radio beams to an airport. The course takes from two to three weeks and we come out with a C.A.A. instrument rating.

Must run along now, will write soon again.

Much love to all,
Scottie

Saturday, 10 August 1941

Dear Family,

    In about a week and a half now I'll be heading toward Miami. Now have 12 hours in the Link Trainer and none in the air on instruments in Squadron iii. I'll get a total of 18 hours in the air (9 flying days) and 15 in the Link. That trainer, by the way, is quite a contraption but very exasperating and a hot box in this kind of weather. I should start flying tomorrow. In a few days now I should get my final orders and know to which carrier I am going. I'll be sent either to Norfolk or San Diego first for a carrier instruction course of about ten weeks and then sent to the squadron to which ordered. Get my orders before leaving for Miami – just why I don't know. Probably saves paper work.

    When are Mother and Helen T. going to Ann Arbor? It should be a swell trip. Ought to come back via Miami – wouldn't that be swell!!!

    Another new flight class with about six of '39 has reported. By the time I leave the place will be humming with my class.

        Much love to all,
          Scottie

Sunday, 17 August 1941

Dear Family,

This is probably the last letter from Pensacola, since I expect to check out of here Friday. Have six more hours and a check in Squadron Three.

This probably won't arrive before Mother leaves for Ann Arbor, but if it does here is a big wish for a wonderful trip. My, but I'm glad that you are going.

Right now in the squadron, I'm in radio instrument flying or, as they say, flying the beam. That is starting out under the hood, orientating by radio, and then coming into the airport on the beam, letting down according to procedure, and, when the hood opens, finding yourself, you hope, directly over and 500 feet above the airport. That is how all of the airlines come into their fields in bad weather and how they keep on their course all the time. It's amazin' to suddenly shake the stick to tell the instructor you are over the airport, open the hood and sure enough be there.

I expect to live off the station in Miami – where remains to be seen. It will be cheaper since I'll be given an extra $40 and will probably move in with the gang already down there.

I'll be quite glad to leave Pensacola – and they say Miami is cooler. It's not that it gets so hot by the thermometer (95° is about average at noon), but the relative humidity is always about 90, as you can see when I tell you it rains every day (for about an hour). All my uniforms started to mildew and, since I had them cleaned and put up in cedar bags only to have to take them out and have them cleaned again, you can see that my cleaning bill is a pain in the neck. Now they get the sun and air once a week.

My address in Miami will be N.A.S. Miami, Florida, I suppose. That should do temporarily, at least.

That's all for now.

       Much, much love to all,
        Scottie

ROBERT SCOTT WHITMAN JR.

Friday, 22 August 1941

Dear Family,

Well, Pop, how do you like a bachelor's existence again? Not much fun, but I'll bet you are making out O.K. and wishing to heck Mother would hurry home - but think how much good the trip is doing her.

This note is primarily to tell you that I'm not going to Miami, but instead to Squadron Four and patrol planes. The reason: well, a complicated set of circumstances surrounding a mistake on the part of a clerk in Squadron Two. He forgot to send my assignment (to carrier duty) to the Training School Office, which, in turn, because of that, did not send to Washington for my orders.

The mistake was not found out until too late to send for them, so they gave me Big Boats instead. I was sort of looking forward to flying the small fast planes, but you should be happy to know that I'm going to the safest flying duty in the big slow two and four engine patrol planes.

I finished up in Squadron Three today, and am now a qualified instrument pilot, authorized to proceed on instruments anywhere (airlines etc.). It is quite a thrill to go under the hood not knowing where you are, having nothing but instruments and radio to guide you, and at an altitude of 4500 feet, orientate by radio and end up over the center runway of the airport at Mobile, 500 feet up. That's what I did today - worked a perfect problem for the check. Then, too, the check pilot puts the plane into all sorts of unusual positions and the student must bring the plane back to normal straight flight at cruising speed. It's all done with a turn and bank indicator, air speed indicator, and rate of climb indicator - and, of course, tachometer and manifold pressure gauges (for he might have changed the throttle setting).

The emphasis in the new squadron is on navigation and bombing and radio work. The newest patrol boats are small ships with a skipper, exec. etc. They are probably quite thrilling, but the crates around here are just trucks, and flying them is equally boring as driving a truck. (So I'm told, for I haven't been up yet.)

I'm enclosing a picture of the best land plane I have soloed

in, and probably the last for some time to come, and a picture
of what I hope to fly soon after graduating and then later.
    Well, at least, I'll be here when Tex arrives - some
consolation.

        No more now, much love,
            Scottie

Pensacola, training on a PBY-5A Catalina Patrol Bomber

Labor Day, 1 September 1941

Dear Family,

Mother's grand letter arrived. It sounds as though it were a grand trip but awfully tiring. I do hope that you are rested up again and feel back to par.

I suppose that George is busy packing three months vacation into one, and having a swell time doing it. When does he start back for the last year? Heavens to Betsy, in another nine months we'll have another engineer, full fledged, in the family.

And in another month there will be an aviator in the family. I should finish up about the first of October if all goes well. I have eighteen hours in Big Boats now – six of it only is pilot time, since three of us go up with one instructor and get an hour each in a three hour hop. They are not much fun (P- boats, I mean), but then they are nice and safe and once I get used to them I suppose I'll like it.

I'm reading Bill Shirer's <u>Berlin Diary</u> – it was given to me, and, if you haven't read it, I'll send it along. When I've finished. Or did you say you had read it?

I have been much concerned, (though why I should be, I know not) about all the to-do in the papers and magazines over the lack of punch behind our so called "defense effort". Of course it may not be as bad as the picture is painted, but where there is so much smoke there must be some fire. And with all the waste and the bungling and ineffectual attempts at "inflation killing", it looks as though we are fast killing off the chances of any successful war effort or post war effort toward normalcy. You can see the same "depression" shaping up only in a magnitude that leaves the last far behind.

The increase in automobiles on the road, the rising cost of food, rent, fantastic rents; it's unhealthy. And still, when there is a call and urgent call for government control of prices, wages, and industry, that government which, when there was no call for it, meddled too much, now turns to a policy of <u>laissez faire</u> – I don't get it.

But maybe I don't know what I'm talking about. It seems to me, now <u>is</u> the time to <u>start</u> running industry, business and transportation – not <u>stop</u> it.

Oh, well, who am I to settle the affairs of the nation – It's hot and I'm tired but well.

> Much love to all,
> Scottie

NAVY DEPARTMENT
Nav-311-ES
82661-6

BUREAU OF NAVIGATION
WASHINGTON, D.C.
5258   September 6, 1941

From: The Chief of the Bureau of Navigation.
To: Ensign Robert S. Whitman, Jr., U.S.N.

Via: Commandant.

Subject: Change of duty.

1.   When directed by the Commandant, Naval Air Station, upon the completion of your training on or about October 6, 1941, you will regard yourself detached from duty under instruction at the Naval Air Station, Pensacola, Fla., and from such other duty as may have been assigned you; will proceed to San Diego, Calif., and report to the Commanding Officer, Transition Training Squadron, Pacific Fleet, for temporary duty involving flying under instruction.

2.   When directed by the Commanding Officer, Transition Training Squadron, Pacific Fleet, you will regard yourself detached; will report to the Commandant, Eleventh Naval District, for first available government transportation to the port in which Patrol Squadron Forty-four may be, and upon arrival report to the commanding officer of Patrol Squadron Forty-four for duty involving flying.

3.   You are hereby authorized to delay for a period of fifteen days in reporting to the Commanding Officer, Transition Training Squadron, Pacific Fleet, in obedience to these orders.

4.   Keep the Bureau of Navigation and your new station advised of your address.

5.   This delay will count as leave. Upon the commencement of the leave, you will immediately inform this bureau of the exact date and upon the expiration thereof, you will return the attached form, giving the dates of commencement and expiration.

6.   These orders constitute your assignment to duty in a part of the Aeronautic Organization of the Navy and your existing detail to duty involving flying continues in effect.

C.W. Nimitz

Copy to:
Bu. Aero.
Cdt., 11th Nav. Dist.
Cdt., 8th. Nav. Dist.
Cdt., Naval Air Station,
    Pensacola, Fla.
C.O., Transition Training
    Sqd., Pacific Fleet
C.O., Patrol Sqd. 44
Cdr., Patrol Wing 4,
Cdr., Aircraft, Sctg. Force.

ROBERT SCOTT WHITMAN JR.

TFP   1st Endorsement   U.S. Naval Air Station
                                                        Pensacola, Florida
                                                         8 September 1941

From: Commandant
To: Ensign Robert S. Whitman, Jr., U.S.N.

            1. Delivered.

                                                    JOHN P. REMBERT, Jr.

                                                    By direction

F R SA

Tuesday, 9 September 1941

Dear Dad,

Happy birthday, Pop – and many, many happy returns of the day. I only wish that I could be home to say it instead of write; but that can't be, so, instead, a letter will have to suffice.

Your letter telling of the "business" has arrived and you can bet that I'm glad that there have been some results; makes work worth while when you get something tangible out of it.

Well, I've about three weeks to go and then where? Since my orders have not come through, I've no idea what sort of a station comes next. It, of course, could be anywhere. Tomorrow I get a check in P-2 Y's. I hope it will be successful, but have found that flying Big Boats is not so easy as it looks. And also it is more fun than I thought it would be.

I'm due to be best man at a huge wedding in Atlanta on the 27th of this month, and hope to have it coincide with my finishing here. It can work out that way if luck is with me. "Rip" Kline, one of the '39ers down here is marrying an Atlanta girl. Very much society – eight ushers and bridesmaids etc. etc. – it should prove fun.

It is still as hot as blazes down here and no promise of a let-up in sight. Hope I get sent to a temperate climate.

Wednesday

Check O.K. and my orders have arrived – Patrol Squadron 44 after additional training at the 'Transition Training Squadron' in San Diego. They are a good set of orders – the best station I've seen yet. Rumor has it that it is a four-engine squadron. Wouldn't that be something?

I have mailed a little birthday package and it should arrive Friday. If it doesn't you'll know it's coming.

Many, many happy returns again – and much love to all,

      Scottie

Friday, 19 September 1941

Dear Family,

Well – there aren't too many weeks left before I leave Pensacola behind me. The "hurricane", so called, held up flying for four days, but now we are back in the swing again and I have 17 hops to go. These can be finished in eleven days, but it will probably be longer than that.

The flights left are bombing, Nav., gunnery and instrument.

Now – as far as leave is concerned; as you know, I have fifteen days. I have been peremptorily ordered to Key West to visit Betty and Bill Maddox and so am going down there for a couple of days – whether to do it on my way up north or on my way west, I don't know – probably on my way north. It is a long haul I have before me – Key West, Binghamton, San Diego. I guess 8000 miles, more or less.

The order of stops is dependent to a great extent on the route I want to take west – north or south. I think I'll get a route mapped out by one of the Oil Company travel bureaus.

Next week-end I'm going to Atlanta for Rip's wedding – (I guess I told you about that).

Tex arrived yesterday, and we spent six hours catching up on 2-1/2 years. There are now about 60 of '39 here, and it seems more like home.

If you have any suggestions as to how I can break up the long trip, and as to route, I wish you would come forth with them. It will be the longest I have ever driven by a great margin, and I should be a good ten days on the road. Driving alone as I shall be, is going to be grim.

       No more now – much love to all,
         Scottie

Tuesday, 30 September 1941

Dear Family,

Have arrived back from the wedding after having adequately acquitted myself; and another one of our boys has fallen by the wayside. It was quite the flossiest wedding I have ever seen, with eight ushers, six bridesmaids, a maid and a matron of honor, and seven groomsmen, and me. Oh, - and the bride and groom showed up as an incidental extra. We were royally entertained by the best people that Atlanta can produce and had a very gay time of it. Now, however, that is over. I'll tell you more about it when I see you, which should be in from two to three weeks. I have twelve more hops, which can be finished in from six to twelve days. Am not going to Key West. Bill and Betty have been transferred to Annapolis and I'm to stop through there on my way up. I want very much to see them and especially Jimmie. Was to spend by week-ends in Key West from Miami, but, of course, couldn't make that.

I may stop overnight in Norfolk, to see Bob and Donna. However, I haven't decided on that yet.

Bought a new set of tires for the car - they were too worn to chance a transcontinental trip, and the prices jump tomorrow (the 1st). It was a blow to the exchequer but a necessity, considering my 7000 mile jaunt.

Dad's suggestion about using Navy travel was good except for one stumbling block. If I ride "Navy", I lose eight cents a mile travel allowance from here to San Diego.

Tex is rooming with me now since Bob Wood has left. It is good to see him again.

Heard from Marsh the other day. He is still in Manila and just as disgruntled as ever. Can hardly blame him - it is tough on all of the people out there. We have sent two married officers and one about to be married from our flight classes; and I, a bachelor confirmed, get those wonderful orders of mine. Really does not seem fair does it?

It is still as hot as blazes here during the day, but the nights are pleasant. It is hard to realize that I must pack prepared for fall weather. Have lost most of my tan - we fly too late to make the beach worth while.

There is a chance that I can get a Kaydet who finishes about the same time I do to ride as far as Norfolk with me - that will

be a break. After that I don't know. I sort of hate to advertise
and get a stranger for a partner. Would like to plan my trip so
I could stop off to see any friends or relatives on the way.
Would save so much expense. However, we'll see.

That's about all for now.

Much, much love to all,
Scottie

Wednesday, 8 October 1941

Dear Family,

Each day I have delayed writing until I could tell you some definite dope on my plans, and each new day comes along with everything just as uncertain as ever. Actually, I should have been finished here two weeks ago, and yet it looks now as though it would be either Monday or Wednesday of next week. The big monkey-wrench in the business is the weather. That hurricane last Monday and Tuesday raised hob with everything here. It did not get here at all, and there were no winds stronger than a summery zephyr (whatever that may be), but it was headed this way. As a result, the whole station went into "condition 1" for hurricane — windows boarded up, all planes secured (tied down), IN the hanger, and 23 of our big boats flown away to Jacksonville. So, even though the storm got perverse and decided not to pay us a visit, we were still delayed another two days.

At this point, I have two bombing, two camera, gunnery, and a Nav hop left — three days of flying if they will schedule me that way and the good weather holds. Since they give out wings (your own that you bought) on Monday, Wednesday and Friday, it looks like either Monday or Wednesday.

If it is Wednesday, I think I'll try to see the Cornell-Navy game in Baltimore next Saturday a week. Since I have promised Betty I'll stop in Annapolis, I'll wire or write when you can expect to have me breeze in with my new wings — a fledgling "junior birdman".

Both of your swell letters arrived, Mother's yesterday and Dad's today. I'm sorry, too, that there were no pictures of the wedding. There were some, of course, but nobody sent them on although we asked. Only one boy got any, and even I haven't seen his copy yet.

I went to see the station team play Saturday — it has an imposing roster of ex college stars — among them McLeod, all American from Dartmouth; but it is a pretty sad looking outfit, principally because none of the players much care one way or the other. They have all had their fill of football. The Pensacola High School team that I saw play Friday night did a much better job.

I'm so glad for George that he got his job, and he must have had a good record to get it. As I have told you, I'll help him along if he needs it. As soon as I get this trip and my uniforms out of the way I'll be pretty well set to pitch into the kitty.

Dad's letter sounded a bit too worried to be to my liking. I know it is easy to say and hard to practice; but, Pop, try not to let things get you down. You know darned well that you'll come out all right.

How about the World Series: wasn't that fourth game – ninth inning – break of Mickey Owen's a heart-breaker! HOLY SMOKE!!!!

The Navy showing against W. Va. was typical: 7-0 at the end of the half, 40-0 at game end. Superior reserve power is what did it, of course. Wonder what will happen when we meet up with a team that can match us reserve for reserve. That Cornell game should be a humdinger.

Yesterday out on a bombing hop I actually hit the target, a two-foot in diameter steel umbrella, from 6000 feet. Very lucky considering all the factors – but a thrill.

That is about all the news except that I'm looking forward to home more than I can say – and it is as hot as the hinges of hades here.

　　　　　Much, much love,
　　　　　　　Scottie

　　　　　　Department of the Navy
　　　　　　　Date 5 Sept., 1941
　　　　　　Naval Aviator No. 8676
　　　　　　　―――――――――――――
　　　　　　　This certifies that
　　　　　　Robert S. Whitman, Jr.
　　　　　　　Ensign U.S. Navy
　　　　　born 1 day of Jan., 1916
　　　　having fulfilled the conditions pre-
　　　　scribed by the United States Navy
　　　　Department, was appointed a
　　　　　　　Naval Aviator
　　　　　　on 28 August 1941
　　　　　　　C.W. Nimitz
　　　　Chief of Bureau of Navigation

3 1 0 6
U.S. Naval Air Station
Pensacola, Florida
station
29 August 1941
date issued
This is to certify that
Robert S. Whitman, Jr.
name
Ensign U.S.N.
rank
has passed the test in instrument flying
prescribed for pilots of
The United States Navy
and is qualified to proceed on instruments in
Single engines
type of plane
A.C. Read
A.C. Read, Capt., U.S. Navy
Commanding

ALSO QUALIFIED FOR
LET DOWN ON
INSTRUMENTS

W E S T E R N	
U N I O N	(50)

NA566 5 TOUR:SANTAANA CALIF 30 500P

1941 OCT 30 PM 9:57

MRS R S WHITMAN-

    51 STJOHN AVE BINGHAMTON NY-

ARRIVED SAFELY NO STRAIN LOVE:

        SCOTTIE

United States Naval Air Station
Pensacola, Florida

Know all men by these presents that

Ensign Robert S. Whitman, Jr., US Navy

has completed the prescribed course of training as a
Student Naval Aviator and having met successfully all
the requirements of the course, has been designated a

Naval Aviator

In Witness Whereof, this certificate has been signed
on this 13th day of October 1941, and the Seal of
the Naval Air Station hereunto affixed

Captain, U.S. Navy
Commandant

Commander, U.S. Navy
Executive Officer

Commander, U.S. Navy
Superintendent of Aviation Training

Naval Aviator Diploma 13 Oct 1941

XIII
S A N D I E G O
NOVEMBER 1941 – DECEMBER 7, 1941

ROBERT SCOTT WHITMAN JR.

Los Angeles California

Sunday, 2 November 1941

Dear Family,

Sunday morning in California, and there is time to turn in a report of the trip across and all that has happened.

The trip to Ann Arbor was uneventful, the lunch that Mother fixed very delicious, and the arrival time about 5:30. George was working, so I waited for him at the house and watched the boys fixing the prize winning home-coming display. He showed up shortly and we cleaned up and had dinner and then had dates for a little while.

The game Saturday was a corker, Michigan – Minnesota – the best I have seen in a long time. Our seats were good, the game swell, and the Michigan Band unbelievable. It, the band, is everything anyone has said it is and then some. Saturday night we had dates again and went to various radio dances at the houses. And I shoved off Sunday morning.

Drove to St. Louis that night and stayed in a tourist court or, as they are called out here, MOTEL. The next day I drove to Oklahoma City expecting to stop there. However, just outside I picked up a boy in an R.O.T.C. uniform. He was heading for Los Angeles and I decided to drive through to Amarillo, since I had a relief driver. Turned out by degrees that the lad had gone to Clemson for a year, but was wearing the uniform now just to help getting rides. He had started out with $3.25 in his pocket to go to the coast to look for a job. His story, as I wormed it out of him, was a perfect pattern of the same old malarkey, but I believed it fully, and do now. And so, I ended up by driving straight through to Flagstaff, Arizona. He wouldn't let me put him up for the night and headed on his way. Happy go lucky, with not a care, and a $1.25, and no money to fall back on. He told me his mother had given him the three dollars – all she had. He had the quarter. His father was a cotton mill worker, and had smashed a foot in an auto accident – couldn't work now. He was on his way to catch a defense job to escape the draft and support his family. Courage – Holy Smoke – and just as happy as a lark. That lad made me do a lot of thinking. And he was intelligent, clean, polite – might have been George or I, or any of our friends. So I let him out at the turn to the Grand Canyon after having offered to see him through the rest of the way. He probably has a job by now - the aircraft industry snaps at bright young unskilled laborers out here. I stopped and saw the Grand Canyon, which was very magnificent, and looked just like the pictures and movies I have seen of it, and stopped at Boulder Dam and finally arrived in L.A. Have seen Betts and Peg, been to San Diego, and am back in L.A. with Paul Holmberg now. We drove up to see the U.C.L.A. - Calif. game yesterday, and he is going back on the train while I stay up for a party at the Van Wormers, which they are having for me. Will report in tomorrow or Tuesday.

I shall write a more detailed account of the trip in a couple of days - but Pablo is awake now and it's time to catch some breakfast and put him on a train - and get out to Peg's.

Much, much love to all,
Scottie

ROBERT SCOTT WHITMAN JR.

V P 44 U.S.N.A.S.

San Diego, Calif.

7 November 1941

Dear Family,

So we'll start where we left off - although I don't exactly remember where that was; but, at least, I had told you about my passenger. Dad's very, very welcome letter arrived today and he asked where I picked him up. Well, as I remember, it was in a little town just west of Oklahoma City - and I rode him to Flagstaff, Arizona. I had planned to spend the night just the other side of Oklahoma City, and it was about seven in the evening. Arrived in Flagstaff about three the next day.

So I went to see the Grand Canyon in a snow storm after staying in a tourist court that night, and then headed on to L.A. after stopping at the Boulder Dam. The dam, by the way, is most certainly a sight. There must be enough concrete in that pile for a superhighway most of the way across the continent. Really, it must be one of the wonders of the world.

Well, I went into California via Las Vegas, which is trying valiantly and with some degree of success to surpass Reno as a naughty divorce city. I stopped there to get a stabilizer bolt for my front wheel assembly, and a sandwich. In the hamburger joint that I patronized I was sitting when in walked a blonde menace all got up in cowgirl clothes a la Saks, Fifth Avenue, with a guy who was very much a cowboy fresh out of John Wanamaker. The gal with a spotless pearl grey sombrero, silk shirt of some bright color, a very short tie tied four in hand made of silk - and black - very much pressed jodhpurs, and shiny and very fawncy cowboy boots. I looked and looked and yet could find no sign "courtesy of Chamber of Commerce". However, I'm darned well convinced that the C of C planted that pair around to create atmosphere. I was in town for about half an hour, but I've put Las Vegas down as a phony.

So, I started out across the desert - sage brush to the right of me, sage brush to the left of me, sage brush all over the place - and automobiles with prepared people riding along with water bags hanging on the front fender. Had me wondering, but "Honeymoon" stood the strain. Suddenly a sign - "welcome to California", but the sage brush was just as sagey on the other side and the road just as desolate - no waving palm trees, soft sunshine, bathing beauties or movie cameramen – and so on and on. I might as well have been in mere Arizona or New Mexico or Nevada – but not in C A L I F O R N I A!!!!!

Hours later I was riding through a little town with an unpronounceable name and saw a woman in the street with long pants – crease and all – T H E N I knew – I was there for shore.

And so, finally, I got to a sign which told me I was entering the city limits of Los Angeles. And then after about fifty miles of driving, I was shunted by the traffic to the entrance to a hotel – and I gave up and stayed right there. Called the Van Wormer tribe that night and went out to see Betts and her husband. Came back – not back but down here the next day after renewing acquaintances with Peg and her nine month old son, David.

Saturday Paul Holmberg and I went back to L.A. to see the U.C.L.A. game and I stayed on over Sunday night for a party that Peg and Betts had planned for me. It was a very nice party and Richmond (Harby) Deyo was there with his wife. Very interesting – Peg's first real boy friend (me), her second (Rich), and her husband. The girls are both very well married and are just as I expected them – quite swell. It was gratifying to find that out, since it bears out a judgment made when I was a little more immature than now.

Well, Patson Forty-Four is here as a part of the Transition School. I spent five minutes in the Transition Training Squadron – long enough for them to endorse my orders and send me to 44. There I have done little but read the various publications that are required. So far have no job and have not flown.

Living conditions are a bit sloppy at present, but I expect that things will straighten out before so very long. Holmberg and Charlie Ridgway are here and so I'm not a complete stranger. Charlie expects to leave for Hawaii around the first of the month. He is learning to run a new type radio apparatus for fighter directing.

All for now,

      Love,
        Scottie

ROBERT SCOTT WHITMAN JR.

Sunday, 16 November 1941

Dear Family,

Since I last wrote another pilot in the squadron and I have moved from the station and are living in town (Coronado). The quarters on the station are so crowded that the skipper is allowing that, and so we now have an apartment. The place we are in now is expensive. However, it is just a stop gap until we can get a small house we have our eye on. When we get that we shall be saving money. As it is now I expect we shall just about break even. (We get our rental allowance now, of course, since the government is no longer furnishing quarters.) It is an upstairs – downstairs place – very, very nice but, as I say, too expensive. Two bedrooms and bath upstairs, living room, dining room kitchen downstairs.

Also, word has come through that the President has approved the Sec. Navy's recommendation that all regular Ensigns, senior to the class of 1940 (N.A.), be promoted immediately to "j.g.". So, before long I'll have a promotion. And there is a very favorable chance that a pay increase bill, which is in Congressional Committee, will be passed. Looks as though I'll be making a little more money before so very long.

So far I have done nothing in the Squadron. Have been given no job and have done no flying. We have turned our planes over to a squadron that flew in from Hawaii, and have taken theirs; and the time this last week has been spent getting our new planes in shape. I must get 600 hours in before I can qualify as a P.P.C. (Patrol Plane Commander), and am told that I'll be getting eighty hours a month until that time. They have changed their minds and have decided to qualify me as quickly as possible – I suppose so I can help take the pilot load and instruction duties off the qualified pilots we have now.

Howard Ady flew in from Hawaii and has been around with Paul Holmberg, Curt Vossler and me. Paul leaves early in December, and Curt soon after. Ady flies back to Hawaii this week.

So far I have met no women and there doesn't seem to be much of any opportunity. I guess it's just as well at present, what with a new home, Christmas, and money to George due. It's going to be a barren Thanksgiving out here, too. Nobody I know – which means Myrt Koivisto (the people I knew in Pensacola) or the Bakers (Donnie's family) – have seen fit to invite me for

Thanksgiving. However, maybe I can get in 18 holes of golf. (if I can borrow clubs) and a dinner with the rest of the gang.

The boy I am living with, whose name, by the way, is Olson, is a very nice guy, and I think we shall get along very well. He is one of the reserve fliers who took a regular commission and will get his j.g. commission at the same time as I – he was the only logical one to get together with, and it is very fortunate that he is so congenial.

You got the dope to send my mail as follows (?)

V.P. Forty-four

U.S. Naval Air Station

San Diego, Calif.

Coronado is a nice little town (on an island, you know) and much, much nicer than Dago, which is a "boom town" if I ever saw it – full of honky-tonk bars and gyp joints, crowded, noisy, and slightly bawdy. High prices – typical of a modern day "defense" town, I suppose – and the 20th century prototype of the 19th century western boom town. Everything is Consolidated Aircraft, the factory that builds my planes. It's a mammoth outfit – 30,000 workers or more, I guess.

It would be fun to write that autobiography; but, compared with so many aviators, my life has been so humdrum. However, just for fun, I might take a crack at it – if I can get the time. Would keep me interested, at least.

> Much, much love to all,
>   Scottie

Sunday, 23 November 1941

Dear Family,

Mother's letter arrived Friday and was certainly most welcome. It is so good to hear from home.

There has very little happened since I last wrote. Slowly but surely things are settling down into an ordered pattern. We go to work at eight and quit at about four-thirty. I have had just two hops so far – one a six hour Nav and the other a primary training hop. There are so many students temporarily attached to the squadron that I seem to be suffering because of them. They must finish their training by a specified time and, since I am here permanently, the theory seems to be to give me my training as best they can after the transients are taken care of.

Had a nice letter from Betty's mother inviting me to visit whenever I could. Probably will sometime. However, there is very little opportunity to get away.

Rip Kline and wife arrived the other day. He will be here for about six weeks, I think.

The apartment is very comfortable and Ollie and I are enjoying it tremendously.

Last night the Junior Chamber of Commerce gave a party for the J.O.'s of all the services. I went but didn't particularly enjoy it. Had a date with a rather nice girl from Pittsburg. She has left (today) for Pittsburg – isn't that always the way?

You asked for Christmas suggestions – Heck, I dunno. I hadn't thought. I would like a pipe. But I can buy a Kaywoodie from the Navy for a dollar less than you could. So it would be silly. I have all the shirts I need. Oh, I don't know. All the things I particularly want are way beyond the combined means of several families – and I always like anything.

My very, very best love to the grandest mother and dad in the world,

        Scottie

Monday, 2 December 1941

Dear Family,

So the Army has to turn in and quit – we have beaten them three in a row. Hooray for our side!

Most of the squadron gathered at the Guruz household – (Guruz is Flight Officer) and listened to the game; then to the Stanford-Cal. Game. It was a nice party and a very satisfactory game.

Mother's letter arrived on Friday and was very, very welcome. Not many letters find their way my way these days.

The new home is grand. Ollie is a very nice guy and our arrangement is working out splendidly. We do our own cleaning – a field day every Sunday morning. Take turns a week at a time getting breakfast. Eat out the rest of the time. It is the nicest quarters I have had and we are breaking just about even.

California weather is really nice. We have had only one day of rain since I have been here. It is very cool in the evening and gets comfortably warm at noon. Have been wearing my green uniforms comfortably, and a top coat in the evening.

You didn't tell me that you were glad about the promotion – word has come through that it is effective as of the 1st of November. So it is just a matter of a bottleneck of clerical work before I am a j.g.

I flew quite a bit since the 10th and finally got in 30 hours by the end of the month, which helps.

I have been assigned as Assistant Flight Officer, and so far my duties have consisted of mapping out a course of instruction for mechanics, radio men, and gunners. The squadron is a training squadron for pilots and enlisted personnel. The powers that be have mapped out a very ambitious program and given us very little to work with, so as a result there are a lot of problems to be met and solved. I have just bit into this thing and am in a maze of difficulties. However, they will straighten themselves out bit by bit.

I haven't heard a word from George since I saw him. Who is "His Marion"? Last I knew he was interested in some "career girl".

The Japanese situation seems to be developing growing pains. I still don't think much will come of it. If there does, console yourself, for my home will become Alaska – quite safe and dull.

Love to all,
Scottie

XIV
ALAMEDA
DECEMBER 7, 1941 – MARCH 21, 1942

Friday, 12 December 1941

Dear Family,

I reckon you've wondered and worried; and the best word I could get to you was to call up Aunt Julie and ask her to write - I have been able to do nothing but fly, fly, fly - and sleep when it was possible, and that wasn't too often. Things have quieted down a little now, and today I haven't been off the ground.

There isn't anything I can tell you - except that I'm not in San Diego but have every prospect of staying here on the coast. I'm well and happy and, except for being a little tired, everything is O.K. We flew out Monday before daybreak and haven't been back. The apartment has been closed and the landlady packed for me. I received today, when the rest of the Squadron arrived by train, the results of her packing - two dirty shirts, a pad of blank paper, and an engine overhaul manual. How I'm going to get the rest of my gear is a problem, but it will work out somehow.

There is no news that I can put out at this point, but I did want to write and tell you that I'm O.K. and that I'm in no danger.

       Lots of love to all,
        Scottie

Until I can find out my best address, send any mail to Aunt Julie. I haven't seen her yet, but if I ever get free will be able to.

Sunday, 21 December 1941

Dear Family,

A very strange Christmas letter - quite appropriate for a very, very strange Christmas. It hardly seems believable that Christmas is only four days away. This year there is not the bustle of getting away for a trip home, no wrapping of Christmas presents, none of the slap happy hurry and scurry that has characterized other Christmases. What little shopping I had done has just arrived from San Diego, and perhaps, if all goes well, can be packed tomorrow. It will arrive late but will arrive; and for George I am enclosing a check - he would like that best, I know, and can use it to make the Christmas rounds.

All of your letters have arrived in good time and the packages arrived in good shape and are reposing unopened on the shelf of my closet. Curious me - I had a hard struggle, but I won over old man temptation, and the packages will be opened Christmas day.

Yesterday, or was it day before? I got away in the evening for a short time and went over to call on Aunt Julie. We had a very pleasant chat. Aunt Julie is grand - just as I expected she would be. It was the first time I had been able to get free at all.

Sure will be a funny Christmas this year. I expect that I shall be flying. I have the duty that day. Reminds me of that picture of the British crew on a Christmas flight that appeared in <u>Life</u>.

So far, after the first jitters that drove the whole coast crazy, the war has been more or less a thing apart - at least, war as one usually thinks of it. Hard work, long hours and very little rest at first - and now lots more of the first two, and a lot more rest.

I'm feeling perfectly swell and am as fit as a fiddle. Was awfully tired for a while, but now am ready to lick my weight in japs or wildcats any day. Have had a couple of very interesting experiences - however - no dope now. I am the Squadron censor and would certainly cut a fine figure putting out censorable stuff myself. I'll try to remember it all though, and tell you some tall tales when I see you next.

My gear is arriving slowly but surely from San Diego - Rip and Libby Kline and Doc and Margie Abbott have certainly come through for me. Doc even sent a check for $25, thinking I might have come off without any money. That little piece of thoughtfulness really got me. You see, I did leave in one heck of a rush – but I bought a shirt and some socks, and now that most of my stuff has arrived I'm all set.

Right now I am flying with the skipper as his navigator. I don't get much flying in for that reason, but still am building up experience.

There is so little I can tell you now for reason of the tight restrictions, that writing seems a little futile – however I am well, happy – and everything is grand – even have "Honeymoon" here – Curt Vossler drove it up.

I wish I could be home with my family for this Christmas, but there is a big job to be done and in my little way I am trying my darndest to do my part.

The very, very merriest of Christmases to the grandest and best family in all the world, with lots of love,

     Scottie

MY ADDRESS.
Mr. R.S. WHITMAN, Jr.
FLEET AIR DETACHMENT
U.S. NAVAL AIR STATION
Alameda, Calif.

FLEET AIR DETACHMENT

U.S. NAVAL AIR STATION

ALAMEDA, CALIF.

Tuesday, 30 December 1941

Dear Family,

Most of my gear has arrived, and I now can use for the first time the typewriter I had overhauled.

On Christmas Eve I opened the package from home, and my, what a wonderful Christmas that package turned out to be. There was the pipe that I wanted so badly, and a whole raft of tobacco in the trickiest package I have ever seen. A billfold just when I was about to break down and buy one because mine was torn and completely worn out. And some beautiful ties and socks – and oh, how I need both – and a tie set when both of mine had been lost somewhere – and nuts – I guess nobody will ever forget how I like nuts – AND that sweater – I remember so well mother asking me what color of sweater I would like – and then she knitted me the prettiest sleeveless sweater I have ever seen. It was the nicest Christmas I have ever had – oh, much the nicest. Bet Mother picked out that tie and sock combination to go with the sweater – they fit like hand and glove.

I'm sorry to say that the package I had started for home has not yet been mailed – it seems that Christmas time has been pretty darned busy around here. Every day I have been either in the air or about to go into the air, and as a result, it hasn't gone into the mail. However, under the circumstances, I know that you will forgive me and will make believe that it is Christmas whenever it may arrive. We have all figured that the holiday season would be just about perfect for a jap surprise out this way and so quite naturally kept pretty much on the alert. There will be no more surprises like that at Pearl Harbor.

It was so grand of Mother to send Jimmy a present and I know that Betty appreciated it tremendously. It is little thoughtful things like that that make Mother Mother. I do hope that my letter home arrived safely – it should have come about the day before Christmas.

Aunt Julie must think that I am horrible unless she understands how very little I can get free. I have been ashore just three times since I arrived here, and hence have called on her just once. She sent me a carton of cigarettes through the mail, and tomorrow, if I can get in at a reasonable hour, I'll call and thank her for them.

If my letters seem uninteresting, blame it on the little yaller fellers - and I'll keep all the good stories stored away for a future and more propitious time.

However, there is one thing of which I would like to convince you of and that is that I'm perfectly safe, well, and happy. There is a lot of hard work to be done and I am trying to do my part of it, but I am just as safe physically as ever. I do know that you worry, and yet there is no cause for worry - so stop. The only cloud lately is that caused by my inability to be home at Christmas, and that is a cloud. However, my last two years at home may be looked upon as sheer gravy, and for them I am thankful.

Christmas Day I spent in the air and had a Christmas dinner of tomato soup and chocolate; but in the evening I was invited to dinner at a Commander Grant's and had turkey and all the trimmins.

A newsless letter I know this is, but at any rate it can serve to tell you that on Christmas Day I was with my family in spirit at least.

       Much love to all,
        Scottie

Saturday, 3 January 1942

Dear Family,

Holy smoke – it's New Years and after. And so commences what will probably be an epoch year. What a helluva lot of changes this world has seen in the past 365 days, and who knows what the next will hold for the crazy darned people that inhabit it.

The perfectly grand birthday package arrived on time and in fine shape. Thank thank you very, very much; but you most certainly should not have splurged so on me. I have started the Bromfield novel and it promises to be a humdinger. Shall faithfully attempt to keep the diary; but will make no promises whatsoever.

Both Mother's and Dad's letters arrived betimes, and were so welcome. It certainly is a treat to hear from home. Letters from my family are a real event in my young life, I can tell you.

As at Christmas, we spent the glad New Year period on the alert, and had our party at BOQ. For an impromptu party that just sort of happened with no planning, it was quite an affair. All of sudden there seemed to be hundreds of people milling around the corridor that most of our squadron occupies. All the wives and gal friends had arrived. One guy would have a cake, another a box of candy, another a bottle of champagne. We just all pooled our resources, packed into two adjoining rooms with the connecting doors open, turned the radio up full blast, and had a swell time.

I have not yet been able to get out to see Aunt Julie again. I don't know what she must think of me. I tried to call her and no one was at home. Maybe, day after tomorrow I'll be able to get out there. Received a birthday card from her with the usual and very welcome money in it, and must soon get to her to thank her for it and the cigarettes.

A little belatedly, but with just that much more feeling,

A VERY, VERY HAPPY AND MOST SUCCESSFUL NEW YEAR TO THE GRANDEST FAMILY AND GUY COULD HAVE.

   Love,
    Scottie

N. Nav. 96-A
(July 1936)

(COPY FOR DISBURSING OFFICER)

ACCEPTANCE

~~PATROL SQUADRON FORTY FOUR~~
(Place of acceptance)

~~January 6~~ _____, 19 42
(Date)

From: ~~Lieutenant (junior grade) Robert Scott Whitman, Jr., U.S. Navy.~~
(Name and rank)

To: SECRETARY OF THE NAVY (Bureau of Navigation).

I hereby accept the appointment as ~~a Lieutenant (junior grade),~~

~~U.S. Navy~~

to rank from ~~November 1~~___, 19 41___, dated ~~December 13~~___, 19 41___

. *Robert Scott Whitman jr.*
(Signature)

OATH OF OFFICE

HAVING BEEN APPOINTED ~~a Lieutenant (junior grade),~~

_____ in the U. S. Navy,

I, ~~Robert Scott Whitman, Jr.,~~ _____, do solemnly swear (or affirm) that I will
(Name in full)

support and defend the Constitution of the United States against all enemies, foreign and domestic; that I will bear true faith and allegiance to the same; that I take this obligation freely, without any mental reservation or purpose of evasion; and that I will well and faithfully discharge the duties of the office on which I am about to enter: So help me God.

Robert Scott Whitman jr
(Signature)

WL Richards

F A Roby jr. ⎤
               ⎦ *ss:*

Subscribed and sworn to before me this ___6th___ day of ~~January~~ ____, 19 42

RC Brixner

BLANK SPACES BELOW TO BE FILLED BY OFFICER ACCEPTING ORIGINAL APPOINTMENT

PLACE OF BIRTH		STATE OR TERRITORY OF WHICH A CITIZEN	DATE OF BIRTH
	STATE		
Town or City ⎱ County			

NOTE.—This duplicate copy to be certified to as a true copy by officer concerned, and turned over to disbursing officer taking up accounts.

U. S. GOVERNMENT PRINTING OFFICE   4—3542a

Acceptance of Appointment as a Lieutenant (jg) U.S. Navy.

Patrol Squadron Forty-four

c/o Postmaster

San Francisco, California

13 January 1942

Dear Family,

It is way past time for a letter home, and I expect that you are provoked and peeved with me beyond all reconciliation. However, the letter writing time that was is no more, and it is a struggle to be able to sandwich in time for even a short note.

Your letters have arrived on schedule and they certainly are more than welcome. Letters and mail of any sort have come to mean more and more to me.

Sunday was a gala day. After some twenty-five years I finally met cousin Paul. He was home after quitting his job in Chico in order to enlist in the Army and dodge the draft which was looming up far too large and close for comfort. I went over in the morning and was taken out to dinner and then to a tea (which was enjoyable but slightly on the boring side). It was a real pleasure to meet Paul, and I found him to be a very nice sort of a person – not dynamic by any means, but really quite O.K. He is now in the Army Air Corps on his way to Texas. Just what he will do there is something nobody seems to know, but I expect that he will be put to some clerical job.

Aunt Julie says that she will see that you get copies of the pictures taken in which I am wearing my J.G. stripes. The commission has not come through yet in fact; but a dispatch authorized our taking oath of office, and so now my days as an Ensign are over.

We are working hard, but everybody in the Squadron is well and safe. How long we stay here is, of course, problematical, but we have had no indication of any move, so you can assume that I'll be here for some time.

I'm afraid that we may as well reconcile ourselves to the fact of a long and very, very hard war. That, I think, is an indisputable truth. The complacency of the American people, which still for some reason endures, is due for an awful jolt one of these days. Even out here on the west coast, where the war is a bit closer, the people don't seem to realize that there is a war. One day I'm afraid that they will.

However, all is well here, and I am getting a lot of invaluable experience in the safest and best way possible.

What little I can tell you in the way of news has been told, and with this very, very barren letter I send all the love in the world to the grandest family I know.

Scottie

Scottie, Aunt Julie and Cousin Paul.

Thursday, 29 January 1942

Dear Family,

The way that time zips by these days is really amazing and a bit confusing. I expect that my letter is way overdue, and do hope that it has not caused you any worry. I have promised myself a half a dozen times that the one thing that I will do is get my letters to you off on time, and now I guess I have slipped again. The current reason for delay is a trip south that I made and have just returned from, plus the addition of a new job. I have taken over the Personnel Office here, and am having the time of my life reorganizing the whole works and generally adding to the confusion. The former Personnel Officer was not quite experienced enough to handle the job, and the Captain seemed to think that perhaps I was – it is not a tough assignment in any sense of the word, but does keep me busy.

George's check will go into the mail tomorrow probably, and since I have not heard from him, I can assume that the current plans are satisfactory to him. If they cramp him in any way, please let me know immediate and he shall have more money within the week.

I have not been able to get away to see Aunt Julie since I saw Paul and the family a couple of weeks ago, but hope to be able to get over there within the next week or two. I have picked up a slight case of gum infection or trench mouth or what have you, and have spent a couple of rather unpleasant hours in the dentist's chair so far, with a couple of more on the way. He tells me that those two cantankerous wisdom teeth must go, and I am looking forward with none too much pleasure to the parting.

The package with the candied nuts arrived, and let me tell you they really made a hit. I passed them out, of course, and they lasted just about ten minutes. The consensus of opinion was that they were by far the best sweets that anybody lucky enough to get a taste had ever tasted. Thank you a million times for them.

I am trying to keep the diary up; and some day maybe I can put into words all the things that have happened, so that you may know of our experiences during the first stages of the war.

Sort of looks as though the Navy has started to work out in the far East. The reports in the papers have sounded quite encouraging. If only the land forces could follow through, we should be in a much better spot.

I suppose that Singapore will fall. The propaganda that Churchill has been sowing about bad news to come certainly points to the fact that the fall is expected. That will make the situation indeed very, very acute, but not, of course, hopeless. It will, I am afraid, lengthen the war by many a month; and the only thing to do is to face the cold hard fact, cinch up the belt, and git goin'.

I have been, of course, indeed very, very fortunate. This present station is probably as fine an assignment in every sense that one could get during these times. Our only war so far, with very, very few exceptions, has been with the weather, and we really do not know what war is. Work we do, and lots of it, and in our own way we are doing a big and an important job – but it is not combat by any means.

It is in the pins that I shall be qualified as a first pilot soon, and as soon as I have enough hours, I shall be a plane commander. I am still flying with the Captain as his Navigator now.

So much for the news (?) for the present. Your letters are the bright spots each day that they arrive. Much, much love to the grandest Mom and Pop any guy ever had.

Scottie

Alameda, piloting a
PBY-5A Catalina,
Patrol Squadron 44.

UNITED STATES PACIFIC FLEET

P2/P17-2/00   AIRCRAFT SCOUTING FORCE

PATROL SQUADRON FORTY FOUR

Fleet Air Detachment,

Naval Air Station,

Alameda, California,

February 3, 1942

From: Commander, Patrol Sqwuadron FORTY FOUR,

To   : Lieut. (jg)(T) Robert S. Whitman, Jr., U.S. Navy

Subject: Physical Examination for Promotion.

Reference:(a) BuNav Ltr. Nav-326-mf, 82661-6, of Dec.

              18, 1941.

1.   In compliance with paragraph 1 of reference (a) you will report to
the Board of Medical Examiners of member, for an examination to determine your
physical fitness for promotion on or about February 3, 1942.

                         (signed)   R.C. Brixner

R

FIRST ENDORSEMENT: PATROL WING EIGHT   February 4, 1942

From: President, Board of Medical Examiners.

To   :   The Squadron Commander.

        1.Reported, examined and found to be physically qualified for
promotion.

                         (signed)   B.V. Leamer

Tuesday, 10 February 1942

Dear Family,

This can be only a hurried note, but I must get something off to you so that you will not worry.

I am in the midst of getting ready for the Captain his recommendation for a general court martial on a lad in the squadron that got himself all fouled up. Having never done that before, I have been busier than a one armed paper hanger, and as a result have had little time for anything but running in circles. Let it suffice to be said that I am well and happy and busy – which business keeps me happy, I expect.

Your letter arrived betimes, and today I received Mother's package. 'Tis a funny thing how Mother knows just what I need when I need it. Thank you a million.

Please Mother don't work so hard that you completely wear yourself out. Your letters sound so sort of tired and discouraged. Remember that I can see George through his school quite easily; and if your teaching is going to wear you down to a frazzle – QUIT IT RIGHT NOW.

This is all the letter I have time for now – but within the next two days, you shall have a long, long one. I think by that time I'll be squared away again.

        Much, much love to all,
         Scottie

Don't worry about my moving somewhere else.
If that comes to pass, I'll let you know before I go----
There is no veiled hint here!!!!

Sunday, 15 February 1942

Dear Family,

It is so hard to find anything to write that would be interesting to you since there is so little of our operations that I can tell you. We are, of course, patrolling and convoying – those two are our missions. Anti-submarine coastal patrol and then outer oceanic patrol take most of our time.

We have been working pretty hard and are getting very little time off; but everybody is well and, of course, more than satisfied with our base. San Francisco is just about as good a place to be during these times as one could hope for.

I have been able to get free sometimes and have gone over the bay bridge to San Francisco and gone dancing or to a movie. That bridge and the Golden Gate bridge are truly marvels of engineering. "Impressive" is under-statement. The toll is just a quarter rather than the fifty cents one would expect if the Hudson tunnels were used as a comparison. I understand that the ferries still run to some points but are slowly going out.

You may wonder whom I go out with in San Francisco. The gal is rather amazing, and you might be interested in hearing about her, I met her through a friend of mine at a Christmas party that we went to. Her name is Josephine Jackson – looks to be about twenty-two. Graduated from Washington State (Theta) was married and her husband died. So she got a job in a dept. store and moved into a boarding house. I imagine that she was reared more or less in the lap of luxury, since she has spoken of things that only happen to people with money. Father and Mother died within a couple of years of each other back when she was in school. She, being educated but not trained, got a job selling sports clothes and modelling sports clothes, and just has the time of her life – loves it. She is the most genuine person I've known and is more fun than a barrel of monkeys. I enjoy going out with her no end, and I expect that I could be really seriously interested. Have met a lot of girls out here, Cal. and Stanford and Mills being so close; but they, (those that I've met) don't hold a patch to Joie. Her "story", as I say, is a patchwork and I guess I'd never have known it had I not got so curious that I pieced it together. It all fits in and is one of those story book jobs. What she needs now to complete it is a happy marriage to some guy who is settled down and can finish off the story. I think you would like her. So much for Joie. (Have no fears I'm not "entangled" and she is a nice girl – very nice – this to quiet any motherly qualms). I just enjoy going out with someone who is intelligent, real, and who gets such a kick out of living even though she has somewhat of an excuse to be a bit sorry for herself – and besides she is an asset on a dance floor – the kind people look at twice.

I'm getting fatter – lack of exercise is the trouble. We can't get away during the day at all, and if I am not at a desk I'm sitting in a plane – just have to starve myself.

I've met a couple of other gals that I mean to look up again and John Andregg's wife knows all the Delta Gammas at Cal. So, when I can get free, I can keep myself busy.

The biggest problem is not being able to get away during the day.

I need new shoes; the car needs work; I need to see a tailor and get some clothes repaired. We are in uniform for the duration now – and when I get a chance I'm going to pack my big box with clothes & moth balls & store it. Maybe Aunt Julie would take it for me.

So much for now.

Lots and lots of love to the grandest Dad & Mom I know,
         Scottie

Monday, 16 February 1942

Dear Family,

Mother's letter arrived yesterday, and the package with some of that swell nut candy, a couple of days before. It was sure thoughtful of you to send that, after I had told you how much we enjoyed it the last time.

The news of George's marks was indeed really good news. That kid has plenty of what is needed. I'm proud as punch of his work and of his coming job. It is certainly grand that I have a brother who, in spite of his troubles, has come through with colors flying high - really high. I'm also certainly glad that George will be spared from all this mess that we are in. He will be doing his part for his country just as much as the lads at the fronts, and probably will end up by doing much more, for aircraft experimentation and development will figure probably most prominently in the credit or debit sides of our ledger when the final story is told. And he will be quite safe to boot. Hooray for a bright spot in the apparent gloom.

My life goes on much of the sameness. Fly every other day - usually twelve hours or more - see lots of ocean and sky - spend the odd days here in the office muddling along through the paper work that has increased rather than decreased since the war began. It is all interesting but I'm afraid that I'm not a very competent person - I forget too many details.

The station has certainly become populated since we got here. For a while our outfit and a handful of station officers were all that occupied B.O.Q. Now the place is full and overflowing. Bob Wood is here - you remember he is the classmate that I roomed with before Tex at Pensacola.

I'm trying to get my affairs so squared away that I won't have any encumbering truck that I'll have to pack or store should I be transferred - which is unlikely now. But the mess I left things in San Diego taught its lesson, and so I'm going to pack all of my civilian clothes and excess gear, and store them. I suppose I could well give my civies away for it looks like a good long time before any of us will be coming out of uniform; but I reckon I'll save them just in case. I haven't figured yet whether to send the stuff home or to store it out here.

Will be sending George another check the first of the month - I gather that our arrangement has worked out okay.

ROBERT SCOTT WHITMAN JR.

Mother's last letter (yesterday) has worried me considerably. Mom, you must must not wear yourself down so. Your letter sounded so completely worn out – and discouraged. For heaven's sake, don't wait for them to get you a relief – just light out. We'll make out all right – you can be sure of that. You must not worry about me – I'm O.K; our outfit started this San Francisco detail; we know all the tricks of the trade, the coast, weather etc. etc., and we are the logical outfit to stay here. If I move I'll let you know. So, if I don't write as often as I did, you'll just know that I'm rushed for time or just too tired (which is my only complaint about anything).

Much, much love to all,
Scottie

```
                    W E S T E R N
                    U N I O N
```

```
   NS27  24  NT - SANFRANCISCO  CALIF 7
   1942 MAR 8  AM 7  10
   MR AND MRS R S WHITMAN-
        51  STJOHN  AVE  BINGHAMTON  NY-

HAY  GUESS  WHAT  WERE  GOING  TO  BE  MARRIED  WHEN?  DASH  WE
DUNNO.  BUT  SOON  WILL  LET  YOU  KNOW  AS  SOON  AS  WE  KNOW
LOVE-
     JOIE AND SCOTTIE.
```

Tuesday, 10 March, 1942

Dear Family,

Well, well, and well - who would have thunk it. I expect that you were a bit surprised by our wire, since I had given you no warning. The whole thing is not quite so sudden as it would seem except perhaps the decision to go ahead and plunge rather than wait. I have known for a long time that I wanted to marry Joie - have been seeing her almost every minute that I could get free. However, I wasn't so sure that it was smart, and she was sort of doubtful too. So 'twasn't until the night that we sent you the wire that we decided to go ahead and take the deep step.

There did seem so many complications: the uncertainty of my movements, the so little time that I get away, George's school to finish - all those things that pointed the other way. So we just decided to muddle along as far as expenses were concerned and hope that I stayed put here. You will be crazy about her, I know. Best I'll be able to do for the time being is a picture that I'll send along right quick like, and after that maybe soon you will be able to get to know her. Everybody in the Squadron is jealous of me (she has done most of the visiting since I haven't been able to get out.)

We have finally decided on April the 2nd, that being a time that looks as though I could get away. Probably something will come up and it won't be then - but now that looks like the first chance, and that is the only way that we can see to do it if we do it at all - grab what we can get while the grabbing is good.

For obvious reasons and for the reason that Joie has no family here, if for no other, it will be a very quiet wedding. I've tried to call Aunt Julie three times since the glad day, and haven't been able to get ahold of her. I hope that she may be able to help us make arrangements - and at least lend us her minister. And I know that you would want her present when the time comes.

Am hoping for some leave but can't bet on it.

Oh, heck, fire folks, she is really wonderful - so much our sort, thinks as I do, acts the way I would want my wife to act, has the same ideas, same likes and dislikes (except bread pudding) and she is mine - so I'm agoin' to get married (to a Theta).

       Lots of love to all,
        Scott

Monday night, 16 March 1942

Dear Family,

At least I can start this letter and perhaps finish it so that it will get off tomorrow. There is so much to tell you and so much to say that I hardly know where to begin.

First, I suppose should come the plans for the wedding. It is to be on Thursday, April 2nd, at five in the afternoon at the chapel in the Presidio. Very quiet of course. The chapel is a beautiful little one setting up on a hill, overlooking the Golden Gate. I am hoping that some of the Squadron will be able to get away to be there, but probably very few will be able to. Some of the wives will be there, of course; women like weddings so. I do so hope that it is a pretty wedding for Joie's sake. You see she has no one to plan it for her and that makes it hard. We do so wish that Mother were here to help - and to be here; and Dad to get in the way, and just be here.

Of course, you don't know my Joie but someday you will; and then you will know how I came to get married (We are going to have some pictures taken and you will, of course, get one immejite)

I have a weeks leave and am planning to take Joie to Del Monte; it is only 2 hours from here - by the sea and close enough so I can get back if called.

We have a place to live, an apartment here in Alameda - 916 Union Street. We were so lucky to get it. Everything is full up and one real estate agent even refused to take my name. Jean Richards the Exec's wife told me about this and we snapped at it. It is sort of nice - three rooms, electric stove, breakfast nook - quite O.K.

Joie is to have a minerature** if it ever arrives. Had to send to Philadelphia for it. The diamond that Mother gave me is to be set in it.

George Ghesquiere, of whom you have heard me speak often, is to be my best man, and Joie's sister is coming up from Los Angeles to be with her. (George and his wife are here now after return from the Islands.)

Joie has had the flu for the last week; but yesterday she got out and we went to see Aunt Julie* . We couldn't stay as long as we would have liked to, but did have a little chat after their other guests had left. Aunt Julie was just as grand and wonderful as ever. I think she passed approval of Joie - but she undoubtedly will write. Joie liked her, at any rate.

Now more news: I now have my own plane, am a qualified pilot with a brand new $250,000 airplane all my own. We have switched to a slightly different type plane, the PBY-5 A, an amphibian, and are now flying off the field rather than the water. We are still doing the same sort of work, and the planes are admirably suited for such, since they can land either on land or on the water. They look just like the PBY-5 except that they also have sidewheels and a nose wheel (all retractable).

We have filed our intention to wed and had our physical exams. Day after tomorrow we shop for a wedding ring and pick up the license. Joie is going to work until the middle of next week - she says she's gotta if she is going to have a new pair of shoes for the 'weddin.'

Oh, I do so hope she will be happy. Right now, she is at least putting up a darn good imitation.

I haven't received any word from Dad since I told you the news - I suppose he has been awfully busy, but it has been a month or more since he wrote last. I would sort of like to feel that I have his blessing too when I jump off the deep end.

There is not much more to say. It's after ten and I have a long day ahead, which will start all too soon, and so I must hop in bed. So, I guess for now it's goo-night to the dearest Mother and the grandest Dad in all the world. You have had a tough time of your life and many's the time my heart has ached for it. Never fear the future - it is always secure so long as I am around, and I do hope that I shall always succeed in being a credit to the parents that I love so much and admire just as much. I want you proud of me; and I'm bringing you a daughter of whom you could be nothing but proud.

> Lots and lots of love,
> Scottie

Scottie and Joie were married March 22, 1942.

"We went to Vallejo last Tuesday. Slipped in and slipped out. It was a perfectly planned and perfectly carried out occasion. Joie of course was the center of all. She looked very pretty - carried a big bunch of American Beauty roses and wore an Orchid as did her maid of honor. Many pictures were taken which you will probably get. Ordered a Vallejo paper which has not come. Everything very merry (except tears in the corner of the eyes of an elderly aunt). We went by bus. Mare Island is thirty-five miles away, and gas and tires must be saved for necessary errands. It was not so pleasant a trip but that was small. Joie called me up the day after - said she collapsed when it was all over, if there are any little details do ask me questions. It is certainly a _real_ honor."

In attendance—Scottie's maternal Aunt Julie

XV
PEARL HARBOR
MARCH 27, 1942 – MAY 21, 1942

```
W E S T E R N
                              (05)
U N I O N


    NS28  22  NT-TDBY  CORONADO CALIF 22
1942 MAR 23 am 7 07
    MR AND MRS R F WHITMAN-
     51 ST JOHN AVE BINGHAMTON NY-
    CONGRATULATIONS YOU HAVE A NEW DAUGHTER WERE MARRIED LAST
NIGHT HAVE TO LEAVE FOR AWHILE NO NEED TO WORRY WILL WRITE LOVE-
        SCOTTIE
```

Sunday, 30 March 1942
Dear Family,

Holy Smoke! When this outfit of mine moves it moves fast – and that isn't any stuff. I suppose the best thing to do is to start at the beginning and relate chronologically all that has gone on.

It all started about 4:15 P.M. a week ago yesterday when I climbed out of my plane from a convoy job and was met with the news: that I was flying to San Diego in the morning; that five other planes were also going; and that there we were to have our wheels taken off and were going "West". The reason is of no import to anybody and need not be related. The whole thing was a complete surprise to everybody – the <u>first</u> word of any sort, rumor or otherwise, came with the actual orders at 11:00 that morning. I was on a "job" and so didn't get the word until afternoon.

My first thought was of Joie, of course. I tried to get her on the phone as soon as I could get my wits together; not home yet. It was the day she was going to quit her job and the girls were saying goodbye and giving her nighties and stuff. I left word with her landlady and she came out to the station about 5:30. She had the car (we were going to the dance on the station that night). There was no doubt in my mind as to what I wanted to do from a personal standpoint, but I was not sure if it would be fair to Joie to be married to a man who immediately shoved off to be gone for an indefinite time. One look at her and I knew – and so we got me packed, dressed, lit for Frisco after leaving a note for George who was standing by for a call if needed.

We stopped downtown and got Joie a plane reservation for San Diego, leaving Oakland at 6:35 the next morning. Finally, home about 8:00. All the girls in the house were waiting for Joie, and whisked her off to get her packed and dressed. I set off in search of flowers, and I finally got what I wanted, white baby orchids. We had already picked out a ring but, of course, couldn't get it. Mrs. Lawler had called a jeweler she knew and had a selection waiting for us. We got a very pretty plain gold one to match Joie's mineature; and Mrs. L. had called a minister – couldn't get hers, so got one out of the classified directory – and was scared stiff for fear he was colored until he turned out to be a very nice Methodist, who performed a very, very nice ceremony at 9:30 in the living room of the house in front of the fireplace banked with flowers from heavens knows where. Then sherry and fruit cake. It was not the wedding my Joie was going to have, but was very lovely "considering", in fact, "considering", it was miraculous.

We took separate planes for San Diego and arrived about the same time. Joie had registered us at the Hotel de Coronado, a very swish place that we couldn't possibly afford except for the special Navy rate. We had a huge room facing the ocean, which for two with meals sells for about forty dollars a day ordinarily. I spent very little time with the Squadron (by permission), and we had a very, very wonderful time, accomplished no end of things, got pictures taken and I have wash prints with me!!! Got the ring engraved and my watch engraved – Joie gave me a very swell watch. Mrs. Lawler broke that jeweler out and got the one which Joie had already chosen.

Wednesday my new brother-and sister-in-law drove down from Los Angeles for the afternoon; and Thursday about five in the afternoon I said goodbye to just about the grandest gal I know and we headed West. I flew all night and about 11:00 this time (18-1/2 hours or so) the island of Maui loomed up, and here we are on Oahu – Honolulu. As far as we know to go no further. Closer to the war, yes, but much safer actually, since the weather is much, much better. It is a lot less comfortable here, of course – complete, and I mean complete, blackout every night, crowded quarters, restrictions of all sorts; but really pleasant enough – except that Joie can't come out here.

Folks, I want to tell you and have you know how completely satisfied I am with the new daughter I have brought you. Joie is just about the finest thing that ever happened to me.

There never was a person whom I so completely respected and admired, aside from the other feelings of "like" and "love" I have for her. She is such a grand person. Oh, I could go on for hours telling you about her. It is going to "be tough for her" while I'm gone I'm afraid, for I'm quite sure she likes me a little bit too. She certainly was a trooper about my leaving and only broke down twice – once when I told her the news and one other time. However it wasn't fun to say goodbye. We are both so very thankful for our time together and are living for the time when I can return – or she can come out. Just know that I am married to the <u>right</u> gal.

Will write soon again. I'm as safe as ever – be <u>sure</u> of that.

      Lots & lots of love,
        Scottie

Lt. (jg) R.S. Whitman, Jr., U.S.N.

Patrol Squadron Forty Four

c/o Postmaster

San Francisco – Calif.

Thursday, 10 April 1942

Dear Family,

Letter writing has devolved itself into a real chore since our move. There is so little that can be told. However, there is lots of time in which to tell it.

No mail has arrived yet - how much has left is a problem, too. I don't know whether you are getting my letters promptly or not. Air mail is very overtaxed and, of course, capacity of the planes is limited so there quite likely are delays.

It is lovely here - quite a wasted paradise at this point. It seems such a shame. However, such are the things one must expect in war time.

I do so wish that Joie could be here (naturally) but the Navy won't let her come. All families are being evacuated as quickly as is possible. Perhaps later the whole thing will shake down and become clarified; I keep hoping so anyway.

Our squadron is living in three houses here on Ford Island (N.A.S.). It is a good arrangement and works out very well. Plane crews stay together - pilots, I mean - and each section - two planes - stay together, have the duty the same time, are off at the same time, etc.

The food at the BOQ mess is good. We get almost everything we would get anywhere - which is a lot more than can be said of the civilian in town. I understand that they are having a pretty tough time of it.

Aside from the strict blackout, and lack of family, life here is quite normal. I have not been in to Honolulu, except the first day, and then had no chance to judge how things went in "civil life"; but I expect that it is much of the sameness.

As you know, I have my own plane now and am doing the same sort of work that I was doing in Alameda - only not quite so often.

So you see, all is well and normal except for the fact that I have a brand new wife and miss her considerably - wonder how long it will be before I see her again. Who know, we may all be together real soon.

There is little else to tell you. Remember all is well and will be. If the mail falls off it's the mail service that is causing it.

       Much, much love to all,

        Scottie

Sunday, 19 April 1942

Dear Family,

A letter from Joie dated the 11th, tells of her receiving my first letters, and so I expect that you have heard from me since the last move. That is a relief, since I know that you must have worried somewhat, even though you did not show it in your letters.

There is so little to relate, that aside from the actual material fact of a letter, there is little excuse for writing. Our life here is much the same as it was on the coast with, of course, one big difference. I am well and reasonably happy, and am very much assured of staying that way – aside from that there is nothing.

Joie has sent out announcements. You probably have received one by now. The pictures had not arrived according to the last word that I had from her regarding them. They probably have by now, and I expect that you have yours.

I think that you have the full explanation of our hurryup wedding rather than as planned. There was nothing else that we could do under the circumstances except not get married, and neither of us wanted that because, you see, we do both of us care quite a bit for the other.

I sent Joie a list for announcements also, but I did not have the addresses or even the names of a lot of the married girls, so it will have to be incomplete – which I guess doesn't matter much.

At this writing we are still all agog with the news of the Tokyo bombing. Have no more details than you, if as many. If it happened as it must have, it was a swell piece of work on someone's part. Probably will help morale no end – detrimentally on one side and, what is more important – beneficially on this side.

We, out here, get less news than you in the States, and it is usually a day or two later – why, I haven't quite figured out except that there probably is a misplaced sense of importance in the eyes of the military government, or crossed wires between the continental and the island censors. At any rate, all the news that we get that is good is first hand; and, of course, there is quite a bit of that for those of us who have friends who are taking part in some of the business that is going on these days.

Out here, I am closer to the old navy that I knew than I have been since I left the old ship – this is the Navy out here.

All of my gear got sent here by mistake. George did not have time to get it packed and stored before the Squadron had taken it away. You see, I shoved off without a chance to pack – just like the last time. I am repacking and shipping everything except what I can carry in my plane back for storage on the Coast. I don't know how much I have lost by these two moves which gave me no chance to pack my own gear, but I'm afraid that it is considerable. However – such are the fortunes --

I will try to send George some money the first of the month – my pay accounts are all fouled up.

When exactly does George graduate? I want to send him a cable of course – and best wishes and all of that – that kid has done himself really 'proud' – and I guess you know that I am as proud as punch that he is my brother.

Much, much love to the grandest mother and dad any guy ever had.

Scottie

Monday, 27 April 1942

Dear Family,

Mother's letter arrived today and comes an answer post haste so maybe I'll get another soon. I have missed hearing from home. Your letters all these years have meant so much to me that when there is a little delay in the mails it seems much longer than actually, and I always worry for fear that all is not well - that either Mother or Dad is sick that something is wrong.

Your letter was the first intimation that the office was to be closed. Gosh that is a shame - and now what. Isn't there something in the defense set up (or now war set up) that Dad could find? I know just what the situation is and you know I'll turn to.

I guess I was selfish to go ahead and get me married and thus take on more responsibility. However, we can make out beautifully so don't have a worry. I know you both are not very happy and we can't have that - after all my family has done for me they are just going to have to stop worrying - so thar!!

Joie has gone back to work. It's a good thing I think - will keep her busy and her mind occupied - she has taken sort of a sock in the teeth herself from life.

You didn't tell me when George finished. I shall write to him within a couple of days and send him a little something as a graduation present, that I think that he will appreciate most a cancellation of his debt. So we'll make that his big present and whatever else I send just something so he'll know that his brother is proud of the grand job he has done. He will probably feel better about stepping off into his career free of debt and so the slate is clean.

Mary Ellen Chase is the one who used to get my letters when I wrote to Mary Jane Chase at Smith. Said she enjoyed them immensely - told Chase's English Lit class so, at least, and I think read one of them or at least part of it.

My life here is very prosaic. It was exciting at first - coming into the "war zone" - but now it is dull - lots of work, not any excitement - the "zone" has moved on out West now. We, of course, "play it close to our chests" and "proceed with caution". There cannot be any repetitions of the disgrace which hit our country - and there will be none.

I see quite a few of my friends from time to time. However the majority of my class doesn't get over here, since most of the classmate aviators are still in training.

Dad asked about "qualifications". In our type of plane there is a comparatively large crew including three or four pilots - a Plane Commander, a First Pilot, a Navigator, and a Third Pilot (sometimes). I flew as Navigator for the Captain for the first couple of months, and now have my own plane - my first command, so to speak. You are supposed to have 1000 hours before qualification as a P.P.C. (Patrol plane Commander). I was qualified actually at 525 and on paper (officially) at 600. It is the exigencies of the work - not my ability.

Five of us are living in a house which used to be "married officers' quarters" - Ollie, Bill Richards (exec officer), Don Guruz, Russell Neil, and I. it is a nice set up. Ollie has a big radio phonograph combination - lots of records. We are all cribbage players, and play a lot of that - usually four handed - haven't been off the station since I arrived. Would like to do some sight-seeing and swimming. There are some pools here on the station, but there hasn't been a lot of time. I have taken over a new job now - "operations" and it is taking some time to get squared away. "Aircraft" is a new business and I'm still as green as grass. It's good to be lazy though - which I am between flying quite some and my new job.

Haven't seen many flowers - but have seen Hibiscus - Gardenias grow wild so I hear. From where I sit though airplanes are a lot prettier than flowers at this point.

We go see the shows now and then - right now there isn't much time for even that.

My "figure" does need trimming, and I hope to get at it before all is lost. I'm afraid I'm getting fatter. Don't eat much - but it still seems to be a losing fight.

Now you two must not worry - everything will be okay - how I wish that I could set you up in a nice place of your own and let you spend the many years to come getting a little back of all that life has taken from you. Perhaps someday I may be able to but until that time I'll see to it that you have everything you possibly can have.

The check enclosed is to do whatever you think best with. If George needs more than anything I send him, please let me know, and I'll try to scrape together some more. I'm at sort of a loss as to my affairs right now – but we'll get along until they get squared away.

All is well here.

Much, much love to my very wonderful Mother and Dad,

Scottie

Thursday, 30 April 1942

Dear Mother,

Today is the last day of April, tomorrow, May Day. Home it is Spring, the grass green, trees budding, the Robins now no longer alone heralds of early Spring, but busy raising a new brood. Gee, how I'd like to see Spring come at home – <u>that</u> is the best time of year.

Here there is no season, just a varying degree of summer; first cool, then warm, and then hot and then hotter. So goes the cycle. Dad would like that sort of weather, but I like the seasons, as they come at home. Perhaps because that is the weather I know best, and, more probably, just because it's home.

It would seem that after all these years of banging around the world – and I have been covering my share – that the attachments of home would become weaker – and that "home" would become that place where hangs the hat; but it's not so. Never more than now is my home with you and Dad. True, I have Joie, and thank heaven for that; for, just as I need my Mother and Dad, so, too, have I come to need her. But Joie has no home either. She has a step-mother for whom she cares not at all – and in whose home she lived but a short while – but no family – and no home. So you see the only home I have or Joie has is the only home I have ever had with you and Dad. And right now I'm just a wee-bit homesick – or maybe it's not such a wee-bit.

I'd like to have a cribbage game, an argument with Dad, a "Dagwood" and a good bull session with you – and especially just to be there and have my gab with my family. It has been too long since the last fest. One day soon we'll have us another over a quart of beer and some cheese and crackers – and I keep wishing for that day.

The thoughts in my mind and the feelings I have all the time about my Mother and Dad are hard to express on paper – and, I'm quite sure have no need for expression were such possible. You know how much I care for and respect my parents – such feelings are those of any man toward a family so grand.

Your lot in life has certainly not been the bed of roses, and how my heart has ached for all of the unhappiness that has come your way. Nobody deserved more of a break than you, Mom, and that break just doesn't seem to come. Someday, I hope, I can make it come - that is another day for which I'm waiting and hoping.

The way in which you have held us four together through thick and thin, the way you have pushed us through our education, and the way you have taken everything that fate can hand out, and come back for more, with always heaping devotion for your two boys, sticking with us through all our relatively minor trials, but minimizing your own, making us the men we are today - not perfect - not even outstanding, but at least with a good sense of what is right, and the fortitude to do it - for giving us a happy home and nothing but pleasant memories of childhood, for setting the standard in our minds "would Mother approve?" - a standard which is an infallible yardstick - for all these things which you have done for George and me, and many more, you must know that you are my nomination for "woman of the year" - every year. Not because it soon comes "Mother's Day", but because around that time it is a little easier to express those thoughts that are with me always.

It's a nasty world these days, and there is a big job ahead. We will do that job - and well. Of that you may be assured. I am doing my part as best I know how. Mine is not an exciting nor a dangerous job, but it is a necessary one. When that is done, I can come home - and bring with me my bride so that she may know the woman whom I most want her to meet - my Mother.

All the love in the world to the greatest woman I know.

    Scottie

XVI
MIDWAY AND BEYOND

Sunday, 17 May 1942

Dear Family,

There has been somewhat of a lull in the correspondence, and I expect that you are wondering what has happened. Rest assured that nothing is amiss, but just a sudden press of trivial things that seem to take most of the time. It is rather hard to find a subject for a letter, because the days happenings are usually very prosaic or, if not that, censorable; and I suppose, that also has its derogatory influence on prolific writing.

Whenever there is a lull such as this last one, you must not feel apprehensive, but just know that the 'press of affairs' precludes dashing off a note.

And with that, I am at a loss. It would hardly be becoming to write a love letter to one's family, and that is about all that Joie gets out of me, and the weather, the movements, the operations are all taboo - and my life at this point is operations - I'm learning a heck of a lot the hard way by making mistakes, but it is interesting in a quaint sort of way.

I haven't been able to send George his graduation present yet, because the pay situation is fouled up again, and I haven't been paid for a while, but that will straighten out within a day or two, and then he will hear from me - so in case he thinks that his brother has forgotten him, you might reassure him.

I can't remember when your last letters arrived, but they were certainly welcome sights - mail from home and from Joie means an awful lot these days - Joie is wonderful about writing, and seems to manage to keep up pretty much a diary of her days doings and writes a bit about twice a day.

My health is good and my disposition lousy, and aside from that there seems to be little to say.

From the papers it seems that the tempo of the war has quickened, and that before the summer is over, we may see great things happen - that is of course all pure surmise on my part, and I think that it is influenced by what the mainland commentators say. I personally would like to see the thing brought to a successful conclusion pronto - but there probably is little chance of that.

There has never, that I can remember, been a time when I felt less prolific, and so perhaps the best thing to do is to stick this sorry excuse in the mail, and hope that inspiration will hit soon.

Much much love to all,

Scottie

Thursday, 21 May 1942

Dear Family,

Mother's letter arrived yesterday - and welcome indeed, it was. Mail is <u>such</u> a comfort and pleasure to a guy who is away from home. Our mail service is necessarily erratic and varies from miraculous to terrible. One way or another it arrives, however, just as must my letters to you. They will continue to arrive you may be sure - some more delay than others - but come they will.

There is hardly a bit of news to relate - life moves on in a now familiar pattern - a pattern which probably appears to the outsider as something exciting and glamorous, but which, to us, often becomes something of a bore. However, every once in often enough something comes up which is new and different, or old with a new twist, to keep the job from becoming too prosaic.

I'm much interested and a bit concerned over George's reapplication for the Army Engineering corps. He can do a much better service to his country by doing just that for which he is slated. The experimentation and resultant development of newer and better aircraft which takes place with N.A.C.A. is of the greatest importance. However, George must needs live his own life, and he won't be happy unless he has done what he wants.

Little by little, as my old numbers of Time arrive, I get a clearer picture of what is happening at home. Gas rationing, sugar rationing, price ceilings, compulsory savings - et al - Perhaps, in our own cumbersome democratic way, we'll forestall too great an inflationary movement.

I've finally become mobile again. My box and trunk have gone back to Joie. (they were went out here by mistake). I have nothing now but two bags that can go into the plane wherever and whenever it goes. It is so much better that way. "Aircraft" is most definitely mobile business, and I think that that fact alone, if no other, makes it a fascinating pursuit. Dull, yes, as any other job becomes so at times, but never a <u>complete</u> bore.

I don't suppose you know much of anything of our operations, and there is little I can tell you for fear that this might fall into unfriendly hands before it reaches its rightful destination. However, I don't suppose that it is any secret that patrol planes patrol and search - which is what I do. How much patrol or search is another thing and will have to be held until "military secrets" such as that are no longer necessary. The plane which I now command is a fair to middling large plane, and I have three other officers besides myself and a commensurate crew. It is one of the more comfortable jobs, and much the least dangerous (which I hope will help to allay the fears that I'm sure you very foolishly but naturally have).

And that, I fear, is all that I can say of our operations. When all this mess is just a couple of chapters in the history books, you shall have all the details.

Since the above, I received the pen with which I'm writing from Joie. It is a very super Parker. I guess maybe she was getting tired of my penciled letters. I have yet to give her her wedding present - and am going to wait until I can get something really nice. She has her minerature now, thank goodness. Bailey, Banks and Biddle were awfully slow.

There seems to be little more else to write so for this time —

Much, much love to the dearest and grandest Mother and Dad in the world,

    Scottie

San Francisco, Calif.

Sunday, June 5, 1942

Dear Mother and Dad Whitman,

    Happy news from out west today and knew you'd be eager to hear. One of the girls had a telephone call, and all's well.

    Scottie's last letter said they would be pretty busy for awhile and he probably wouldn't have a chance to write – that was a couple of weeks ago, so it was grand to get first hand news today. . . . .

            Affectionately

                Joie

San Francisco, Calif.

Friday, June 12, 1942

Dear Folks,

    Your letter just came and these pictures of Scottie are so precious I could weep! Do you mind if I keep them for a little while?...............

    I still haven't had a letter, but the grape vine keeps me informed that everything is hunky dory. They are working hard, busy practically all the time - ....

           Affectionately

              Joie

San Francisco, Calif.

Wednesday, June 17, 1942

Dear Mother and Dad Whitman,

Your letter just came, Dad, and I hasten to correct your mistaken idea that I have information which I refuse to pass along.

Here's the straight dope –

Scottie's executive officer called his wife in Long Beach from Honolulu early Sunday morning, June twelfth, saying the squadron was having its first breather in two weeks on that day. They had taken part in the Midway battle, and all was well.

Day before yesterday one of the wives up here got a letter saying they were all fine, and had had their first chance at "smacking the japs".

That is absolutely all I know. My last letter from Scottie was written May twenty – second, so you've heard since I have.

I know only too well how you feel when you say "this sort of thing can't go on", but it could go on for the duration of the war, and we've just got to take it with our chins up, and not let Scottie know what slow torture it is to sit back home and wait – and wait.

I think – tho' it's only a guess – that Scottie's base is still Pearl Harbor, and that he patrols between there and Midway. However, I'm sure if he'd gotten into Honolulu for more than a nap we'd have heard from him. ....

Love,

Joie

```
                W E S T E R N
                         (24)
                U N I O N
                                        1942 JUN 18 AM 2  36

NS20 82 GOVT-WASHINGTON DC JUNE 18 132A

R S WHITMAN-

     7 JOHNSON AVE BINGHAMTON NY-

-THE NAVY DEPARTMENT DEEPLY REGRETS TO INFORM YOU THAT YOUR

SON LIEUTENANT JUNIOR GRADE ROBERT SCOTT WHITMAN JUNIOR

UNITED STATES NAVY WAS KILLED IN ACTION IN AIRCRAFT

ENGAGEMENT WITH ENEMY IN THE PERFORMANCE OF HIS DUTY AND IN

THE SERVICE OF HIS COUNTRY ON JUNE FOURTH X BODY NOT

RECOVERED X THE DEPARTMENT EXTENDS TO YOU ITS SINCEREST

SYMPATHY IN YOUR GREAT LOSS X TO PREVENT POSSIBLE AID TO

OUR ENEMIES PLEASE DO NOT DIVULGE THE NAME OF HIS SHIP OR

STATION X-

                    REAR ADMIRAL RANDALL JACOBS

                    THE CHIEF OF NAVAL PERSONNEL.
```

1942 June 18 – Western Union Telegram from Rear Admiral Randall Jacobs.

THE BINGHAMTON PRESS, FRIDAY EVENING, JUNE 19, 1942.

LIEUT. ROBERT WHITMAN, BINGHAMTON

FLIER, KILLED IN ACTION AT MIDWAY

Killed in action against the Japs at Midway Islands was LIEUT. Robert Scott Whitman, Jr., 26, son of Mr. and Mrs. R.S. Whitman of 51 St. John Avenue. A graduate of U.S. Naval Academy, he was piloting a Consolidated P.B.Y. bomber when it was shot down in the Pacific.

Body Unrecovered, says Navy Department in Message to Parents

Lieut. (junior grade) Robert Scott Whitman, Jr., 26, of Binghamton, was killed in action June 4 in an air engagement with the Japanese over the Pacific – the epic battle of Midway Island, in which an enemy invasion fleet was shattered and a threatened attack upon Hawaii forestalled. His parents, Mr. and Mrs. Robert Scott Whitman, of 51 St. John Avenue, were informed of Lieutenant Whitman's death in a telegram from the Navy Department yesterday.

Broome County's 11th son to be lost in action was a graduate of the U.S. Naval Academy at Annapolis in 1939. He was the pilot of one of America's crack PBY-5A bombers and when last heard from was stationed at Hawaii.

The Navy Department communication read:

"The Navy Department regrets to inform you that your son, Lieut. (junior grade) Robert Scott Whitman, Jr., U.S. Navy, was killed in action in aircraft engagement with the enemy in the performance of his duty and in the service of his country on June fourth. Body not recovered. The Department extends to you its sincerest sympathy in your great loss."

It was signed by Rear Admiral Randall Jacobs, chief of Naval personnel.

Lieutenant Whitman went down to an unmarked grave in the Pacific after

ROBERT SCOTT WHITMAN JR.

taking part in one of the most glorious sea-air battles in American history – a battle which ended with the U.S. forces victorious over the fleeting, crippled remnants of a formidable invasion armada.

The Binghamton pilot apparently was at the controls of one of the big land-based Consolidated PBY bombers which were cited by the Navy Department for gallant action after they had intercepted the two columns of enemy ships and battered them to pieces off Midway Island, June 3 and 4.

In this battle the Japs lost at least two aircraft carriers and a large number of cruisers, destroyers, transports and supply vessels. Three big battleships were badly damaged. It was estimated the 90 per cent of the Jap planes launched in the attempt to surprise and capture Midway Island were lost. Ten thousand Japs, many of them air pilots, were left to die as the broken fleet turned tail and scurried away in flames and damaged beyond early repair.

A dispatch from the U.S. Army Air Corps Headquarters at Hawaii, June 11, described how land-based bombers on June 4, "dumped explosives 'smack on the nose' of Japanese aircraft carriers and utterly smashed an enemy invasion fleet unofficially estimated at more than 50 warships of all types."

Lieutenant Whitman, a flight Commander, was piloting one of those bombers, which dispatches said scorned the attempts of Zero fighters to protect the trapped Nipponese battle fleet.

Lieutenant Whitman was well known in Binghamton. He attended Old St. John Avenue School, a predecessor to Alexander Hamilton.

He was graduated from Binghamton Central High School in 1933, after playing tackle n the varsity football team for two years, ranking 29th in a large graduating class, serving as business manager of the school paper and writing for the Panorama. He also managed the baseball team and was a delegate to the Red Cross convention at Washington in his sophomore year.

After a year at Dickinson College, Carlisle,)Pa., in which he played football, he entered the U.S. Naval Academy in 1935 and was graduated with credit – in the top third of his class – in 1939.

He played Plebe football and was on the Junior Varsity in the second year before Quincy before applying for transfer to the Naval Air Training School at Pensacola, Fla. Last October he was awarded his wings and assigned to Coronado air base near San Diego, Calif.

Before being transferred to Hawaii, three months ago, he married Miss Josephine Jackson, of San Francisco, March 21, 1942. Almost immediately his squadron flew to Hawaii and his bride remained in San Francisco.

Lieutenant Whitman is survived by his wife, his parents and a brother George S. Whitman, a graduate of the University of Michigan, who is now employed as an aeronautical engineer.

PLEBE TO WWII HERO, MY JOURNEY FROM ANNAPOLIS TO MIDWAY

THE BINGHAMTON PRESS, FRIDAY, JUNE 19, 1942.

BINGHAMTON NAVAL AIRMAN MISSING IN PACIFIC ACTION

LOCAL FLIER
    WAS LEADER
        OF SQUADRON

NAVY DEPARTMENT NOTIFIES
    PARENTS OF LIEUT. ROBERT
    S. WHITMAN, JR.

ANNAPOLIS GRADUATE

VICTIM WAS SENT TO HAWAII
    DAY AFTER WEDDING ONLY
    FEW MONTHS AGO

Lieut. (junior grade) Robert S. Whitman, Jr., Binghamton Annapoli graduate and a U.S. Navy flier, has been listed as "missing" afte action against the enemy in the Pacific.

The Navy Department notified his parents, Mr. and Mrs. Robert S. Whitman of 51 St. John Avenue, by wire yesterday.

Lieutenant Whitman was married a few months ago in California to a San Diego girl. The day after his wedding he was transferred to Hawaii.

GRADUATED IN 1939

It is believed that the naval flier took, part in either the Coral Sea or the Midway engagements. He was a bomber squadron leader and presumably based on an aircraft carrier.

Twenty-six years of age, Lieutenant Whitman graduated from the Naval Academy in 1939. He was a classmate of Lieut. (junior grade) Charles DeWitt McCall,

formerly of 14 Newton Avenue and now stationed in the Pacific on submarine duty.

The naval flier entered Annapolis in 1935, two years after he graduated from Binghamton Central High School. Following a post graduate course at the high school he spent one year at Dickinson College.

29th in Class

In his senior year at Central he ranked 29th in his class. He was on the Panorama staff in his sophomore year and became assistant business manager of the school paper in his junior year.

While at Central he played on the junior varsity and varsity football teams and managed the baseball team. He was a delegate to the Red Cross Convention in Washington during his sophomore year.

Lieutenant Whitman is the fourth Binghamton aviator to be listed as missing or killed in action since the war broke out.

Lieutenant Whitman is survived by his parents and one brother, George, who recently graduated from the University of Michigan.

ROBERT SCOTT WHITMAN JR.

PATROL SQUADRON FORTY FOUR   /jrp

                                        %Postmaster,
                                        San Francisco, Calif.,
                                        15 June 1942.

Mr. Robert S. Whitman,
51 Saint John Ave.,
Binghamton, N.Y.

Dear Mr. Whitman:-

     I deeply regret having to inform you that your son, Robert Scott
Whitman Jr., Lieutenant (junior grade) U.S. Navy, was killed in action
with the enemy on June 4, 1942.

     The officers and men of Robert's squadron feel a deep personal
loss in his passing. I had grown to know him well in the time he was
in the squadron. I leaned heavily on him giving him responsibility
after responsibility; he accepted them all cheerfully and did
everything he attempted, excellently.

     He died bravely and with no thought of self. His last words were
of warning to his crew of impending crash. This he did after being
wounded and while endeavoring to bring his crippled plane down safely.
His every action was in accord with the best traditions of our Naval
Service and of our country.

     His remains were carried down with his plane.

     You may communicate with me at the address below:

          Commander, Patrol Squadron FORTY FOUR,
          % Postmaster, San Francisco, California.

                    Most sincerely yours,

                    (signed) R C Brixner.

Plebe to WWII Hero, My Journey From Annapolis to Midway

THE BINGHAMTON PRESS, MONDAY EVENING, JUNE 22, 1942

LIEUT. ROBERT WHITMAN DIED

WARNING CREW, PARENTS TOLD

Lieut. (junior grade) Robert Scott Whitman, Jr., 26, of Binghamton, who was killed in action in the battle of Midway Islands, June 4, warned his bomber crew members of the impending crash before going down into the Pacific at the controls of his plane, according to a letter received by his parents, Mr. and Mrs. Robert Scott Whitman of 51 St. John Avenue from Lieutenant Whitman's commander.

The Binghamton Navy pilot, a graduate of Annapolis, was wounded, but made a gallant attempt to save his bullet-ripped PBY Consolidated bomber.

The letter, signed by R.C. Brixner, commander of Lieutenant Whitman's patrol squadron, reads:

"I deeply regret having to inform you that your son, Robert Scott Whitman, Jr., Lieutenant (junior grade) U.S. Navy, was killed in action with the enemy on June 4, 1942.

"The officers and men of Robert's squadron feel a deep personal loss in his passing. I had grown to know him well in the time he was in the squadron. I leaned heavily on him giving him responsibility after responsibility; he accepted them all cheerfully and did everything he attempted excellently.

"He died bravely and with no thought of self. His last words were of warning to his crew of impending crash.

"This he did after being wounded and while endeavoring to bring his crippled plane down safely. His every action was in accord with the best traditions of our navy service and of our country. We are proud of him in his squadron.

"His remains were carried down with his plane."

San Francisco, Calif.

19 June 1942

Dearest Joie

    I am so deeply grieved and shocked over the loss of Scotty I hardly know what I am doing.

    I just received a letter from Red, and he said that he had written you an official letter the day before, which you no doubt have received by now (my letter was written on the 15th). He said he knew you would want to know the details which could not be written in an adequate way in a letter of that sort – so he and the Captain talked it over and asked me to tell you the details that will make you prouder than ever of Scotty. I will quote him word for word.

    "Scotty took his plane out on a mission the morning of the battle well knowing the dangers involved. He carried out his mission, and died valiantly doing it. He was jumped by three jap fighters, and fought them for about thirty minutes before he was shot down. And, he got one of the japs first. With three of his crew already dead and another badly wounded, himself badly wounded, but the co-pilot dead, the plane out of control and on fire, he did a wonderful job of bringing it down, and his last words were for the safety of his crew. Due solely to his efforts three members of his crew got out of the plane to a rubber boat and were rescued two days later. Scotty and four others of his crew went down with the plane.

    Scotty died carrying out his duty. It was his information, coupled with that of other planes in the same area which was responsible in a large part for the success of the whole battle. Without the dope he was sending, even as they crashed, it would have been a very sad story for the whole fleet."

             (signed)   Jeanne

PLEBE TO WWII HERO, MY JOURNEY FROM ANNAPOLIS TO MIDWAY

THE BINGHAMTON PRESS, THURSDAY EVENING, JUNE 25, 1942

Except from

SPINNING

THE S P O R T S   T O P

BY AL LAMB

Whitman was a Central Grid Star

The writer was a trifle slow, as perhaps some sports fans were, in recognizing the name of Lieut. Robert S. Whitman, Jr., U.S. Navy aviator who gave his life in the Battle of Midway, as that of Scott Whitman, a former football star at Binghamton Central High School.

Scott, as he was always known in athletics, played a strong game at tackle on the Blue elevens of 1930 and '31.

We were talking about him yesterday to Richard L. Schuster, vice principal of Central, who was head football coach when Whitman played there. During the conversation, "Dick" cited an incident in his own career to prove a point about the value of football. After he was graduated from Penn State College, a major, trying to induce Schuster to enter West Point, said that the army was anxious to have athletes attend the Military Academy because it had been found that they make the best officers.

Commander, Schuster Laud Him

So perhaps Whitman's football experiences at Central and at the U.S. Naval Academy at Annapolis, where he was a member of the squad, stood him in good stead. His parents received a letter from his squadron commander in which it was stated that he died bravely and his last thoughts were of his crew; that, although wounded, he gamely tried to bring his crippled bomber down safely and, when realizing that would be impossible, warned his crew of the impending crash.

"Scott was a fine team man - he had a great team spirit - when he played football at Central," said Mr. Schuster. "He was a fine fellow and a dandy lineman. He always played much better in a game than he did in practice, because he had a fighting heart and an ideal competitive spirit under pressure, and I am sure that he was giving his country the best that he had in his final game."

Those who didn't see Whitman play for the Bulldogs a dozen years ago should be assured that he had real ability by the statement that he was good enough to be selected for the Annapolis squad by "Rip" Miller, the line coach.

Several Football Incidents Recalled

I met him one day when he was home for a visit after a Navy football season. He was praising "Monk" Meyer, the Army's star half-back. "He's a skinny fellow," he told us, "and I sat on the Navy bench feeling sorry for an Army man when he played West Point. Every time I saw a couple of our big linemen bury him into the ground I expected him not to be able to get up. But the way he'd bound back, he must be made of rubber."

Excerpt from
Mr. Schuster recalled that in 1930 his Central High eleven had Norwich and had barely beaten the Morrisville Aggies. The boys found themselves, he said. Elmira was rolling up big scores against formidable opposition. Some of the Central players received uncomplimentary letters from Elmira. They put them in their helmets before the game with Elmira. "I remember Scott tearing off his helmet after Central upset Elmira 21-0, running around out there on the middle of the gridiron and, when he found his man, waving the letter in his face," said the former coach.

Fought Best on Gridiron Against Odds

"Norwich came down here the next season with another strong team and expected to trim us. But they pointed most all of the plays at our tackles, and Whitman and Rudach stopped them, playing like all-scholastics all afternoon.

I recall both of those games distinctly in connection with Scott, for we were underdogs in both contests and he arose to the occasion wonderfully."

I feel that the best way to conclude this is to say amen to an opinion expressed by Schuster; "I think that the war will be won on American gridirons."

Alameda, California,

Sunday, January 10, 1943

Dear Mother and Dad –

You letter just reached me, what with my having new headquarters again, and I hasten to answer for I am overwhelmingly full of proud news.

I received a wire yesterday from the Bureau of Naval Personnel requesting that I act as sponsor to an escort vessel named Whitman to be launched on the 19th of this month. It is a great honor that makes me feel quite humble and at the same, exceedingly proud.

It seems to right that the navy should have a ship named after our wonderful Scottie.

....

All for now –

      Lots of love,

        Joie

ROBERT SCOTT WHITMAN JR.

THE BINGHAMTON PRESS, FRIDAY EVENING, JANUARY 14, 1943.

NAVAL VESSEL IS NAMED WHITMAN

IN TRIBUTE TO BINGHAMTONIAN

A U.S. Navy escort vessel, the Whitman, has been named in tribute to the memory of Lieut. Robert Scott Whitman, Jr., of Binghamton, who was killed June 4 in an air engagement with the Japanese during the epic battle of Midway Island.

His parents, Mr. and Mrs. R.S. Whitman, Sr., 51 St. John Avenue, learned of the naming of the vessel in a letter today from the lieutenant's widow, Mrs. Josephine Whitman, of Alameda, Cal., who wrote that she had received a telegram from the Bureau of Naval Personnel "requesting that I act as sponsor to an escort vessel named Whitman to be launched on Jan. 19." No further details were given.

The engagement in which the Binghamton hero lost his life saw the shattering of an enemy invasion fleet and the forestalling of a threatened attack on Hawaii.

The battle ended with the U.S. forces victorious over the fleeing, crippled remnants of a formidable invasion armada.

Lieutenant Whitman, a flight commander was piloting one of the big land-based Consolidated PBY bombers which were cited by Navy Department for gallant action after they had intercepted the two columns of enemy ships and battered them to pieces off Midway Island, June 3 and 4.

In the historical engagement, the Japs lost at least two aircraft carriers and a large number of cruisers, destroyers, transports and supply vessels. Three big battleships were badly damaged and it was estimated that 90 per cent of the enemy planes launched in the invasion attempt were lost. Japanese casualties were estimated at 10,000.

Dispatches at the time said Lieutenant Whitman was piloting one of the bombers which scorned Zero fighters trying to protect the Nipponese fleet.

A graduate of Binghamton Central High School, where he played tackle n the football team, Lieutenant Whitman attended Dickinson College, Carlisle, Pa., and then entered the U.S. Naval Academy at Annapolis, from which he was graduated in the top third of his class - in 1939.

After graduation he saw service on the heavy cruiser Quincy for a year and a half before applying for transfer to the Naval Air Training School at Pensacola, Fla. He was awarded his wings in October, 1941, and subsequently was transferred to Hawaii.

SAN FRANCISCO CHRONICLE   Saturday January 16, 1943

SHIPS NAMED

AFTER HEROES TO

BE LAUNCHED SOON

First combat ships to be named after slain heroes of this war will be launched at Mare Island next week.

They are the ....
And the Robert Scott Whitman Jr., named after a Naval Lieutenant (jg), also decorated posthumously for heroism.
....
The Robert Scott Whitman Jr., which will slide down the Navy Yard's ways Tuesday, will be sponsored by the Officer's widow.

In making the announcement, the yard's public relations office described the vessels as "combat ships of the destroyer-escort type."

POSTAL

TELEGRAPH

To COMMANDANT   Monday, Jan. 18, 1943
Navy Yard   2:30 P. M.
Mare Island, California.

We deeply regret our inability to be present at the launching of the U. S. S. Whitman. However to the prospective commanding officers and crew we send our hearty greetings and best wishes. We know the ship will be worthy of him for whom she is named.

Robert S. and Margaret S. Whitman.

N. B. I took this first to the Western Union but they declined to accept it, stating that under the new rule they could not accept any greeting messages and would not make any exception. I then took it to the Postal who accepted it without question and took my money for it. We do not yet know whether it was received and perhaps read at the launching ceremonies or not. If Postal took my money for send-it and did not send the message I shall get a refund or tear their local office down around their heads.

ROBERT SCOTT WHITMAN JR.

THE BINGHAMTON PRESS,

Tuesday Evening, January 19, 1943

NAVY FLIER'S WIDOW

TO SPONSOR SHIP

LAUNCHING TODAY

With his widow, Mrs. Josephine Whitman of Alameda, Cal., as the sponsor, a U.S. Navy escort vessel, the Whitman, was launched today in tribute to the memory of Lieut. Robert Scott Whitman, Jr., of Binghamton, who was killed in action June 4 during the historic battle of Midway Island.

The ceremony in the navy yard at Mare Island, Cal., opened at 12:20 (P.W.T.) this afternoon, with the actual launching at 12:42.

Mrs. Whitman acted as sponsor at the request of the Bureau of Naval Personnel.

Lieutenant Whitman, the son of Mr. and Mrs. R.S. Whitman, Sr., 51 St. John Avenue, piloted a big land based Consolidated P.B.Y. bomber in the engagement that shattered a Japanese invasion fleet. The action of the American forces forestalled a threatened attack on Hawaii.

Lieutenant Whitman and other fliers in the engagement were cited for gallant action.

Christening of U.S.S. Whitman, January 19, 1943

```
      NAVY DEPARTMENT                              penalty for private use
          -----                                    to avoid payment of
   Office of the Commandant                           postage, $300.00
         Navy Yard
    Mare Island, California                       MARE ISLAND
          -----                                     STATION
       Official Business


                   Mr. and Mrs. R.S. Whitman

                      51 St. John Avenue

                      Binghamton, N.Y.

   _____


                       THE COMMANDANT

             requests the honor of your presence

                          at the

        LAUNCHING OF THE UNITED STATES SHIP WHITMAN

                          at the

             Navy Yard, Mare Island, California

               Tuesday, January 19,1943

   Ceremonies twelve twenty P.M.    Launch at twelve forty-two P.M.

                          - - -

           Mrs. Robert Scott Whitman, Jr., Sponsor
```

Launching of U.S.S. Whitman

TIMES-HERALD, VALLEJO, CALIFORNIA – Wednesday, January 20, 1943.
LAUNCHING OF M.I. SHIP HONORS HERO OF WAR
MARE ISLAND NAVY YARD yesterday launched the U.S.S. Whitman, the second destroyer-escort vessel to be launched in two days at this West Coast Navy Yard. Mrs. Robert Scott Whitman is shown above christening the vessel which was named in honor of her late husband and naval hero, Lt. (jg) R.S. Whitman. Left to right on the launching platform during the ceremony are Captain W.E. Malloy, USN, Planning Officer; Rear Admiral W.L. Friedell, USN, Yard Commandant; and Mrs. J.N. Andregg, Matron of Honor. (Official U.S. Navy Photograph.)

Dear Scottie:

I've wanted to write to a place unnamed,
As my letter to you was returned unclaimed.
That was after June fourth, during Midway too –
But what they say has occurred couldn't happen to you!
You're up there somewhere, in the clouds, flying high –
A person like you darling never could die.
The world has acclaimed you a 'hero', my dear –
Not just for the present, but through all of the years.
So many have told me I've lost a dear friend –
They don't know us, my dear one, I'll find you again.
But until then my darling, if they only knew
My heart went down with you, at Midway too.

Anonymous

Alameda, California
Wednesday evening,
January 27th, 1943.

The Admiral's car came for me at 7:00 A. M., and we proceeded
to Piedmont to pick up my matron of honor (Betty Andregg, with whom I
stayed for awhile last summer) and then went on to Mare Island.

When we arrived at the main gate of the Navy Yard, we were instructed to go right to the ship. The Admiral was waiting us there, and we
arrived exactly on schedule at 11:15. We were taken to the sponsor's
platform and were told the procedure, and I broke a trial bottle on the
ship. Then the Admiral took us to his quarters, where we met Mrs. Friedell,
and combed our hair etc and put on our flowers. We each had a corsage of
two beautiful white orchids, and I had a boquet of about four dozen roses.

At about 12:10 the four of us went back to the ship, and my knees
really felt peculiar-like when I got up on the platform. First there were
pictures, then the band played, then speakers (Admiral Friedell read your
telegram during his speech) then a prayer, then the Star Spangled Banner.
After that was a scheduled wait while the last whatever it is was removed
from under the ship, before the Admiral held out the bottle, and Captain
Malloy said "now". I broke the bottle just after the ship started to
move, and really splashed champagne all over beautifully, then they handed me a microphone into which I said "I christen thee Whitman", and she
slid down the ways as perfectly as could be, and"bowed to her sponsor."
And you can imagine my feeling when the Captain said, after she was afloat -
"There's your ship Mrs. Whitman."
After the ship was launched, the bottle I'd broken ('twas encased in silver) was brought back by a little motor boat, and presented to me in a

beautiful velvet lined mahogany box, with a silver plate engraved the same as is on the bottle -

U.S.S. WHITMAN

launched

NAVY YARD, MARE ISLAND

January 19, 1943

Sponsor: Josephine Porter Whitman

I'm enclosing a schedule - Oh yes - I also wore a "rosette" of blue and gold ribbon, which all sponsors at Mare Island traditionally wear.

Opposite page:

In letter dated October 11, 1936 reference is made to the article in the October issue of <u>Forum</u> by James Oliver Brown entitled <u>Annapolis Stronghold of Mediocrity</u>. Enclosed with the manuscript at the end is a copy of an article by Scottie published in the October 16th, 1936 issue of the <u>Log</u> entitled <u>Mediocrity</u> a reply to and refutation of the Brown article.

T H E   L O G
Of the
UNITED STATES
NAVAL ACADEMY
October 16, 1936

MEDIOCRITY

By R.S. Whitman

    Behold Brethren, a dissenter in the ranks. One of our
distinguished (?) alumni (whether by reason of his interest
in the welfare of our fair school, or for reasons best known
to himself) has brought to the intelligentsia a highly
entertaining dissertation - better, a critical attack - aimed
at the institution of which we of the regiment are a vital
part. I refer to the much discussed "Annapolis, Stronghold
of Mediocrity" from the pen of James Oliver Brown ('33), and
published in the current issue of FORUM.

    Contrary to Mr. Brown's assertion that we have no time
for anything but "cheap fiction," his article has been widely
read, and now is a notable topic of conversation throughout the
regiment. Opinion as to the truth of this superbly written and
highly unconstructive thesis is divided. Some agree rabidly with
Brown's ideas, and others just as radically would derive great
pleasure from presenting him with a punch in the nose.

    I do not feel that we should jump to conclusions in
the spirit of the moment. Because one man, and he a highly
problematical authority on educational methods, brings his
learned criticism to bear upon a school reputed to be the best
of its kind in the world, is no reason why we should ally
ourselves so violently to the either side.

    Though I make no claims as an equal to the intellectual
powers of a Harvard graduate, and feel quite incompetent to
match myself in debate with such a mental giant, I still cannot
let his assertions go unrefuted.

    Criticism is easy, but constructive criticism is a different
matter. Brown has done it the easy way. His denouncement to the
public, his explosion of the taxpayer's "erroneous knowledge"
seems to resolve itself into three main issues. I quote from his
article.

"Obscured by all this activity are three great shortcomings
in the academy training: the failure to develop the thought
process, the failure to provide a broad education, and the
failure to develop character, initiative, and individuality."

Let this not resolve itself into a debate for the negative,
but rather a brief rebuttal for Brown's main points of issue.

Of main importance to the case for the negative, is the fact
that in his eagerness to pick apart our educational system,
Brown has forgotten that the Naval Academy is an institution
set up for the express purpose of training men to become
officers in the United States Navy, to take a job in a highly
specialized and professionalized business, that the government
pays a huge amount of money each year for the maintenance of
this institution, and pays qualified men a salary while they are
learning their business. Because of this, the government demands
- and rightfully - that results be obtained. We must remember
that we are here for a purpose. Does our school attain what it
attempts? Are the results satisfactory? If so the school is far
from mediocre.

Now to examine his issues separately. The first which I shall
attempt to discuss concerns our disciplinary system.

Brown cites petty rules which in his opinion have no
constructive purpose rather than perhaps to serve as an irksome
burden on the men affected. These regulations coupled with a
strict routine fail, according to Brown, to develop initiative,
character, and individuality.

Last year, the Academy celebrated its 90th anniversary.
During the past 90 years, many men have gone through the mill,
and have taken their place in the fleet. Their actions alone
should prove beyond question that the Academy produces the
desired results, but let us go a little further. From long
experience, these rules have been laid down. If a regulation
has been instituted, it has been to facilitate the output of
efficient Naval officers. Our curriculum is full - too full
to allow any waste of time. Many of the cited "nagging and
senseless rules" are designed to save time, or to keep men from
becoming too lax with the discipline which is such an important
cog in any military organization. How without a strict routine
could we get our full day's work done? Human nature is not such
that man can hold himself to such a fast pace without the help
of a routine strictly enforced. We must do each day's work in

order to bring about in the given time, the desired end. It is hard to keep 2000 men keyed to the pitch necessary to produce finished officers in four years. How can it be done if not by regulations and enforcement of these regulations? And how, without initiative, character, and individuality, have our officers since time immemorial taken such a great place in the development of our country?

Secondly, we are told that the Academy does not develop the thought process. Here, I think Brown has stepped far beyond reason. The lecture system which he so heartily endorses has not been adopted here wholly because mightier brains than mine – or yours, Mr. Brown, deemed it not conducive to the development of that same thought process. Is not far more mental exercise provided that a man is handed a book and told to dope it out for himself rather than have a professor do the problem for him. We recite frequently, we are marked frequently, and we dope it out for ourselves. You were a midshipmn. How can you make such a grossly absurd statement as when you accuse the Naval Academy of failing to develop the thought processes of its students?

Lastly, Brown states that the Academy fails to provide a broad education. To this, I can make no negative reply. True, we do not come into intimate contact with the classics. Nor do we meet with "psychology, philosophy, or biology." Our course is too packed with highly technical and specialized subjects which are of immediate and essential importance to us in our career. We must learn to shoot guns, to navigate, and a hundred other things. We cannot spare time for a classical education which, as desirable as we admit it to be, does not run battleships.

Brown's one constructive thought has been voiced many times before. It is no brain child of his own. He asks that the course either be lengthened or that the Naval Academy become a post-graduate school.

At present, both seem inadvisable, and so for the present, let us be content with that "mediocre" school which produces the leaders of a navy reckoned as equal at least to any – a navy noted throughout the world for its efficient and high caliber officers.

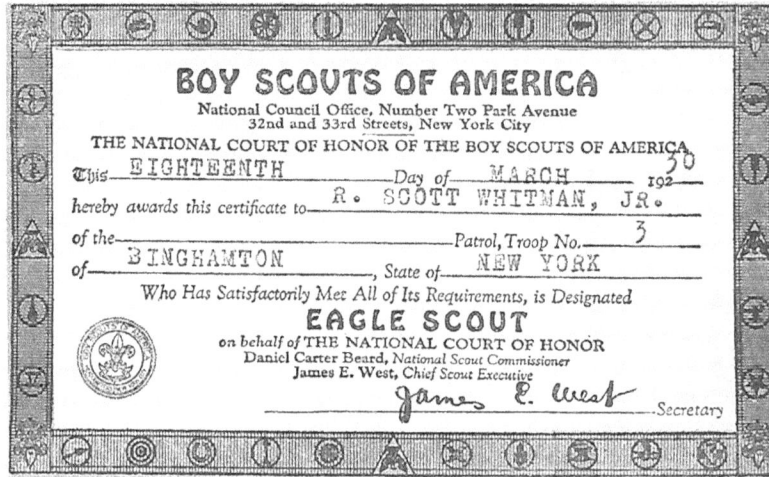

BOY SCOUTS OF AMERICA

National Council Office, Number Two Park Avenue
32nd and 33rd Streets, New York City

THE NATIONAL COURT OF HONOR OF THE BOY SCOUTS OF AMERICA

This EIGHTEENTH Day of MARCH 1930

hereby awards this certificate to R. SCOTT WHITMAN, JR.

of the—————————— Patrol, Troop No. 3

of BINGHAMTON, State of NEW YORK

Who Has Satisfactorily Met All of Its Requirements, is Designated

EAGLE SCOUT

on behalf of THE NATIONAL COURT OF HONOR

Daniel Carter Beard, National Scout Commissioner
James E. West, Chief Scout Executive

James E. West —————Secretary

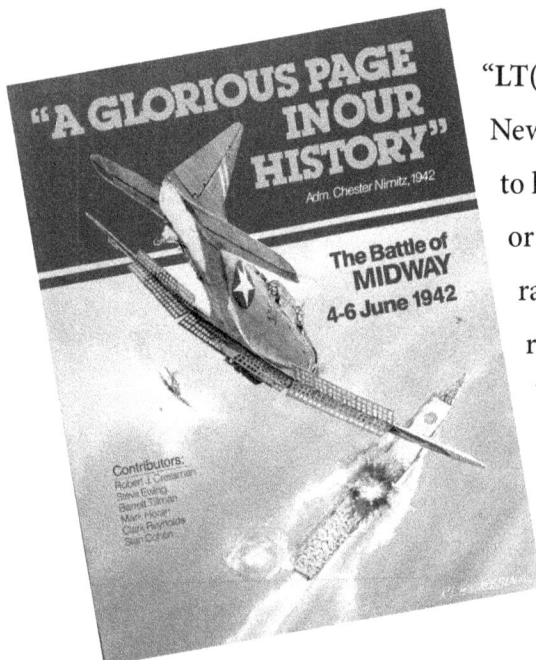

"LT(jg) Robert S. Whitman (a husky New Yorker, from Binghamton, known to his classmates at the USNA as "Whit" or "Scottie"), flying 44-P-12 (BuNo 04975), ran across the Occupation Force. He reported antiaircraft fire, and that he was being attacked by enemy planes …
page 74

www.ingramcontent.com/pod-product-compliance
Lightning Source LLC
Chambersburg PA
CBHW080658110426
42739CB00034B/3321